Technology Transfer and U.S. Foreign Policy

Henry R. Nau

Technology Transfer and U.S. Foreign Policy

PRAEGER PUBLISHERS
Praeger Special Studies

New York • London • Sydney • Toronto

Library of Congress Cataloging in Publication Data
Main entry under title:

Technology transfer and U.S. foreign policy.

   (Praeger special studies in U.S. economic, social, and political issues)
   Includes bibliographical references and index.
   1. Technology and state—United States.
2. Technology transfer. 3. Technical assistance, American. 4. United States—Foreign relations.
I. Nau, Henry R., 1941-
T23.T4   309.2'233'73   76-2908
ISBN 0-275-56790-7

PRAEGER PUBLISHERS
PRAEGER SPECIAL STUDIES
383 Madison Avenue, New York, N.Y. 10017, U.S.A.

Published in the United States of America in 1976
by Praeger Publishers,
A Division of Holt, Rinehart and Winston, CBS, Inc.

9   038   98765432

© 1976 by Praeger Publishers

All rights reserved

Printed in the United States of America

ACKNOWLEDGMENTS

I wish to acknowledge a special debt to the graduate students who worked with me on this study and authored the case studies that appear as separate chapters of this volume. These individuals persevered through numerous discussions, debates, and drafts of their respective studies. They neither asked for nor were given any quarter. They went about their work with a sense of professionalism and commitment to excellence that says a lot about them as individuals and as future participants and analysts of the public policy process. I hope that they learned as much from this experience as I did. I list them here (alphabetically) and congratulate them on this fine beginning of their youthful careers:

>Mary M. Allen
>Ann L. Becker
>Harlan S. Finer
>Howard J. Gobstein
>George D. Holliday
>James P. Lester
>Carol A. Ulinski

PREFACE

Technology has been acknowledged throughout the postwar period as a linchpin of U.S. foreign policy. Indeed, much of U.S. postwar leadership has been based on the supremacy of U.S. military and civilian technology. Despite this critical role of technology, however, few attempts have been made to assess the full range of national interests involved in the use of American technology in foreign affairs. Instead, American technology has been employed and evaluated in several separate and largely unrelated policy contexts. The most important perhaps has been the role of technology in U.S. military strategy. Another has been the use of technology to enhance U.S. diplomatic influence and prestige (foreign aid, Apollo, and so on). A third has been the role of technology in private foreign investment. The utilization and assessment of U.S. technology in these separate contexts have masked a number of broader trends in the relationship between technology and foreign policy interests and contributed to the lack of an underlying framework or perspective for evaluating trade-offs among the various foreign policy uses of technology. The lack of such a perspective is evident in contemporary debates about technology transfer where some participants define the national interest as synonymous with strategic uses of American technology while others view the national interest in terms of the commercial benefits of technology.

This study cannot resolve these debates since they are endemic to a pluralistic system in which no single person or group has a monopoly on the definition of national interest. What it can do, however, is to establish a framework for identifying the full range of issues and actors concerned with the outflow of U.S. technology abroad and, on the basis of this framework, to point out broad trends that cut across individual policy sectors and lend perspective to some of the confusion and conflict of contemporary debates. Accordingly, the study examines historical (postwar) and contemporary practices associated with the use of U.S. technology in foreign affairs, whether this use involved strategic, diplomatic, commercial, or other aims and whether the technology was destined for advanced, socialist, resource-rich or resource-poor developing countries. In addition, it examines several specific case studies of recent technology outflows (or the potential for such outflows) to various groups of countries.

These inquiries reveal the increasing economic as well as strategic and diplomatic significance of U.S. technology in foreign affairs. Whereas in the past technology was largely at the service of strategic and diplomatic objectives, today it may have to be viewed increasingly in terms of its economic costs and consequences. To be sure, technology remains a major resource of U.S. diplomacy and military strategy. Indeed, as American goods and money assume a less dominant role in international economic relations, given the shift of wealth to Western Europe, Japan, and most recently the OPEC countries, American technology (advanced know-how and skilled people) becomes an even more important asset of U.S. diplomacy (as Secretary Kissinger seems to have recognized). Nevertheless, this asset can be preserved in a more competitive economic world only if its use acknowledges the economic costs and consequences involved. This is especially true if foreign customers begin to demand U.S. technology increasingly in its "purer" forms (that is, embodied in information and people) apart from capital and management control (that is, direct investment). Current U.S. legislation offers no means to assess the economic worth of technology, independent of strategic or foreign policy considerations. The present study highlights the urgency to consider such means and to make the appropriate decision whether new guidelines or legislation is needed to incorporate commercial criteria into current policy.

The national foreign policy focus of this study inevitably ignores other aspects of the international transfer of technology and may seem to slight the interest of those more concerned with international organizations or recipient country aspects of international technology flows. No study, of course, can include all interests and perspectives. And we are led to adopt a source country focus, in particular U.S. national interests, because most existing studies of technology transfer ignore this focus in favor of global or recipient country approaches. Yet an understanding of all of these aspects of technology transfer, we believe, is necessary to advance present international alignments toward a more satisfactory distribution of technological resources and capabilities. Our hope is to clarify the incentives and mechanisms of U.S. national policy toward technology outflows in order to facilitate a more constructive and coherent response to international needs. Indeed, as we argue in the last chapter of this study, a sober understanding of U.S. interests in this area should lead to a more balanced U.S. policy of technological interdependence with other countries (involving import as well as export of technology), rather than the one-sided and chauvinistic policy of technological leadership or independence which the United States has pursued throughout most of the postwar period and continues to pursue today in such areas as energy.

This study was sponsored by a grant from the National Science Foundation (NSF Grant ST-44205) and was directed by Henry R. Nau, associate professor of Political Science and International Affairs and member of the Graduate Program in Science, Technology and Public Policy at George Washington University. It was administered under the auspices of the University Policy Studies (UPS) program of the Science and Technology Policy Office (STPO) of NSF. The UPS program represented a unique attempt to bring together faculty-student university teams to conduct research in the Washington policy milieu on issues of interest and relevance to current policymakers. The program called for each team to spend at least a portion of its research time in the Washington area interacting closely with STPO project officers and other government officials responsible for policy in the individual areas of research. The objectives were twofold: to prepare research reports more closely attuned to the immediate concerns and problems of policymakers and to assist in the professional training of graduate students by introducing them to the governmental policy process and to subject areas of increasing policy interest for the future. In the summer of 1974, five UPS research teams spent up to ten weeks in the Washington area. These teams then returned to their individual campuses during the academic year of 1974-75 to do further background research and prepare final reports. Participants included teams from Harvard, University of Washington (Seattle), State University of New York (Binghamton), Harvard-MIT (a combined team), and George Washington University (GWU). The overall program was administered by the Graduate Program in Science, Technology and Public Policy at George Washington.

The GWU team, which I headed, wishes to thank the Science and Technology Policy Office and its director, Russell Drew, for sponsoring this novel approach to policy-relevant research and graduate student training. We are particularly indebted to Hylan Lyon, who was our original project officer in STPO when the research began. Dr. Lyon not only contributed substantially to the early conceptualization of the study but also took a personal interest in the graduate student training aspects of the program. He spent many long hours with the team as a whole and with individual students offering his own insights and experience in the policy areas we were investigating. When Dr. Lyon left STPO to become the deputy director of the Science, Technology and Industry Directorate of the Organization for Economic Cooperation and Development (OECD) his role was ably assumed by Ernest Powers and Richard Gray who saw us through the many difficult weeks of drafting the final reports and bringing the project to a fruitful conclusion. For the patience and wisdom of these individuals, as well as the entire STPO staff, we are profoundly grateful. There are extremely busy professionals who nevertheless recognized the need and the long-term payoff of helping to influence university research and graduate training in directions relevant to future policy concerns.

In addition, we owe thanks to numerous other government officials who assisted us with interviews and materials for our research. We are unable to acknowledge all of them, and many asked that they remain anonymous. The student members of the team have cited individuals and institutions that helped them in their respective case studies. I wish here to acknowledge a few additional people whose assistance was particularly helpful to me: Leo Packer, Justin Bloom, and Oswald Ganley of the Department of State; Nelson Sievering and Jack Vanderryn of the Energy Research and Development Administration; William Porter of the Federal Energy Administration; Maurice Mountain of the Defense Department; Tom Ward and Arthur Morrissey of the Central Intelligence Agency (Morrissey is now with State); John Shepard of the Department of Commerce; James Urano, Keith Byergo, Guy Baird, and Edgar Owens of the Agency for International Development; and Richard Price and Arthur Shantz of the General Accounting Office.

I am also grateful to professional colleagues who read and criticized portions of this study: Herbert Kleiman of Battelle Memorial Institute; Herman Pollack of the Graduate Program in Science, Technology and Public Policy, George Washington University; various individuals at the Rand Corporation in Santa Monica where I spent a day discussing an early draft; and members of the panel on American Power and the International System at the 1975 Political Science Association Convention where I presented a paper summarizing the results of this project.

In addition to those students acknowledged earlier who authored the case studies of this volume, I also benefited from the assistance and contribution of other students. They include Alan Buckley, Harold Federow, Roland Fung, Dana Peck, Henry Resnikoff, and Dean Sagar. For administrative and staff support, we all owe special thanks to Barbara Claassen and Rose Limbrick of the George Washington University Graduate Program. None of us could have retained our sense of direction or good humor without their steady and sensitive guidance.

CONTENTS

	Page
ACKNOWLEDGMENTS	v
PREFACE	vi
LIST OF TABLES	xiii
LIST OF FIGURES	xv

Chapter

1   A NATIONAL PERSPECTIVE ON TECHNOLOGY TRANSFER   1

     The Need for a National Perspective   1
     Broad Trends and Specific Cases   5
     Issues and Actors   9
     Notes   19

2   POSTWAR HISTORY OF U.S. PRACTICE TOWARD TECHNOLOGY TRANSFER   21

     Technology Transfer and Military-Strategic Policy   21
     Technology Transfer and U.S. Foreign Assistance Programs   29
     Technology Transfer and the Private Industrial Sector   40
     Notes   48

3   CONTEMPORARY DEVELOPMENTS IN U.S. PRACTICE TOWARD TECHNOLOGY TRANSFER   55

     From Strategic to Economic Issues   55
     From Government to Industrial Actors   65
     Notes   82

Chapter		Page
4	KamAZ: U.S. TECHNOLOGY TRANSFER TO THE SOVIET UNION Harlan S. Finer, Howard Gobstein, and George D. Holliday	87
	Exploratory Contacts	90
	Contract Negotiations	99
	Contract Implementation	105
	KamAZ: Implications for Future U.S.-Soviet Commercial Relations	110
	Notes	116
5	ENERGY R AND D: U.S. TECHNOLOGY TRANSFER TO ADVANCED WESTERN COUNTRIES James P. Lester	120
	R and D and the Energy Crisis	121
	R and D Discussions: A Multilevel Drama	125
	The Goal Setting Environment: U.S. Strategy in the Energy Crisis	128
	The Intergovernmental Level: The Washington Energy Conference	129
	The Intragovernmental Level: Bureaucratic Policymaking in the United States	132
	The Transgovernmental Level: The Energy Coordinating Group	144
	The International Organization Level: The International Energy Agency	153
	Conclusions: Implications for Future Collaboration	158
	Notes	163
6	BAUXITE-ALUMINUM INDUSTRY: U.S. TECHNOLOGY TRANSFER TO RESOURCE-RICH DEVELOPING COUNTRIES Mary M. Allen	171
	Bauxite Supplies and U.S. Interests	172
	International Bauxite Association	178
	Domestic Economic Issues for the United States	180
	Foreign Economic Issues for the United States	182
	National Security Issues for the United States	184
	Foreign Diplomatic Issues for the United States	185
	U.S. Government Options	187

Chapter		Page
	Foreign Bauxite Supplier Options	191
	U.S. Aluminum Industry Options	195
	Conclusions	199
	Notes	205
7	IRRI SMALL AGRICULTURAL MACHINERY PROJECT: U.S. TECHNOLOGY TRANSFER TO RESOURCE-POOR DEVELOPING COUNTRIES Ann L. Becker and Carol A. Ulinski	208
	Stages of the IRRI Project	212
	The Research and Development Stage	213
	The Manufacturing Stage	220
	The Farmer Stage	234
	The Role of Government Policies	237
	An Evaluation of the IRRI Project	246
	Notes	259
8	NATIONAL AND CASE STUDY PERSPECTIVES ON TECHNOLOGY TRANSFER: AN INTEGRATED VIEW	265
	Economic-Social Criteria for Evaluating Technology Exports	266
	Growth of Disembodied Technology Exports	271
	Declining Government Funding of Industrial R and D	274
	Adjustments in Government-Industry Relations	281
	Notes	286
9	U.S. FOREIGN POLICY FOR TECHNOLOGY TRANSFER: RESEARCH NEEDS AND POLICY DIRECTIONS	288
	Research Needs	289
	Policy Directions	295
	Notes	301
APPENDIX: TECHNICAL COMPONENTS OF ALUMINUM		303
INDEX		316
ABOUT THE AUTHOR AND CONTRIBUTORS		327

LIST OF TABLES

Table		Page
1.1	Motivations of Technology Transfer	12
1.2	Definition of Technology and Technology Transfer	15
2.1	Foreign Policy Motivations and Initiatives in Technology Transfer	33
2.2	Direct Investment Abroad and Income Flows, All Areas, 1948-74	44
3.1	Trends in Funds for Total Research and Development, by Source of Funds, 1953-75	66
3.2	Trends in Funds for Industrial Research and Development, by Source of Funds, 1953-75	67
3.3	Trends in Research and Development Funds for Manufacturing and Non-manufacturing Industries, by Source of Funds, 1963-73	69
3.4	Trends in Research and Development Funds for Manufacturing Industries Only, by Sector and Source of Funds, 1963-73	70
3.5	Trends in Funds for Total Research and Development, by Sector of Performance, 1953-75	75
5.1	Transgovernmental System of Action (ECG Phase)	122
5.2	International Organization System of Action (IEA Phase)	122
5.3	Current U.S. Cooperative Programs in Energy Research and Development	123
5.4	Federal Energy Research and Development Funding, Fiscal Years 1969-75	133
5.5	Energy Research and Development Administration: R and D	134

Table		Page
5.6	Office of Coal Research Energy Research and Development, Fiscal Years 1975-79	136
5.7	U.S. Lead Agencies and the Ten Priority Areas for Cooperation	140
5.8	Energy Research and Development Expenditures in ECG Countries, Fiscal Year 1974	152
6.1	U.S. Net Imports of Bauxite, Manganese, and Tin	176
7.1	IRRI/AID Contracts	210
7.2	Sales of Briggs and Stratton 7-8 hp Engines, 1970-73	222
7.3	CB:IBRD Credit Financing, May 15, 1974—June 30, 1975	246
8.1	AID Expenditures, Fiscal Years 1962-73	279
8.2	Food for Peace Total Expenditures	280
A.1	Aluminum Shipments Distribution by Market, 1972 and 1973	304
A.2	Types of Bauxite	305
A.3	Compositional Range of Bauxite Ore for Some Major World Producers	306
A.4	World Mine Production and Reserves, 1973	307
A.5	U.S. Imports of Bauxite, by Source, 1973	308
A.6	Major U.S. Suppliers and Reserves	308
A.7	U.S. Imports of Alumina, by Source	309
A.8	Alumina Production, Worldwide	310
A.9	National Strategic Stockpile of Bauxite	312

Table		Page
A.10	Major Potential Domestic Sources of Aluminum	313

LIST OF FIGURES

Figure		Page
1.1	Stage and Level of Technology Application	17
5.1	Analytical Framework: Four Subsystems of Action	126
7.1	First Sequence of Relationships, IRRI Project	213
7.2	Second Sequence of Relationships, IRRI Project	214
7.3	Third Sequence of Relationships, IRRI Project	214
7.4	First Sequence: Primary Linkages	249
7.5	Second Sequence: Secondary Linkages	253
7.6	Third Sequence: Tertiary Linkages	255
7.7	Governmental Role in Indigenization of Technology	258

Technology Transfer and U.S. Foreign Policy

CHAPTER 1

A NATIONAL PERSPECTIVE ON TECHNOLOGY TRANSFER

"In a global economy of physical scarcity," Secretary of State Henry Kissinger said to the Sixth Special Session of the United Nations General Assembly in April 1974, "science and technology are becoming our most precious resource."[1] He was undoubtedly referring to the particular importance of science and technology to U.S. foreign policy. Recent discussions on technology transfer with Latin American countries, the concern over outflows of U.S. technology to the Soviet Union and Eastern Europe, the promotion of American technology to the Middle East, the new emphasis on technical assistance and expertise in U.S. aid policy—all point to the increasing salience of science and technology in U.S. diplomacy. The <u>International Economic Report of the President</u> submitted to Congress in March 1975 refers to technology as "a valuable and saleable national asset."[2] Indeed, in the more competitive world economic situation today, U.S. technology may be assuming some of the role that U.S. goods and capital played in an earlier U.S. dominated economic world. As Kissinger himself is reported to believe, "America's ability to contribute money and run the world in the old-fashioned way of the 1950's and 1960's is now over. What we can contribute—and what the world wants—is our technological capabilities."[3]

THE NEED FOR A NATIONAL PERSPECTIVE

In short, U.S. technology in foreign affairs today is significant not only in terms of its military-strategic value but also increasingly in terms of its commercial and social value (that is,

its relationship to international economic competitiveness and to
national development). In view of this expanded significance, the
present study set out to review postwar U.S. policies or nonpolicies
toward the transfer of U.S. technology across national boundaries
and to assess the current issues and trends with respect to these
policies. Specifically, it sought to address two broad questions:

1. When viewed from an overall national perspective, what
are the issues and objectives that have guided U.S. policies toward
the international transfer of U.S. technology, and is there a basis
in the current debate and discussion of these issues for formulating
overall national guidelines toward the use of technology in future
U.S. foreign relations?
2. Related to the first question, what are the mechanisms and
institutions by which U.S. technology has been transferred and
managed in postwar foreign affairs, and are there discernible shifts
in these mechanisms in current developments, suggesting some
redistribution of influence among U.S. groups (actors) in the making
of technology transfer policy?

In posing these questions, we took note of the fact that, in the
postwar period, the outflow and evaluation of U.S. technology across
national boundaries has taken place in three separate and largely
unrelated policy contexts:

1. The strategic-military context emphasizing the role of
U.S. technology in maintaining a qualitative strategic superiority
over communist and other adversaries.
2. The foreign assistance context involving the use of U.S.
technology to influence domestic and foreign policy conditions in
friendly or neutral countries.
3. The private industrial context reflecting, in large part,
the transfer of technology within the integrated organizational
structure of the multinational company but also including significant
transfers between independent enterprises (as, for example, in
industrial relations with Japan).

Policy in these different contexts has not been consistent. Nor
has it been formulated by the same actors. In the first context, U.S.
policy has been largely restrictive and heavily influenced by high-
level governmental agencies. In the third context, policy has been
largely liberal and formulated chiefly in the board rooms of private
multinational corporations. In the second context, policy reflects
a mix of restrictive (conditional) and liberal (humanitarian) considerations and public and private organizations.

Policy in these different contexts was also discussed in different terms and applied to different regions of the world. For example, the term technology transfer normally referred to industrial exchanges, primarily among advanced, industrialized countries—United States, Canada, Western Europe, and Japan (essentially member countries of the Organization for Economic Cooperation and Development—OECD). The term technical assistance referred to foreign assistance efforts primarily in developing countries but also, as in the case of nuclear reactors and satellite communications, in Western European countries. The term technology export referred to strategic materials and export controls, chiefly in relations with communist countries. In this study, we use these terms interchangeably to refer to the <u>outflow</u> of U.S. technology across national boundaries in whatever context for whatever reason to whatever country. We are seeking to assess the rationale and mechanisms for the use of U.S. technology in foreign relations from an overall national perspective. A national perspective, it should be noted, is not the same as a U.S. government perspective, any more than it is identical with a private industrial perspective. The only assumption we make is that it is worthwhile examining technology outflows from a territorial, nation-state perspective.

We are led to this assumption less by a conviction that the nation-state is an indestructible unit of action and analysis in present and future international relations than by an awareness that a comprehensive perspective has been sorely neglected in previous studies of U.S. technology in foreign affairs. These studies have either reflected the heavy preoccupation of postwar U.S. policy with defense and space technology,[4] or they have looked at only specific contexts or issues of U.S. technology policy, such as technology in the foreign aid context[5] or technology in global health, population, and resource areas.[6] No study has attempted to assess or compare technology policies across different contexts. There has been little generalization within each of these contexts (for example, as we note subsequently, a case law approach has dominated the strategic-military review of technology exports), let alone among them. It was broadly assumed that technology transfers could not be abstracted either from the particular political relationship in which they were embedded (that is, the adversary, neutral, or friendly nature of the recipient country) or from the economic form in which they were embodied (that is, product or capital outflows).

There were good reasons to hesitate in abstracting technology transfer from its political and economic context. As this study reveals, the range of issues and expertise required to deal with the task is enormous. Two considerations, however, made the effort at conceptualization seem worthwhile, despite the high level of abstraction and difficulty involved.

First, an analogy with the evolution of trade policy in the United States suggests that the consideration of technology policy from a national perspective, while premature, nevertheless may not be wholly irrelevant or without practical consequence for policy developments in the future. There are only four types of economic factors exchanged in international relations—products, capital (short and long term), information, and people—and we have slowly, over the last 50 years, developed a national perspective and a set of national guidelines to deal with one of these, the international exchange of goods. This perspective, embodied most recently in the 1974 Trade Reform Bill, did not emerge overnight. For a long time, we had trade policies for specific products, industries, and countries, but no overall framework for assessing these policies across individual product or industrial sectors. Today, this framework exists, though there is continued debate about its specific contents. By contrast, we continue to evaluate capital exchanges from a narrower balance of payments perspective. However, with the advent of floating exchange rates (nullifying the effects of capital controls) and the growing domestic and international interest in the multinational corporation, this perspective is expanding to embrace broader economic and social criteria. It is not unthinkable that debate over these criteria might someday yield a consensus and perhaps minimal guidelines for capital exchanges.

To be sure, we are nowhere near this point for exchanges of information (know-how) and people (professional skills and services). Thus, it is clearly premature to consider technology policy before we understand investment flows in which so much technology is embodied. Nevertheless, a second consideration urges us to go ahead. As part of the reevaluation of investment exchanges going on in contemporary international relations, some countries, developing but also developed ones, are seeking to unbundle or disembody technology from international product and capital flows. They wish to obtain economic resources from various countries in separate packages—technology or know-how from one supplier, capital from another, management and marketing services from a third, and so on. If this tendency grows (and, at the moment, we have only scattered, case study evidence of it), the United States may be asked to sell its information and expertise increasingly apart from its products and investment control. This development would quickly focus policy questions on technology apart from trade and investment flows.

Thus, it may not be too early, even from a political point of view, to begin to identify the common issues and practices affecting technology transfer across U.S. national boundaries, irrespective of

A NATIONAL PERSPECTIVE

the context or destination of these transfers. This effort need not lead to nationalistic or restrictive policies (which is the most common criticism of the national perspective as a basis of analysis). Indeed, to continue the analogy with trade policy, it may be the only way to salvage technology flows from the mercantilist and restrictive practices that crippled trade flows in the interwar period. The development of national perspectives in trade policy provided the necessary framework to weigh overall gains and losses from trade flows and to stanch the protectionist claims of individual product and industrial groups.

BROAD TRENDS AND SPECIFIC CASES

Accordingly, the study set out to pull together the multiple issues and characteristics attending the technology transfer process. To do this, we operated at two different levels. One level involved a high degree of abstraction and conceptualization. At this level, we first sought to review, compare and synthesize U.S. postwar experience in technology transfer across diverse and largely unrelated policy sectors. Chapter 2 of this study lays out this historical background in strategic-military, foreign assistance, and private industrial policy areas. We then sought to identify, again at a high level of synthesis, the principal contemporary issues and trends suggesting deviations from this historical experience. These issues and trends, we thought, might help to clarify longer-term developments contributing to the current debate about technology transfer policy. This debate is multifaceted and confusing. The confusion is compounded by the historically fragmentized context for discussing and evaluating technology transfer policy. There is an evident need to step back from the immediate discourse and to look for broader, perhaps secular phenomena underlying the discontent and dissension among policy groups. Chapter 3 of this study presents this broader view. It identifies several patterns, some advanced, others incipient, that are already evident in technology transfer events and that suggest a set of hypotheses and projections telling us what to look for in individual cases of technology transfer policy in the future.

These latter hypotheses and projections were particularly useful to us at the second level of our work. This was the level of specialization and detailed case studies. Because we were operating at a high level of abstraction in the conceptual part of the project with few previous studies to guide us, there was a need to balance our effort with more specialized empirical investigations. We undertook, therefore, four very specific case studies of technology transfer issues. We were guided in our selection of these studies by the conceptual aims of the project. For example, it seemed reasonable, in connection with our comparison and synthesis of U.S. policy in strategic-military, foreign assistance, and private industrial areas, to do case studies in each of these areas. The case studies might then offer illustrations or correctives of the patterns we identified in our broad historical and contemporary review of technology transfer policy.

With some modifications, that is the strategy we followed. In selecting a case study to illustrate strategic-military issues or technology transfer relations with communist countries, we had to defer to the nonclassified, open, university context in which we were operating and pick a study which would focus more on the recent and novel economic issues in technology relations with socialist or planned economy countries than on traditional strategic-military issues. We selected the participation of a U.S. company, Swindell-Dressler of Pittsburgh, Pennsylvania, in the construction of the Kama River truck plant in the Soviet Union. While, at the very beginning, Swindell's participation in this project raised some defense or, at least, foreign policy issues, the principal issues after an export license was approved were commercial and economic. Chapter 4 presents this case study.

Economic issues in technology transfer, of course, are most important in relations among advanced, industrialized countries. Ideally, to illustrate technology transfer practices in private contacts among industrialized countries, we would have liked to do a case study of technology transfer within the multinational company or between independent enterprises. Once again, however, our situation and resources dictated otherwise. We were unlikely in a university context to secure the cooperation of private industry concerning the transfer of proprietary information. In the case of Swindell, there was a public record of sorts due to export licensing procedures for technology transfers with communist countries. For industries operating within the free world, there is no such record. We struck a compromise. Instead of looking at an exclusively private transfer of technology among advanced countries, we looked at a government-initiated effort among these countries which also involved private company participation and thus illustrated some of the commercial issues at stake. This effort was the U.S.-initiated discussions of international cooperation or technology transfer in energy R and D, begun under the auspices of the Energy Coordinating Group of the Washington Energy Conference and continued within the recently established International Energy Agency (IEA). Government participation in these discussions not only facilitated our

A NATIONAL PERSPECTIVE 7

research effort but also seemed appropriate in light of one of our conclusions in this study. If, as one analyst notes, there is "a currently accelerating, worldwide trend toward the expansion of the public sectors of national economies and increased governmental intervention in the market process,"[7] the U.S. government may be increasingly encouraged into some novel partnerships with U.S. industry. At the least, as we argue subsequently in this study, the government-industry interface may be a more interesting place to look for significant developments in future use of U.S. technology in foreign affairs than the industrial sector alone. The energy R and D study, in fact, revealed some novel departures in government-industry relationships. Chapter 5 gives the details of this case study.

To illustrate technology transfer in the foreign assistance sector, we decided to do two case studies to reflect the new distinction between the third world, developing countries rich in raw materials that can be expected to pay for their technology imports, and the fourth world, poor developing countries that will continue to require foreign aid. For third world countries, we did a case study of the bauxite-aluminum sector to examine the potential of nonpetroleum raw material sectors for OPEC-type cartelization and large-scale technology transfer, such as is currently taking place between industrialized and OPEC countries. Foreign suppliers have dramatically increased the price of bauxite, raising familiar issues of import dependence and development of alternative supplies. Chapter 6 lays out the options for U.S. government and industry in meeting this further challenge to resource supplies.

With regard to poor fourth world countries, we did a case study of the concept of appropriate technology transfer, looking specifically at a ten-year-old project funded by the Agency for International Development (AID) at the Internation Rice Research Institute (IRRI) in the Philippines to develop small farm, labor-intensive agricultural equipment. This project has acquired new significance in light of 1973 amendments to the Foreign Assistance Act. These amendments placed new emphasis on technical assistance and employment of the poor majority in foreign aid to developing countries. Appropriate technology transfer, illustrated by the AID/IRRI project, emphasizes adaption and development of technologies uniquely suited to labor and resource conditions in developing countries. The AID/IRRI project therefore deserves careful analysis as a possible model of future U.S. aid programs to implement the 1973 amendments. Chapter 7 evaluates this project in light of these new conditions.

The case studies leave a significant gap between our interest in economic issues and our investigation of private sector technology transfers, either within the multinational company or between independent enterprises. We have compensated for this to some extent by broader inquiries into the role of technology in contemporary economic theory (see Chapter 3). We have also availed ourselves of recent studies of private sector technology issues.[8] Our purpose, however, is less to add anything new to the ongoing effort to develop theoretical economic explanations or standards for evaluating technology transfers than to show what the likely policy and institutional issues may be while economic theory in this area continues to be underdeveloped and under development. Policy, it is clear, does not always wait for theory in these matters. For example, practices and institutions to screen technology transfers to socialist and planned economy countries on purely economic-commercial grounds may emerge long before there is a generally accepted set of theoretical economic-commercial criteria to evaluate these transfers. Some may deplore this rush to policy before theory, and some may deplore this study for trying to understand policy and institutional issues before clarifying prior economic issues. Suffice it to note here, however, that seeking to analyze policy issues, whether or not adequate theoretical understanding exists, is not the same as advocating particular policies. The principal author of this study is not at all convinced that the government should have a role in the economic evaluation of technology transfers. But he is willing to report as accurately as possible existing trends that may be pushing public policy in this direction.

Chapter 8 draws together the reviews and findings of the four case studies. It discusses examples from these studies that illustrate the broad trends identified in Chapter 3. The case studies suggest there can be no substitute for intensive analysis of individual policy issues when the latter arise. But these studies also suggest, when reviewed in the context of an overall conceptual framework, that technology transfer policy involves issues and problems that go far beyond the specific details of individual cases. It is important to have a framework that cuts across and identifies broader and frequently novel issues.

Chapter 9 seeks to address some of these larger and still relatively unexplored issues that underlie contemporary and future U.S. policy toward technology transfer. In one sense, Chapter 9 is a reflection of the gap in our general understanding between a national and individual case study perspective on technology transfer policy. The gap itself is not surprising. As we noted, this study constitutes the first effort we know of to deal with technology policy across the board. We have had to proceed deductively as well as inductively to sketch out the gray area between individual case studies and macroeconomic trends. Many of the arguments we make, therefore, are speculative. They suggest patterns we must

A NATIONAL PERSPECTIVE

test out empirically, in particular through more aggregate data analysis. Only then can we confirm them or understand their full implications. More experts and resources will be required to do this testing. In one sense, an effort at synthesis, such as I and my assistants attempted in this study, has to be the product of a single mind. Threads have to be drawn together from many sources and directions. Confirming or disproving the patterns woven by these threads, however, is now the task of multimember professional interdisciplinary teams and larger-scale information processing and data analysis centers. Indeed, there may be a serious need, as we argue in the last chapter, to dedicate the same kind of resources to the analysis of foreign economic and technology policy problems that the U.S. government, in particular the Defense Department, has dedicated over the past 30 years to the analysis of strategic problems. Technological and industrial problems, especially struggles over natural resources and over domain of nonnational, nonterrestrial space, may pose as serious a threat to world peace in the future as strategic problems posed in the past.

ISSUES AND ACTORS

To classify and begin to relate technology transfer issues at both the general and specialized case study levels, the study evolved a framework of issues (motivations or rationales for technology transfer) and actors (mechanisms) involved in the technology transfer process. This framework had to be broad enough to capture the wide scope of the technology transfer debate but also specific enough to introduce some precision into the ofttimes confusing language of this debate.

A critical step in establishing this framework was to define the various perspectives from which technology outflows might be evaluated by different actors. The debate over technology transfer policy derives in large part from the different ordering of these perspectives by individual actors. We identified five such purposes or perspectives for evaluating technology outflows. Our definition of these perspectives is critical, we believe, for introducing greater clarity into the technology transfer debate.

1. military-strategic—use or value (positive or negative) of technology transfer for the development, manufacture, or deployment of military weaponry and forces. There are two ways in which a technology transfer may contribute to military-strategic capabilities: (a) directly enhance military capabilities—this is the end-use issue in technology export

review cases; (b) improve civilian capabilities and release resources to increase military expenditures, or help to offset adverse civilian effects of existing military expenditures—this is the fungibility issue in technology export review cases.

2. foreign policy-diplomatic—use or value of technology transfer for exercising influence in the international arena. From this perspective the transfer of technology not only has an effect on military-strategic capabilities, it may also affect political-diplomatic intentions. For example, technology transfer may affect the will to use certain capabilities no less than the actual level of such capabilities. It may also enhance the prestige, leadership, and image of the country initiating the transfer. In short, technology is not just an instrument of power, that is, coercive force; it is also an instrument of influence, or psychological force. Frequently, these uses of technology in foreign affairs are incompatible; for example, the decision to deny a technology export to a recipient country because of its capability- or power-enhancing potential may also deny to the source country the diplomatic or influence-enhancing potential of the export. This conflict has been particularly noticeable in U.S. policies toward the export of atomic energy technology—such exports being restricted, on the one hand, for fear of their power-enhancing effects (that is, proliferation) and promoted, on the other, to enhance U.S. prestige and influence in world affairs (that is, Atoms for Peace). This conflict, of course, represents the difficult foreign policy or political-diplomatic trade-off issue of technology export review cases, that is, whether to grant the technology in anticipation of uncertain political returns or to deny the technology and perhaps contribute to independent development.

3. economic-commercial—use or value of technology transfer for profit or commercial gain.

4. social-environmental—use or value of technology transfer for the "quality of life," that is an evaluation of the transfer not just in terms of commercial gains and losses but in broader social and environmental terms.

5. administrative-institutional—use or value of technology transfer to affect organizational or bureaucratic interests within the United States. Just as technology transfer may be used as an

A NATIONAL PERSPECTIVE

instrument of influence in the international arena, it may also be used as an instrument of influence among agencies within the United States. For example, some elements in Congress may use the technology transfer issue to pursue a power struggle with the executive or, in the case of individual presidential aspirants in Congress, to affect their image and influence in the political system as a whole (an uncharitable interpretation of Senator Jackson's interest in technology transfer to the Soviet Union). Similarly, as we note in Chapters 8 and 9, technology transfer or, more broadly, resource transfer issues are the source of an increasing tug-of-war between free market oriented government agencies, such as Treasury, Agriculture, and Commerce, and foreign policy oriented agencies, such as State. While these institutional conflicts are always based to some extent on substance, they also reflect the operation of checks and balances within the U.S. governmental system, in which bureaucratic tendencies to defend and expand organizational turf serve to check excess as well as, at times, to thwart efficiency.

This definition of perspectives for evaluating technology transfers (Table 1.1 summarizes these perspectives) deliberately avoids the use of the term national security. The latter is not irrelevant, as we note in a moment, but it is a vague, umbrella concept which is used interchangeably by all of the disputants in the technology transfer debate. For example, industrial spokesmen frequently imply that national security requires maximization of wealth and hence liberal policies toward technology transfer, while defense officials place strategic superiority in specific weapons technology above overall maximization of economic output and call for technology export controls. Or labor spokesmen view national security as a function of the distribution rather than maximization of economic returns from technology transfer and advocate controls on investment outflows. What is involved in these different definitions of national security is a different ordering of the perspectives listed above. The definition of national security results from a subjective weighting by each group of the relative importance of power, influence, profit, social consequences, and organizational interests in overall returns from technology transfer.

Now, in a pluralistic society, each group is entitled to participate in the definition of national security. A study that seeks objectivity, therefore, should not load the concept of national security automatically in favor of one group or another. Through debate among these groups, a consensus may emerge on what constitutes national security. This type of consensus prevailed for a good part of the postwar period during which military-strategic concerns outweighed all others and defense officials exercised primary influence over the

TABLE 1.1

Motivations of Technology Transfer

Motivation	Definition
military-strategic	use or value of technology transfer for the development, manufacture, or deployment of military <u>capabilities</u>, i.e., weaponry and forces: a. directly enhance military capabilities b. improve civilian capabilities and release resources to military outlays or to offset adverse civilian effects of existing military outlays.
foreign policy-diplomatic	use or value of technology transfer for influencing <u>intentions</u> (as compared with capabilities) in the international arena.
economic-commercial	use or value of technology transfer for <u>profit</u> or commercial gain.
social-environmental	use or value of technology transfer for improving the "<u>quality of life,</u>" i.e., consequences for equity and ecology (as compared with commercial gain).
administrative-institutional	use or value of technology transfer to advance <u>organizational or bureaucratic interests</u> within U.S. domestic system.

Source: Compiled by the author.

definition of national security. With the onset of detente, however, this consensus broke down, and, as we argue in this study, economic-social concerns weigh more directly today in calculations regarding technology transfer. The current debate reflects this broadening of concerns or interests affected by technology transfer and undoubtedly represents the first step toward shaping a new consensus that incorporates these additional concerns.

National security, then, as we use it in this study, refers to a composite judgment by a particular group (or individual) of the relative importance of the different purposes or perspectives for evaluating technology transfer which we have listed above.

The various groups or actors involved in the technology transfer debate include government agencies, industrial groups, labor unions, foundations (especially in foreign assistance areas), and even, in some instances, consumer groups. Our focus in this study is primarily on U.S. actors. Foreign actors, such as bauxite supplying countries, are also included insofar as their behavior raises various options for U.S. actors. But we undertook in this study an assessment of technology transfer issues from the point of view of U.S. interests, not foreign interests or the interests of the international system as a whole. Once again, this focus was chosen less because we believe U.S. interests are the only ones that matter than because previous studies have relatively neglected these interests. Much of the theorizing about technology transfer to developing countries, for example, has been done from a systemic rather than a national vantage point.[9]

The principal actors we are concerned with in this study are government agencies and private industries. Whether public or private actors are involved in the transfer process constitutes one of the important ways to distinguish among various mechanisms of technology transfer. These mechanisms may be further contrasted in terms of three principal features:[10]

1. scope—bilateral versus multilateral
2. function—whether the transfer aims at
   a. acquiring a new capability (R and D)
   b. making effective use of an existing capability (operation)
   c. coping with the consequences of the use of a capability (regulation)
3. instrumentality—whether the transfer calls for
   a. coordination of independent policies
   b. joint facilities
   c. a common policy integrating specific policies
   d. a fully unified policy substituting for independent policies.

In our discussion of historical and contemporary patterns associated with technology transfer policies, we look for shifts in these various features of technology transfer mechanisms. For example, in the private industrial sector, what has been or is today the relative preference for the following instrumentalities of technology transfer?

1. market-sharing or other cartel-like agreements representing coordination of policies of independent partners
2. common prototype or pilot plants representing joint facilities of two partners
3. specialization agreements, in which each partner produces only one component or product utilized by both, reflecting an integrated policy
4. merger agreements or direct investment representing a single, unified structure and policy.

Finally and crucially, we need to define what we mean in this study by technology. Technology is most usefully defined in terms of a spectrum ranging from scientific publications and exchanges, at one end, to proprietary information and professionally-qualified people, at the other. Indeed, technology, it would seem, is always embodied in one of four primary forms: publications, products, proprietary information, and people. Table 1.2 lists these principal <u>forms</u> of technology, together with a twofold classification of <u>types</u> of technology and a representative (not exhaustive) listing of practical <u>modes or mechanisms</u> of technology transfer. In some sense, Table 1.2 suggests that the different forms of technology incorporate higher and higher levels of technology and accordingly represent increasing value. Scientific publications are widely available and generally of small value to the recipient unless the latter has a broad background to interpret and apply basic knowledge. Products embody more visible and useful forms of know-how, but again this know-how is available, without accompanying information and personnel exchanges, only through a difficult process of reverse engineering. Proprietary information offers the know-how to reproduce specific products and processes but also requires personnel exchanges to yield maximum benefit. Finally the transfer of people may constitute the most valuable form of technology since people embody the very ability to create new products and processes.

By the same token, the different types of technology, since they embody larger and larger proportions of people-related know-how as one moves from the bottom to the top of Table 1.2, also represent an ascending order of value. Firm specific technology is

TABLE 1.2

Definition of Technology and Technology Transfer

Forms of Technology	Types of Technology	Area of Technology Use	Mechanisms of Technology Transfer
People	firm specific (information specific to firm's experience and activities not attributable to any specific item firm produces)	R and D	training and education
		Management and Planning	management services
			cooperative R and D agreements
		Manufacturing and Production	know-how and technical assistance agreements
			direct investment
			coproduction/joint venture
		Marketing and Distribution	turnkey plant sales
Proprietary information	system specific (information about manufacture of product or item that any manufacturer would obtain)		patent and license (without know-how) agreements
		Design and Construction	capital equipment
			intermediate products
			final products
			scientific meeting
Products	general (information common to an industry or trade)	Maintenance and Service Manuals	
Publications			professional journals

Source: Compiled by the author.

Approximate Relative Value of Technology Transfer

usually more valuable than general technology, or technology used in establishing an R and D capability (which can produce new innovations on its own) is more valuable than technology contained in maintenance and service manuals. The mechanisms of technology transfer listed in Table 1.2 reflect this scale of value in the actual transfer process. Again, training programs or technical assistance agreements are likely to be more valuable to a recipient country over the long run than specific products or license agreements without know-how provisions.

The ordinal ranking suggested here is by no means precise. The forms, types, and mechanisms of technology transfer all shade into one another. The most valuable packages are those which incorporate, in some proportion, all of these ingredients. For example, turnkey plant sales usually incorporate not only the items falling below the turnkey entry in Table 1.2 but also some know-how, management (at least, in the construction phase), and training services. To the extent, however, that the transfer terminates at the time of start-up of the plant, the mechanism may involve less technology transfer and hence be less valuable than a direct investment mechanism or a long-term technical assistance agreement in which technology is exchanged on a continuing basis. This assumes, of course, that direct investment mechanisms are utilized fully in terms of their technology transfer potential. In individual cases, perhaps overall as some developing countries contend, little or no technology may be transferred through the multinational company. Table 1.2 merely suggests that the possibility of ongoing and hence more valuable people-embodied exchanges is present in the case of direct investment, while it is not in the case of individual product or plant sales.

The value of the technology transferred may also vary depending on the stage of the industrial cycle at which the technology is applied. Figure 1.1 adds a horizontal dimension of value to the vertical dimension of Table 1.2. It suggests that technologies applied at the exploration stage, such as earth resource satellite monitoring technology, may be more valuable than technologies specific to certain manufacturing processes, because the former technologies may affect a wider range of industrial sectors than the latter. Presumably, new resource discoveries could stimulate all sorts of industrial activities from mining to manufacturing sectors. Similarly, innovations in distribution systems could affect the utilization of a whole range of consumer products, whereas innovation in the utilization of a single product would have a more limited impact.

Obviously, value here is a function of bottlenecks in a particular economy as well as the stage of various industrial sectors at which principal value is added to a particular product (that is, the

FIGURE 1.1

Stage and Level of Technology Application

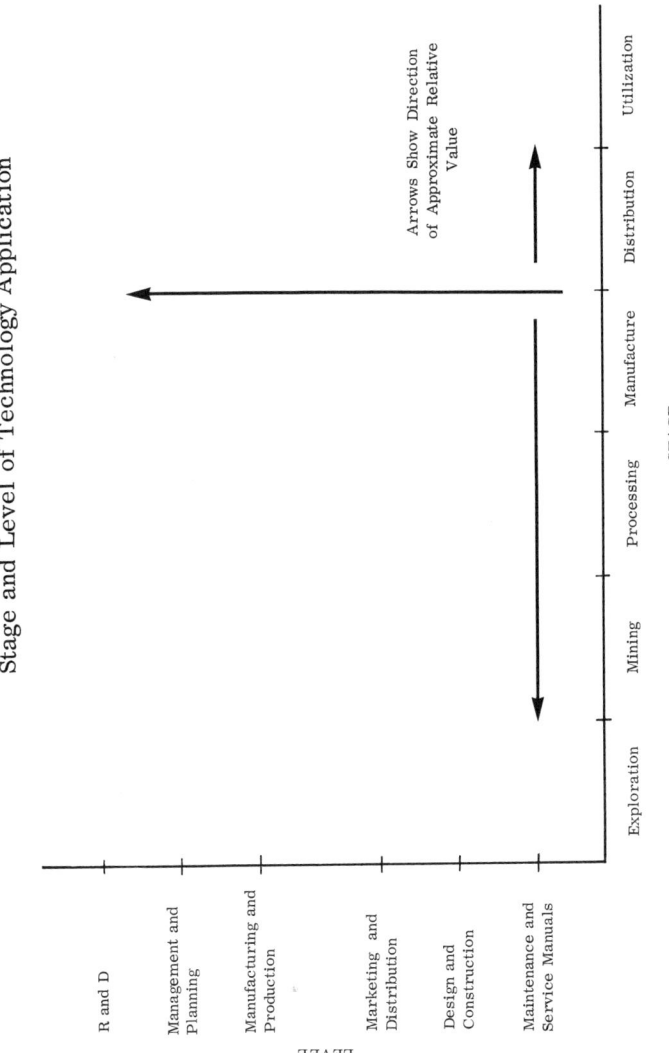

Source: Compiled by the author.

principal value-added stages). Moreover, as we note in Chapter 3 of this study, the value of individual technology transfers may be quite different for recipient as compared to source countries. What Table 1.2 and Figure 1.1 try to suggest is that, from an American point of view (that is, as a source country), it may not be too early to begin to make and to clarify these types of value distinctions. If, as we discuss later, U.S. technology transfer in the future assumes more of a people-embodied than product- or capital-embodied form and if recipient countries, especially developing countries, increase their demands for value-added technologies in certain industries (for example, the bauxite-aluminum industry where principal value is added to the final product beyond the mining stage), the issue of how to price technology outflows from the United States so as to capture their "true" value (whatever that is, as we discuss later) may become a critical as well as controversial public policy question. The rough effort in this study to suggest initial value distinctions seeks to anticipate this coming controversy. As we argue in our recommendations for further research, much more effort is needed to develop and refine the admittedly rough initial categorizations we have proposed.

One last word about the focus of this study. We have looked at U.S. policies toward the outflow or export of American technology, not the import of foreign technology the the United States. The latter is an increasingly important subject in its own right, but postwar U.S. experience has been primarily in the area of technology export. There is export control legislation and a complex policy review mechanism to govern technology outflows (potentially all outflows to designated adversary countries). There is no comparable mechanism for technology imports. This reflects postwar U.S. technological dominance which may of course be rapidly disappearing. If one of the conclusions of this study holds, namely that it will be increasingly difficult for the United States to trade technology assets for political-diplomatic returns (since this assumes a monopolistic position in the traded technologies), it will become increasingly necessary to trade technology for technology. This should create a new interest in the analysis of problems and policies for technology import into the United States.

For the purposes of this study, however, technology transfer is synonymous with technology export. Moreover, we are interested in technology transfer not technology diffusion. The latter suggests a natural, uncontrolled spread of technology throughout the international system, which probably occurs to some extent. To what extent, of course, is a policy issue. To assume that diffusion is the norm and transfer or the controlled export of technology the exception

A NATIONAL PERSPECTIVE

is no more justified than to assume the reverse. We intervene in natural processes all the time, and natural processes constantly arise to foil our best efforts at intervention.

NOTES

1. See News Release, Bureau of Public Affairs, Department of State, April 15, 1974.
2. Obtainable from Superintendent of Documents, U.S. Government Printing Office, Washington, D.C. Quote is from p. 105.
3. See Nicholas Wade, "Kissinger on Science: Making the Linkage with Diplomacy," Science 184 (May 17, 1974): 780-81.
4. See, for example, Eugene B. Skolnikoff, Science, Technology and American Foreign Policy (Cambridge: MIT Press, 1967). In his last chapter, Skolnikoff foresaw the broader implications of technology going beyond traditional defense and space sectors.
5. See Rutherford M. Poats, Technology for Developing Nations (Washington, D.C.: The Brookings Institution, 1972).
6. This is the focus, for example, of an interesting series of studies by the Congressional Research Service of the Library of Congress entitled "Science, Technology, and American Diplomacy" and directed by Dr. Franklin Pierce Huddle, senior specialist in science and technology with the Congressional Research Service. For a complete listing of these studies, which began to appear in 1970, see the latest of the series, Science and Technology in the Department of State, prepared for the Subcommittee of International Security and Scientific Affairs of the Committee of International Relations, U.S. House of Representatives (Washington D.C.: U.S. Government Printing Office, June 1975). The last study of the series is a summary and overview of the individual reports currently being prepared by Dr. Huddle.
7. Theodore Geiger, "On Not Pushing A Good Thing Too Far: Or Avoiding a Neomercantilist International Economic System," Looking Ahead 1 no. 5 (July 1975). Published by the National Planning Association, Washington, D.C.
8. For a selected bibliography of this literature, see Robert Gilpin, Technology, Economic Growth, and International Competitiveness, a report prepared for the Subcommittee on Economic Growth of the Joint Economic Committee, Congress of the United States, 94th Congress, 1st sess. (Washington, D.C.: U.S. Government Printing Office July 9, 1975), pp. 77-79.

9. Samuel N. Bar-Zakay, "Technology Transfer Model," Rand Publication P-4509, Santa Monica, Calif., n.d.

10. On the definition of the last two of these features, see John Gerard Ruggie, "International Responses to Technology: Concepts and Trends," in John Gerard Ruggie and Ernst B. Haas (eds.), "International Responses to Technology," <u>International Organization</u>, special issue (Summer 1975): 570-73.

CHAPTER 2

POSTWAR HISTORY OF U.S. PRACTICE TOWARD TECHNOLOGY TRANSFER

This chapter reviews the postwar American experience with technology transfer in the three separate and largely unrelated policy sectors of strategic-military, foreign assistance, and private industrial relations. Following our conceptual framework for this study, we assess in each sector the issues or perspectives (motivations) for evaluating technology transfer and the principal actors (mechanisms) involved in transfer policymaking and implementation.

TECHNOLOGY TRANSFER AND MILITARY-STRATEGIC POLICY

Technology was first recognized as a major national asset in the context of defense policies during World War II. As Daniel Greenberg has written:[1]

> The utility of science and technology in the economic crisis of the early New Deal was never clear-cut. . . But in mid-1940, with radar just beginning to play a critical and dramatic role in the aerial battles over Britain, there was no difficulty in demonstrating that science and technology were indispensable ingredients of modern warfare.

The subsequent mobilization of science and technology under The Office of Science Research and Development (OSRD) confirmed the importance of technology in military-strategic policy. It did not, however, spark an immediate awareness of technology's role in more general diplomatic, commercial, or social areas. After the war, proposals were made for a National Science Foundation which would direct the application of science and technology to civilian areas, such as national health, creation of new jobs, and betterment of the national standard of living. Despite the efforts of prominent scientists (such as Vanneuver Bush, wartime head of OSRD), however, no action was taken on these proposals. Instead, science and technology continued to serve primarily military needs, funded mostly by the Navy and the newly created Atomic Energy Commission (AEC). The National Science Foundation was finally established in 1951 but its funding was sharply limited. By contrast, the Korean war stimulated another massive increase of funding for weapons development.[2]

Given the focus on military uses of technology, attitudes toward the transfer of technology in this period were dominated by the requirement of secrecy. In atomic energy, even wartime collaboration with allies was discontinued in 1946, and the AEC slapped stringent controls on handling of all atomic energy technology. More general wartime controls on commercial exports and technology were also extended, but these were intended primarily to deal with inflationary short supply situations arising in the wake of the war. They were considered to be temporary and were housed in the International Trade Office of The Department of Commerce.

It was not until the outbreak of the cold war that the United States developed a more comprehensive policy toward the protection of its technology on national security grounds. The Export Control Act of 1949 provided the first multiple-year authorization for export controls. The Act granted general authority "to restrict the export of goods and technology which would make a significant contribution to the military potential of any other nation or nations which would prove detrimental to the national security of the United States." In addition, it authorized the use of export controls to further the foreign policy of the United States and to protect the domestic economy from the excessive drain of scarce materials and the inflationary impact of foreign demand.[3] The intent of the Act at the time was to impose sweeping controls on exports of strategic materials and technology to communist countries.* Unilateral U.S. controls were to be

---

*The Act distinguishes among various communist countries with Romania and Poland the most lightly controlled communist countries, the Soviet Union, China, and Eastern European countries in a middle group, and North Korea, North Vietnam, and Cuba the most stringently controlled group.

backed up by multilateral controls, administered by NATO through COCOM, the Consultative Group-Coordinating Committee. In addition, in 1951, the Mutual Defense Assistance Control Act (Battle Act) provided authority to cut off U.S. military and economic assistance to any country transhipping or reexporting controlled products to communist countries. Treasury regulations in 1953 issued under the Trading with the Enemy Act of 1917 extended the same controls to U.S. citizens and corporations residing abroad, even if the goods in question were of alien origin. Finally, the Mutual Security Act of 1954 authorized the State Department to control export of arms, ammunition, implements of war, and related technical data.[4]

Issues

The effect of these multiple regulations was to cast a restrictive net around U.S. strategic technology to prevent the export of a perceived U.S. technological advantage. The justification in theory and as reflected in the language of the Export Act was that technology produces advances in military weaponry or command and control systems which contributes significantly to the military potential of other nations which, in turn, if the latter are hostile or potentially hostile, is detrimental to the national security of the United States.

It would be inaccurate to say that a consistent rationale has motivated or guided the actual administration of U.S. export controls in the postwar period. The Export Act itself suggests multiple intentions (military-strategic, foreign policy, short supply, and so forth), and, as we note below, the mechanisms for export control are highly decentralized and, in practice, often competing. Case law, rather than any framework of common criteria, has guided the review of export applications. Nevertheless, the consensus, at one time, to prevent technology exports on military-strategic grounds was much stronger than it has ever been either to promote or prevent technology exports on foreign policy or economic grounds. The argument behind the military-strategic approach to technology transfer (or more actually technology nontransfer) needs to be further examined.

The first step in this argument is that technology is a primary motor of weapons development. In the postwar period, the United States has relied on a technological or qualitative superiority in weapons to offset a perceived Soviet advantage in conventional and quantitative forces. Thus, technology or, more precisely, a technology gap in the U.S. favor weighs crucially, it is thought, in the deterrence balance. The development of new technology must be continuously promoted, and the diffusion of existing technology to adversary countries prevented or, at least, delayed. To accomplish the latter, U.S. export control policies must determine what technologies are used primarily for military purposes and what the "state of the art" of these technologies is, that is, what technology is indeed "new" and otherwise not available to adversary countries. In practice, these determinations have usually been made in terms of what products and technologies have military use in the United States (not the Soviet Union), who is the end-user seeking to import U.S. technology and is he clean (that is, not a front for military end-users), and what are the current capabilities of the adversary country in the particular product or industrial area. Judgments of the state of the art, U.S. uses, and current capabilities abroad tend to be highly technical. In addition, if the export is approved, complicated safeguards may be required to insure that specified end-use is maintained and diversion to military uses prevented.[5] Postwar U.S. practices have relatively ignored the issue of availability of technology from non-U.S. sources.[6] An assessment of adversary country capabilities sufficed to approve or deny the export, even if the technology was available from another country. The United States sought to regulate the export of the technology by allied countries through COCOM. But allied countries have at times resisted COCOM restrictions by noting that the technology would be exported in any case by some non-COCOM country.

The second step in the argument is that such advances contribute significantly to military potential. The particular weapon or software advance is not just technically significant but militarily important. This requires an evaluation of the technology in the context of the military strategy and planning of the recipient country. It may also require an evaluation of the broader civilian context of military policies and capabilities. As we noted in Table 1.1, technological advances may influence military capabilities both by contributing directly to weapon systems and by freeing resources to be applied to military uses or to offset civilian effects of existing military expenditures. At one time, U.S. export controls prohibited any contribution to the military or economic potential of adversary countries. Known as the Kitchin amendment (after Congressman Paul Kitchin who introduced it), this provision was struck from the legislation in 1969 when the Export Control Act was liberalized and renamed the Export Administration Act.

In practice, the attempt to evaluate the contribution of technology to an adversary's military potential is more difficult, not to mention more subjective, than determining military end-use or technical state of the art. The value depends ultimately on factor conditions in the recipient country and on that country's ability to absorb the technology. Analysts currently disagree, for example, about the contribution large-scale U.S. computer systems might make to Soviet military potential. Preliminary evidence of a Rand study "suggests that any such enhancement would probably be modest."[7] The argument is based on the fact that large computers are of less value to the Soviet Union than to the United States. Factor costs, defense budget constraints, and military situation and strategy are so different that the Soviets can obtain militarily equivalent outcomes without large computers.[8] Conversely, a Hudson Institute study concludes that Russian assimilation of large-scale systems in electronics and transportation "could have a major impact in enhancing the efficiency of the Soviet military and civilian sectors."[9] Here the argument is that the standard to be applied is not value to the Soviets versus value to the United States but value to the Soviets in terms of their own industrial and technological base. Even a small contribution to Soviet capabilities when measured against comparable contributions to U.S. capabilities may constitute a giant step forward in terms of Soviet capabilities alone.

In some circumstances, the export rather than embargo of technology may entail security benefits. For example, if the Soviet Union is less efficient utilizing large computers than smaller ones, exporting large computers to them may raise their relative costs and divert some of their scarce resources, such as software capabilities, to less efficient uses. Obviously, this reasoning, which stands the traditional military-strategic argument on its head, is no more a standard for all technology exports than the traditional argument. What it suggests is that evaluation of technology transfer is never simply a matter of military end-use or contribution to technical capabilities alone. It is also a matter of priorities for resource allocation, and these are determined by broader domestic and foreign policy objectives.

Thus, the third step in the military-strategic argument is the determination that a significant contribution to the military potential of another country through U.S. exports is detrimental to U.S. national security. This is clearly a matter of assessing adversary intentions and trying to determine the trade-off between political conditions and technological contributions. Encouraging the export of technology may enhance an adversary's capabilities but diminish his desire to use these capabilities. Further trade-offs may be involved between these military and diplomatic consequences and commercial gains from technology transfer. How does one compare these fundamentally use these capabilities. Further trade-offs may be involved between these military and diplomatic consequences and commercial gains from technology transfer. How does one compare these fundamentally

incommensurable entities ? That it is difficult to do so does not
avoid the fact that it is also essential to do so. Technical judgments
independent of political context are sterile. If these judgments
sufficed in export review procedures in the past, it was in large part
because there was a widespread consensus about the political context
of containment, if not confrontation, with communist countries. Today
this consensus no longer exists, and the calculus of national interests
is more complicated. It will do little good, therefore, to call simply
for a clearer definition of national interests. The fact is that there
is no central organ in the U.S. government which has sole responsibility
to define the national interest. Instead the national interest emerges
from a process of bargaining, compromise, and sometimes simply
confusion among the various governmental and private groups involved
in the administration and conduct of technology exports.

Actors

The basic export control mechanism continues to be centered
in the Department of Commerce. The Office of Export Administration
(OEA) in the Bureau of East-West Trade has overall responsibility
for export licensing of all industrial products and technical data.
General licenses apply to most goods and require no formal application
or approval; validated licenses are required for controlled products.
In approving applications as well as establishing control lists (Commodity Control List—CCL), Commerce consults with other interested
agencies. At the working level is an Operating Committee consisting
of staff people from OEA, Defense, State and other interested agencies. If disagreement exists at this level, the case may be referred
to the Advisory Committee on Export Policy which meets at the
assistant secretary level. If disagreement still persists, it may be
appealed to the East-West Foreign Trade Board at the Secretary
level. Finally, in unusual cases but also the most important ones
from the point of view of precedence, the President may get
involved.*

---

*This was the case, for example, in the decision in July
1971 to approve U.S. company participation in the Kama River
Truck Plant in the Soviet Union. See the case study of Kama
in Chapter 4.

POSTWAR HISTORY   27

There is also a parallel appeals mechanism for U.S. export control decisions in COCOM. As we note below, State represents the United States in COCOM, and it has happened that an export license has been approved (or denied) by the State-led mechanism and denied (or approved) by the Commerce-led mechanism.

Since 1969 and reflecting the shift toward liberalization of export controls that year, industry representatives participate in the export licensing process. They sit on Technical Advisory Committees (TACs) which provide technical inputs on the formulation of "state of the art" judgments of various technologies. They have no policy role and frequently complain about the classified and perfunctory nature of TAC meetings. To strengthen these meetings, Congressional legislation in 1974 stipulated that government representatives on TACs should specifically include Defense and State Department officials. Before that, government representation was unspecified, and industrial spokesmen complained that the people they spoke to were not the same ones subsequently making decisions. Industry groups also complain that export controls involve time delays and cost increases for U.S. business. In the face of growing economic competition for international sales and evidence of direct government support of industry in other countries, they want U.S. government agencies to rationalize the export control process and to promote more vigorously rather than to restrict U.S. exports.[10] The confusion of current U.S. policy is marked by the fact that responsibilities to promote and to restrict exports are both administered within the same bureau in Commerce (Bureau of East-West Trade was set up in 1972 to advance detente through trade).

While Commerce is the center of the export control system, it is by no means predominant. As we noted, the Department of State has responsibilities for licensing exports of arms, ammunition, implements of war, and related technical data. The Office of Munitions Control in the Bureau of Political-Military affairs is the administering authority for these licenses. Characteristic of the fragmentation of export control administration, this office is not the same one that represents State on the Commerce interagency committee and supplies the U.S. representative to COCOM meetings in NATO. The latter are the responsibilities of the Office of East-West Trade in the Bureau of Economics and Business Affairs. Likewise, State's responsibilities often overlap with those of Commerce. During the 1960s, for example, the Munitions Control Board fought a running battle with some elements of NASA and the aerospace industry over export of air and space technologies abroad. The latter felt that these technologies were militarily insensitive and believed that "Munition Control Board officials were restricting commercial technology that might give others a competitive position, a position distinct from military threats and, hence, supposed to be under the jurisdiction of the officials of the Department of Commerce."[11] In truth, of course, Commerce and State are evaluating the same thing, albeit from different starting points. State controls military items and data which may also have commercial applications; Commerce looks at commercial products that may also have military uses.

Curiously, Defense has never been the administering agency for strategic export controls, even though it has played an important role.* It sits on the Commerce interagency group and assists State at the working level in administration of munitions controls. Responsibility lies in The Office of International Security Affairs, assisted on technical matters by the Defense Directorate of Research and Engineering and The Office of Economic Research of The Central Intelligence Agency. Until the relaxation of export controls in 1969, the Defense position in the export review process was a strong one. After the Administration decided in 1971 to relax trade restrictions with the Soviet Union and China, however, its role became more one of rearguard sniping than frontline generalship. In 1974 Congress added some amendments to the export control legislation to strengthen Defense. These amendments required that Defense be informed of every request for a validated export license, meaning in practice that Defense would review the various delegations of authority made to OEA to facilitate what had been considered before to be "routine" validated applications. Defense then had thirty days in the case of each request to recommend action to the President. If the President overruled Defense, he would have to submit an explanation to Congress within thirty days of receiving the recommendations of Defense.[12] These changes added further delays and requirements to export review procedures, clearly displeasing industrial groups already critical of these procedures.

---

* Part of the historical explanation for this may lie in the fact that already during the war the precedent was set to establish civilian control over development of military technology. OSRD worked on military objectives (exclusively as we noted in the text) but was independent of military control. This was necessitated by the need to rely primarily on private university and industrial organizations to mobilize scientific and technological talent and resources. OSRD also operated with minimum control from State, setting the precedent for conflict between technical agencies and foreign policy organs in the administration of technology-related international programs (see section on foreign assistance programs).

The scattering of technology export responsibilities for military-strategic and other purposes (see next section) does not end here. As we noted, exports of U.S. citizens and corporations originating abroad are controlled by Treasury (which also licenses gold exports). Nuclear fuel materials and related data are licensed by the Nuclear Regulatory Commission (before, by the AEC), vessels (other than vessels of war) by the Maritime Administration of the Department of Commerce, natural gas and electric energy by the Federal Power Commission, tobacco seeds and plants by the Department of Agriculture (which also must approve Commerce actions on any agricultural commodities), narcotic drugs and marijuana by the Department of Justice, and endangered wildlife species by the Department of Interior.

Internal administration of export policies is thus highly fragmented. External administration is multilateral and takes place through COCOM (NATO allies plus Japan minus Iceland). The latter meets weekly in Paris and reviews exception requests to the controlled commodity list. Decisions are by unanimous vote, although an individual member may override a COCOM veto on a particular transfer if it judges the transaction to be "essential" to its interests.[13]

The list itself is reviewed every three years. Historically, the U.S. list has been much more extensive than the COCOM list. Consequently, disputes with allies have marked COCOM activities since the beginning. With the relaxation of U.S. policy in 1969, the lists have been brought more in line. Today, the U.S. list contains only 73 categories of products not on the COCOM list, and these categories themselves have been narrowed as to the products they include. The COCOM list has itself been drastically reduced (40 percent in 1968-69 and 30 percent in 1971-72). It will be further reduced in the current review (1974-75). For the moment, however, it continues to prohibit trade in many highly desired commercial products, such as large computers, magnetohydrodynamic equipment, telecommunication gear, and integrated circuits.

TECHNOLOGY TRANSFER
AND U.S. FOREIGN ASSISTANCE PROGRAMS

The value of technology as an instrument of foreign policy was not immediately recognized after World War II. Even, with the inauguration of the Marshall Plan in 1948, which reflected the first major use of U.S. economic resources for foreign policy purposes in peacetime, technical assistance or productivity programs were viewed as only minor supplements to production efforts based

primarily on larger inputs of capital and labor. The European
Recovery Program, as economists repeatedly noted, was primarily
a program of investment to restore prewar levels of output, not an
effort to promote growth through technological advance. Technical
assistance activities under the Marshall Plan amounted to less than
1.5 percent of the $12 to $13 billion of total U.S. aid.[14]

In the case of Marshall Plan aid to China and Southeast Asia
and, more importantly, in the case of the Point IV Program announced
by President Truman in 1949, technical assistance received greater
emphasis. In aid to less developed countries, it was believed, "the
need was for extensive technical assistance and relatively small quantities
of material aid."[15] As President Truman noted, this need was
prompted as much by limitations on U.S. capital resources as by an
understanding of the value of technology as a U.S. foreign policy
asset:[16]

> The United States is preeminent among nations in the
> development of industrial and scientific techniques.
> The material resources which we can afford to use
> for the assistance of other peoples are limited. But
> our imponderable resources in technical knowledge
> are constantly growing and are inexhaustible.

The resource crunch which followed the outbreak of the Korean
War gave even greater emphasis to the idea of technical assistance.[17]
In the reorganization of U.S. aid programs, however, defense needs
overshadowed civilian and developmental uses of American technology.
It was not until after the Korean War that civilian technology emerged
as a central element in U.S. foreign policy initiatives.

The first such initiative was the Atoms for Peace Plan announced
by President Eisenhower at the United Nations in December 1953. This
plan called for the sharing of peaceful benefits of U.S. nuclear
technology to preempt the independent development of military uses of
atomic energy and to improve the U.S. foreign policy image which
still suffered from the memory of Hiroshima and Nagasaki. This
nuclear initiative was followed shortly by the Apollo effort to beat
the Russians in space and land the first man on the moon. Quickly,
by the end of the 1950s, civilian as well as military technology had
become the new index of world power. As Alastair Buchan wrote
in 1967, "The products of its science and technology have become,
for better or worse, the source of a nation's pride, as pig-iron
production statistics were in the late nineteenth century or figures
of dreadnaught launchings in the early twentieth."[18] Technology was
a currency which could be traded directly to obtain political gains
(that is, to achieve specific objectives) or indirectly to enhance

general prestige and access in the world community (to achieve general objectives). (In the rest of this section, we include under our definition of foreign assistance programs any initiative that contains this element of trading technology primarily for political or foreign policy gains.)

Issues

Today technology serves multiple purposes in U.S. foreign policy, from an instrument of detente and a subject of dialogue with Latin America to a focus of cooperation in allied energy diplomacy. These foreign policy purposes or motivations of technology transfer may be classified into several broad categories. Specific uses of technology are:

1. strengthening free world allies against communist and other adversaries (for example, OPEC)
2. promoting economic growth and stability in developing countries
3. preempting independent foreign development of peaceful technologies with military applications
4. signaling competitive or cooperative changes in relations with foreign countries
5. influencing the internal policies of foreign states, preferably in a democratic direction
6. improving the quality of human and social life in the international system.

General uses of technology include:

1. enhancing overall prestige and leadership in the world community
2. maintaining open lines of transportation, communications, and economic exchanges around the globe
3. expressing an American sense of humanitarianism and noblesse oblige.

There are clearly conflicts between some of these diplomatic uses of technology. For example, the desire to use technology to signal a turn toward less friendly relations with one foreign country (an embargo on exports of products and technology) may reduce the image and hence influence of the United States among other countries as a reliable supplier of technology. Or the desire to share peaceful uses of technology to promote economic progress may conflict, in the absence of adequate safeguards, with the desire to prevent proliferation of military uses. Foreign policy programs are designed to serve many objectives, and much of the debate in evaluating these programs stems from a different ordering of priorities among these various objectives (not to mention the relative importance of foreign policy objectives as a whole in relation to military and commercial objectives—see discussion in previous and following sections).

Table 2.1 gives some representative initiatives from the postwar period reflecting aspects of these various foreign policy motivations of technology transfer. Technology has been only a part of these initiatives and, in some instances, a relatively minor part. But if in an earlier period diplomacy largely served the interests of science and technology, today science and particularly technology are perceived by many as important instruments of diplomacy. One indication of this is the proliferating number of bilateral science and technology agreements the United States has concluded since 1961. By early 1975, the United States had signed upwards of 28 bilateral agreements or understandings of one sort or another in the fields of science and technology.[19]

Science and technology are also becoming more important in the diplomacy of other countries. The socialist countries, recognizing the importance of technology in productivity growth, have initiated policies to import technology from the West. The developing countries are also increasingly taking the view that "the acquisition of science and technology is the key to an improved economy in their impoverished world."[20] In fact, with the planning for a second United Nations Conference on Science and Technology, the role of science and technology in development may assume in the late 1970s the same policy importance for developing societies that capital growth and import substitution policies did in the 1960s.

As the cold war has waned, conflictive, prestige-enhancing uses of technology transfer in foreign policy have given way to somewhat more practical, productivity-enhancing uses. Whereas military assistance programs and the space race were the chief, if not sole, foreign policy expressions of technology during the cold war period, science and technology agreements today are the symbols of detente with Moscow (the U.S.-USSR Science and Technology Agreement of 1972) and of "friendly" relations with economic adversaries in the Middle East (OPEC countries such as Saudi Arabia, Iran, and Egypt). To be sure, foreign military assistance, especially sale of military equipment, remains a large part of U.S. agreements (particularly with some Middle East countries like Iran).[21] Moreover, technology retains its use as an indication of dissatisfaction with foreign

TABLE 2.1

Foreign Policy Motivations and
Initiatives in Technology Transfer

Motivation	Initiative
Specific Uses	
1. strengthening free world allies	NATO weapons coproduction programs
	Military assistance and foreign military sales programs
	Marshall plan
	International Energy Agency
2. promoting economic growth and stability in developing countries	Point IV Program
	AID economic assistance
3. preempting independent foreign development of military-related technologies	Atoms for Peace Plan
	Proposals for internationalization of nuclear fuel facilities
4. signal change in foreign relations toward conflict or cooperation	Export Control Act
	Bilateral science and technology agreements
5. influence internal policies of foreign states	1973 Foreign Assistance Act's emphasis on poor majority
	Jackson amendment to 1974 Trade Bill
6. improving the quality of human and social life in the international system	Population and pollution control programs
General Uses	
1. enhance prestige	Apollo
2. maintain access	Satellite Applications Program (Comsat)
	Law of the Sea policies
3. express humanitarianism	Disaster relief assistance

Source: Compiled by the author.

policies of other countries. As we noted in the previous section, export control legislation provides explicit authorization to use export controls on product and technology "to the extent necessary to further significantly the foreign policy of the United States and to fulfill its international responsibilities." Amendments to this legislation in 1974 extended these controls specifically "to secure the removal by foreign countries of restrictions on access to supplies...." Such retaliatory imposition of technology export controls, however, was to take effect only after "the President shall make every reasonable effort to secure the removal or reduction of such restrictions, policies, or actions through international cooperation and agreement...."[22] It is also questionable how substantive and not just symbolic science and technology agreements with the Soviet Union and other potential adversaries may be. From the side of the Soviet Union and OPEC countries, however, the interest in Western technology seems to be as practical as it may be political.[23]

In another area, that of foreign aid, U.S. motivations also show a gradual shift toward more specific and practical uses of technology transfer. In the 1950s, U.S. aid was a primary instrument in the ideological campaign against neutralism; in the 1960s, it was tied more closely to overall domestic economic and institutional development (the emphasis on democratic institutions added by Title IX of the Foreign Assistance Act of 1966); today it is concerned with the still more specific social and distributional consequences of growth. The emphasis of the 1973 Foreign Assistance Act on technical expertise, as opposed to large-scale capital transfers, and on employment and the poor majority, as opposed to industrialization and affluent elites, suggests that technology is being viewed increasingly in relationship to the practical problems of the common citizen, as opposed to such lofty goals as the prestige and wealth of the state.[24]

Actors

The implementation of U.S. foreign assistance programs may be discussed in terms of internal administration of programs within the United States (public versus private actors, Congress versus Executive, technical versus foreign policy agencies) and international administration of these programs outside the United States (bilateral versus multilateral).

From the beginning, foreign assistance legislation emphasized heavy reliance on private industry to transfer resources to recipient countries. The Economic Cooperation Administration (ECA), for example, set up to implement the Marshall Plan, delegated procurement authority to recipient governments which in turn purchased commodities and equipment directly through private channels. A primary reason for establishing ECA as an autonomous agency of government was to maximize the "businesslike" features of the recovery program and to minimize bureaucratic competition with the private sector. The Point IV program and all subsequent technical assistance efforts likewise stressed private sector participation. The desire to divorce early technical assistance programs from conventional government administration was also a factor in the establishment in 1947 of the Institute of American Affairs, a public corporation to administer technical assistance programs with Latin American countries.[25]

As foreign assistance programs became an increasingly central aspect of U.S. defense policy following the Korean War, aid legislation began to provide government guarantees and tax incentives for private investment abroad. By 1958, it was recognized that technical assistance alone could not accomplish very much. The Development Loan Fund was established to finance larger capital projects at lower interest rates and longer repayment terms. In the mid-1950s, the Department of Agriculture also began to supply commodity assistance to developing countries through the Food for Peace Program set up to disperse agricultural surpluses generated by U.S. farm price support programs. The increasing importance of capital and commodity assistance reinforced the role of private industry in implementation of U.S. aid programs.

The Atoms for Peace Plan likewise stressed private sector participation. Under bilateral and multilateral (Euratom) agreements concluded through this program, loans from the Export-Import Bank and fuel guarantees from the Atomic Energy Commission (AEC) helped American nuclear industries expand into foreign markets. Although diplomatic objectives were primary in these nuclear initiatives, commercial objectives were also well served.[26]

The U.S. space program had more explicit technical and commercial objectives. While the Apollo program was primarily scientific and technical in nature, there were also commercial spinoffs from this program. In the communications satellite field, U.S. policy was predominantly commercial. In 1963 Congress chartered Comsat as a private corporation to develop an operational satellite communication system and to negotiate the necessary agreements with foreign countries. In these negotiations, Comsat was required to seek only "counsel" from the Department of State. This meant, as a former U.S. official noted, that "from the outset—U.S. foreign policy objectives and perceptions in this field would be filtered through a private entity with divergent goals and perceptions."[27]

As a result, Comsat dominated the International Telecommunications Satellite Consortium (Intelsat) established under interim agreements in 1964 to operate a global communications satellite system.

Congress, of course, has played a primary role in insuring the place of private industry in implementation of foreign assistance programs. Traditionally skeptical of programs to spend money abroad, unless for defense, Congress has sought through provisions of tied aid, shipment on U.S. bottoms, and so on, to convert as much of U.S. aid appropriations as possible into purchases of private U.S. goods and services. During the 1960s, commodity assistance consisting largely of shipments of U.S. goods to developing countries became a principal instrument of U.S. aid programs.[28]

The close coupling of economic assistance with military programs (necessitated by Congressional reluctance to appropriate funds for foreign use except for defense purposes) led to some Congressional questioning of the role of U.S. companies in foreign assistance programs, particularly in the wake of Vietnam. Today there is an interest in separating economic and military aid appropriations. The role of private industry in implementing these programs seems assured, however. As the 1973 Foreign Assistance Act continues to suggest, benefits to private industry remain a principal justification for U.S. foreign aid.

If Congress has looked out for the interests of private industry in technically related foreign policy activities, it has also given primary operational responsibility for these activities to the executive branch and within the executive branch, to technical rather than foreign policy agencies. The Atomic Energy Act of 1954, the National Aeronautics and Space Act of 1958, and the Comsat Act of 1962—all delegated to the domestic operating agency (in Comsat's case, as we have seen, a private corporation) authority to negotiate foreign agreements without the approval of the Senate. Other agencies were also given this authority, but these three agencies have the largest international programs. Each of these agencies (AEC, NASA, Comsat) quickly established an ascendance over the State Department in foreign policy related areas of their activity. The operating agencies, controlling budget expenditures and responsible to Congress, placed technical efficiency and maximum industrial benefits above diplomatic considerations in the administration of foreign programs. The White House and State Department, on the other hand, sought to coordinate these programs to promote broader diplomatic and political ends, even at the cost, if necessary, of technical and commercial efficiency. Conflict between operating and foreign policy interests became acute in the case of peaceful nuclear explosions (PNEs) and the Comsat negotiations. The AEC promoted peaceful nuclear explosions while some groups in State worried about the consequences for nonproliferation objectives, the Comsat pursued commercial objectives and a single global satellite system while some diplomatic officials deplored the problems these policies caused in relations with our European allies.[29]

As we have noted, the White House had few difficulties initiating foreign policy-related technological programs (such as Atoms for Peace) but was less able to control these programs during implementation. The State Department, with no operating mandate and little expertise in technical areas, was a weak and ineffective ally and indeed relied on the White House for whatever clout it could muster.* A most recent example of this pattern is offered by the U.S.-USSR Science and Technology Agreement. While the original agreement was negotiated in 1972 with the idea that the White House Office of Science and Technology (OST) would exercise some supervision over the various R and D programs, the subsequent abolition of OST left these programs primarily in the charge of the individual operating agencies (health to HEW, transportation to DOT, agriculture to USDA, and so on). The Bureau of International Scientific and Technological Affairs in State, recently upgraded and reorganized as the Bureau of Oceans and International Environmental and Scientific Affairs (OES), picked up the task of coordinating and evaluating these programs to insure balance and integration with broader U.S. foreign policy objectives. While it has had some success, coordination remains a problem. One result is that few trade-offs are possible between various programs (such as, health and agriculture), reducing the level of benefits in each program to a lowest common denominator.[30] As a recent study concludes with reference to bilateral science and technology agreements in general, "only by a vigorous and competent management, supplied on an overall basis by the executive branch, can these agreements ultimately be assured of yielding more good than harm."[31]

Conflict between domestic-oriented industries and operating agencies, on the one hand, and foreign policy-oriented agencies, on the other, has had a primary impact on U.S. preferences concerning the

---

* For example, the White House was instrumental in 1962 in upgrading the Science Adviser's Office in State to operational status. State science officials, of course, recognized this dependence and at times maneuvered the White House into supporting their objectives.

external organization of foreign assistance programs. While a
number of U.S. foreign assistance initiatives such as the European
Recovery Program and the Atoms for Peace Plan sought multilateral
responses to international problems, the vast majority of these
initiatives including the Atoms for Peace Plan, have been dominated
by bilateral arrangements. The only exceptions perhaps are European
programs which, beginning with the Marshall Plan and continuing
through the U.S.-Euratom joint agreement in peaceful nuclear energy
(which gave Euratom inspection rights over U.S. supplied nuclear
materials), encouraged the formation of regional institutions to
administer U.S. aid and to integrate national economic and technological efforts in Western Europe. Since the early 1960s, however, U.S.
enthusiasm for European technological multilateralism has waned.
Reflecting on U.S. behavior in the negotiation of a final Intelsat
agreement from 1964 to 1970, one analyst noted that "the U.S. does
not appear to have made up its mind whether it wants Europe to be
a first class power (or collection of powers) and thus provide it
with the necessary aid to achieve this position, or whether it would
prefer to let Europe lag."[32]

Bilateralism seems to be preferred by most technical agencies
as well as some elements in the foreign policy agencies. Under this
pressure, multilateral objectives have often suffered. For example,
despite the multilateral character of the Atoms for Peace Plan and
the International Atomic Energy Agency (IAEA) set up to implement
this plan, "bilateral agreements preempted much of the scope for
multilateral action, and the potential role of IAEA as a supplier of
nuclear assistance in its own right was undercut."[33] There were
both foreign policy and domestic bureaucratic reasons for this.
The IAEA was one of the few international arenas in the 1950s where
U.S. and Soviet officials dealt with one another. There was a
desire on the U.S. side not to make IAEA activities any more controversial than they already were. Giving IAEA a primary technical
assistance role in nuclear materials would have sharply increased
its sensitivity. Moreover, AEC officials were not eager to see
IAEA emerge as a competitor in the supply of nuclear assistance
to foreign countries. Bilateral agreements maintained AEC leverage
and control. As one AEC commissioner explained, "if [other
countries] deal with us under an individual bilateral agreement we
have some control over where this material goes and for what purpose it is used, and we do not have that if it is channeled through
the International Agency...."[34]

In the case of NASA, "U.S. cooperative programs were clearly
designed to bypass UN machinery." As one source explains, "the
use of bilateral agreements instead of multilateral or international
arrangements for international cooperation was a fundamental

decision that directly affected space application programs as well as scientific ones."[35] The NASA director of international programs gave the reasoning behind this decision.[36]

> ...the basic orientation of international forums is likely to be formalistic rather than operational.... Above all, there will be a tendency to be regulatory and restrictive rather than facilitative...

Multilateral arrangements, in short, were not ways to get things done. For those initiatives, mostly scientific, which required cooperation, NASA worked through the National Academy of Sciences which represented the United States on COSPAR, the space committee of the International Council of Scientific Unions. This link emphasized NASA's preoccupation in international programs with efficiency rather than any form of foreign assistance.[37]

Foreign assistance programs to developing countries have also been implemented, for the most part, bilaterally. By the late 1960s, this was beginning to change somewhat. But, from 1970-72, U.S. aid disbursements through international organizations dropped dramatically (from $480 million to $180 million to $142 million); these disbursements picked up again in 1973-74 (to $775 million and $814 million respectively, the latter representing about 20 percent of total economic assistance for that year).[38] As these figures suggest, however, the multilateralization of U.S. aid is an extremely uneven process and depends critically on unpredictable attitudes in Congress toward organizations like the United Nations.

When technology-related U.S. foreign policy initiatives led to multilateral arrangements in the past, as in the case of IAEA, these arrangements were limited chiefly to a regulatory as opposed to R and D or operational role (confirming the suspicions of NASA's director of international programs that international forums were regulative rather than facilitative). The IAEA, from the U.S. point of view, was designed primarily to cope with the consequences of existing nuclear capabilities. It was denied a significant technical assistance function which, as some have noted, probably weakened its safeguard or regulatory role.[39] When R and D, operational, and especially commercial activities were at stake, as in the case of Comsat, the United States showed a preference for establishing national institutions first and then seeking international participation in an essentially U.S. owned and operated system. This same pattern is evident today, for example, in U.S. proposals for international arrangements to produce enriched uranium. Since 1969, the AEC has pursued a policy of commercializing the enrichment of uranium and encouraging private industry to build a fourth U.S. plant. Proposals for international cooperation, put forward in 1971 and again in 1974, clearly depended on the prior establishment of a new U.S. manufacturing entity (if not fully commercial, perhaps, as some proposed, a government chartered enrichment corporation—like Comsat) before international participation could be permitted. At latest report, U.S. policy seems to be aimed at nothing more than foreign financial participation in an otherwise U.S.-dominated facility.[40]

In terms of the instrumentalities of cooperation in technology-related activities, the United States has favored the coordination of national policies rather than the establishment of joint facilities or integrated multilateral policies. In the joint nuclear agreement between the U.S. and Euratom, for example, no common facilities were established, which might have competed with the domestic operating agencies. Instead the agreement called for coordination or parallelism in U.S. and European expenditures for nuclear reactor development, with each party spending money only on its side of the Atlantic.[41] Similar coordination of national policies has characterized the U.S. approach to international cooperation in foreign aid programs. The principal instrument for rationalization of aid programs of industrialized countries has been the Development Assistance Committee of the Organization for Economic Cooperation and Development, where periodically national policies are reviewed and, to some extent, harmonized with one another.

Whether this pattern will prevail in the future is still unclear. As we discuss in the next chapter, some developments suggest that the United States may be required in the future to undertake more institutionalized forms of international cooperation in technology-related activities.

TECHNOLOGY TRANSFER AND THE PRIVATE INDUSTRIAL SECTOR

As we note later in this section, the preferred postwar mechanism for U.S. technology transfer in the private industrial sector has been foreign direct investment or the multinational company. Important private transfers have also occured through licensing, principally with Japan, which until recently sharply limited foreign direct investment.* These transfers, however, though sometimes controversial as in the case of aerospace technology to Japan, have not been as important as direct investment in terms of total returns on technological exports. In the next chapter, we suggest that licensing transfers may become more important in the future, as countries other than Japan seek to buy technology separately without accompanying foreign equity control. If this should happen, one might expect the licensing of U.S. technology to attract greater attention and analysis, as well as to spark greater controversy particularly concerning the pricing of technology in licensing agreements.

In the postwar period, international economic theory has had to give more explicit recognition to the influence of two factors on economic growth: technology and the organizational structure of the multinational company. Classical economic theory treated technology as a neutral factor of production, accounting for growth largely in terms of increases in physical and human inputs.[42] International disparities in output per worker were explained solely by differences in factor endowments. As Richard Nelson noted, this left "no real room... for a meaninfgul concept of a technological gap."[43] Economic research in the 1950s, however, and official disputes among industrialized countries over R and D and technology gaps in the 1960s sparked growing awareness of the importance of technology. Today, it is widely acknowledged that technology is a nonneutral factor and contributes importantly to economic growth and productivity. What remains in dispute is a commonly accepted methodology for measuring technology and its contribution to growth. As we discuss in a moment, this raises difficult issues concerning the pricing of technology in international economic exchanges.

Classical theory also excluded the possibility of the multinational company. As John Dunning emphasizes,[44]

> in the classical model of static comparative advantage, there is no room for the multinational enterprise at all. With completely free movement of goods but immobility of factors of production... there is little incentive for international direct investment.

---

* For example, as a single country, Japan accounted for a large and growing percentage of all U.S. returns from royalty and licensing arrangements with <u>unaffiliated</u> foreign residents. This percentage amounted to 20 percent in 1964, growing to 33 percent in 1974 (compared to 24 percent for all six of the original member countries of the European Common Market). (Data available from Bureau of Economic Analysis, Department of Commerce.)

In the postwar period, of course, the multinational company has extended its "global reach" to all corners of the world.[45] It has created a new organizational structure for the exchange of goods, technology and personnel in world markets, a structure which makes obsolete the competitive two country, two product model of classical economic theory. Instead of having to deal in open markets, multinational companies may transfer resources internally, treating their respective affiliates as departments of the same commercial enterprise rather than independent buyers and sellers. Thus, it is not only that technology and information are more important factors in growth, but also that they constitute the nerves of a centralized structure of decision-making and planning within the multinational company.

The parallel emergence of technology and the multinational company in world economic exchanges has raised a whole series of new and, as yet, only partially answered questions:

1. What role does technology play in foreign direct investment and hence the creation of the multinational company?
2. How does the multinational company manage its technology in international exchanges?
3. What impact does the transfer of technology by the multinational company have on source and recipient countries?

The first question highlights the principal issues associated with the outflow of technology in the private sector, and the last two questions concern the actors and mechanisms involved in private technology transfers.

Issues

Recent studies indicate that the more technology-intensive industries (measured in terms of R and D expenditures as a percentage of sales) are also the more active industries abroad; in short, technology intensive industries are the multinationals.[46] They tend to export more (both in terms of absolute levels and rates of change), invest more abroad (only in absolute, however, not relative terms since technology-intensive firms are also more active in domestic investment as well), and license more often in foreign markets (usually a second best alternative to direct investment).

Explanations concerning the role of technology in direct investment and the creation of the multinational enterprise vary. One explanation suggests that foreign direct investment is basically defensive to preserve export markets. At some point, it is argued, foreign or local competitors may enter the export market. Or foreign governments may impose tariff and other import restrictions to encourage local manufacture of imported products. Under these circumstances, exporting companies face either a loss of external markets or the need to shift production facilities to foreign locations. This explanation suggests that traditional competitive factors, including government policies affecting market access, may be more important in motivating direct investment than technology. [47]

A second explanation stresses supply conditions or factor endowments in foreign markets. According to this explanation, firms invest abroad to take advantage of lower production costs, principally cheaper labor and transportation costs. In the early stages of the development of a new technology or product, firms find it advantageous to keep production at home, close to R and D facilities, component and equipment manufacturers, end-users, and innovation-oriented financial markets. Once the product and technology are standardized, however, the firm can exploit traditional factor differences in international markets and shift production activities abroad. If anything, this explanation suggests that new technology, at least initially, may be a hindrance rather than an incentive to invest abroad. [48]

A third explanation sees technology as the primary engine of foreign direct investment, creating a monopoly advantage which firms use to capture and dominate foreign markets. As Richard Cooper notes, "a major motivation for direct investment is undoubtedly the desire by an investing firm to exploit some quasi-monopoly it holds, whether special skills, patent rights or 'good will'."[49] To benefit from lower production costs while still protecting technological secrets, the multinational firm sets up wholly-owned or majority-controlled subsidiaries abroad and seeks to exclude foreign competitors from sharing monopoly rents. Indeed, the apparent preference of many multinationals for direct investment over licensing adds weight to this explanation (see Table 2.2 below). Lower production costs alone should appeal neutrally to all firms. Instead, technology-intensive or multinational firms have a greater incentive to invest because they have a technological edge to exploit. [50]

Actors

In the last explanation, at least, motivation of technology transfer is closely linked with the mechanism of transfer, namely, majority-owned direct investment. More broadly, there are other

TABLE 2.2

Direct Investment Abroad and Income Flows, All Areas 1948-74
(Current Dollars in Millions)

Year	A Direct Investment Abroad to Foreign Owned Affiliates	B Fees From Licensing, Royalties and Management with Foreign-Owned Affiliates	C Interest, Dividends and Branch Earnings From Foreign-Owned Affiliates	D Fees and Royalties From Unaffiliated Foreigners	E Other Private Services From Unaffiliated Foreigners
1948	721	213	1,064	292	
1949	660	220	1,112	244	
1950	621	246	1,294	267	
1951	508	272	1,492	286	
1952	852	292	1,419	309	
1953	735	305	1,442	314	
1954	667	328	1,725	307	
1955a	823	373	1,912	324	
1956	1,951	438	2,171	133	378
1957	2,442	446	2,249	140	424
1958	1,181	442	2,121	168	444
1959	1,372	543	2,228	166	449
1960	1,674	403	2,355	247	486
1961	1,598	463	2,768	244	521
1962	1,654	580	3,044	256	513
1963	1,976	661	3,129	273	551
1964	2,328	756	3,674	301	589
1965	3,468	924	3,963	335	668
1966	3,625	973	3,467	353	777
1967	3,072	1,123	3,847	393	911
1968	2,880	1,245	4,151	437	984
1969	3,190	1,356	4,819	486	1,118
1970	4,281	1,561	4,992	573	1,228
1971	4,738	1,757	5,983	618	1,481
1972	3,530	1,911	6,416	655	1,689
1973	4,968	2,309	8,841b	725	1,874
1974	7,268	2,783	17,679b	781	2,088

Technical Notes and Sources

Column A—Direct Investment Abroad to Foreign Owned Affiliates

This column represents capital transactions by U.S. residents with foreign enterprises in which the U.S. residents by themselves or in affiliation with other U.S. residents own 10 percent or more of the voting securities or of other ownership interests. Included are net increases in capital stock and capital contributions, in intercompany accounts, and in owner's home office accounts; excluded is the U.S. parent's share of the reinvested earnings of foreign incorporated affiliates.

Source:
1948-1959 — DRI Inc., central data bank, March 1975 (Note 2)
1960-1974 — Survey of Current Business, June 1975, pp. 30-31 Table 2 line 39

Column B—Investment Fees From Royalties, Licensing and Management

This column represents U.S. receipts and payments entered into intercompany accounts of U.S. corporations and their foreign affiliates and foreign corporations and their U.S. affiliates for the use of intangible property such as patents, trademarks, copyrights; rentals for the use of tangible properties and charges for professional, administrative and management services excluding film and tape rentals.

Source:
1948-1959 — DRI Inc., central data bank, March 1975
1960-1974 — U.S. Department of Commerce SESA, Bureau of Economic Analysis, June 1975

Column C—Investment Income Interest, Dividends, and Branch Earnings

This column measures receipts by U.S. parent organizations from their foreign affiliates of interest and dividends (after withheld foreign taxes) and branch earnings (after foreign income taxes). Receipts include not only actual transfers but also other amounts due in the reporting period that are not actually transferred. In the latter case, the amounts are offset by contra-entries in Column A.

Source:
1948-1949 — DRI Inc., central data bank, March 1975
1960-1974 — Survey of Current Business, June 1975, pp. 30-31, Table 2 line 11.

Column D—Fees and Royalties From Unaffiliated Foreigners

This column represents U.S. receipts and payments arising out of agreements by U.S. residents or governments of foreign countries to sell or buy outright or provide or be provided with the use of intangible assets or rights such as patents, techniques, processes, formulas, designs, trademarks, copyrights, franchises, manufacturing rights, or other similar intangible property or rights excluding firm rentals.

Source:
1948-1955 — See Note 1
1956-1959 — DRI Inc., central data bank, March 1975
1960-1974 — U.S. Department of Commerce, SESA, Bureau of Economic Analysis, June 1975

Column E—Other Private Services

This column measures all receipts by U.S. private residents from foreign residents who are not affiliated with the U.S. recipient and from foreign governments for various miscellaneous services rendered domestically or abroad. Such services include international reinsurance operations of U.S. insurance companies; international cable, radio and telephone operations provided by U.S. communications companies, and foreign contract operations of U.S. construction, engineering, consulting and other technical services.

Source:
1948-1955 — See Note 1
1956-1959 — DRI Inc., central data bank, March 1975
1960-1974 — Survey of Current Business, June 1975, pp. 30-31, Table 2, line 9

Note: 1948-55 Royalties received from unaffiliated foreigners and Other private services were reported as one statistic.
Source:
1948-55 DRI, Inc., central data bank, March 1975

Note: DRI, Inc. central data bank is a private terminal linked data source which is based upon a one-for-one statistical translation of revised U.S. Department of Commerce data updated monthly.

[a] The U.S. balance of payments statistics are customarily revised each June to incorporate new information. The 1975 revision involved changes in methodology as well as the inclusion of new information. The series displayed in Table 2 was revised to correspond to the 1966 benchmark survey of U.S. direct investment. Each revision is explained in the technical notes appended to "U.S. Balance of Payments Developments: First Quarter 1975, Revised Historical Statistics 1960-1974." Survey of Current Business, June 1975, pg. 25.

[b] The abrupt rise in investment income is due to increased incomes of petroleum affiliates and world wide money inflation. However, net investment income in the first quarter of 1975 has declined as a result of reduced incomes of petroleum affiliates.

mechanisms of transfer—export of product, licensing of proprietary information, and equal or minority share-holding in joint ventures. What mechanism a firm chooses to manage its technology abroad is largely a function of external markets and internal organization.

If property rights are protected and perfect markets exist for goods and factors, firms should be indifferent between using the technology to produce goods and services or selling it to other producers.[51] If they sell to other producers abroad, some analysts argue, it is only because they are frustrated by domestic market obstacles from applying this technology at home.[52] This argument implies that all other things being equal, firms prefer to utilize their technology at home and sell their product abroad. This minimizes the risk of transferring the technology to foreign competitors and maximizes control of commercial returns on final product.

In the real world, of course, "all other things" are seldom equal. Economic as well as political conditions in international markets create varying preferences for industrial mechanisms to manage technology transfer. Studies show that the more competitive foreign markets are or the smaller the size of these markets, the more willing firms may be to license their technology.[53] On the other hand, if firms enjoy a monopoly advantage or if the anticipated market is large, the more likely they may be to direct invest.[54]

The choice of transfer mechanism is also affected by internal firm characteristics. Large and single product firms seem to prefer to direct invest. Small and multi-product firms tend to do more licensing and joint ventures. Design firms are more likely to license than product firms.[55]

Perhaps as a reflection of U.S. technological superiority in the past, American companies, on the whole (semiconductors, for example, is an exception—see note 53) have preferred direct investment to licensing. Direct investment, studies show, is the most advantageous way to exploit monopoly benefits of new technology.[56] "Unlike portfolio investment," as Joseph S. Nye, Jr. notes, "the contribution of the multinational corporation is not so much the movement of capital as the organization of capital, management, technology, and access to rich country markets into an economic package which is greater than the sum of its parts."[57] By transferring technology through wholly- or majority-owned subsidiaries, the multinational firm internalizes the control and pricing of resources. International economic exchange becomes more a matter of internal company organization and strategy than competitive arms-length market forces. Under these circumstances, it is possible, though not inevitable, that firms can extract monopoly rents for their special skills, whether the latter consist of superior access to knowledge, factor inputs, scale economies, or consumer markets.

The preference of U.S. firms for direct investment is apparent from Table 2.2 which compares U.S. receipts from direct investment in foreign affiliates with U.S. receipts from licensing, management, and other arrangements with unaffiliated foreign firms. For 1973, these totals were approximately $11 billion (Columns B and C) and $2.5 billion (Columns D and E) respectively. If we try to isolate payments for technology only (royalties and fees), the figures for 1973 are $2.3 billion (Column B) and $0.7 billion (Column D) respectively. The attempt to separate out payments for technology, of course, is plagued by problems of definition and accounting. What seems clear is that, in the case of direct investment, income on royalties and fees represents only the tip of the iceberg of technological payments. In addition, payments for technology may be received through dividends on equity, interest on loans, and sale or purchase (at discounted prices) of products for affiliated firms. There is evidence that these payments are quite substantial. For example, as Table 2.2 shows, receipts from dividends and interests (Column C) are by far the most important part of repatriated earnings from U.S. direct investment. What portion of these receipts (plus unrepatriated earnings) may be attributed to technology is difficult to say (which spotlights again the unresolved problem of measuring the separate contribution of technology to output), but it is no doubt considerable. The sale or purchase of products among affiliated firms may also be considerable. Commerce studies estimate that in 1970 multinational corporation (MNC) merchandise exports from the United States to majority-owned foreign affiliates made up about 41 percent of all MNC merchandise exports from the United States and about 20 percent of total (MNC plus other U.S. exporters) merchandise exports from the United States. In absolute amount, this totaled some $8.6 billion worth of exports. This covers exports from U.S.-based operations only; in 1970 MNCs controlled total exports from operations in all countries about five times this amount.[58] These figures give an upper limit on the total levels of MNC exports that may be subject to discount or transfer pricing.

The issue of transfer pricing, of course, concerns the price parent firms charge affiliates for resources transferred internally within the same commercial enterprise. "The guiding principle in deciding the price which a user division should be charged...," according to A.M. Alfred, "should be...the open market price." Otherwise it would be impossible to judge the commercial efficiency of that division. "But," as he goes on to note, "where there is no effective open market price, the two divisions are, for commercial purposes, linked."[59] In practice, it is likely that transfer pricing is affected by many other factors besides commercial markets, for example, government tax, investment, and other policies.

Direct investment, the preferred mechanism for U.S. industrial transfers in the past, represents a fully unified economic structure and hence a high degree of institutionalization in international economic relations. However, U.S. direct investment has been chiefly limited to operations or manufacture. Multinationals conduct few of their R and D activities overseas.[60] Thus, while government initiated international transfers have been loosely structured and confined largely to regulation of technological activities, industry initiated transfers have been tightly structured and aimed mostly at operation of technological capabilities. The next chapter looks at some possible shifts in these patterns.

NOTES

1. Daniel S. Greenberg, The Politics of Pure Science (New York: The New American Library, 1967), p. 76.
2. Even scientists in this period were preoccupied by military issues, in particular, the controversy over the hydrogen bomb. See Robert Gilpin, American Scientists and Nuclear Weapons Policy (Princeton: Princeton University Press, 1965).
3. The Act has been revised every three years or so since 1949. The latest revision was in 1974. For a copy of the 1974 legislation, see Export Administration Report, Fourth Quarter, 1974, 110th Report on U.S. Export Controls to the President and the Congress by the Domestic and International Business Administration Bureau of East-West Trade, U.S. Department of Commerce, Appendix B.
4. For details of these various controls, see Howard Gobstein, "The Export Control System: 1945-1975," paper prepared for the project on "Technology Transfer and U.S. Foreign Policy," National Science Foundation Grant ST-44205, Henry R. Nau, Principal Investigator, Graduate Program in Science, Technology and Public Policy, The George Washington University, Spring 1975.
5. This has occurred only once or twice, a notable case being the sale of a U.S. computer to the Soviet research center at Dubna. See Howard Margolis, "Notes on Technical Advice on Political Issues," (Arlington, Virginia: Institute for Defense Analyses, April 1972).
6. See Richard Huff and Robert E. Klitgaard, "Controlling Exports on National Security Grounds," prepared for the Commission on the Organization of the Government for the Conduct of Foreign Policy as part of the Defense and Arms Control Study directed by

Graham T. Allison. This study is part of a larger classified case study drafted by Robert E. Klitgaard and contains helpful insights into a policy area where there is little publicly available literature.

7. See Charles Wolf, Jr., U.S. Technology Exchange with the Soviet Union: A Summary Report, prepared by the Rand Corporation for the Defense Advanced Research Projects Agency, R-1520/1 ARPA, August 1974, p. vii.

8. For a full development of this argument, see Huff and Klitgaard, op. cit., pp. 59-60.

9. See Herman Kahn and William Schneider, Jr., National Security Policy Issues in U.S.-Soviet Technology Transfer, prepared by the Hudson Institute for the Defense Advanced Research Projects Agency, HI-2016-RR, June 14, 1974, pp. 5-6.

10. See testimony before Congress in 1974 on Amendment of the Export Administration Act. U.S. Senate, Subcommittee on International Finance, Committee on Banking, Housing and Urban Affairs, Hearings, The Role of the Export-Import Bank and Export Controls in U.S. International Economic Policy, 93d Cong. 2d Sess., April 2, 5, 10, 23, 25, and May 2, 1974; and U.S. House of Representatives, Subcommittee on International Trade, Committee on Banking and Commerce, Hearing, International Economic Policy, 93d Cong. 2d sess., April 22 - 26, 29, 30, and May 1 - 2, 1974.

11. See Judith Tegger Kildow, Intelsat: Policy-Maker's Dilemma (Lexington, Mass.: Lexington Books, 1973), p. 31. As we noted, until 1969, Commerce had authority under the Kitchin amendment to block technologies that had commercial as well as military significance.

12. See the Conference Report on final amendments to the Export Administration Act of 1974, U.S. House of Representatives, Report No. 93-1412, 93d Cong., 2d Sess., October 2, 1974. Amendments to the Defense procurement authorization bill in summer 1974 also sought to strengthen the position of Defense on export controls. Senator Jackson, who originally proposed these amendments, sought to give Defense the right to block exports unilaterally subject only to Presidential review and to give Congress the right to override a Presidential decision if it disagreed with the latter. The last provision was retained, but the Export Administration Act, which was subsequently passed and did not include this provision, is the controlling legislation on export issues.

13. What is "essential," of course, is highly controversial on disputes of this sort. See Jack Behrman, National Interest and the Multinational Enterprise: Tensions Among the North Atlantic Countries, (Englewood Cliffs, N.J.: Prentice-Hall, 1970).

14. For an account of the role of technical assistance in the European Recovery Program, see Harry Bayard Price, The Marshall Plan and Its Meaning (Ithaca: Cornell University Press, 1955); and

European Productivity and Technical Assistance Programs: A Summing Up (1948-1958). A report by the International Cooperation Administration, Technical Cooperation Division, USRO, May 15, 1958.

15. See Price, op. cit., p. 203.

16. Quoted in William Adams Brown, Jr. and Redvers Opie, American Foreign Assistance (Washington, D.C.: The Brookings Institution, 1953), p. 389.

17. Price, op. cit., p. 156.

18. The Implications of a European System for Defense Technology, ISS series on Defense, Technology and the Western Alliance, no. 6 (London: Institute for Strategic Studies, October, 1967): 3.

19. See Science and Technology in the Department of State, prepared for the Subcommittee on International Security and Scientific Affairs of the Committee on International Relations, U.S. House of Representatives by the Congressional Research Service, Library of Congress (Washington, D.C.: U.S. Government Printing Office, June 1975), chapter IV.

20. See International Science Notes, published by the Bureau of Oceans and International Environmental and Scientific Affairs, Department of State, no. 34 (June 1975): 2.

21. For a recent analysis and critique of military assistance programs, see Robert J. Pranger and Dale R. Tahtinen, Toward A Realistic Military Assistance Program. Foreign Affairs Studies (Washington, D.C.: American Enterprise Institute for Public Policy Research, December 1974).

22. The 1974 Trade Bill also contains a controversial provision denying trade preferences to developing countries participating in supply access restrictions (such as Latin American OPEC countries). For precise wording of the export control legislation, see reference in note 7.

23. See, for example, John P. Hardt and George D. Holliday, U.S.-Soviet Commercial Relations, prepared for the Subcommittee on National Security Policy and Scientific Developments of the Committee on Foreign Affairs, U.S. House of Representatives, by Congressional Research Service, Library of Congress (Washington, D.C.: Government Printing Office, June 10, 1973). This study is part of series on "Science, Technology and American Diplomacy" directed by Franklin P. Huddle.

24. For copies of Foreign Assistance legislation through 1973, see Legislation on Foreign Relations, printed for the use of the Committees on Foreign Affairs and Foreign Relations of the House of Representatives and Senate, respectively, 93d Cong., 2d sess., March 1974. For a discussion of the significance of the 1973

amendments to the Foreign Assistance Act, see address by the author, "The New Directions of U.S. Technical Assistance Programs: A Critique," before the Society for International Development, American University, Washington, D.C., March 21, 1975. (Available from Graduate Program in Science, Technology and Public Policy, George Washington University.)

25. See Price, op. cit., p. 78; and Brown and Opie, op. cit., passim. Also see Government Utilization of Private Agencies in Technical Assistance, Staff Study No. 5 of the Subcommittee on Technical Assistance Programs, Committee on Foreign Relations, U.S. Senate (Washington: U.S. Government Printing Office, January 9, 1956).

26. See Lawrence Scheinman, "Security and a Transnational System," in Robert O. Keohane and Joseph S. Nye, Jr., Transnational Relations and World Politics (Cambridge: Harvard University Press, 1972), pp. 290-92. See also this author's National Politics and International Technology: Nuclear Reactor Development in Western Europe (Baltimore: Johns Hopkins Press, 1974), chapter 5.

27. Comment by Abram Chayes, former Legal Adviser in the Department of State. See Kildow, op. cit., p. 10.

28. See Joan M. Nelson, Aid, Influence and Foreign Policy (New York: Macmillan, 1968), p. 77.

29. On peaceful uses of nuclear energy, see Eugene B. Skolnikoff, Science, Technology and American Foreign Policy (Cambridge: M.I.T. Press, 1967), pp. 43-45; and on Comsat, Kildow, op. cit., pp. 11-16.

30. A study by the General Accounting Office concludes for example, that "to date the exchange of information has been limited and of little technical benefit to the United States." A Progress Report on United States-Soviet Union Cooperative Programs by the Comptroller General of the United States, January 8, 1975.

31. See Science and Technology in the Department of State, op. cit., p. 86.

32. Kildow, op. cit., p. 26.

33. See Mason Willrich, Global Politics of Nuclear Energy (New York: Praeger, 1971), p. 51.

34. See Commercial Nuclear Power in Europe: The Interaction of American Diplomacy with a New Technology, prepared for the Subcommittee on National Security Policy and Scientific Developments of the Committee on Foreign Affairs, U.S. House of Representatives, by Warren H. Donnelly, Science Policy Research Division, Congressional Research Service, Library of Congress, (Washington, D.C.: Government Printing Office, December 1972), p. 62. This study is part of series on "Science, Technology, and American Diplomacy" directed by Franklin P. Huddle.

35. Kildow, op. cit., p. 24.
36. Ibid., p. 25.
37. NASA explicitly rejected the foreign aid approach of the AEC in international agreements. NASA's director of international programs believes this decision had fundamental consequences and wonders "what might have been the character and course of cooperation in the nuclear field had scientific channels, rather than a political structure such as the IAEA, been utilized." See Arnold W. Frutkin, International Cooperation in Space (Englewood Cliffs, N.J.: Prentice-Hall, 1965), p. 39.
38. See U.S. Overseas Loans and Grants: Obligations and Loan Authorizations July 1, 1945 - June 30, 1973, prepared by the Statistics and Report Division, Office of Financial Management, Agency for International Development, May 1974. The figures for 1974 were also obtained from the Office of Financial Management.
39. See Commercial Nuclear Power in Europe, op. cit., chapter VI.6.
40. See Edward F. Wonder, "Competition in Collaboration: Uranium Enrichment and American European Relations," Ph.D. dissertation, University of Virginia, July 1975, especially chapter 4. Mr. Wonder wrote a preliminary draft of chapter 4 for the project on "Technology Transfer and U.S. Foreign Policy" focusing on specific concerns of the project. See also Washington Post, June 27, 1975.
41. For details on the joint agreement, see Nau, National Politics, op. cit., chap. 5.
42. Economists working outside the classical tradition, of course, have long stressed the importance and contribution of technology to economic growth. The work of these economists include the seminal contributions of Joseph Schumpeter and Thorstein Veblen. See, in particular, Schumpeter, The Theory of Economic Development (Cambridge: Harvard University Press, 1934), especially chap. II; Business Cycles (New York: McGraw-Hill, 1939), especially chap. III; and Capitalism, Socialism and Democracy (New York: Harper and Row, 1947). See also Veblen, The Theory of Business Enterprise (New York: New American Library, 1958).
43. Richard Nelson, The Technology Gap: Analysis and Appraisal (Rand publication P-3694-1; Santa Monica: Rand Corporation, December 1967), section I.
44. John H. Dunning, "The Determinants of International Production," Oxford Economic Papers, vol. 25 (November 1973): 305.
45. For an interesting if somewhat sensational treatment of this expansion, see Richard J. Barnet and Ronald E. Miller, Global Reach: The Power of the Multinational Corporations (New York: Simon and Schuster, 1974).

46. See, among others, Michael Boretsky, U.S. Technology: Trends and Policy Issues. Monograph No. 17, Program of Policy Studies in Science and Technology, The George Washington University, October 1973; and United States Tariff Commission, Implications of Multinational Firms for World Trade and Investment and for U.S. Trade and Labor, vols. I, II, and III. Report to the Committee on Finance of the United States Senate, TC Publication 537, Washington, D.C., January 1973, especially vol. III, chapter VI.

47. A study done for the Organization of American States (OAS) provides support for this explanation. In an analysis of chemical, electrical, and pharmaceutical investments in Latin America, it concludes "that tariff-jumping motivations predominate in the investment decision." See The Transfer of Technology to Latin America (Summary) by the Science Policy Research Unit of the University of Sussex, Brighton, England. Available from Department of Scientific Affairs, OAS, Washington, D.C. 1972, p.15.

48. This scenario, of course, is the now familiar product-cycle theory of foreign direct investment. See Raymond Vernon, "International Investment and International Trade in the Produce Cycle," Quarterly Journal of Economics, 80 (May 1966): 190-207.

49. Richard Cooper, The Economics of Interdependence: Economic-Policy in the Atlantic Community (New York: McGraw-Hill, 1968), p.88.

50. The work of the late Stephen Hymer supports this explanation. See "The Multinational Corporation and the Law of Uneven Development," in Jagdish Bhagwati (ed.), Economics and World Order (New York: Macmillan, 1972), pp. 113-40.

51. See G.R. Hall and R.E. Johnson, "Transfers of United States Aerospace Technology to Japan," in Raymond Vernon (ed.), The Technology Factor in International Trade (New York: National Bureau of Economic Research, distributed by Columbia University Press, 1970), p. 309.

52. See, for example, the argument of Lewis M. Branscomb, "Technological Consequences of Barriers to the Flow of Technology in World Trade," June 4, 1974. mimeographed.

53. Implications of Multinational Firms, op. cit., pp. 596-97. See also John E. Tilton, International Diffusion of Technology: The Case of Semiconductors (Washington, D.C.: The Brookings Institution, 1971).

54. Implications of Multinational Firms, op. cit., pp. 595-96.

55. See Robert B. Stobaugh, "Summary and Assessment of Research Findings on U.S. International Transactions Involving Technology Transfers" in The Effects of International Technology Transfer on U.S. Economy. Papers and Proceedings of a Colloquium,

Washington, D.C., November 17, 1973. Published by National Science Foundation, July 1974, pp. 19-22. The evidence on most of these points is at best fragmentary but nevertheless suggestive.

56. Implications of Multinational Firms, op. cit., pp. 595-96.

57. Joseph S. Nye, Jr., "Multinational Corporations in World Politics," Foreign Affairs, LIII (October, 1974): 170.

58. For the figures and calculations discussed here, see Leonard A. Lupo, "Worldwide Sales by U.S. Multinational Companies," Survey of Current Business, vol. 53 (January 1973): 33-41.

59. A. M. Alfred, "Company Pricing Policy," Journal of Industrial Economics, vol. 21 (November, 1972): 9.

60. The Tariff Commission study estimates this figure for manufacturing industries at about 6 percent. See Implications of Multinational Firms, op. cit., p. 581.

CHAPTER

3

CONTEMPORARY DEVELOPMENTS IN U.S. PRACTICE TOWARD TECHNOLOGY TRANSFER

In this chapter, we examine contemporary developments in U.S. technology transfer policy and seek to contrast these developments with the historical experience outlined in the previous chapter. There is a temptation to identify current developments that seem to deviate from past experience as incipient trends and to project these trends into the future. If we succumb to this temptation in this chapter, it is for the salutary purpose of suggesting possibilities which have not been identified in more specialized studies of technology transfer problems and which perhaps ought to instruct our investigations of these problems in future studies (some of which we recommend in Chapter 9). We use the term trend or pattern, therefore, very loosely. A few of the developments we note do, in fact, constitute trends (for example, declining role of government funds in industrial R and D). For most of our observations, however, neither sufficient time has lapsed nor are the requisite aggregate data available to permit these observations to be labeled trends. The observations, nevertheless, strike us as being important and seem to deserve further efforts to collect the data and to construct the relevant time series.

Our discussion in this chapter follows the same framework of issues and actors used throughout this study.

FROM STRATEGIC TO ECONOMIC ISSUES

Two trends emerge with respect to issues or perspectives for evaluating U.S. technology transfers:

1. an expansion from exclusive military perspectives for evaluating technology transfer to broader economic and social perspectives
2. a lack of consensus on the substance of new economic criteria to evaluate technology outflows, causing the debate to be conducted in the earlier terminology of military-strategic criteria with a resultant increase in confusion

The first trend marks a broadening of perspective from the exclusive military-strategic point of view, which prevailed immediately after World War II, to the much broader economic-commercial and, in an incipient way, social-environmental point of view that exists today. As we noted in the previous chapter, technology in the 1940s and early 1950s was valued and funded largely for its contributions to military strength. In the middle and late 1950s it began to acquire a broader foreign policy significance, being valued as a symbol of American leadership and prestige, as well as a substantive contributor to military systems. In foreign assistance programs, technology could be used to win friends and influence adversaries in ways that might maximize world order and make unnecessary the recourse to advanced military weaponry.

In the 1960s, however, the economic costs and benefits of using technology transfer for foreign policy purposes began to be perceived. At first, arguments by U.S. allies about R and D and technology gaps suggested that economic and industrial advantages went hand-in-hand with foreign policy supremacy.[1] In the Gaullist version of this argument, U.S. industry was said to have benefitted enormously from U.S. government R and D subsidies, largely for defense and foreign policy (space) purposes, as well as from the U.S.-constructed, dollar-dominated world monetary system, which encouraged foreign countries to hold U.S. dollars and thereby finance U.S. military and industrial ventures abroad. Toward the end of the 1960s, however, the technology gap argument was being reversed. American businessmen and government officials were complaining that the large balance-of-payments deficits which afflicted U.S. accounts throughout the 1960s were due not only to military and foreign policy outlays in places like southeast Asia, but also to a fundamental and growing weakness in U.S. technological capabilities. U.S. capital and technology, exported during the early postwar period to allied and other countries to strengthen free world foreign policy, had also contributed to building up commercial rivals in Japan and Western Europe. These rivals were now competing against U.S. companies in foreign export markets and, particularly in the case of Japan, in certain key home markets as well (for example, radios and other

CONTEMPORARY DEVELOPMENTS 57

transistorized electronic equipment).[2] Industrialists not only resented the give-away of American technology for foreign policy purposes but also the tighter restrictions U.S. companies faced in developing export markets in the communist countries. Allied governments, they noted, were both more relaxed in their implementation of export controls and more vigorous in their financial and institutional support of industrial contacts with the East. American companies, on the other hand, were continuing to pay the price for U.S. government programs and restrictions imposed in an era when foreign policy objectives superseded commercial considerations. In the new era, these commercial costs and benefits could no longer be ignored.

Finally, in the 1970s, some awareness of the social-environmental value and consequences of technology transfer may be emerging. Just as technology transfer in the 1960s could no longer be valued for foreign policy purposes alone irrespective of commercial costs, so in the 1970s it can no longer be valued for commercial gains irrespective of social and environmental costs. Perhaps the best example of this is found in recent foreign aid legislation. As we noted in the previous chapter (in connection with broader shifts from prestige- to productivity-enhancing uses of technology in foreign affairs), amendments to the Foreign Assistance Act of 1973 place new stress on the plight of the poor majority and rural masses in developing countries. While total GNP in developing countries grew at unprecedented rates during the 1960s, the social inequities of growth, in particular the distribution of resources between urban elites and rural masses, grew worse. As one analyst has noted, "the unparalleled economic growth achieved by most developing countries during the 1960s had little or no effect on most of the world's people, who continue to live in desperate poverty." Instead of overall growth trickling down to these people, "economic growth policies in most developing countries have led to a dual economy, which provides considerable benefits for a sizable part of the population—civil servants, favored farmers, and industrial workers—but allows the underprivileged majority to share very little (if at all) in the new prosperity."[3] A new assessment of the social consequences of foreign aid has thus led to altered guidelines for the outflow of U.S. technology in foreign aid programs.

Environmental concerns are also figuring into current controversies about technology transfer, as evident, for example, in the export of nuclear technology and the import of supersonic (SST) aircraft. These concerns are quite new, but the increasing interest in technology assessment, at both the international and national levels, suggests that the transfer of technology abroad, no less than this transfer within national boundaries, will have to meet stiffer social and environmental standards in the future.

Tracing this evolution during the postwar period reveals the increasing stress that has been placed on the national consensus concerning technology transfer. (This stress has also affected the national consensus on domestic technology as priorities have shifted from defense and space technologies to economic and social R and D.) During the cold war, as analysts have noted, military-strategic and economic issues were linked hierarchically within the U.S. domestic system.[4] The dominance of military-strategic concerns permitted American political leaders to throw a blanket of national security around most economic issues, including technology transfer. At one point, as we noted, national security was stretched to preclude export of any technology that might contribute to the military or economic potential of an adversary. Today, however, military-strategic threats are reduced and alternative perspectives have emerged. There is, accordingly, growing dissatisfaction over exclusively or predominantly military-strategic and foreign policy standards for evaluating technology transfers.[5]

Yet, for the moment, military-strategic and foreign policy considerations are the only standards recognized in export control legislation (except for short supply situations). The legislation contains no general economic standards to judge technology transfer and, what is worse, as we note below, economic theory offers no commonly accepted basis to establish such standards. There may be no need for such standards. Some industrialists prefer that, except in clear national security cases, existing standards simply be removed, opening the way for the law of comparative advantage to work in technology no less than in trade. They doubt that macro-economic generalizations are possible and urge that decisions be made on a case-by case basis.[6]

Whether this desire to avoid broader economic standards can withstand the pressures acting in the world to reduce U.S. leverage in technology transfer is another question. Direct investment, the preferred mechanism of U.S. private transfers in the past, is under increasing attack around the world. As C. Fred Bergsten notes, "virtually every country in the world which receives direct investment—which means virtually every country in the world, big or small, industrialized or developing, communist or non-communist, left or right—is levying increasingly stringent requirements on foreign firms."[7] At stake is the relative distribution of gains or losses from direct investment, both between source and recipient countries and among groups within these countries. Direct investment, it is believed by many, skews these gains in favor of source over recipient country and, within source countries, in favor of business over labor groups.

Recipient country officials complain that technology transferred through direct investment is both overpriced and accompanied by so many restrictive practices that it contributes little to local development. Payments for technology, they contend, exceed real costs. Multinational firms have already developed and exploited this technology in advanced markets. Hence, the marginal cost to them to transfer it to developing countries is close to zero.[8] Yet direct (visible payments for licenses, and so on) and indirect (transfer pricing) costs of technology to developing countries are enormous and rising at a rate of about 20 percent per year. Moreover, the technology received in return for these payments, it is argued, is often obsolete and inappropriate to local needs. Foreign subsidiaries fail to employ local suppliers and resources, conduct little R and D in local markets, and operate under all sorts of restrictions, including tied purchases of intermediate and capital goods from parent firms, limitations on exports, patent and licensing restrictions, and so on. Through transfer pricing, these subsidiaries may also minimize tax payments to local governments.[9]

Source country groups, particularly labor, complain that the technology transferred through direct investment is underpriced or indeed "given away." They note that the export of capital and technology rather than products results in the loss of jobs and hence the loss of national income from domestic production. If, on top of this, they argue, the technology is sold at bargain basement prices, the loss of income may be greater.[10] Some government and multinational representatives also fear that U.S. firms, particularly in relations with strong bargaining partners such as Western European and Japanese firms and increasingly foreign trading corporations in socialist countries, may not be able to obtain adequate returns for their technology. If these firms are unable to extract monopoly rents from new technology, the sale of this technology may eventually reduce the income and incentive for funding technological innovation in the U.S. and contribute to an erosion of U.S. technological leadership. What is more, it may contribute to the creation of foreign rivals which subsequently compete with U.S. products in both export and home markets.[11]

The issue here is one of private versus social yields on technology transfer and how to discount current and future benefits of technology. Does the price that returns a profit for an individual firm adequately reflect the numerous externalities arising from public investments in R and D, education, and general technological infrastructure? Does it take account of risk from future competition? Does it compensate for job displacement and retraining which may be occasioned by production shifts from declining to accelerating export sectors (and which might be financed through a tax on profits)?[12]

As the Tariff Commission study of multinational companies reports, "the procedures by which firms establish 'prices' at which technology is transferred are notoriously noneconomic."[13] On the basis of imprecise knowledge, however the study suggests that payments for technology through direct investment may overstate the value of the technology involved, while payments through indirect investment (licensing of unaffiliated firms) may understate the value. Since, as we noted, U.S. returns on direct investment are several times larger than returns on indirect investment, the United States (and some other source countries as well) may be receiving more for their technology than this technology would be worth if it were all made available through competitive licensing arrangements. As a result, recipient countries are showing increasing disillusionment with U.S. (as well as other countries') direct investment as a mechanism of technology transfer.

Developing countries seem to be inspired increasingly by the Japanese example in which technology was imported but direct investment was, for the most part, prohibited. They are talking more and more about unbundling the direct investment package. Capital, management, and technology, they find, are available from an increasing number of European, Japanese, and, in the case of capital, OPEC countries. U.S. multinationals no longer hold the monopoly position which permitted them earlier to package technology invisibly within the bowels of the multinational company accounting system. Thus, the various elements of the direct investment package can be bargained for separately, making more competitive and discrete the pricing and conditions of the specific technology component. This development, as Bergsten notes, "is further along in extractive than in manufacturing industries... [and] within manufacturing, it is further advanced for low-technology investments and those which use the country as an 'export platform.'" But, as he concludes, "the trend appears inexorable."[14]

The disillusionment with foreign direct investment may be part of a larger disillusionment with the private sector in both developed and developing countries. As Theodore Geiger has noted, this is leading to an accelerating expansion of the public sector in national economies.

> Currently, in more and more OECD nations, including Canada and the United States, some politicians are pressing for —and some governments are already undertaking—further nationalization of private economic activities or establishment of subsidized state-owned corporations to compete with them, greater control over private investment both indigenous and foreign,

CONTEMPORARY DEVELOPMENTS

more extensive regulation of production and marketing as part of new attempts at comprehensive national economic planning, and stricter mandatory price and wage controls if and when rapid inflation resumes.[15]

The same is true, if not more so, in developing countries. "In the last few years," Geiger notes,

the expansion of the public sector and the restriction of the market process has been intensified as more and more developing countries have been trying to bring about a redistribution of world income in their favor through nationalization of their raw-material producing industries, the formation of commodity-exporters' cartels, and higher taxes on and tigher controls over their private sectors, especially foreign-owned firms and subsidiaries.[16]

Another trend may be working against the direct investment mechanism for future industrial technology transfers, this time within source countries. As analysts have noted for some time, the relative importance of service compared to manufacturing industries has been increasing in the United States and other industrialized countries.[17] Aside from exporting less, service industries, when they transfer technology abroad, may prefer to license rather than direct invest.[18] For them, technology is a product rather than a factor of production. As a consequence, they may be more willing to sell it in an open market without the numerous restrictions imposed to protect a proprietary production asset.

If, under these pressures in both recipient and source countries, the transfer of technology moves away from direct investment toward "purer" forms of proprietary and personnel transactions (upper end of spectrum in Table 1.2), the pricing of technology may become more visible (that is, no longer a matter of intrafirm accounting) and also more controversial (since the debate over proper costing and/or pricing of technology will now become more than theoretical). Faced by political restrictions on foreign investment and, in the case of advanced markets (such as Japan), by close government-industry collaboration to expand export markets, U.S. private industry may be in an increasingly weak bargaining position in international economic exchanges. The unbundling of technology from capital investment takes away a principal source of payment for technology, namely receipts on dividends, loans and other branch assets (see Table 2.2). Technology may have to be paid for increasingly in terms of royalties on sales, cash (lump-sum or installment payments), or buyback of resultant products (an arrangement favored by the Soviet Union). In the latter two cases, negotiation of price is an extremely critical exercise, since such negotiation is influenced primarily by immediate market positions and bargaining strength with little hedge against future market contingencies, as would be the case in equity or royalty (tied to sales) arrangements.*

In some instances, therefore, intervention on the part of the U.S. government or quasi-public institutions may be desirable, both to support private companies abroad and to insure adequate public returns from technology exports at home. The alternative to broad economic criteria for technology transfer is arbitrary government intervention motivated by economic concerns but masked by national security justifications (such as the actions of the Munitions Control Board in aerospace technology). Indeed, if, as Bergsten believes, sniping at foreign direct investment represents an "inexorable trend" (see text and Note 14), private industry may be increasingly exposed to arbitrary action, from foreign governments as well as the U.S. government.

Today, the only economic basis for government intervention to control exports is to protect against short supply. Changes in 1974 to the Export Administration Act make it easier to utilize this provision, but the provision is meant to deal with agricultural and raw material products primarily, not with exports of industrial technology or know-how. Is there a need to develop similar criteria

---

* Prices of buyback products are frequently tied to an index of world prices, but this type of hedge is less certain than participation in management or profits of the enterprise. For example, even if the price is indexed, the world price may still fall so low or rise so high as to make the entire venture unprofitable. In these circumstances, the Western partner could not terminate the venture as it might in the case of management control. One solution may be an agreement, under such eventualities, to renegotiate the buyback arrangement to equalize reductions in gain or overall losses between the two partners. This seems to be the type of solution reached by Occidental Petroleum Company in its multibillion dollar fertilizer deal with the Soviet Union. (See Angelo Leparulo, "East-West Technology: A Case-study of Industrial Co-operation," prepared for the Seminar on the Management of the Transfer of Technology Within Industrial Co-operation, UN Economic Commission for Europe, Geneva, July 14-17, 1975. Mr. Leparulo is Vice-President for Science and Technology at Occidental.)

CONTEMPORARY DEVELOPMENTS 63

to protect against a depletion or short supply of U.S. know-how? As in the case of strategic-military and foreign policy standards for technology transfer, the establishment of new economic and perhaps also social criteria will take place through debate and consensus. In this debate, which has already begun, it would be helpful to distinguish carefully among three different measures of the economic and social worth of technology: cost, price, and value.[19]

Cost refers to the material and human resources consumed in the development of technology (chiefly R and D costs). As we noted, many developing countries (and some U.S. corporations for tax purposes) argue that these costs in the case of technology exports are zero, since R and D expenditures have already been recaptured through domestic exploitation of the technology. The only relevant costs, therefore, are transfer costs, that is the actual costs of physically moving and adapting the technology to a foreign environment.[20] On the other hand, a full cost notion would require the apportionment of original development costs against the price of technology exports. These costs would include public investments in social and economic infrastructure (for example, education) and in private R and D expenditures (for example, federal R and D contracts). This notion is apparently what motivates the Department of Defense from time to time to impose a recoupment fee on private technology exports when the technology involved has been developed in part through defense R and D contracts.* The difficulty with a cost approach to the worth of technology is the absence of any commonly accepted or practiced method of cost accounting. This varies from firm to firm and becomes more difficult as one moves from product to design and service firms. How ultimately does one cost out the accumulated education and experience of a professional engineer or management consultant?

Instead of cost accounting, most firms rely on the concept of price to determine the worth of technology. Price is a function of the competitive depth of supply and demand markets and may have little to do with cost. Here is where issues arise, on the supply side, concerning monopoly rents and, on the demand side, concerning monopsonist buyers. In dealing with Soviet trading corporations, for example, should U.S. firms be freed from U.S. antitrust restrictions

---

*A most recent example of this is current Air Force policy to recoup R and D costs on the F-16 fighter. Reportedly, a recoupment fee of $470,000 will be imposed on each F-16 aircraft for export. About 500 planes are expected to be exported. (See Aviation Week and Space Technology, Sept. 15, 1975.)

so as to confront Soviet monopsony with U.S. monopoly?[21] The answer is not simple. Some analysts argue that such combinations of U.S. firms for export purposes are already permissable under Section 2 of the Webb-Pomerene Act of 1918. This section exempts firms from antitrust regulations if they engage in associations for the sole purpose of export trade and if such associations do not result in any restraint on trade within the United States. The exemption nevertheless is a carefully guarded one, and other sections of the Webb-Pomerene Act actually have the effect of extending U.S. antitrust jurisdiction over activities outside the United States, since the Federal Trade Commission is authorized to investigate foreign activities that potentially violate Section 2. In an increasingly competitive economic world, monopoly concerns may be less justified than in the heyday of the U.S. multinational, when there were few alternative suppliers to U.S. firms. Similarly, monopsony concerns may be exaggerated. Soviet trading corporations, though single buyers within the Soviet Union, are only one of several buyers in world markets. Presumably U.S. firms are under no pressure to accept worse terms from these buyers than they would from their least desirable customer elsewhere in the world. Nevertheless, the increasing influence of governments in economic exchanges may manifest itself most clearly in the pricing area. As the OPEC example has demonstrated, the price of many commodities and services in the future may have to be negotiated between governments rather than set in the private market place.

Finally, there is the concept of value in determining the worth of technology exports. The technology may have a value to the exporting country which goes beyond mere cost or price. Value is often a social or noneconomic concept, which, as in the case of the military-strategic role of a piece of technology, may be considered to be so high as to preclude the sale of the technology at any price. Being a social measure, the value of technology may also vary considerably between different societies. Knowing the value of a piece of technology in some other country, as we noted in the case of military-strategic evaluations of technology transfer, may be even more difficult than determining that value in one's own country. What is more, if the technology cannot be absorbed in the recipient country, real value may be far less than abstract value. As Paul Hoffman once noted, "technical assistance cannot be exported; it can only be imported."[22] Once we take into account the social and cultural dimensions of technology transfer, we become aware of inherent limitations in the transfer of technology. And the export of technology becomes less threatening from the point of view of either compromising a military-strategic advantage or giving away an essential economic asset.

CONTEMPORARY DEVELOPMENTS 65

FROM GOVERNMENT TO INDUSTRIAL ACTORS

Three points can be made about possible trends in current actor relationships and mechanisms associated with U.S. technology transfer.

1. Industry's share (that is, the multinationals since they account for most R and D spending by U.S. industry) in the funding of industrial research has grown over that of government, strengthening the hand of private actors in influencing technology transfer policy.
2. This is happening at a time when foreign policy coordination of private industrial transfers, as well as of foreign activities of government technical agencies, may be more necessary than ever before to deal with a world economy increasingly influenced by political forces.
3. To meet these new conditions, U.S. technology transfers in the future may have to be implemented more through multilateral than bilateral means and may have to assume altered functional and instrumental characteristics. For example, in the case of government transfers, multilateral mechanisms may be required to undertake R and D and operational, as well as regulatory, functions and to involve joint facilities and common policies, as well as coordination of separate policies. In the case of industrial transfers, multilateral mechanisms may have to undertake R and D and regulatory, as well as operational, activities and to involve joint ventures and looser forms of policy coordination, as well as tightly unified instrumentalities such as direct investment.

Tables 3.1 and 3.2 show the enhanced role of industry over the federal government in funding the development of new technology. From 1965-75, industry's contribution to total national R and D expenditures rose from 33 to 43 percent, while the federal government's share dropped from 65 to 53 percent, as shown in Table 3.1. In R and D activity most relevant to industrial uses, namely R and D performed in the industrial sector (Table 3.2), industry's contribution increased even more, from 45 to 62 percent, while the government's share dropped from 55 to 38 percent (or from 59 to 38 percent since 1959).

The latter figures, in particular, suggest (if one assumes R and D expenditures are a reasonable measure of innovative success—a large assumption, to be sure, but one of the few measures we have) that considerably more new technology is being developed in the private industrial sector today, which lies outside the

TABLE 3.1

Trends in Funds for Total Research and Development,
By Source of Funds, 1953-75
(Current Dollars in Millions)

Year	Total	Federal Government		Industry		Other[a]	
		Federal	Percent of Total	Industry	Percent of Total	Other	Percent of Total
53	5,128	2,759	54	2,239	44	130	2
54	5,651	3,138	56	2,367	42	146	2
55	6,182	3,509	57	2,513	41	160	2
56	8,375	4,859	58	3,336	40	183	2
57	9,791	6,119	62	3,460	35	212	3
58	10,734	6,791	63	3,700	34	243	3
59	12,384	8,059	65	4,057	33	268	2
60	13,551	8,752	65	4,508	33	291	2
61	14,346	9,264	65	4,749	33	333	2
62	15,426	9,926	64	5,114	33	386	3
63	17,093	11,219	66	5,449	32	425	2
64	18,894	12,553	66	5,880	31	461	3
65	20,091	13,033	65	6,539	33	519	2
66	21,894	13,990	64	7,317	33	587	3
67	23,205	14,420	62	8,134	35	651	3
68	24,669	14,952	61	8,997	36	720	3
69	25,686	14,914	58	9,998	39	774	3
70	26,047	14,764	57	10,434	40	849	3
71	26,745	14,982	56	10,817	40	946	4
72	28,402	15,875	56	11,508	41	1,019	3
73	30,427	16,472	54	12,880	42	1,075	4
74	32,045[b]	16,955	53	13,916	43	1,174	4
75	34,345[b]	18,160	53	14,935	43	1,250	4

Notes: [a] Other comprises universities and colleges, and other nonprofit institutions.
[b] Estimated

Source: National Science Foundation, National Patterns of R and D Resources: Funds and Manpower in the United States, 1953-1975, NSF 75-307 (Washington, D.C.: U.S. Government Printing Office, 1975); Table B5.

TABLE 3.2

Trends in Funds for Industrial Research
and Development, by Source of Funds, 1953-75

(Current Dollars in Millions)

Year	Total R and D Amount	Federal Amount	Federal Percent of Total	Industry[a] Amount	Industry[a] Percent of Total
53	3,630	1,430	39	2,200	61
54[b]	4,070	1,750	43	2,320	57
55[b]	4,640	2,180	47	2,460	53
56	6,605	3,328	50	3,277	50
57	7,731	4,335	56	3,396	44
58	8,389	4,759	57	3,630	43
59	9,618	5,635	59	3,983	41
60	10,509	6,081	58	4,428	42
61	10,908	6,240	57	4,668	43
62	11,464	6,434	56	5,029	44
63	12,630	7,270	58	5,360	42
64	13,512	7,720	57	5,792	43
65	14,185	7,740	55	6,445	45
66	15,548	8,332	54	7,216	46
67	16,385	8,365	51	8,020	49
68	17,429	8,560	49	8,869	51
69	18,318	8,451	46	9,867	54
70	18,062	7,779	43	10,283	57
71	18,311	7,666	42	10,645	58
72	19,437	8,090	42	11,347	58
73	20,937	8,257	39	12,680	61
74	22,020	8,320	38	13,700	62
75	23,860	9,150	38	14,710	62

[a]Company funds include all funds for industrial research and development performed within company facilities except funds provided by the Federal Government. The data do not include company-financed research and development contracted to outside organizations such as research institutions. Universities and colleges, or other nonprofit organizations. In 1972 industrial firms contracted $221 million in company-financed R and D projects to outside organizations.

[b]Estimates derived from related information because either no sector survey was conducted for this year or this item was not obtained in survey.

Sources: National Science Foundation, Research and Development in Industry, 1972, NSF 74-312 (Washington, D.C.: U.S. Government Printing Office, 1974).
National Science Foundation, National Patterns of R and D Resources: Funds and Manpower in the United States, 1953-1974, NSF 75-307 (Washington, D.C.: U.S. Government Printing Office, 1975).

influence of federal R and D contracts. Federal contract monitors have access to a smaller proportion of the total R and D activity being conducted by industry and may know less about the full range of new developments in industrial technology. Accordingly, the federal government's ability to influence technology transfer in the private sector for military-strategic or foreign policy purposes may have been relatively diminished.

In the past, government funds dominated R and D spending in defense and space industries. As Table 3.3 shows, the federal share of R and D funding was highest in the electrical equipment and communications sector (65 percent in 1963) and the aircraft and missiles sector (90 percent in 1963). In manufacturing industries as a whole, the federal share was well over one-half (57 percent in 1963). If one allows for some spin-off from defense and space research (the exact amount, of course, is controversial), government influence over the direction and output of private industrial R and D may have been even higher. This placed government agencies in an advantageous position to establish the conditions and policies governing international technology transfer from the private sector. Government knew the nature of the technology involved and did not have to rely on industry to supply it with this information. Information in such circumstances is influence. Federal contract agencies could readily monitor technological outputs in the private sector and have some prior understanding of the military and perhaps even economic worth of the technology before this technology was offered for export. In the case of R and D conducted within federal laboratories and contract centers themselves, government's position was even stronger. Here federal agencies could set down the terms of international technology transfer at the same time they released the technology to industry for commercial exploitation. (This was done, for example, by the AEC when it authorized in 1954 direct industrial contacts abroad in nonclassified nuclear reactor areas and extended this authorization in 1964 to nonclassified nuclear fuel areas. The AEC had to redefine the latter authority, however, when private industries began to supply in the late 1960s unclassified data on reprocessing technology to foreign countries.)[23]

Today, as Tables 3.2 and 3.3, and 3.4 indicate, much of the technology U.S. firms seek to export abroad is being developed increasingly through investment of private funds. In the electrical and aerospace sectors, the government's share of R and D funding is down by some 12 to 15 percentage points, although the absolute share is still quite high (50 percent and 78 percent respectively in 1973). In manufacturing industries as a whole, however, the government's share is now less than 40 percent, almost 20 percentage

TABLE 3.3

Trends in Research and Development Funds
for Manufacturing and Non-Manufacturing Industries,
by Source of Funds, 1963-73
(Current Dollars in Millions)

	All Industries Manufacturing and Non-Manufacturing				All Industries Manufacturing SIC 19-39					Non-Manufacturing			
Year	Total	Percent of Total	Percent Federal	Percent Industry	Total	Percent of All Industries	Percent Federal	Percent Industry	Total	Percent of All Industries	Percent Federal	Percent Industry
1963	12,630	100	58	42	12,354	98	57	43	276	2	69	31
1964	13,512	100	57	43	13,193	98	57	43	319	2	72	28
1965	14,185	100	55	45	13,801	97	54	46	384	3	70	30
1966	15,548	100	54	46	15,051	97	53	47	497	3	74	26
1967	16,385	100	51	49	15,826	97	50	50	559	3	69	31
1968	17,429	100	49	51	16,826	97	48	52	603	3	71	29
1969	18,318	100	46	54	17,653	96	44	56	655	4	68	32
1970	18,062	100	43	57	17,357	96	42	58	705	4	68	32
1971	18,311	100	42	58	17,602	96	41	59	704	4	64	36
1972	19,437	100	42	58	18,726	96	41	59	711	4	61	39
1973	20,937	100	39	61	20,181	96	39	61	756	4	59	41

Source: For the years 1963-72, see Research and Development in Industry, 1972, National Science Foundation, Publication No. NSF-312, pp. 26, 28, 31, 33, 34; for 1973, see Science Sources Studies Highlights, National Science Foundation, Publication No. NSF-74-319, December 4, 1974, p. 2.

TABLE 3.4

Trends in Research and Development Funds
for Manufacturing Industries Only,
by Sector and Source of Funds, 1963-73
(Current Dollars in Millions)

	Motor Vehicles and Transportation SIC 371, 373-375, 379				Aircraft and Missiles SIC 372, 19				Petroleum and Refining SIC 29, 13			
		Percent of Manufacturing Industries Only	Percent Federal	Percent Industry		Percent of Manufacturing Industries Only	Percent Federal	Percent Industry		Percent of Manufacturing Industries Only	Percent Federal	Percent Industry
Year	Total				Total				Total			
1963	1,090	9	27	73	4,712	38	90	10	317	3	7	93
1964	1,182	10	27	73	5,078	38	91	9	393	3	16	84
1965	1,230	9	26	74	5,148	37	87	13	397	3	12	88
1966	1,344	9	26	74	5,526	37	85	15	371	3	5	95
1967	1,354	9	27	73	5,669	36	80	20	371	2	4	96
1968	1,491	9	25	75	5,776	34	79	21	437	3	8	92
1969	1,558	9	18	82	5,909	33	77	23	467	3	2	98
1970	1,582	9	19	81	5,245	30	77	23	515	3	4	96
1971	1,756	10	17	83	4,912	28	79	21	505	3	3	97
1972	1,982	11	15	85	5,014	27	81	19	473	3	3	97
1973	2,437	12	16	84	5,051	25	78	22	504	2	3	97

		Chemical and Allied Products SIC 28					Machinery SIC 35					Electrical Equipment and Communications SIC 36, 48			
		Percent of Manufacturing Industries Only	Percent Federal	Percent Industry			Percent of Manufacturing Industries Only	Percent Federal	Percent Industry			Percent of Manufacturing Industries Only	Percent Federal	Percent Industry
Year	Total					Total					Total			
1963	1,239	10	19	81		958	8	26	74		2,866	23	65	35
1964	1,284	10	16	84		1,015	8	24	76		2,972	23	63	37
1965	1,356	9	14	86		1,065	8	22	78		3,200	23	62	38
1966	1,407	9	13	87		1,217	8	24	76		3,626	24	61	39
1967	1,507	10	14	86		1,326	8	24	76		3,867	24	59	41
1968	1,588	9	13	87		1,477	9	23	77		4,105	24	57	43
1969	1,659	9	12	88		1,536	9	17	83		4,401	25	55	45
1970	1,766	10	10	90		1,649	10	14	86		4,352	25	52	48
1971	1,819	10	10	90		1,773	10	16	84		4,534	26	51	49
1972	1,909	10	10	90		1,964	10	18	82		4,946	26	51	49
1973	2,079	10	10	90		2,141	11	16	84		5,330	26	50	50

continued

(Table 3.4 continued)

	Other Manufacturing* SIC 20, 21, 22, 23, 24, 25, 26, 27, 30, 31, 32, 34, 39				Other Metals SIC 33				Professional and Scientific Instruments SIC 38			
		Percent of Manufacturing Industries Only	Percent Federal	Percent Industry		Percent of Manufacturing Industries Only	Percent Federal	Percent Industry		Percent of Manufacturing Industries Only	Percent Federal	Percent Industry
Year	Total				Total				Total			
1963	703	6	41	59	183	2	5	95	284	2	29	71
1964	745	6	25	75	195	1	4	96	331	3	29	71
1965	790	6	24	76	213	2	4	96	403	3	33	67
1966	860	6	33	67	232	2	3	97	468	3	31	69
1967	951	6	11	89	242	2	3	97	542	3	35	65
1968	1,040	6	34	66	251	1	4	96	660	4	35	65
1969	1,123	6	34	66	257	1	4	96	734	4	32	68
1970	1,237	7	33	67	275	2	4	96	745	4	27	73
1971	1,293	7	31	69	272	2	2	98	744	4	23	77
1972	1,370	7	31	69	254	1	5	95	804	4	21	79
1973	1,470	7	18	82	273	1	4	96	896	4	20	80

* SIC codes included in Other Manufacturing are not the same each year, making the annual comparisons inconsistent. The bulk of R and D, nevertheless, is done in the following industrial sectors: SIC 20 - Food and Kindred Products, SIC 30 - Rubber Products, SIC 32 - Stone, Glass and Clay, and SIC 34, Fabricated Metals. The data for all years in these four sectors are complete and represent more than 90 percent of R and D in the category of Other Manufacturing.

Source: For the years 1963-72, see Research and Development in Industry 1972, National Science Foundation, Publication No. NSF-312, pp. 26, 28, 31, 33, 34; for 1973, see Science Sources Studies Highlights, National Science Foundation No. NSF 74-319, December 4, 1974, p.2.

points down from 1965. It is difficult to know without further inquiries (some of which we recommend in Chapter 9) what this decline in government funding of private R and D actually means in terms of relative influence over the total range of technological activities in private industry. To be sure, a 55 or 38 percent funding share does not translate directly in that much or that little influence. We do not know what constitutes a threshold of government access or leverage in R and D relations with private industry. This threshold will undoubtedly vary by industry and by type of R and D contract. But, without further study, it is not unreasonable to conclude that the dropoff of government funding reflects a secular trend reducing government access to private R and D developments and causing some of the concern expressed by government, particularly defense, officials in recent years that private industries may be exporting valuable know-how without a proper assessment of the public costs involved.

As more information about new technology is tucked away in the private sector on a proprietary basis, it is less available to government officials. It is true, as Commerce officials point out, that this information is sometimes available from private companies in individual cases and on a strictly confidential basis (which means that it may not be shared even with other agencies, such as Defense, unless the latter ask—and it is difficult to ask for something you do not know exists). But individual cases may not reveal the larger developments most significant for public policy. And even then, information in these cases is usually provided only on an ex post facto basis and may thus arrive too late to develop timely policies. As has been evident in the recent oil crisis and in relations established by U.S. manufacturing companies with the Soviet Union under Article 4 of the U.S.-USSR Science and Technology Agreement of 1972 (which encouraged direct contacts between U.S. firms and Soviet customers), government has had to go to industry to obtain information about technology transfer and other private company policies after private industry has taken the initiative or established certain conditions which enable it to operate even when governments cannot (as in the activities of the multinational oil companies to soften the embargo against the United States and the Netherlands). Not only is government re-acting in these circumstances, instead of acting, but it is wholly dependent on industrial estimates and communications as to what is happening in these private transactions.*

---

*The effort to get more of this information into public view already preoccupies some public officials. Senator Church engineered the passage in fall 1974 of an amendment to the Senate Trade Bill calling for multinational companies to disclose their total direct investment

There is nothing unusual in a private enterprise economy in government playing a reactive role. The point we are making is that, in the particular policy area of technology transfer and in contrast to the earlier position of government in the development and transfer of new technology in the private sector, government knowledge about and influence over international technology transfer through the private sector today may be diminished. This decline might be less significant than Tables 3.2, 3.3, and 3.4 suggest if government R and D in its own laboratories and federal contract centers, which have remained approximately constant as a percentage of total national R and D (see Table 3.5), paralleled work being done in the private sector. Then government officials making policy with respect to technology exports might have knowledge from their own laboratories about the nature and significance of technology in the private sector. That in-house government R and D overlap substantially with private sector R and D is unlikely, however. While government R and D have also diversified away from exclusively defense and space areas, they remain focused, for the most part, on public service activities. New industry R and D, by contrast, are oriented toward private market opportunities.

Many may feel that the reduction of government's role in the development and transfer of private industrial technology is a good thing and a long awaited corrective to the unusual, defense-induced R and D role assumed by government after World War II. Others may feel that this reduction represents an irresponsible shift of further influence and initiative to an already strong and powerful private sector. In this study, we take neither position. For us, the possible decline of government influence over private technology transfers is most significant in light of a second development, this one international in scope, that seems to suggest increasing government influence over industrial activities in most other countries of the world today. As we noted earlier in this chapter, government intervention or, more broadly, the public sector is expanding rapidly in both developed and developing countries. Under these circumstances, U.S. private industries may encounter international markets in the future more and more influenced by political forces. To deal with these forces, at least from a macrolevel, closer and more effective coordination between private industry and the U.S.

---

in each foreign affiliate, the net income and foreign tax payments of each affiliate, and the gross sales of the parent corporation and foreign affiliate by country. The amendment was struck from the bill in the House-Senate Conference Committee. (See "New Controls Asked for Multinationals," National Journal Reports, 7 (May 10, 1975): 695.)

TABLE 3.5

Trends in Funds for Total Research and Development by Sector of Performance, 1953-75
(Current Dollars in Millions)

Year	Total R and D Performed	Total R and D Performed by Government	Percent	Total R and D[a] Performed by Industry	Percent	Total R and D[b] Performed by Other	Percent
53	5,128	1,010	20	3,630	71	488	10
54	5,651	1,020	18	4,070	72	561	10
55	6,182	905	15	4,640	75	637	10
56	8,375	1,040	12	6,605	79	730	9
57	9,791	1,220	12	7,731	79	840	9
58	10,734	1,374	13	8,389	78	971	9
59	12,384	1,640	13	9,618	78	1,126	9
60	13,551	1,726	13	10,509	78	1,316	10
61	14,346	1,874	13	10,908	76	1,564	11
62	15,426	2,098	14	11,464	74	1,864	12
63	17,093	2,279	13	12,630	74	2,184	13
64	18,894	2,838	15	13,512	72	2,544	14
65	20,091	3,093	15	14,185	71	2,813	14
66	21,894	3,220	15	15,548	71	3,126	14
67	23,205	3,396	15	16,385	71	3,424	15
68	24,669	3,493	14	17,429	71	3,747	15
69	25,686	3,503	14	18,308	71	3,875	15
70	26,047	3,855	15	18,062	69	4,130	16
71	26,745	4,156	16	18,311	69	4,278	16
72	28,402	4,482	16	19,371	68	4,549	16
73	30,427	4,619	15	20,937	69	4,871	16
[c]74	32,045	4,900	15	22,026	69	5,119	16
[c]75	34,345	5,200	15	23,860	70	5,285	15

[a]Expenditures for Federally Funded Research and Development Centers (FFRDC) Administered by industry and by nonprofit institutions are included in their respective sectors.

[b]Other includes (1) Universities and Colleges (2) FFRDC's associated with Universities, Colleges and nonprofit institutions (3) other nonprofit institutions

[c]Estimated

Source: National Patterns of R & D Resources, Funds and Manpower in the United States, 1953-1975 National Science Foundation—NSF 75-307, (Washington, D.C.: U.S. Government Printing Office, 1975).

government would seem to be required. Yet the U.S. government today is in a weaker position than before to know about and influence private industrial, especially technological, transactions abroad; and private industry, though in a stronger position to carry out such transactions, faces a traditional reluctance to participate in, let alone initiate, macrolevel policy coordination. The result is that other countries may increasingly relate technological and industrial issues to larger political and diplomatic purposes, while the United States drifts between external pressures to respond to changing political requirements and internal traditions inhibiting such a response.

The situation is best understood in contrast to the postwar historical experience of U.S. foreign policy and industrial activities in technological areas. In the 1940s and 1950s, as we discussed in the previous chapter, foreign policy-oriented government agencies often initiated programs of technology transfer to support foreign policy objectives, while domestic-oriented government agencies and private industry largely implemented these programs. Internally, high level government agencies (White House, State Department) had sufficient leverage over new technologies (nuclear energy, space technology, and so on) to couple these technologies effectively with foreign policy purposes, while private industry was eager enough to obtain access to these technologies to go along with government incentives and guidelines. Externally, technical government agencies (AEC, NASA, and so on) and private U.S. industries (multinational companies) were, for the most part, well received, so that with only loose and indirect supervision by high level government officials, lower level actors were able to transfer products and technology abroad largely in line with U.S. foreign policy interests (the case, for example, in foreign aid programs). As Richard Cooper has noted, a two-track system existed in which "the establishment of rules governing international trade permitted trade issues to be discussed and resolved in their own realm, without intruding into other areas of policy...."[24] This system was particularly advantageous for the United States since the post-war international economic system was set up largely in line with U.S. foreign policy interests and thus operated for the most part in support of these interests, without requiring high level government attention.

The type of economic world we face today is quite different. It is often characterized as one of accelerating interdependence.[25] While the meanings of this concept are multiple and imprecise,[26] interdependence most generally refers to the growing interpenetration of national societies and various social groupings within national societies. Many more actors are involved in foreign activities, and their activities often take place outside the control or oversight of traditional government agencies responsible for foreign policy.[27] The interplay of these transnational actors, it is thought, makes it increasingly difficult to insulate national societies from one another and to pursue historical objectives of independence and national sovereignty. National societies, in other words, are inextricably enmeshed in one another and have no choice but to respond and become increasingly sensitive to one another.

In economic areas, where interdependence is believed to be strongest, the deepening and multiplication of relationships among all levels of society are said to make it more difficult for governments to contain the effects of economic events, which spread rapidly throughout a society and from one society to another. Thus, if governments want to control economic disturbances such as inflation, unemployment, commodity market fluctuations, and so on, they are increasingly required to concert policies across national boundaries. Moreover, these policies must be liberal and open, since the very objectives of economic well being which are responsible for the upsurge of transnational contacts require that further obstacles to economic exchanges be removed. Much like the argument that more technology is the answer to the problems of technology, more interdependence and transnationalism are seen as the solution to the current resistance of some groups and countries to existing levels of interdependence.[28]

In this new world, it might be argued, export controls, whether military-strategic or commercial in nature, are increasingly inappropriate. Transnational actors must be free to interact openly and continuously. Even if governments desired to impose such controls, these controls would be unlikely to succeed (since transnational actors, as we noted in the case of private multinational companies, often confront governments with faits accomplis) or would only invite retaliation. In contrast to the postwar situation in which foreign policy interests set the context for low-level government and private industrial relations, low-level government (transgovernmental) and private industrial (transnational) actors now set the framework for foreign policy interests and responses. Unless governments are willing to incur large economic and commercial losses, with resultant unemployment and popular discontent, they will have to defer to the reality and interests of numerous interlocking transnational economic relationships.

The interdependence argument is widespread and in many respects convincing. As put forth by many analysts, however, its central deficiency is the failure to recognize that interdependence is a vertical as well as horizontal phenomenon and that it is a two-way street permitting governmental influences to be projected through transnational relationships, no less than the reverse. As transnational links have multiplied <u>between</u> countries, subnational links have multiplied within countries. Governments, by assuming greater and greater responsibilities for social and economic problems in individual societies, have come to occupy an increasingly central place in these subnational networks. As such, governments may be in a better position to influence transnational relations today than in the past. As long as international interactions were largely an activity of government and business elites, transnational links could be divorced from domestic social and political pressures. Now that many more domestic groups are involved in international relations, governments may face stronger requirements than before to defer to internal groups even at the expense, if necessary, of external groups. The increasing voice of inward-oriented labor groups in advanced Western societies may provide a good illustration.

Vertical interdependence or, what is another way of saying the same thing, the expansion of the public sector in national economies today (referred to by Geiger) is clearly more advanced in many foreign countries than in the United States. Indeed, as we noted in the case of technology transfer policy, U.S. industry may now have the upper hand over government, at least in terms of control of information about new technology and hence influence over the external as well as internal disposition of this technology. The point we are making here is that these external and internal developments facing technology transfer policy in the United States seem to run counter to one another. If vertical interdependence continues apace in foreign markets, it seems unlikely that, in foreign relations at least, U.S. policy will be able to maintain traditional distinctions between public and private interests and responsibilities. Thus, new internal arrangements may have to be found to couple U.S. foreign policy interests, which dictate a response to changing political requirements in world markets, with U.S. industrial and political purposes. Unless this is done, U.S. industry will be increasingly subjected to conditions in foreign markets exclusively determined by foreign governments. In a foreign environment that increasingly demands public accountablility of private activities (as in the case of codes of conduct for multinational companies), the least harmful alternative for U.S. industry may be self-restraint or establishment of internal mechanisms of coordination between public and private interests in the United States. Such mechanisms need not involve government control. The latter is not only impractical, given existing political forces in this country, but it would also do little to alleviate foreign concerns about private corporate activities abroad. Indeed, as we have seen in instances where the U.S. government has been perceived as acting too closely with U.S. multinationals (for example, Chile), it would undoubtedly exacerbate these concerns.

Consequently, it is a mistake to respond to foreign pressures for codes of conduct and other regulations of the multinational companies, including codes of conduct for the international transfer of technology, by interpreting these pressures as demands for U.S. government control of private industry. Foreign actors may be asking only that the U.S. government and private industries accept the same standards of self-restraint and limited regulation in international markets that they apply in their relationships to one another in domestic markets. Even if wrong in certain cases (and this will become apparent quickly in specific negotiations), this assumption directs our attention to what may be the real problem, namely the need to develop imaginative quasi-public or quasi-private institutional and procedural devices to coordinate public and private interests in an increasingly interdependent environment at home as well as abroad. Interdependence, as we have argued, is an intra-national no less than an inter-national phenomenon. And, as developments in the energy sector most recently demonstrate, there is a growing need to establish improved public-private mechanisms of accountability between government and private industry within the United States, as well as with other countries.

Just as private industrial actors face new conditions abroad, so do government of quasi-public technical agencies such as the Energy Research and Development Administration (ERDA), NASA, and Comsat. Dominance of these agencies in international arrangements can no longer be assured. The final Intelsat agreement provides one example. Comsat was stripped of its majority voting control of Intelsat and required to turn over its exclusive management role of the satellite system within six years (that is, by 1977) to an international secretariat. U.S. influence in future technology-related international agencies is likely to follow this same pattern. Discussions to establish international mechanisms to exploit the oceans and to operate a full-scale earth resource satellite system reveal strong opposition, from advanced (that is, Western European) as well as developing countries, to significant, let alone controlling, U.S. influence in such agencies.[29] This tougher international bargaining situation may call for increasing trade-offs between U.S. interests in various international organizations. This, in turn, may require closer coordination of U.S. technical agency and foreign policy activities. Foreign policy interests need not and probably should not dominate in these internal government arrangements, any more than public interests should dominate in government-industry arrangements. The point is simply that both sets of interests will have to be considered together and will not be easily separated as in the earlier postwar period.

Secretary of State Kissinger appears to have recognized some of these new imperatives of interdependence of U.S. foreign policy.

In the past two years, he has increasingly used this term to explain U.S. foreign policy interests in the areas of technology, economics, and commodity issues.[30] In energy and food, which he has often referred to as the primary illustrations of the new interdependence, interdependence seems to imply both the need to maintain common perceptions of the legitimacy of the existing international political (detente) and economic (liberal) system and the requirement for all countries to share increasingly in the material cost of operating this system (for example, the need for OPEC countries to assume international financial responsibilities more in line with their new wealth).[31] To attract other countries to support this concept of interdependence, Secretary Kissinger has repeatedly offered to share American technological and professional resources. To date, however, U.S. policy has been relatively unsuccessful in establishing concrete follow-up programs to support its concept of interdependence (as in the International Energy Agency). Instead, at the moment, we seem to be pursuing two separate policies: at the political level, a policy of rhetorical interdependence and, at the physical level, a policy of resource independence (for example, Project Independence). Part of the reason for, as well as problem of overcoming, this separation of policies is the difficulty of coordinating public and private interests which we have noted. In many areas of new technology, private industry controls more of the critical resources and must be encouraged and persuaded through new public-private mechanisms to invest these resources in international ventures beneficial to U.S. foreign policy interests. In the next chapter, we review some of the specific ways in which government and industry have tried to respond to these requirements in the energy sector. As that discussion suggests, the problem is not one of private sector interests alone but also government technical agency activities (such as ERDA). As these agencies lose their ability to dominate in related international organizations, they may become less enthusiastic about participating in such organizations or, what is more likely, reduce their concerns in managing problems and relationships within these organizations to narrow technical issues, perhaps at the expense or certainly to the neglect of broader foreign policy requirements.

What might be the consequences of a failure to address these problems of adjustment in government-industry and internal government relations? Let's assume that the trends we have discussed in this chapter continue unabated without adjustments at the interface of U.S. public-private relationships. Under circumstances in which foreign countries would continue to demand U.S. technology but prohibit U.S. direct investment, U.S. industries would be faced with two alternatives: 1) convert to a role as management and technology suppliers to world markets, or 2) decide to rely less on foreign markets altogether.

In the first case, the export of technology may partially replace the export of capital, just as, within mature industrial sectors during the postwar period, the export of capital partially replaced the export of U.S. know-how (technology) and expertise (services) would become more important in the balance of payments, perhaps even more important than exports of products (see Note 17). The pricing of technology would consequently become a more critical factor in determining overall balance of payments returns as well as contingent domestic economic progress. At the moment, we have little idea what the specific returns on sale of know-how and management services are. There are three problems connected with our lack of knowledge in this area. There is a structural problem in knowing what proportion of productivity and hence commercial profits to attribute to technology. Thus, as we noted in Chapter 2, licensing, royalty, and management fees from direct investment undoubtedly understate the real returns on technology through direct investment. Second, there is a definitional problem in knowing whether all fees and royalties are related to technology.^{32} This obviously varies by firm and by type of contract. Third, there is an operational problem in knowing where technology returns might be hidden in the balance of payments through transfer accounting of various sorts within the multinational company. All of these problems make it difficult to say what we are getting for our technology or what trends may be taking place with respect to these returns. Is demand for U.S. know-how and services increasing, as foreign preferences for unbundling the direct investment package would suggest? Or is U.S. know-how and expertise country-specific and hence less transferable than real goods, as some argue who believe that American organizational and managerial techniques are irrelevant to the needs of many foreign buyers, particularly socialists or planned economy countries.*

Whatever the case, the pricing of "purer" or disembodied forms of technology export is more critical precisely because these exports may be more valuable. If competitive markets which encourage licensing over direct investment tend to understate the value of

---

* The argument here is not that socialist countries do not want U.S. technology but merely that they prefer hard products to soft services. The more mobile character of modern services (professional and management consulting, and so on) is something that few economists have looked at very seriously. There is a textbook assumption that services are not exportable. This was certainly true of traditional services (such as civil construction) but it is clearly untrue of modern professional services.

technology, as the Tariff Commission study tentatively suggests (see text following note 13), American returns on technology exports may decline. Without government incentives to offset this decline, investment in new technology and correspondingly U.S. competitiveness may suffer (since investment in new technology may be in part a function of export returns on mature or standardized technology).[33] Increasingly outgunned by foreign competitors, U.S. industries may choose the second option of reducing depedence on foreign markets.

Industry support of U.S. foreign policy initiatives in technology may thus decline. Not only is the federal government's domestic leverage over industry less (due, as we noted, to industry's greater role in funding of new technological development) but foreign governments are increasingly suspicious of U.S. companies and their imputed or actual role in U.S. foreign policy activities. If, under these circumstances, the U.S. government wanted to keep a private presence abroad, federal officials would have to provide new incentives to private industry as well as to Congress to maintain this presence. For example, if U.S. aid in the future is increasingly channeled through multilateral institutions, how will this affect private industrial benefits and related Congressional incentives traditionally supporting bilateral aid appropriations?

Taken together, the decline of federal government leverage over U.S. industry and increasing foreign hostility to U.S. direct investment suggest that technology may be a less fungible political asset in the future than it has been in the past. Its technological advantage reduced (or reversed, as more extreme analysts argue), the United States may have to share more official influence in technology-related international institutions (as in the case of the revised Intelsat agreement) and to relinquish more private influence in industrial arrangements entering into joint ventures and servicing contracts instead of direct investments.

Some of these possibilities emerge in the specific case studies we conducted in this project. These case studies are the subject of the next four chapters. Chapter 8 then seeks to synthesize and integrate the case study results with the broader trends we examined in this chapter.

NOTES

1. See an earlier article by this author, "A Political Interpretation of the Technology Gap Dispute," Orbis 15 (Summer 1971): 507-27.

2. Concern about these matters was evident in the Nixon Administration. As Judith Kildow wrote in 1973, "The current U.S. administration believes that the country's economic position has been

weakened because too much technology has been given away already...".
See Kildow, Intelsat: Policy-Makers Dilemma (Lexington, Mass.:
Lexington Books, 1973), p. 28. For a recent development of the
argument that U.S. technological leadership has vanished, see
Michael Boretsky, "Trends in U.S. Technology: A Political-Economist's view," American Scientist (January-February 1975): 70-82.
We comment on Boretsky's view in the last chapter of this study.

    3. James P. Grant, "Development: The End of Trickle Down,"
Foreign Policy, no. 12 (Fall 1973): 43-65.

    4. See C. Fred Bergsten, Robert O. Keohane, and Joseph S.
Nye, Jr., "International Economics and International Politics: A
Framework for Analysis," in C. Fred Bergsten and Lawrence B.
Krause (eds.), "World Politics and International Economics",
International Organization, vol. 29 (Winter 1975): 18-22.

    5. See, for example, testimony before Congress during
hearings on technology transfer. U.S. House of Representatives,
Subcommittee on International Cooperation in Science and Space,
Committee on Science and Astronautics, Hearings, The Technology
Balance: U.S.-U.S.S.R. Advanced Technology Transfer, 93d Cong.,
1st and 2nd sess., December 4,5,6, 1973 (Washington, D.C.: U.S.
Government Printing Office, 1974). Also U.S., Senate, Subcommittee on Multinational Corporations, Committee on Foreign Relations,
Hearings, Multinational Corporations and U.S. Foreign Policy:
Trade Between the U.S. and the Soviet Union, Part 10, 93rd Cong.,
2d sess., July 1974, (Washington, D.C.: U.S. Government Printing
Office, 1975).

    6. See, for example, the views of three industrial representatives, E. L. Ginzton, Ralph Landay, and Lewis Branscomb, expressed on a panel entitled "U.S. Technology and International Trade," at
the annual meeting of the National Academy of Engineering, Washington, D.C., April 24, 1975. Papers obtained from the National
Academy of Engineering.

    7. C. Fred Bergsten, "Coming Investment Wars?",
Foreign Affairs 53 (October 1974): 136.

    8. See, in particular, the writings of Constantine V. Vaitsos,
"Bargaining and the Distribution of Returns in the Purchase of Technology by Developing Countries," Bulletin, Institute of Development
Studies, University of Sussex 3 (October 1970).

    9. See A Catalogue of Issues Involved with The Transfer of
Technology to Latin America, a background paper prepared for
the Science and Technology Policy Office of the National Science
Foundation and the Office of Technology Policy and Space Affairs of
the Department of State by the project on "Technology Transfer and U.S.
Foreign Policy," NSF Grant ST-44205, Graduate Program in Science,
Technology and Public Policy, George Washington University, August
13, 1974.

10. See testimony of I. W. Abel, Chairman of AFL-CIO Economic Policy Committee, before the House Ways and Means Committee, May 16, 1973. Contained in pamphlet "A Program to Build America's Jobs and Trade in the Seventies" obtained from AFL-CIO headquarters, Washington, D.C.

11. See various testimony in the U.S. Senate, Committee on Finance, Hearings, The Trade Reform Act of 1973, parts 1-6, 93d Cong. 2d sess., March 4-7, 21, 22, 25-29, April 1-5, 8-10, 1974 (Washington, D.C.: U.S. Government Printing Office, 1974).

12. These issues were debated during 1974-75 before the Technical Assistance Board (TAB) of the Department of Commerce. See, in particular, the paper presented to TAB by Raymond Vernon and Marshall I. Goldman, "U.S. Policies in the Sale of Technology to the U.S.S.R.," September 15, 1974; and a preliminary critique of this paper by Thomas A. Wolf, "Preliminary Assessment of Vernon and Goldman Paper," October 10, 1974.

13. United States Tariff Commission, Implications of Multinational Firms for World Trade and Investment and for U.S. Trade and Labor. Report to the Committee on Finance of the United States Senate, T C Publication 537, Washingtin, D.C. January 1973, vol. 3, pp. 597-98.

14. Bergsten, op. cit., p. 139.

15. Theodore Geiger, "On Not Pushing a Good Thing Too Far: Or Avoiding a Neomercantilist International Economic System," Looking Ahead 1, no. 5 (July 1975). Published by the National Planning Association, Washington, D.C.

16. Ibid.

17. See, for example, Lawrence Krause, "Why Exports are Becoming Irrelevant," Foreign Policy, no. 3 (Summer 1971); pp. 62-70; and Daniel Bell, The Coming of Post-Industrial Society (New York: Basic Books, 1973), chapter 2.

18. The evidence is very preliminary, and further study is needed. See Robert B. Stobaugh, "Summary and Assessment of Research Findings on U.S. Internation Transactions Involving Technology Transfers," in The Effects of International Technology Transfer on U.S. Economy. Paper and Proceedings of a Colloquium, Washington, D.C., November 17, 1973; The National Science Foundation, July 1974, pp. 19-20.

19. I benefitted from discussions on this point with Hylan Lyon, formerly with the Science and Technology Policy office of NSF and now Deputy Director of Science, Technology and Industry, OECD, Paris.

20. For an assessment of these costs which are actually quite substantial, see Edwin Mansfield, "International Technology Transfer: Forms, Resource Requirements and Policies," Papers and Proceedings, The American Economic Review 65 (May 1975): 372-75.

21. See Raymond Vernon, "Apparatchiks and Entrepreneurs: U.S.-Soviet Economic Relations," Foreign Affairs (January 1974): 249-62.

22. Quoted in Harry Bayard Price, The Marshall Plan and its Meaning (Ithaca: Cornell University Press, 1955), p. 108.

23. See Commercial Nuclear Power in Europe: The Interaction of American Diplomacy with a New Technology, prepared for the Subcommittee on National Security Policy and Scientific Developments of the Committee on Foreign Affairs, U.S. House of Representatives, by Warren H. Donnelly, Science Policy Research Division, Congressional Research Service, Library of Congress, (Washington, D.C.: U.S. Government Printing Office, December 1972), pp. 30, 37, and 43.

24. Richard Cooper, "Trade Policy is Foreign Policy", Foreign Policy, no. 9 (Winter 1972-73): 19.

25. For recent studies of international interdependence, see, among others, Seyom Brown, New Forces in World Politics (Washington, D.C.: The Brookings Institution, 1974); and Miriam Camps, The Management of Interdependence, Council Papers on International Affairs (New York: Council on Foreign Relations, 1974).

26. For a helpful attempt to clarify some of these meanings, see John Gerard Ruggie, "International Responses to Technology: Concepts and Trends," International Organization, special issue, 29 (Summer 1975): 557-85.

27. For the pathbreaking study in this area, see Robert O. Keohane and Joseph S. Nye, Jr. Transnational Relations and World Politics (Cambridge: Harvard University Press, 1972).

28. Some analysts recognize the pitfalls of unrestrained liberalism and, instead of another "great leap forward" toward liberalization, call for "the rationalization of a system of limited interdependence that would be consistent with political reality." See Robert O. Keohane and Joseph S. Nye, Jr. "World Politics and the International Economic System" in C. Fred Bergsten (ed.), The Future of the International Economic Order: An Agenda for Research (Lexington, Mass.: Lexington Books, 1973), p. 140.

29. See with respect to ocean issues, Ann Hollick and Robert E. Osgood, New Era of Ocean Politics (Baltimore: Johns Hopkins Press, 1974); and with respect to earth resource satellite systems, Valerie A. Hood, "A Global Satellite Observation System for Earth Resources: Problems and Prospects." A report on research carried out under NSF Grant GI-41472, "The Application of International Regulatory Techniques to Science/Technology Problems," under the direction of David A. Kay, American Society of International Law, July 1975.

30. See, among others, Kissinger's speech "Energy: Toward A New Cooperative Era", before the Ministerial Meeting of the International Energy Agency, Paris, France, May 27, 1975. Press Release, Bureau of Public Affairs, Department of State.

31. See the author's "U.S. Foreign Policy in The Energy Crisis," The Atlantic Community Quarterly 12 (Winter 1974-75), pp. 26-39; and "Interpreting U.S. Foreign Policy in Food and Energy," paper presented at the Annual Convention of the American Association for the Advancement of Science, Americana Hotel, New York, New York, January 30, 1975.

32. For a discussion of definition problems in the technological balance of payments, see Mary Frances Teplin, "U.S. International Transactions in Royalties and Fees: Their Relationship to the Transfer of Technology," Survey of Current Business 53 (December 1975): 14-18.

33. On the relationship of innovation to growth and international economic competitiveness, see Robert Gilpin, Technology, Economic Growth and International Competitiveness, a report prepared for the Subcommittee on Economic Growth of the Joint Economic Committee, Congress of the United States, 94th Cong., 1st sess. (Washington, D.C.: U.S. Governmental Printing Office, July 9, 1975).

CHAPTER 4

KamAZ: U.S. TECHNOLOGY TRANSFER TO THE SOVIET UNION

Harlan S. Finer
Howard Gobstein
George D. Holliday

Soviet plans to construct a mammoth truck plant on the Kama River were officially unveiled in April 1971 at the Twenty-Fourth Congress of the Soviet Communist Party. The truck plant, which promised to be the largest in the world, was designated by the Congress as the single most important industrial project in the Party's 1971-75 Five-Year Plan. As such, it was to enjoy the highest civilian priority in the government's financial and supply programs throughout the plan period.

The announcement of the Kama River Truck Plant (abbreviated as "KamAZ") came as no surprise in the West. Rumors of such a project had reached Western ears as early as the spring of 1969. Development of the KamAZ trucks had begun in 1968, and by mid-1969 the decision to locate the project at Naberezhnyye Chelny, a small village on the Kama River, had been reached. Construction

---

A number of people rendered invaluable assistance to the authors. We are especially indebted to Mr. Donald Stingel, then President of Swindell-Dressler, Inc., who addressed a seminar at George Washington University and related the experiences of his company's involvement in the Kama River Project; to Dr. John P. Hardt of the Congressional Research Service, Library of Congress, who provided valuable advice and information; and to Mr. Herbert Meyer, associate editor of Fortune Magazine, who shared his useful insights during several conversations. In addition, many officials of the Departments of Defense, State, and Commerce gave us much needed information.

of the project began immediately after the Party's Politburo gave its approval in September 1969. The Soviet press reported the following month that the project was already underway with 2,000 workers on site.[1] Shortly afterward, contacts with Western industrial firms were initiated. By the time of the project's official unveiling, negotiations were well under way with a number of potential foreign contractors, including the Ford Motor Company, Mack Trucks, Inc., and the Swindell-Dressler division of Pullman, Inc.

From the beginning, KamAZ has been a project of epic proportions. Indeed, superlatives seem unavoidable when discussing its size, cost, and personnel. When the $5 billion facility goes into operation, it will consist of six huge installations: foundry; forge; pressing and stamping; tooling and repair; engines, gears and transmissions; and assembly. Together, these installations will cover 23 square miles of land, with 11 million square feet of working space under roof. The plant's buildings will be connected, from within and without, by 170 to 185 miles of fully automated, computer-controlled conveyor belts. When it reaches full capacity, the Kama plant will produce 150,000 three-axle, heavy-duty trucks of various designs, including single-unit trucks, trailer trucks, and truck tractors designed to pull semitrailers. It will also produce 250,000 engines (of which 100,000 will be supplied to other Soviet automobile factories) in three basic models: a 260-horsepower, ten-cylinder engine, a 210-horsepower, eight-cylinder engine, and a 180-horsepower, eight-cylinder engine. Finally, it will produce a large variety of spare parts.[2] This will represent a full 25 percent increase over the current level of Soviet automotive production and a vast increase in heavy-duty truck manufacture.

In addition to the plant's six installations, the project will include factories to produce the building materials required for construction, a huge 1,100 megawatt hydroelectric generating station, and an entire city to house the plant's 80,000 workers and their families. The city will have apartments, stores, schools, theaters, hospitals, a sports palace, a vodka distillery, and a 560-room hotel. Nine collective farms have been organized to supply the city with food, and a modern, surface rail, mass transit system has been constructed to transport the project's 125,000 construction workers to and from the construction site. When completed, this city-factory complex will cover an area of approximately forty square miles.

The total costs of the project have been variously estimated (with earlier estimates being lowest) at between $5 billion and $6 billion. Approximately 25 percent of this amount has been set aside for the construction of the city. Another $1.6 billion has been allocated for the purchase of foreign equipment (although the final cost figure may be much higher due to rising costs in the West and escalator clauses in many foreign contracts). Since the construction and equipping of KamAZ is being managed by Soviet officials (unlike the Tol'yatti automobile project in which FIAT held a turnkey contract), only subcontracting agreements have been negotiated with Western firms. The largest single subcontractor for KamAZ is the French firm, Renault. The largest dollar value of foreign contracts has gone to the West Germans. The American share of the foreign contracts has been alternatively estimated at anywhere from $200 million to $500 million. The true amount is probably close to $400 million. The Soviets have awarded approximately 100 contracts to some 50 American firms. These contracts range in size from Swindell-Dressler's $40 million in contracts for foundry designs and equipment to Federal Products Company's two contracts totaling less than $5,000.

American involvement in the Kama River project represents an important development in U.S.-Soviet industrial cooperation. It deserves careful analysis for a number of reasons:

1. It reflects a new attitude on the part of U.S. policymakers toward technology transfer to the Soviet Union.
2. Large-scale Western involvement in the Kama project has highlighted a number of problems faced by U.S. and other Western firms which sell technology to the Soviet Union.
3. It has focused attention on the important role of Western technology in the Soviet economy and on some of the shortcomings of existing Soviet techniques for absorbing that technology.

The following case study provides an analysis of the issues and problems associated with American participation in the Kama River project. This participation is analyzed during three successive stages of U.S.-Soviet interaction: 1) exploratory contacts; 2) contract negotiations; and 3) contract implementation. It concerns primarily the experiences of the Swindell-Dressler division of Pullman, Inc. As the major American contractor for the project, Swindell's experience illustrates most of the difficulties encountered by participating U.S. firms. In our discussion of the exploratory phase of negotiations, we also consider the involvement of two other American firms—Ford Motor Company and Mack Trucks. Neither firm signed a contract with KamAZ but their early contacts with the Soviets, compared to those of Swindell, help to illustrate the substantial, if not dramatic, changes that occurred in Soviet-American trade and technical relations in the short period between the spring of 1970 and the summer of 1971. The sections dealing with contract negotiations and contract implementation discuss the considerable problems that remain in U.S.-USSR industrial relations despite these changes. The final section discusses some of the implications of KamAZ for future U.S.-Soviet commercial relations.

EXPLORATORY CONTACTS

Ford Motor Company and Mack Trucks

Soviet contacts with US firms concerning KamAZ were initiated in early 1970, a year prior to the project's official unveiling. At this time, the Soviet State Committee for Science and Technology extended an invitation to the Ford Motor Company to engage in exploratory talks in Moscow. The subject of these talks was not publicly disclosed until April 20, 1970, when Henry Ford II announced from the American Embassy in Moscow that Ford Motor Company was considering a Soviet offer to undertake the construction of a truck plant on the Kama River.[3] In this announcement, Ford emphasized that the talks were exploratory and were concerned primarily with technical assistance. The Soviets had proposed, he later explained, that his company "might help them on the kinds of machine tools that they might use to best advantage from the production standpoint" in the complex that they were planning.[4] Ford added that the Soviets also requested his company's participation in the design of the heavy-duty trucks to be produced.[5]

While these initial statements by Henry Ford suggested a somewhat limited role for the Ford Motor Company in the Kama project, a company press release issue on April 29 presented the Soviet offer in a different light. According to the release, the company had been asked to undertake the entire construction project alone or in conjunction with other Western companies. The Soviets had emphasized, however, that even if construction was undertaken by a consortium of foreign contractors, one company was to act as an overall project manager.[6] The release futher announced that the Ford Motor Company had invited a small Soviet delegation to tour its U.S. facilities and to engage in additional talks concerning the technical details of the Soviet proposals.[7]

Despite these initial efforts, Ford Motor Company announced two weeks later that it had rejected the Soviet offer of participation in the truck project.[8] Speaking before an annual stockholders meeting in Detroit, Henry Ford cited public criticism of Ford Motor Company's involvement with the Soviets as a major influence on the company's decision (see next section). Ford stated, however, that the company was "continuing to study the many considerations involved in other Russian proposals."[9] Ford also stressed that he strongly supported increased U.S. trade with Eastern Europe and with the Soviet Union.

Following the rejection of the Soviet offer by Ford Motor Company, the Soviets engaged the Satra Corporation to assume the task of finding American firms to assist in the Kama project. Satra soon initiated conversations with Mack Trucks, Inc., a subsidiary of the Signal Corporation of Los Angeles. As a result of these initial conversations, representatives of Mack Trucks traveled to Moscow in November 1970 where they were first introduced to the specifics of the Soviet proposal. At this time, the Soviets were requesting that Mack assume a general contracting role for four of the seven functional subdivisions of the proposed facility. It was also proposed that Mack assume responsibility for obtaining low-interest, long-term credit financing for the project.

On May 18, 1971, after several months of preliminary discussions, Mack Trucks signed a protocol letter of intent with representatives of the Soviet Ministry of Foreign Trade.[10] This protocol agreement was reported to have been so generally worded that Mack officials regarded it as little more than "an agreement to agree."[11] The content of the protocol, however, was reported to have assigned to Mack the responsibility for "designing key elements of the complex, deciding what equipment should be installed, purchasing and shipping that equipment and providing help on other aspects of truck production."[12] The monetary value of such activity was reportedly estimated at approximately $750 million. As part of the agreement, Mack was given until June 25 of that year to formally commit itself to the project and to secure U.S. government approval.

At this point, Soviet involvement with Mack Trucks should have progressed into the negotiation phase. However, a complex of difficulties intervened. Mack's participation in KamAZ was first brought into doubt when it failed to meet the June 25 deadline for securing government approval for an export license. Officials of the Office of Export Administration (OEA) in the Department of Commerce reportedly required additional time to process Mack's application and suggested that Mack obtain an agreement extension. Mack's parent company, Signal Corporation, announced that, despite this difficulty, it had no desire to pull out of the deal with the Soviets.[13] In response to Mack's desire to continue negotiations, the Soviets agreed to an extension until July 25, and subsequently granted a second extension until September 15.[14] During this period, the OEA approved various licenses for the export of some $250 million worth of truck manufacturing equipment (including equipment for the Kama facility) but failed to clear Mack's application. As a result, Mack officials informed the Soviet Ministry of Foreign Trade on September 16 that "since approval from the U.S. Government had not been received," it was in the "mutual interest" of both parties to consider the May agreement terminated.[15]

While Mack did indeed encounter difficulties in securing an export license, it is not altogether certain that the failure to secure such official approval was the real reason behind Mack's rejection of the Soviet proposal. Complaints by Commerce officials that Mack had failed to provide information relevant to the application have led some informed observers to believe that it was Mack, and not the OEA, that had been the reluctant party. As explained in greater detail below, it may well have been the inability of Mack Trucks to assume the general contracting role proposed by the Soviets that prompted it to seek a termination of the May protocol agreement.

Swindell-Dressler

Shortly after contacts with Mack Trucks had been established by Satra in mid-1970, the Soviets initiated contacts with Swindell-Dressler. In September 1970, while attending the International Foundry Congress in Brighton, England, E. Stanley Haynes, director of Swindell's foundry department, met informally with two representatives of the Soviet State Committee for Science and Technology. Two days after this initial contact, Haynes met in London with a representative of Metallurgimport, the Soviet trading corporation responsible for the importation of metallurgical equipment. Both of these meetings entailed lengthy but inconclusive discussion about foundry designs and equipment, with the Soviets displaying particular interest in the specifics of Swindell's involvement in the design and engineering of Ford Motor Company's new auto foundry at Flat Rock, Michigan.[16] The Soviets, however, made no mention of the Kama project, nor did they indicate any interest in contracting for Swindell's services.

Two weeks after these meetings, Haynes received a call asking him to fly to Zurich for discussions concerning a possible project. In Zurich, Haynes' discussions once again turned to Swindell-Dressler and its foundry operations. On this occasion, however, without mentioning KamAZ by name, one Soviet representative spoke about "a big project which a foundry could be a part of."[17] With nothing more definite than this, Haynes returned to Pittsburgh. Six weeks passed during which he continued to correspond with several Soviet officials involved in the still undisclosed "big project." In

November, Swindell-Dressler finally received an official letter from Metallurgimport which outlined the Kama project and requested that Swindell bid on a contract to design the truck plant's foundry. The letter also asked that Swindell send representatives to Stuttgart to discuss the proposal.

The Stuttgart meeting marked the final phase of exploratory talks between Swindell-Dressler and the Soviets. At this meeting, Haynes was accompanied by Donald Stingel, then senior vice president and now president of Swindell-Dressler. Meeting with Haynes and Stingel was a delegation from the Soviet Ministry of Foreign Trade which included V.N. Sushkov, the Ministry's director of machinery and equipment imports. (Sushkov's presence in the Soviet delegation is noteworthy in that he had been closely associated with Soviet dealings with Swindell's parent firm, Pullman, Inc., during World War II). Once again the discussion focused on Swindell-Dressler—**its skills, its financial resources, and its position** within the Pullman corporate family.[18] At the meeting's end, Haynes and Stingel were told to expect an invitation to Moscow and to be prepared to present designs for the proposed foundry. Haynes and Stingel returned to Pittsburgh to prepare for the forthcoming negotiations.

Issues and Problems

The exploratory stage of U.S.-Soviet negotiations concerning the Kama River project was marked by the necessity for each American firm to assess possible participation in the project in light of a number of important political and commercial issues. The most salient of these issues was that of determining the political and strategic implications of U.S. involvement in the Kama project. This issue focused upon two considerations: 1) the direct military value of the technical information and equipment to be exchanged with the Soviets, and 2) the indirect political significance of the exchange on U.S.-Soviet relations. During the period of exploratory talks in 1970, the first of these two considerations was publicly emphasized by U.S. officials. The transfer of technical information and equipment to the Soviet Union was heavily criticized for the benefits it offered in strengthening Soviet military power. As explained below, such criticism was instrumental in inducing Ford to withdraw from participation in KamAZ. By late 1970, however, this criticism had abated somewhat. Official emphasis began to shift to the second consideration. This permitted Mack Trucks and Swindell-

Dressler to begin exploratory talks with the Soviets without the degree of pressure experienced by Ford.

When Ford Motor Company announced in April 1970 that it was considering an offer to participate in KamAZ, U.S.-Soviet relations, though not hostile, were far from that state of cooperation which subsequently became associated with the concept of detente. Differences on Vietnam, the Middle East, the arms race, and other issues served to bolster the argument of those in the government who opposed transfers of U.S. technology to the Soviet Union. The transfer of truck-building technology was singled out for criticism as an example of military-related technology that should not be exported. Secretary of Defense Melvin Laird became the primary Administration spokesman against the involvement of U.S. firms in the Kama project. In an interview printed in May 1970, he remarked:

> Some people believe the best way to succeed with the Soviet Union, for example, is to go to Russia and build trucks for them. Before giving away the technology to construct trucks in the Soviet Union, and establishing plants for them, there should be some indication on the part of the Soviet Union they're not going to continue sending the trucks to North Vietnam by the shiploads for use on the Ho Chi Minh trail.
> We have many American pilots who are today prisoners of war in North Vietnam because they had to attack trucks provided by the Soviet Union to North Vietnam.[19]

Henry Ford II responded angrily to Laird's comments. The statement of the Secretary of Defense, he noted, "is not only highly misleading, but appears to be a gratuitous attack upon my common sense and patriotism. Based on preliminary studies we have made to date," he added, "the program proposed by the Soviet Union calls for no product design requirements or manufacturing technology not already available in Russia, Western Europe or Japan."[20] Ford concluded his remarks by stating that no decision had yet been made on the Soviet proposal and that his company "would not consider entering into any engagement with the Soviet Union without the complete endorsement of the government of the United States."[21]

Despite Henry Ford's protests, Melvin Laird continued to make it clear that he opposed the participation of Ford Motor Company in the Soviet truck project.[22] Laird's opposition was apparently a factor in Ford's withdrawal from the negotiations. In his speech announcing the rejection of the Soviet proposal, Henry Ford emphasized that public criticism, particularly by Laird, had been a major influence on the company's decision.[23]

While the Laird view prevailed within the Nixon Administration in 1970, there were clearly forces at work to change the direction of U.S. policy on trade with communist countries. The Export Administration Act of 1969 had signaled a major reorientation of U.S. export control policy. While previous export control laws had been designed to restrict U.S. trade with communist countries, the new law was intended to foster such trade. It required removal of controls on technology that is freely available to communist countries from non-U.S. sources and on items that are only marginally of military significance. The new law was a congressional initiative which the Nixon Administration first resisted but finally accepted. The Administration's ultimate acceptance was apparently motivated by the belief that changes in political relations with the Soviet Union were possible and that an expansion of trade could be an important element in a new relationship. Administration supporters of a more liberal U.S. East-West trade policy apparently believed that any expansion of trade should be timed to coincide with an improvement in overall political relations. As Secretary of State Henry Kissinger noted later, "The Administration then took the view. . . that intensified trade should grow out of a generally improved relationship—in short that our relations with the U.S.S.R. should proceed on a broad front."[24] Consequently, proponents of expanded commercial relations did not publicly articulate their views until progress was achieved in other aspects of U.S.-Soviet relations.

A second issue which arose during exploratory talks concerned the Soviet insistence on formal protocol agreements as a framework for subsequent negotiations. The purpose behind these agreements is poorly understood in the West. One view is that they serve both to legitimize contacts with Western firms within the Soviet Union, as well as to provide assurance to reluctant Soviet bureaucrats that Western firms will act in good faith throughout the period of negotiations. It is also possible that the Soviets have sought in such protocols (many of which take the form of technical cooperation agreements) a justification to retain designs and technical information presented during negotiations and to utilize such materials in subsequent discussions with competing firms. To be sure, this is the more skeptical view, but it is not without some degree of substantiation in Soviet practice.

Of the three U.S. firms studied, only Mack Trucks signed a protocol agreement with the Soviets. Ford's negotiations were terminated before such a protocol could be arranged. It would appear likely, however, that Ford was also subjected to requests for such an agreement. For its part, Swindell-Dressler refused to sign a protocol with the Soviets. Despite this refusal, the Soviets continued the negotiations. The Soviet attitude in this case may be explained, as we noted above, by the Soviet government's long experience in dealing with Swindell-Dressler's parent firm, the Pullman Company. The required level of trust in the Western partner already existed.

It is interesting to note that the protocol agreements which have been signed with the Soviets have not been uniform in form or content. They have varied from what Mack executives describe as their "agreement to agree" with the Soviets,[25] to more specific agreements on technical areas of cooperation. An example of the more extensive form of protocol was signed in July 1972 between Occidental Petroleum and the Soviet State Committee for Science and Technology.[26] In this agreement, five years of technical and scientific cooperation were outlined and the various methods of cooperation were defined. Cooperative efforts were to range from "mutual consultations" to the exchange of know-how and licenses for technology development and the production of products.[27]

It is important to add, however, that none of these agreements amounts to a commercial transaction in the sense that they involve actual sale or exchange of know-how. They may encourage or envision such sales, as in the case of the Occidental agreement, but they do not themselves finalize these sales.

A third issue which arose during exploratory talks focused upon the need for each U.S. firm to determine the role which it would assume in relation to its Soviet counterparts. In Soviet proposals for KamAZ, both general contracting and subcontracting roles were offered. The choice between these roles was important in the sense that it was to determine not only the amount of company resources to be invested in the project, but also the type and extent of know-how to be transferred. A general contracting role, for example, is likely to entail not only the transfer of technical information and equipment, but also some transfer of management know-how and techniques for scheduling and integrating large-scale manufacturing systems. A subcontracting role, on the other hand, is often more limited in scope, focusing primarily upon the transfer of specific products or component parts of larger systems.

For Ford Motor Company and Mack Trucks, the issue was one of whether or not to assume a general contracting role. The Soviets offered Ford overall responsibility for the project, while proposing that Mack assume a general contracting role for four of the facility's seven functional subdivisions. In both cases, the

the proposals were rejected. Ford apparently rejected a general contracting role as too limited in scope. The terms offered by the Soviets were in all probability insufficient in Ford's opinion to compensate for the technical and managerial know-how to be provided. Instead, the Ford Company sought some form of continuing exchange with the Soviet Union, suggesting, for example, a management contract to handle sales of Kama trucks outside the Soviet Union.[28]

The situation involving Mack Trucks was more complicated. Whereas Ford found the Soviet offer of a general contracting role to be too little, Mack apparently found such a role to be too much. Mack seemed willing initially to accept the general contracting role outlined by the Soviets. This acceptance was in all probability embodied in the understandings which accompanied the signing of the May 1971 protocol. It appears, however, that when the full scope of the Soviet proposal became apparent, Mack officials realized that such a role would tie up too much of the company's resources and personnel. Accordingly, Mack officials sought release from the May agreement. The problem was compounded, however, by the fact that Mack was simultaneously negotiating with the Soviets for the sale of large, off-the-road utility vehicles. In order not to prejudice these negotiations by an act of bad faith, Mack may have thought it convenient to let the U.S. government bear the onus of the voided protocol. Mack could thus point to OEA's lengthy deliberations over granting the necessary export license, and not to its own limited capacity, as the explanation for terminating the May protocol.

The situation involving Swindell-Dressler was different in that the question of accepting a general contracting role was never involved. From the outset of discussions, Swindell was to assume a subcontracting role involving only designs and equipment for the project's foundry. It is apparent, however, that Swindell sought to expand this role. At one point, it insisted that it be authorized to act as the sole purchasing agent for all foundry equipment. This request came at a time when the Soviets, having failed in their negotiations with Mack Trucks, had decided to organize and supervise all aspects of the project themselves. As a result, the request was denied. Swindell's willingness to accept a limited role was in all likelihood premised on its hope that this initial contract might lead to subsequent, more involved participation in Soviet industrial projects. This rationale was suggested in March 1973 when Donald Stingel stated that Swindell-Dressler was ultimately interested in construction engineering jobs in the Soviet Union in which it would have the opportunity to sell some of its own know-how.[29]

In addition to the general problems discussed above, U.S. companies encountered several more limited, but nevertheless frustrating, difficulties. The first of these involved the fact that American businessmen in dealing with the Soviets find themselves confronted not with comparable Soviet economic managers, but rather by government officials (often of high rank) and technical specialists. These Soviet representatives are usually described as possessing considerable knowledge not only about the activities and technology of the firm involved, but also about the general conditions within the firm's field of operation. In the case of Swindell-Dressler, its representatives met with a number of officials of the Ministry of Foreign Trade and the prestigious State Committee for Science and Technology. On all occasions, the conversations centered upon Swindell-Dressler's activities and upon recent advances in American foundry technology.[30] In each instance, the Soviet representatives were described as being extremely well informed.[31]

A second problem centered upon the Soviet's penchant for secrecy during initial discussions. At the beginning of exploratory talks with Swindell, the Soviets gave no indication of the reason for their interest in the firm's activities and capacities. As the discussions progressed, they dropped hints of a "possible project" or a "big project."[32] But, only after a number of meetings, did they finally disclose the content and dimensions of this project. Through this tactic, Swindell's representatives were kept at a disadvantage in that they were forced to negotiate with the Soviets while possessing little idea about what the Soviets were after. Under such circumstances, U.S. companies may be tempted to table more information than they would under normal, more direct commercial discussions.

A third and related difficulty centered upon the Soviet refusal to permit U.S. observers to visit the proposed Kama site. As the Soviets explained to Swindell-Dressler, the Kama site was not "available" for inspection.[33] While Metallurgimport did offer to provide Swindell with soil samples and other pertinent information, this proved to be less than adequate. As a result, Swindell was forced to prepare detailed proposals with insufficient information on which to base design and cost estimates. These designs were to require numerous changes as addition information became available. As will be discussed in following sections, this problem was to continue to plague Swindell's activities during all three phases of its participation in KamAZ. Indeed, Soviet reluctance to allow foreign technicians to tour construction sites has proven to be one of the most frequently cited problems of U.S.-Soviet industrial cooperation.

CONTRACT NEGOTIATIONS

The negotiation phase of Swindell-Dressler's involvement in KamAZ began on March 13, 1971. On that date, Haynes and Stingel arrived in Moscow to present Swindell's design proposal for the Kama River foundry. Meeting with Haynes and Stingel was a Soviet delegation headed by N. P. Maximov, the president of Metallurgimport. This meeting, while productive, proved to be only the first of many negotiating sessions. It was not until December 1971, nine months after the start of contract negotiations, that agreement was achieved. On December 22, 1971, after three days of final discussions, Maximov and Donald J. Morfee, president of Swindell-Dressler, signed a $10 million contract. The contract called upon Swindell-Dressler to provide design and engineering specifications for the Kama River foundry, to be delivered within one year's time. The contract also required that Swindell evaluate various equipment designs offered by other firms for use in the foundry.[34] The agreement constituted the first U.S. contract for the Kama project as well as the project's second foreign contract (Renault had already signed a contract for the design of the diesel engine plant).[35]

Shortly before obtaining a final agreement, the Soviets attempted to persuade Swindell to lower its price, using the possibility of future foundry equipment sales as a lure. Swindell rejected these overtures, insisting that either a profit would be realized on the first contract or it would not be signed.[36] Despite Swindell's refusal to bargain lower terms for future sales, its executives expressed confidence that subsequent equipment sales would be contracted. In May 1972, for example, Donald Morfee remarked that Swindell "was still confident that we will be the main supplier of most of the equipment that will be used in the foundry."[37] Company officials openly speculated that Swindell would obtain contracts for up to $40 million in foundry equipment.[38] The reasons for such confidence remain undisclosed. It appears, however, that despite the claims of Stingel and Morfee that the December contract had been concluded independently of any subsequent contracts, some degree of agreement on possible future sales had been involved. As noted earlier, the December contract had called upon Swindell to evaluate the various equipment designs offered for use in the project's foundry. Did such an inclusion in fact provide a built-in mechanism for Swindell to insure future sales for itself? Was it to evaluate its own equipment as well as its competitors?

Whatever the answers to these questions, Swindell's favored position as the evaluator of foundry equipment designs appears to have been a decisive factor in subsequent discussions concerning equipment sales. In mid-June 1972, negotiations began in Moscow on the foundry contracts, with some 25 to 30 American firms participating. When the process was concluded, Swindell-Dressler held a second contract, this time for $16 million in furnace equipment. In this contract, Swindell agreed to provide 15 electric arc furnaces as well as to fabricate the furnances, supervise their installation, assist in start-up operations, train personnel, and provide initial spare parts.[39] The contract, which was to be financed jointly by the Chase Manhattan Bank and the Export-Import Bank, was described as the world's largest sale of arc furnaces on record.[40]

In concluding the contracts, Swindell encountered problems in Washington as well as in Moscow. The sections which follow discuss first the problems involved in procuring an export license from the Office of Export Administration of the Department of Commerce and second the plethora of problems which characterized Swindell's negotiations with the Soviets.

Procuring the Export License

In order to export foundry designs to the Soviet Union, Swindell-Dressler had to obtain a validated license from the Office of Export Administration of the Department of Commerce. Efforts were directed toward this end shortly after the initiation of contract negotiations. Upon the return of Swindell's negotiators from the March 1971 meeting in Moscow, Swindell began the lengthy lobbying process necessary to obtain the license. Swindell's lobbyists argued that the technology the Soviets wanted was not unique: it could be provided by Japanese and European firms which were bidding for the project. They also argued that a contract for the foundry designs would open the way for subsequent equipment contracts totaling perhaps in the hundreds of millions of dollars.[41] Finally, they maintained that the technology had no direct military applications. Thus, the issue in Swindell's view was an economic one: should Swindell, and the U.S. economy in general, benefit from the sale of its technology?

Although Swindell hoped that their arguments would lead to rapid government approval, U.S. participation in the Kama project once again became the topic of heated debate among government officials. Generally, the Departments of State and Commerce argued in support of Swindell's participation, while the Defense Department continued to express its disapproval. Defense officials again emphasized the benefits which Kama trucks afforded the Soviet defense establishment and pointed to their potential use in aiding Communist forces in South Vietnam.

In the summer of 1971, however, U.S. civilian officials proved less willing to accept the arguments raised by the Defense Department. It had become apparent that the U.S.-Soviet political relationship which had prevailed in 1970, when Laird's comments could effectively halt U.S. participation in the project, had been altered. It had been replaced by an emerging new relationship fostered by a variety of domestic and foreign policy considerations in both countries. In the United States, the view within the Nixon administration that accomodation was possible with the Soviet Union on a number of issues, such as arms limitations, Berlin, and Vietnam, became the overriding consideration. Progress on those issues was perceived as a valuable means of attaining both foreign policy and domestic political objectives. The economic benefits of expanding trade with the Soviet Union, while decidedly marginal in terms of overall economic problems, were considered by some of the administration to be significant. Specifically, it was believed that expanded trade with the Soviet Union would help reduce the U.S. balance of payments deficit and provide a stimulus to selected sectors of the U.S. economy.

For the Soviet leadership concerns about the international political situation also provided the primary rationale for seeking improved relations with the United States. However, they clearly expected the economic benefits of a new relationship to be substantial. For a number of years, they had carefully cultivated commercial ties with Japan and the West European industrial countries, primarily to gain access to industrial technologies that were admittedly superior to their own. Soviet economic planners had expressed concern about a slowdown in economic growth and about technological obsolescence in the civilian sectors of the economy. Western technology was assigned an important role in modernizing a number of critical industries, including the automotive industry. For some of their needs, the Soviets probably considered U.S. technology to be the best available.

In short, by the summer of 1971, relations between the two countries had created a more propitious atmosphere for expanding commercial relations. Swindell had the good fortune to seek export licenses for the Kama project at a time when the Administration was changing its approach to trade with the Soviet Union. Secretary of Commerce Maurice Stans had suggested a new approach in February 1971, when he urged an increase in trade with the Soviet Union as a means of improving the balance of trade.

By July of 1971, Swindell's involvement in KamAZ had thus become a question of political and economic significance rather than a strategic one. The argument that the Kama trucks, which were

not scheduled to roll off the assembly lines until 1976, would assist
forces engaged against U.S. troops in Vietnam now appeared incon-
sequential in light of administration efforts to remove those troops
some time in 1972. In addition, the use of Kama trucks to strengthen
the Soviet military could hardly be viewed as a serious threat to
the strategic superiority enjoyed by the United States. On the basis
of these considerations, the National Security Council recommended
approval of American participation in the Kama project. In July,
President Nixon directed that Swindell be granted the authorization
necessary to facilitate its participation in KamAZ should it receive
the contract.

Subsequent events suggested that KamAZ had become a showpiece of U.S.-Soviet detente. In the second half of 1971 and early
1972, the value of licenses issued for exports to the Soviet Union
escalated rapidly, primarily because of approvals of proposals
for participation at KamAZ. On October 18, 1972, when the U.S.-
Soviet Commercial Agreement was signed the U.S. Government
approved establishment of a special Soviet purchasing commission in
the United States for concluding contracts for the Kama project.
Secretary of Commerce Peter Peterson wrote to Soviet Foreign
Trade Minister N.S. Patolichev: "We believe the Kama River
Purchasing Commission is a good example of our mutual desire to
improve trade between our two countries and to provide necessary
facilities and organizations to achieve that objective."[42] Later,
in March 1973, the U.S. Export-Import Bank extended one of its
first loans to the Soviet Union for the purpose of buying machinery
and equipment for KamAZ.

Problems with the Soviets

The Soviet style of negotiation proved to be the source of
considerable frustration for Swindell's representatives. Particularly
disturbing was the Soviet practice of inviting a large number of
competing firms to Moscow at the same time and then negotiating
with each firm in turn. This resulted in waiting periods between
negotiating sessions which sometimes amounted to several weeks.
Given the inadequate communication facilities in Moscow, foreign
businessmen have found it impossible to conduct other business
matters while waiting to meet with the Soviets. Indeed, even
routine contacts with the home office have often proven difficult
and costly. As a result, foreign company officials have been forced
to either lose a significant amount of time amusing themselves in

Moscow between negotiating sessions, or to arrange for numerous, short-notice trips to Moscow. Either option, of course, is expensive and time-consuming. In Swindell-Dressler's case, the second option was chosen. During the nine month period between the start of contract negotiations and the signing of the first contract, Swindell officials (principally Stingel) were forced to make numerous trips between Pittsburgh and Moscow.

Equally frustrating for Swindell's representatives was the fact that throughout the period of negotiations the Soviets were simultaneously meeting with representatives of competing firms. Swindell executives complained that the Soviets provided little feed-back as to their standing in the negotiations. At the same time, the Soviets dropped hints that certain unnamed competitors were offering more attractive terms. This psychological technique of playing one competitor off against another served to provide the Soviet negotiators with a significant advantage over individual Western firms. Indeed, it enabled them to manipulate the competitive instincts of Western businessmen to obtain the best possible terms for the Soviet Union. As a result of such tactics, Swindell executives reportedly thought on several occasions of pulling out of the negotiations. On each occasion, however, the Soviets persuaded them to continue.

The competitive advantage enjoyed by Soviet negotiators is in large part the product of the monopolistic character of Soviet trading corporations. Instead of dealing directly with the specialized personnel who will ultimately use the transferred products and know-how, Western firms are required to negotiate with trading corporations organized along product lines by the Ministry of Foreign Trade. The negotiators themselves are not associated with the end-users. The former have a primary concern to obtain the best possible terms of transfer for the Soviet Union. This arrangement results in significant delays during negotiations, as the Soviet negotiators must continually consult with specialists concerning design and specification proposals and changes. It also creates a situation in which Western firms are given little indication of Soviet end-user response to their proposals. Indeed, the poker-faced negotiators often act as a screen which conceals any show of interest or preference by end-users until the negotiations have been concluded.

The inability of Western firms to negotiate with Soviet end-users may also compel their representatives to provide a wider assortment of information and specifications than would otherwise be considered necessary or prudent. With little knowledge of the specific demands and interests of the end-user, Western negotiators may deem it necessary to provide additional information in an effort to cover all contingencies and to insure acceptance of their designs and proposals. Such actions, however, can result in uncompensated losses of proprietary know-how. Throughout their meetings with the Soviet negotiators of Metallurgimport, Swindell's representatives considered it necessary not only to provide detailed designs, but also to answer numerous technical questions concerning the specifications and processes involved.[43] All this was done prior to any commitment by the Soviets to contract for Swindell's services.

Language difficulty was also encountered in Swindell's negotiations with the Soviets. On several occasions, translation errors resulted in misunderstandings which required unnecessary changes in Swindell's design and cost estimates. On one occasion in particular, a translation error almost caused Swindell to lose the contract. This occurred in August 1971, when Haynes and Stingel returned to Moscow after receiving their export license from the Department of Commerce. Upon their return they were confronted with what appeared to be a significant change in the Soviet negotiating position. Where previously the Soviet proposals had involved only foundry designs, they now appeared to be demanding engineering designs for the buildings that would house the foundry and for auxiliary equipment such as conveyors and cranes. In light of this change, Haynes and Stingel raised Swindell's cost estimates by more than 50 percent. When the Soviets saw the change, Stingel later explained, "they hit the ceiling...they said it was exorbitant."[44]

What had in fact occurred was an error in the translation of the term "technological design." To American engineers, this is a broad concept which includes the design of the machinery and techniques employed in the production process, as well as the support equipment and buildings. To the Russians, however, the term applies only to the first category of designs. At early meetings, this difference in interpretation required that the Russian term "technological" be translated into the English "process." On this occasion, however, a new Soviet-supplied interpreter had put the term into English as "technology," thus implying to the Americans a broader meaning than intended by the Soviets. As Stingel later explained the resulting problem: "We were miles apart in price because to us the term meant design of machinery and techniques employed in the production process; but the Russians...interpreted our offer to mean only the first category and not the support equipment and buildings."[45] When the misunderstanding was discovered, Swindell's cost estimates were revised back to their original level. Although seemingly minor, the error had almost brought about a break in negotiations.

Two additional sources of difficulty deserve mention at this point. The first involves the Soviet practice of frequently changing or expanding technical designs and proposals during the course of negotiations. In many instances, the Soviets have made such revisions in an effort to obtain additional and often unecessary equipment. This has required comparable changes in design and cost specifications and has served to further lengthen the negotiation period. While this posed only minor problems for Swindell-Dressler, it has been a significant factor in the conduct of negotiations by other Western firms. The second difficulty pertains to the Soviet insistence that all designs provided by Western firms be prepared in compliance with the more complicated Soviet standard specifications for equipment. This results not only in additional preparation costs, as Western suppliers are forced to prepare special designs and estimates, but also contributes to additional production costs, as the equipment to be provided no longer conforms to standards which had been developed to minimize cost.[46]

As a result of these problems, and indeed all the problems described, the conduct of negotiations with the Soviet Union entails higher costs than comparable negotiations among Western firms. While the costs of Swindell-Dressler's negotiations have not been revealed, it is known that the West German firm, Verzahntechnik, invested almost $500,000 in preliminary studies for the design of the proposed Kama transmission plant. This expenditure was made, it must be remembered, before the firm received a contract and without any assurance of success in the contract bidding.

A final area of difficulty pertains to the specifics of the contract itself. The contracts which the Soviets work out with Western firms are considerably more lengthy and detailed than comparable contracts among Western firms. As a result, considerable time is required to prepare the contract and to verify its detailed translations. In addition, the Soviets insist upon including in the contract stringently worded sanctions to cover any breach of contract by the Western firm. These sanctions often amount to 6 percent of the value of the contract (often the total profit margin) and cover defaults in quality, shipping damage, or late delivery. While the Soviets have not strictly enforced these sanctions, they continue to pose a source of irritation for Western contractors. For as is often the case (as will be illustrated in the Swindell-Dressler experience), delays are caused by factors attributable not to the Western firm, but to Soviet planning errors and bureaucratic inefficiency. Should such penalties be invoked, considerable loss would be incurred.

CONTRACT IMPLEMENTATION

At the end of 1975, the construction and equipping of KamAZ was far behind schedule. Originally scheduled for completion in 1974, the project had been delayed by at least two years. Much of the delay was the result of the centralized and vertically compartmentalized nature of Soviet economic planning and management, which generated a number of problems in the contract implementation phase of KamAZ. Problems in this phase were also the result of the limitations of the particular methods and techniques used to absorb foreign technology at KamAZ.

Problems with Designs

Swindell-Dressler's experience in carrying out its contractual obligations at KamAZ provides a good illustration of some of the problems inherent in the compartmentalized nature of Soviet planning and management. The difficulties encountered by Swindell stemmed principally from 1) the separation of the design of plant equipment from the design of plant buildings; 2) the separation of the design of plant equipment from responsibility for purchase of such equipment; 3) the separation of the design of plant equipment from the design of connecting parts and equipment; and 4) the separation of the design of equipment from the design of product components.[47]

The separation of equipment design from building construction posed considerable problems for Swindell-Dressler. Before the December 1971 contract had been signed, the construction of the building to house the Kama foundry had already begun.[48] It was therefore necessary for Swindell to design the foundry to fit into pre-existing spaces. Since the equipment in the foundry encompasses a complex integration of many component parts, the standard practice in the West is to design the building with the equipment designs in mind. The mode of design required for Kama reversed this practice and was thus foreign to anything in Swindell's experience. It required significant revision of Swindell's original designs. In cases where the designs could not be altered, the delivered equipment had to be stored in crates at the Kama site while Soviet construction engineers tore up and rebuilt existing structures to permit installation.[49]

It had become obvious that the Soviets were in a rush to complete their Kama showpiece. This rush, however, served not only to minimize construction efficiency and to increase costs, but also to cause significant delays in the completion of the project. Although the Soviets attempted to explain this process of "building and designing at the same time" as a new "bold experiment" in industrial development, they have been forced to recognize its drawbacks.[50] As one Soviet writer conceded, the process does mean that "in some cases it is necessary to alter the foundation under the machine toll or transfer line or in other cases to introduce changes into a project." He dismissed such problems, however, by the fact that "they are compensated for a quicker introduction of the plant into service."[51]

Additional difficulties were caused by the failure of the Soviets to provide information necessary for the completion of the foundry designs. By the terms of the December 1971 contract, the designs were to be delivered by August 1972. In March 1973, however, the designs were still incomplete. Acting through foreign newsmen, the Soviets publicly expressed their dissatisfaction with Swindell's performance.[52] For its part, Swindell could only explain that, despite the design delays, the arc furnaces would be ready on schedule in late 1973 or early 1974.[53] In late 1973, Moscow again pressured Swindell for the designs. On this occasion, Swindell explained that it had not completed work on several aspects of the designs which depended upon the complicated integration of machinery purchases from several different countries. Some of this equipment, Swindell complained, had not yet been contracted for by the Soviets.[54]

In the summer of 1974 the question erupted anew. On this occasion the Soviets were openly accusing Swindell-Dressler of delaying work on the foundry designs, charging that their failure to supply the designs was playing havoc with the planned production schedules at Kama.[55] The Soviets now threatened to invoke the sanctions provided in the 1971 contract. Swindell responded that it could not possibly complete the designs without the technical information which the Soviets refused to provide. Swindell needed to know, for example, the specifications of Soviet machinery with which U.S.-designed foundry equipment was to connect. It had also not been provided information concerning the maximum-load capacity of the floorings in the foundry buildings.[56] Ultimately, the imbroglio was solved due to the intervention of L.B. Vasiliev, general director of KamAZ, who convinced the reluctant bureaucrats of Metallurgimport to provide Swindell with the information Swindell needed.

Only part of Swindell's inability to obtain technical information can be attributed to the Soviet penchant for secrecy. It soon became evident that in some instances (particularly with regard to the specifications of the foundry flooring) the Soviets did not possess the required information themselves.[57] Planning delays, together with insufficient inter-Ministry cooperation, had caused the preparation of equipment designs and the completion of plant facilities to fall behind schedule. In some cases, these delays were the result of the failure of other agencies to meet schedules or to conclude negotiations with foreign firms.

Problems with Personal Contacts

Swindell's implementation of its two foundry contracts was further impeded by the continued refusal of the Soviets to permit American engineers to tour the Kama construction site. As noted earlier, Swindell had been forced to prepare its preliminary designs for the foundry with insufficient information because, as a Soviet communication noted, the Kama site was "unavailable" for inspection.[58] This problem was to continue throughout the period of contract implementation. The first look that Swindell's engineers got of the constuction site was in late February 1973, almost two years after the start of serious discussions concerning the Kama foundry. On this occasion, Frank Cavalier, Swindell's project leader, and some of his associates were taken on a five-hour tour of the plant site. The tour proved to be largely ceremonial and provided Swindell's engineers with only limited information. According to the terms of the 1971 contract, Swindell was to have sent as many as 25 technical observers to the Kama site in the fall of 1973. By November 1974, however, "few, if any" of the observers had been allowed to arrive at the site.[59] Swindell executives were later to announce that their engineers would not be sent until the summer of 1975.[60] It appears that this delay in permitting foreign observers to the construction site was reflective of Soviet embarrassment at the two-year delay in the project's construction schedule. In addition, the Soviets may have been embarrassed by the fact that there continued to be a shortage of adequate facilities at Kama to house large numbers of Western visitors.

To compensate for the inability of Swindell's engineers to obtain technical information on a first-hand basis, the Soviets arranged for a number of Soviet engineers to reside in Pittsburgh. The Soviets were to provide Swindell's designers with information concerning site conditions, equipment specifications, and construction procedures.[61] While the resident Soviets did provide considerable advice, their presence proved to be as much a hinderance as a help. Swindell's problems in dealing with the resident Soviet engineers stemmed from a number of Soviet practices. First the Soviets were on duty in Pittsburgh for tours of only six months. This required significant time not only to orient the Soviets to Swindell's operations, but also to brief them on the progress of the foundry designs. Second, the Soviets proved to be extremely cautious in providing information and in suggesting changes in Swindell's designs. It was obvious that none wanted to take the responsibility for making a mistake. Even when such changes had to be made, the decision was to be made by a committee in order to spread responsibility throughout the group. Despite the fact that this procedure was responsible for considerable delays, the Soviets were less concerned about the delay than with making a mistake.

Additional difficulty was caused by the highly specialized training of the Soviet engineers. Such training had become the logical end-product of the extreme compartmentalization of Soviet design procedures. A situation arose, for example, in which a Soviet specialist responsible for compressed air systems refused to deal with plans for natural gas or water lines. Since all three of these problems are handled by one engineer at Swindell, each American specialist was required to develop a working rapport with as many as three different Soviet specialists. This had to be done, it should be remembered, at six-month intervals. Because of the highly specialized orientation of the resident Soviet engineers, it often became necessary to consult with additional Soviet personnel in Moscow. If a Soviet specialist was needed in Pittsburgh to approve a design or a specification change, the State Department sometimes took three to four weeks to grant clearance for his travel to this country. This was done, in part, as retaliation for Soviet access restrictions. Naturally, it added to overall delays, as work on specific designs would have to be tabled pending the arrival of the Soviet specialist.

Looking Ahead: Start-up Problems

Perhaps the biggest potential problem in the implementation of subcontracting agreements with the Soviet Union arises in the subsequent phase of equipment installation and plant start-up. In none of the industrial contracts with Western firms have Soviet partners relinquished control over civil construction and equipment installation. There is little evidence that they are likely to do so in the future. It is clear that the Soviet penchant for strong central direction over all aspects of economic activity will continue to exclude any foreign private control of local capital assets and labor forces. As a result, Swindell-Dressler (as well as other Western firms in the Soviet Union) has no formal responsibility beyond the equipment delivery stage. Beyond that, it performs only advisory functions. This does not exclude, however, Swindell's continued responsibility for equipment performance. Such responsibility is retained despite the fact that Swindell possesses no formal authority to insure that such performance is not impaired by delays or by errors in assembly at the construction site.

A situation thus arises in which considerable loss may be incurred by foreign firms due to circumstances entirely beyond their control. A major potential problem in this regard pertains to possible losses attributable to equipment deterioration prior to installation. As evidenced at the Kama construction site, foreign equipment may be allowed to stand idle and unhoused for long periods of time while Soviet engineers complete housing facilities or attempt to make structural changes in completed facilities. Further delays may also result from periodic relocations of Soviet workers to higher priority projects. Given the weather extremes of most industrial regions of the Soviet Union, considerable equipment damage is likely to result.

Such problems will most likely find informal solutions, as one would assume that the Soviets possess an equal, if not greater, interest in seeing that foreign equipment is expeditiously installed and performs properly. In the meantime, however, the arrangement clearly presents risks for foreign firms. The problems inherent in this situation have only begun to be experienced by Swindell-Dressler, as its engineers have only recently arrived on the Kama site to monitor equipment assembly and start-up operations.

KamAZ: IMPLICATIONS FOR FUTURE U.S.–SOVIET COMMERCIAL RELATIONS

Since Soviet foreign trade representatives first opened negotiations with U.S. firms about possible participation in KamAZ, the attitudes of U.S. Government policymakers and U.S. businessmen toward selling technology to the Soviet Union have undergone a profound change. The past political and strategic rationales for restricting such technology transfers are now clearly much less influential. To be sure, export controls in military-related technology remain, and the political implications of U.S.-Soviet commercial relations are considered no less important. However, the impact of strategic export controls on U.S.-Soviet commercial relations has been markedly reduced, and the primary policymakers of the present Administration appear convinced that an expansion of trade is politically desirable. Moreover, the U.S. business community is increasingly regarding the Soviet Union as a profitable market for U.S. technology.*

---

*The momentum of U.S.-Soviet business transactions was slowed in early 1975 by the breakdown of the U.S.-Soviet Trade Agreement. Linking trade conditions to Soviet emigration policies

In this new environment, the economic and commercial issues of U.S.-Soviet technology transfers are receiving more attention. What is the balance of economic benefits when U.S. firms sell technology to the Soviet Union? Will the long-run costs to the U.S. U.S. economy outweigh short-run benefits? What are the future prospects for expanding sales of technology to the Soviet Union and improving the institutional framework in which they take place? While no definitive answers to these questions are attempted, the following discussion of the role of KamAZ in the Soviet economy and its implications for future Soviet commercial relations with the West may provide some insights.

Role of KamAZ in the Soviet Economy

KamAZ is being built to meet a crucial need of the Soviet economy—to boost rapidly the production of trucks in order to provide a more balanced freight transport system. Soviet economic planners have long recognized the need for expanded truck transport capacity to complement their rail and marine transportation systems. Before KamAZ was initiated, they had allocated substantial resources to fulfill that need. However, previous efforts had failed in several respects. The primary problem was simply the inability to expand production of trucks fast enough to meet the rapidly growing needs of the economy. In 1975 a Soviet planning official reported that motor freight transport was increasing 7 to 10 percent annually, while the number of vehicles was increasing by only 3 to 5 percent.[62] The greater volume of freight was being carried by outdated trucks which required frequent, expensive repairs. The necessary increases in output will be provided partially by expansion of existing facilities. However, it is KamAZ which is expected to provide the major part of the increase. Truck production at KamAZ will increase Soviet output by a full 25 percent, while 100,000 diesel engines will be supplied to other parts of the Soviet automotive industry.

A second major problem in the Soviet automobile industry is that Soviet trucks are obsolete by world standards. For example, Soviet industry has proven incapable of producing modern, high-

---

for Jews, Congress imposed limits on export-import financing of sales to the Soviet Union. Nevertheless, large segments of government and business opinion continue to favor more liberal trade with the Soviet Union.

performance diesel engines that equal the efficiency standards of Western engines. Soviet trucks are heavier, constructed with lower grade materials, and require more frequent repairs than Western trucks. Soviet engineers believe that they have designed a technologically superior truck for KamAZ. The KamAZ trucks are basically modifications of other Soviet vehicles, redesigned by engineers from various parts of the Soviet automotive industry. Although initially inclined to seek assistance in designing a new diesel engine through a licensing arrangement with a Western firm, Soviet officials decided that their own engineers at the Yaroslavl Engine Plant could provide a better design.[63] They did, however, enlist the help of Renault in 1972 to make improvements in the engine designs.[64]

Another major problem in Soviet truck production is an inadequate assortment of trucks. Because Soviet industry had concentrated on production of medium trucks, the economy is especially deficient of heavy-duty trucks for use in intercity transport and in the agricultural and construction sectors. This problem is exacerbated by the inadequacy of Soviet roads. At the beginning of the Ninth Five-Year Plan (1970-1975), about three-fourths of all Soviet roads were unsurfaced dirt roads or roads with gravel surfaces.[65] Soviet specialists estimate that in the 1970s, 70 to 80 percent of all Soviet truck cargo will be carried on roads on which Soviet standards permit trucks with no more than six tons of freight per axle.[66] Most Soviet heavy trucks exceed that weight, while medium trucks are inefficient freight carriers for many operations. KamAZ trucks are designed specifically to fill this gap. The three-axle design will provide improved cross-country capabilities, while combinations of more powerful engines and trailers will permit greater load capacity. KamAZ vehicles are, in short, designed precisely for Soviet road conditions.

Western automobile manufacturers have expressed concern that a part of KamAZ's future output will be sold on world markets in competition with their own products. The example of FIAT-designed Soviet cars being sold in Western Europe has convinced some Western businessmen that it is not in their interest to build up a Soviet commercial competitor. To some extent, their fears seem well founded. In recent years, Soviet officials have shown considerable interest in expanding their exports of manufactured goods. The directives of the Tenth Five-Year Plan, for example, mention an increase in the output of products for export as one of the primary goals in Soviet foreign trade.[67] A number of factors have convinced Soviet economists of the need to expand industrial exports. Among them are growing scarcities of some raw materials which have constituted the bulk of Soviet exports in the past, the prestige factor of exporting manufactured goods, and the advantages of scale in some industries.

Soviet officials have not publicly discussed the prospects of exporting KamAZ trucks. It seems probable that an attempt will be made in the future to market some of them in the West. However, the barriers to exporting large numbers of trucks to Western industrial countries are formidable. First, Soviet domestic needs will clearly require the bulk of KamAZ's output. Second, KamAZ trucks are designed specifically for Soviet road conditions. They will not, for example, be the most efficient carriers for the intercity superhighway transport needs of most Western industrial countries. Finally, the Soviets have serious problems in providing the necessary quality and after-sale servicing needed to remain competitive in the West. For these reasons, it appears likely that any exports of KamAZ trucks will go primarily to traditional markets for Soviet trucks—Eastern Europe and developing countries—and not to the industrial West.

The completion of KamAZ should result in a major gain for the Soviets in their attempt to modernize and expand their truck transport system. However, Western technology transfer to KamAZ will not solve other important problems in the Soviet automotive industry. For example, the Soviets have been searching for more efficient ways to manage their industrial enterprises and have shown an interest in Western management techniques. For example, a Soviet specialist observed that KamAZ managers would imitiate the best of Western and Soviet management practices in operating the plant.[68] Yet there is no evidence that the KamAZ contracts provide a framework for Western firms to transfer directly managerial skills to the project. Western firms apparently have no responsibility for seeing that the plant is operated efficiently after start-up.

After start-up at KamAZ, other traditional problems in the Soviet automotive industry are likely to remain. Among these is an inability to maintain the rate of technological progress that is achieved by firms in the West. In the past, a number of Soviet industries, including the automotive industry, have been modernized with large-scale imports of Western technology, only to fall behind technically after a few years.[69] Another remaining problem is an infrastructure in the Soviet economy that is inadequate for increased truck production. Construction of roads and service facilities and improvement of the supply system for materials and spare parts will require increased attention. Finally, although completion of KamAZ will provide the economy with a wider assortment of trucks, important gaps will still exist. For example, there will still be deficiencies of trucks with very large cargo-carrying capacity, special vehicles, semitrailers, trailers, and small trucks.[70] It is likely that the Soviets will continue to turn to Western firms for technical assistance in solving these problems.

Prospects for New Forms of Technology Transfer

The problems involved in transferring Western technology to the Kama project suggest that a somewhat different institutional framework would serve the interests of both the Soviet and Western firms in future projects. The Soviets, on the one hand, are likely to conclude that additional transfers of technology are needed in the automotive industry and other sectors and that more effective ways can be found to absorb technology. On the other hand, future Western partners will probably want assurances that the problems encountered at KamAZ are not a permanent feature of Soviet commercial relations with the West. Thus, there appears to be a confluence of interests in finding better forms for future U.S.-Soviet technology transfers. An improved arrangement would presumably involve closer ties between the Western seller of technology and the Soviet end-user in each stage of commercial interaction. It might also include longer-term and deeper involvement of Western firms in the Soviet economy.

To some extent, improved arrangements for industrial cooperation between the Soviet Union and Western firms may be facilitated by Soviet domestic economic reforms. Since the 1950s, the Soviets have been experimenting with a variety of measures to improve economic planning and management. A common goal of past attempts at reform has been to strengthen the role of enterprise managers in relation to the central bureaucracies and to create incentives to encourage more efficient management. None of the past reforms has proved particularly successful. The most recent institutional reform, initiated in the early 1960s but given primary impetus by a Party decree in April 1973, is the creation of industrial associations. Associations are amalgamations of smaller enterprises producing similar or complementary products. The primary goal of the new reorganization is to increase efficiency by combining relatively small-scale operations into large conglomerates under a unified management and increasing the authority of the managers.

It is too early to assess the net impact of associations on commercial and technical relations with Western firms: the experience of KamAZ, which was organized as an association from its inception, provides some contradictory evidence. For example, Soviet officials have already complained of the difficulties of managing very large associations,[71] and the decision to concentrate the huge Kama complex in a single location was the subject of heated debate among Soviet officials.[72] Judging from some of the problems experienced during construction of KamAZ, the Soviets may yet conclude that it is too large to be managed effectively. In any case, the size of the Kama complex seems to have been a deterrent for Mack Truck and other Western firms which were offered the role of general contractor for KamAZ.

KamAZ's organization as a production association apparently has also had some beneficial effects on industrial cooperation with Western firms. A striking feature of the Kama project has been the authority exercised by its general director, L. B. Vasiliev. While the autonomy inherent in the production association scheme of organization requires that local directors exercise a certain degree of initiative and responsibility, the amount of authority exercised by Vasiliev is indeed impressive. This authority stems in part from the fact that Vasiliev, unlike other plant or association directors, is a Deputy Minister of the Automotive Industry and a member of the USSR Supreme Soviet. As such, he possesses a considerable amount of authority with which to deal with the often inattentive central ministries. Such authority has enabled Vasiliev to conduct the business of constructing KamAZ in a manner that has been described as similar to a top executive of a large Western corporation.[73] He has, for example, been effective at solving contractual disputes between Western firms and Soviet bureaucrats, thus minimizing delays in equipment installation. If Vasiliev's role as association director is typical, Western firms may find it easier to deal with enterprise directors who have both the authority to make decisions and the expertise to negotiate on technical matters.

Equally important with Soviet domestic industrial organization are the actual contractual arrangements between Soviet foreign trade enterprises and Western firms. The Soviets have shown some flexibility in recent years in providing for longer-term, deeper involvement of Western firms in the Soviet economy. While foreign ownership or full managerial control over industrial projects in the Soviet Union appears to be precluded by Soviet law and custom, other forms of Western managerial participation are possible. For example, the general contractor role of FIAT in the construction of the Volga Automobile Plant appears to have involved some participation in management functions. Although this arrangement was not used at KamAZ, Soviet officials have indicated that they prefer it for similar projects in the future.[74]

In recent years, science and technology cooperation agreements have provided a framework for continuing involvement of some Western firms in the Soviet economy. Agreements with FIAT, which recently signed its third five-year agreement, and Renault, which has been involved in the modernization of the Soviet automotive industry since the 1960s, are examples of long-term ties. Likewise, various product payback or compensation agreements signed in recent years provide for long-term involvement of Western firms in the Soviet economy. Such long-term arrangements may provide a more profitable basis for Western firms to transfer technology to the Soviet Union. They reduce fears that the Soviet Union, after effecting a huge infusion of Western technology, will return to their former policy of restricting commercial ties to the West. While such arrangements do not remove all the problems involved in technology transfer to the Soviet Union, they do represent some movement toward a more flexible approach to technical and commercial relations with the West.

NOTES

1. Trud, October 11, 1969.
2. Chase World Information Corporation, KamAZ: The Billion Dollar Beginning, New York, 1974, pp. 58-61.
3. New York Times, April 21, 1970.
4. Henry Ford II, "Exclusive Interview," American Review of East-West Trade, March-April 1970, p. 38.
5. New York Times, April 21, 1970.
6. Ford Motor Company News Release, April 29, 1970.
7. Ibid.
8. New York Times, May 15, 1970.
9. Ibid.
10. Signers of the agreement were: V.N. Sushkov, Ministry of Foreign Trade; A.C.R. Hanson, Chairman of the Board and President of Mack Trucks; Ara Oztemel, President of Satra Corporation; and James Giffen, Vice President of Satra Consulting Corporation. See Wall Street Journal, June 18, 1971.
11. Wall Street Journal, June 18, 1971.
12. New York Times, June 18, 1971.
13. Wall Street Journal, June 28, 1971.
14. Washington Post, September 17, 1971.
15. Ibid.

16. Herbert E. Meyer, "What It's Like To Do Business With The Russians," Fortune, May 1972, p. 1968.
17. Ibid.
18. Ibid.
19. U.S. News and World Report, May 11, 1970, p. 71.
20. Ford Motor Company News Release, May 6, 1970.
21. Ibid.
22. New York Times, May 15, 1970.
23. Ibid.
24. U.S. Congress, Senate, Committee on Finance, Trade Reform Act of 1973, part 2, Hearings before the Committee on Finance, 93d Cong., 2d sess., March 6 and 7, 1974, p. 455.
25. Wall Street Journal, June 18, 1971.
26. See Angelo Leparulo, "East-West Technology Transfer: A Case-Study of Industrial Co-operation," prepared for the Seminar on The Management of the Transfer of Technology within Industrial Cooperation, U.N. Economic Commission for Europe, Geneva, July 14-17, 1975. Mr. Leparulo is Vice President for Science and Technology at Occidental.
27. Ibid.
28. Washington Post, April 21, 1970.
29. Business Week, March 17, 1973.
30. See Meyer, op. cit., p. 168.
31. Ibid., p. 167.
32. Ibid., p. 168.
33. Ibid.
34. New York Times, December 23, 1971.
35. Ibid.
36. Remarks by Donald Stingel at George Washington University, Washington, D.C., on February 25, 1975.
37. Business Week, May 6, 1972.
38. Meyer, op. cit., p. 237.
39. New York Times, October 20, 1972.
40. Ibid.
41. See Meyer, op. cit., p. 169.
42. Letter from Secretary of Commerce Peter G. Peterson to Soviet Minister of Foreign Trade N.S. Patolichev, U.S.–Soviet Commercial Agreements, 1972. Washington, D.C., U.S. Department of Commerce, January, 1973, p. 100.
43. Meyer, op. cit., pp. 169, 234.
44. Ibid., p. 236.
45. Remarks by Donald Stingel before the East-West Trade Forum of the 59th National Foreign Trade Convention, New York City, November 15, 1972.

46. See Angelo Leparulo, op. cit., p. 7.
47. For further details see Eric W. Hayden and Henry R. Nau, "Manufacturing Enterprise Relationships in East-West Technology Transfer: Theoretical Models and Practical Experiences," Columbia Journal of World Business 10, no 3 (Fall 1975): 70-83.
48. Meyer, op. cit., p. 168.
49. See Stingel's remarks (note 36); also see Herbert E. Meyer, "A Plant That Could Change The Shape of Soviet Industry," Fortune November 1974.
50. See M. Troitskiy, "Ne novom etape," ("At a New Stage,") Novyi Mir, no. 1, January 1975. See also Washington Post, January 24, 1974.
51. M. Troitskiy, op. cit.
52. New York Times, May 26, 1973.
53. Ibid.
54. New York Times, January 16, 1974.
55. Herbert Meyer," A Plant That Could Change the Shape....," op. cit., p. 155.
56. Ibid.
57. Ibid.
58. Meyer, "What Its Like To Do Business....," op. cit., p. 168.
59. Washington Post, November 25, 1974.
60. Stingel's remarks, February 25, 1975, Note 36.
61. See Business Week, March 17, 1973 and Wall Street Journal, January 25, 1974.
62. V. Karpunenkov, "Main Directions in the Future Development of Motor Transport in the U.S.S.R.," Avtomobil'nyi Transport, August 8, 1975, p. 2.
63. L. Bliakhman, "Glavnyi vyigrysh--vremia: zametki o problemakh uskoreniia nauchno-technicheskogo progressa," ("The Principal Gain is Time: Notes on Problems of Speeding up Scientific-technical Progress.") Neva, no. 1, 1973, p. 173.
64. Imogene U. Edwards, "Automotive Trends in the USSR," in U.S. Congress, Joint Committee, Soviet Economic Prospects for the Seventies, Joint committee Print (Washington, D.C.: U.S. Government Printing Office, June 27, 1973), p. 309.
65. Ibid., pp. 311-312.
66. V. Petrushov, "Pochemu tak nuzhen KamAZ, " ("Why KamAZ is Needed,") Za rulem, No. 4, April 1971, p.4.
67. Pravda, December 14, 1975, p. 6.
68. B. Mil'ner, "On the Organization of Management," Kommunist, no. 3, February 1975.
69. See Antony C. Sutton, Western Technology and Soviet Economic Development, vols. I-III, (Stanford: Hoover Institution Publications, 1968, 1971, 1973).

70. Karpunenkov, op. cit., p. 2.

71. "The Production Association—The Basic Independent Industrial Unit," Interview with A.V. Bachurin, Deputy Chairman of the U.S.S.R. Gosplan, Ekonomika i organizatsiia promyshlennogo proizvodstva, no. 4, 1975.

72. Troitskiy, op. cit., pp. 170-71 and 178-79. For further discussion of this point see John P. Hardt and George D. Holliday, "Technology Transfer and Change in the Soviet Economic System," paper delivered at a Conference on Technology and Culture at Villa Serbelloni, Bellagio, Italy in August 1975. Publication of the conference proceedings is forthcoming.

73. Meyer, "A Plant That Could Change the Shape....," op. cit., p. 151.

74. East-West Markets, January 27, 1975, p. 11.

CHAPTER 5

ENERGY R AND D: U.S. TECHNOLOGY TRANSFER TO ADVANCED WESTERN COUNTRIES

James P. Lester

This case study was selected to illustrate technology transfer among advanced Western countries. It highlights governmental initiatives and involvement in such transfers while at the same time suggesting the commercial interests and changes in government-industry relationships affecting the use of technology in foreign affairs.

The central thesis of this chapter is that U.S.-initiated R and D cooperation in the energy sector represents a classic example of the use of technology transfer for political or diplomatic purposes. While U.S. policy in this case has been relatively successful in achieving such purposes, it has been less successful in establishing concrete programs of international energy R and D cooperation. Unless such programs are forthcoming, the diplomatic uses of technology transfer remain limited and potentially counterproductive.

I gratefully acknowledge the help of several officials in Washington, D.C. who took time out of their busy schedules to discuss technology transfer in energy R and D. I also wish to thank the National Science Foundation for their financial support of this study, and the Department of State and the Energy Research and Development Administration for providing initial research materials. I am also grateful to Jack Vanderryn, William Crentz, William Porter, Harry Johnson, and Martin Prochnik, whose assistance was invaluable to me. None of them bears the responsibility for accuracy or approach.

R AND D AND THE ENERGY CRISIS

Looking for an effective response to the oil exporters' embargo and price cartel, the United States convened a conference of major oil importers in February 1974. From this Washington Energy Conference emerged the Energy Coordinating Group (ECG) committed to considering cooperative measures. (ECG members were Canada, Japan, Norway, the European communities less France, and the United States.) The ECG met six times between February 25 and August 30, 1974. It arranged for nine working groups to produce proposals for cooperation in the following areas:

1. conservation and demand restraint
2. accelerated development of conventional energy resources
3. oil-sharing measures to deal with supply interruptions
4. producer-consumer relations
5. role of international oil companies
6. financial implications of the energy problem
7. relations with the less developed countries
8. possible areas of international cooperation in uranium enrichment
9. prospects for cooperative development of energy R and D programs

These nine working groups had both differing temporal perspectives and task orientations. That is, most of the working groups were oriented toward the development of near-term policy solutions to the immediate international energy situation. Two of the working groups, however, focused on long-term cooperation as an endeavor to respond to future energy contingencies. One of these working groups was concerned with the development of international cooperation in energy R and D; the other was concerned with international cooperation in uranium enrichment.[1]

The working group on international energy R and D cooperation (known as ECG/ERD) was broken down during the spring and summer of 1974 into ten subworking groups, each dealing with a separate potential area for energy R and D cooperation, as shown in Table 5.1. These expert groups collaborated to submit a report to the ECG on June 6, 1974.[2] The ECG then reached a tentative agreement in September 1974 on an International Energy Program (IEP). The agreement included:

1. an integrated emergency arrangement to limit vulnerability to actual or threatened embargoes by the producers
2. a long-term cooperative program to reduce dependency on imported oil

3. an oil market information system aimed at improving knowledge of the operation of the world oil market and establishing a framework for consultation with individual companies

4. a program for coordination of relations with producing countries and the less developed consuming countries

An agreement embodying government commitments for these arrangements was signed on November 18 and accepted provisionally by 16 OECD countries.[3] With the establishment of the International Energy Agency in November 1974, the ECG/ERD report became the basis for further discussions within the International Energy Agency's (IEA) Committee on Long-Term Cooperation. (See Table 5.2.)

TABLE 5.1

Transgovernmental System of Action (ECG Phase)

Orientation	Perspective	
	Near and Medium Term	Long-Term
Policy Oriented	1. Oil-Sharing 2. Development of Conventional Energy Sources 3. Energy Conservation and Demand Restraint 4. Financial Implications of Energy Problem 5. Role of International Oil Companies 6. Producer/Consumer Conference 7. Relations with LDCs	
R and D Oriented		8. Uranium Enrichment 9. International Energy R and D Cooperation*

*This group was further subdivided into ten subworking (or expert) groups, including the following areas: coal technology, solar energy, radioactive waste management, controlled thermonuclear fusion, hydrogen production, nuclear safety, waste heat utilization, energy conservation, municipal and industrial waste utilization, and overall energy systems analysis.

Source: Compiled from working documents of the Energy Coordinating Group (ECG). See Energy Coordinating Group, "Terms of Reference," (ECG/5), (Brussels, February 24, 1974).

TABLE 5.2

International Organization System of Action (IEA Phase)

Orientation	Perspective	
	Near Term	Long Term
Policy Oriented	1. Oil Market 2. Emergency Questions 3. Producer/Consumer Relations	4. Long-Term Cooperation a. Alternate Sources b. Conservation c. Uranium Enrichment
R and D Oriented		d. International Energy R and D Cooperation*

*The identical subworking (or expert) groups set up during the ECG phase were maintained during this phase of the energy exercise.

Source: Compiled from working documents of the Committee on Long-Term Cooperation. See Agreement on an International Energy Program, in U.S. Congress, Senate, Committee on Interior and Insular Affairs, International Energy Program, Hearings, 93d. Cong., 2d sess., November 26, 1974, pp. 72-96.

Our purpose in this chapter is to examine the evolution of these R and D discussions up to the early spring of 1975. This examination proceeds at four different levels of analysis: 1) the intragovernmental level, looking at the major U.S. agencies involved in formulating U.S. policy toward energy R and D cooperation; 2) the intergovernmental level, looking at the overall policies of the 13 nations engaged in energy R and D discussions within the Washington Energy Conference; 3) the transgovernmental level, looking at the expert working group activities under the ECG; and 4) the international organization level, looking at the expert working group activities under the IEA. A more detailed explanation of these levels of analysis and their interrelationship is provided later in this chapter.

Intergovernmental cooperation in energy R and D has encompassed a broad range of technical fields and approaches. Most of this cooperation in the past has been bilateral and confined to the nuclear sector (if one excludes transfers in oil and gas technologies by multinational corporations).[4] Some multilateral cooperation also existed in the nuclear sector through cooperative agreements between the United States and the European Atomic Energy Community (Euratom).[5]

Cooperation in nonnuclear areas, whether bilateral or multilateral, is a more recent phenomenon. Since the mid-1960s, bilateral programs have been signed in previously ignored sectors such as solar, coal, and geothermal energy R and D (see Table 5.3). These

TABLE 5.3

Current U.S. Cooperative Programs in Energy Research and Development

Mechanism	Type					Resource Development
	Nuclear	Solar	Coal	Geothermal	Hydroelectric	
Bilateral	20	3	3	1	2	10
Multilateral	4	1*	2	1*	1	4

Note: The table excludes agreements in miscellaneous energy R and D agreements such as energy conversion, transmission, and conservation, and includes only those agreements signed prior to the Washington Energy Conference except where otherwise noted.

*Signed under agreements of the NATO Committee on the Challenges to Modern Society.

Source: Herman Pollack and Michael B. Congdon, "International Cooperation in Energy Research and Development," Law and Policy in International Business, (July/August 1974).

agreements have been negotiated with both Western European countries, (for example, United Kingdom, Italy, and Germany) and Eastern European countries, (for example, USSR, Poland, and Romania).[6]

Multilateral cooperation has also been initiated, largely under the auspices of two alliance organizations. First, the NATO Committee on the Challenges to Modern Society (CCMS) has launched development projects in three fields of energy technology—solar, geothermal, and conservation.[7] The CCMS approach to cooperation is unique within NATO in that not all NATO members are obliged to participate. Rather, those countries whose needs would be served by a particular project participate in an R and D effort in which one pilot country assumes the responsibility to link and to coordinate programs for maximum efficiency and to reduce overlaps among the participating countries. As an alternative to a research contribution, a participating country may choose to share in the development costs. The results of the research are then made available to all interested countries and international groups.[8]

A second alliance organization, the Organization for Economic Cooperation and Development (OECD), has also contributed to multilateral cooperation. Its Energy Committee has undertaken a long-term study of energy programs in member countries with the intention of proposing cooperative programs to pool national resources.[9] Finally, the recent U.S. initiative at the Washington Energy Conference suggests a growing emphasis on multilateralism.

This increased interest in nonnuclear and multilateral R and D cooperation is related to America's (and Western Europe and Japan's) increasing dependence on oil imports to fuel their expanding consumption. Despite rising prices, the United States found imported oil to be still considerably less expensive than alternate sources.[10] In addition, U.S. officials assumed that, just as oil gradually replaced coal as the major source of energy in the first half of this century, oil would gradually lose its primacy to nuclear power in the last half of the century. In the interim, they believed, increasing amounts of cheap oil would be forthcoming to meet the world's growing energy needs.[11] With oil consumption rising and domestic production leveling off, a continued increase in U.S. dependence on imported oil seemed virtually certain, and the United States gradually shifted from a position of near self-sufficiency in energy to one of substantial dependence on imported oil.

It has often been observed that the energy problems which the United States now faces, and especially U.S. dependence on imported oil, were due primarily to the failure of public policy. In addition to the recent Arab oil boycott, it is argued, there are at least four other causes of U.S. dependence.[12] First, shipments of natural gas,

ENERGY R AND D   125

which provide about 32 percent of present U.S. energy needs, showed no growth in 1972. Second, the enforcement of regional air quality standards and of motor vehicle emission standards has led to higher petroleum demands, the former because several large coal users found that these standards could be satisfied only by switching to low sulphur residual fuel oil, and the latter because they reduce automobile mileage.[13] Third, the economy has grown at an unusually rapid rate since the last quarter of 1972, resulting in abnormally high energy demands together with inefficient and wasteful use of energy by consumers encouraged by the ready availability of formerly cheap fuels.[14] Finally, and perhaps most importantly, because of the government's oil import quota controls, refineries were uncertain about where they would be able to secure additional supplies of crude oil. Because of this uncertainty, prudence dictated that they delay making commitments to building new refineries.[15]

In response to the energy crisis, the Administration has taken a number of short-term policy steps designed to "reduce unnecessary consumption, equalize the burden throughout the economy, and plan for the future".[16] In addition, long-term responses by the administration include R and D shifts in order to provide funding for alternative sources of energy such as solar, geothermal, coal, and nuclear fusion technologies. To deal with these longer range problems on the domestic level, the Administration has proposed an $11 billion program for energy R and D during the next five years, and a reorganization of government energy agencies to attain greater coordination—both part of Project Independence. On the international level, President Nixon "instructed the Department of State, in coordination with the Atomic Energy Commission, other government agencies, and the Congress to move rapidly in developing a program of international cooperation in R and D on new forms of energy and in developing new international mechanisms for dealing with energy questions in times of shortages."[17] This initiative was followed by the Washington Energy Conference of February 11-13, 1974, an endeavor to respond to the energy crisis on a multilateral basis.

R AND D DISCUSSIONS: A MULTILEVEL DRAMA

Figure 5.1 represents the conceptual framework used in this chapter to analyze the decision-making process of multilateral energy R and D discussions.[18] The framework assumes that four "subsystems of action" exercised primary influence on U.S. foreign policy toward multilateral agreements for energy R and D cooperation.

FIGURE 5.1

Analytical Framework: Four Subsystems of Action

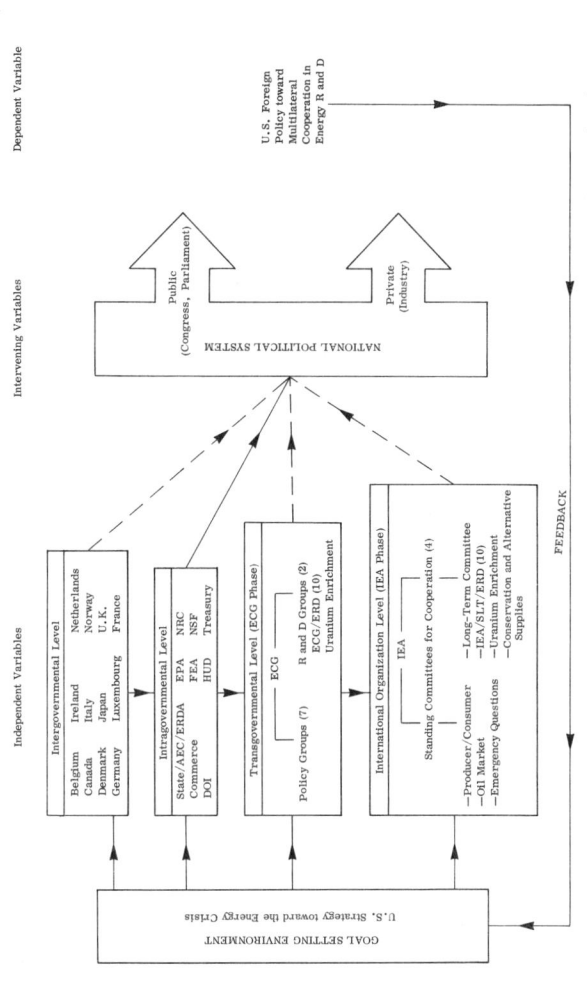

*France refused to join the Energy Coordinating Group (ECG), and during the IEA phase six additional countries became members of the IEA, (Austria, New Zealand, Spain, Sweden, Switzerland, and Turkey). Norway is an associated member of IEA, and France has, in effect, associate status.

Source: Compiled by the author.

These four subsystems include: 1) internal actor inputs derived from U. S. executive agencies (the intragovernmental level), and 2) external actor inputs from foreign governments at different points in time during the energy exercise (the intergovernmental level, the transgovernmental, and the international organizational level). The intergovernmental level applies to the period of time preceding the Washington Energy Conference (December 1973 to February 1974): the transgovernmental level refers to the ECG/ERD phase (February 1974 to November 1974); the international organization level refers to the IEA phase (November 1974 to the present). The intervening variable—the national political system—provides for inputs into actor behavior stemming from specific agency-industry and agency-legislative relationships that vary within each individual national system.

The primary lines of analysis we follow are 1) a discussion of U.S. strategies and goals in dealing with the energy situation; 2) an identification of U.S. agency positions in energy R and D cooperation; 3) the identification of U.S. agency-industry relationships and how these relationships may have facilitated (or impeded) R and D cooperation, as well as the interaction of government agencies with Congress during the energy discussions; and 4) an examination of the decisions (or nondecisions) on multilateral energy R and D cooperation resulting from these energy discussions.

Our discussion of the policies of other countries at the intergovernmental level is somewhat less detailed. We are interested in the position of these government and industrial actors only as they affect the position of U.S. actors. Our dependent variable is U.S. foreign policy toward energy R and D cooperation as affected by internal, domestic variables and external positions of foreign actors.

Although for analytic purposes each subsystem is discussed separately, they are clearly interrelated and feed back upon one another, as Figure 5.1 suggests. At all levels of analysis, particular attention is directed toward identifying, classifying, and investigating the interrelationships of issues raised for U.S. foreign policy by the possible export of energy technologies across U.S. boundaries. The issues with which we are concerned include domestic economic and commercial issues, domestic administrative issues, military-strategic issues, foreign policy issues, foreign economic issues, and social-environmental issues. The internal issues (domestic economic and commercial and domestic administrative) are examined and discussed at the intragovernmental level of analysis, while external issues (foreign policy, military-strategic, and foreign economic) are discussed at the transgovernmental and international organization levels of analysis.

THE GOAL-SETTING ENVIRONMENT:
U.S. STRATEGY IN THE ENERGY CRISIS

In the energy crisis, the United States offered to share its energy R and D technology as a lure to hold together the fragile international economic and political system threatened by the repercussions of spiraling oil import prices.[19] In particular, the United States sought to reassure three separate groups of countries which were alienated or in danger of being alienated from a U.S.-managed system of international detente. The first was the Western allies (Western Europe and Japan) whose relations with the United States had been frayed by the superpower diplomacy of the first four years (1968-72) of the Nixon-Kissinger administration, exacerbated by the "Year of Europe" dialogue initiated in the spring of 1973, and severely threatened by allied differences which emerged during the Mid-East War in October of 1973. The second group was the energy importing countries, both developed and developing, which faced enormous balance-of-payments deficits from higher energy costs and might be lost to the international system unless they could be assured that existing trade (General Agreement on Trade and Tariffs [GATT]) and monetary (International Monetary Fund [IMF, World Bank]) institutions and negotiations were adequate to deal with these problems. The third group was the Arab oil-producing countries which had yet to acquire a stable place in the new international order of superpower detente but now had to be included because of the disruptive effect of continuing Middle East conflicts and because of the increased financial revenues of Arab states.

Improved relations with these states were objectives of U.S. policy before the energy crisis. Indeed, our argument is that the U.S. response to this crisis was not aimed, in the main, at the specific problems created by events of October 1973, namely the problems of price, production cutbacks, and selective embargo of oil. Rather, U.S. diplomacy used the energy crisis as an occasion to mobilize agreement in support of pre-existing policies seeking rapprochement with various alienated and potentially alienated states in the international system. In each case, the bait Washington used to hold or entice these states into the system was American science and technology. Offers of American technology, however, were aimed more at achieving diplomatic solutions than technical contributions to energy problems.

This fact may account for the relative lack of progress achieved thus far within the International Energy Agency (IEA) on cooperative R and D projects (no less than on cooperative programs to develop alternative, medium-term, energy sources). By contrast, progress on institutional and political issues, including the establishment of IEA and the International Energy Program (IEP), has been quite marked. From the beginning, however, these institutional successes have been vulnerable as long as they were not supplemented by concrete programs of action.[20] Indeed, in August 1975, a reappraisal of U.S. energy policy seemed to be under way.[21] Given slow progress in implementing proposals for price floor schemes and R and D consortia, the alliance-based IEA approach was being modified to accommodate a more conciliatory, direct approach to OPEC oil producers. In his speech to the United Nations Special Session in September 1975, Secretary of State Kissinger proposed an International Energy Institute, which would include oil producers as well as consumers and to which the IEA and the International Atomic Energy Agency (IAEA) would make supporting contributions.[22]

THE INTERGOVERNMENTAL LEVEL: THE WASHINGTON ENERGY CONFERENCE

Several months prior to the Arab embargo of October 1973, President Nixon sent his first major energy message to Congress. In that message he instructed the Department of State, in coordination with the Atomic Energy Commission and other appropriate government agencies "...to move rapidly in developing a program of international cooperation in research and development...and in developing international mechanisms for dealing with energy questions in times of critical shortages."[23] In his statement of June 29, 1973, President Nixon announced that the Department of State was "...working closely with other major oil-consuming nations in studying ways of meeting growing world demand for energy supplies."[24]

During the summer and fall of 1973, the Department of State, at the request of the White House,[25] chaired an interagency task force to study the possible expansion of U.S. efforts in energy-related cooperative R and D.[26] The purpose of this study was to identify those energy technologies that offered the greatest promise for cooperative R and D efforts, to determine the potential for involving U.S. industry, and to identify those countries that were the most desirable partners for cooperation in energy R and D.[27]

On October 16, 1973, the Arab oil-producing countries announced an embargo on oil shipments to the United States and initiated a series of oil price increases and production cutbacks affecting all major oil consumers. These actions seriously threatened the economic and political survival of many oil consuming states and led to an increasing number of bilateral government-to-government oil deals. With each consumer country scrambling for its own supply, oil prices were bid up even higher. These developments provided an added incentive for the development of a program of international cooperation in energy R and D.

In early December 1973, the interagency task force completed its study of the problems and prospects for international collaboration in energy R and D (known as the Love Report after John Love, former governor of Colorado and assistant to the President on energy). This task force found that not all energy technology sectors were equally suited for international R and D cooperation. In various sectors, levels of technological progress differ from country to country, priorities vary, and a number of sectors exhibit economic or proprietary barriers to future cooperation.[28] Furthermore, sectors differ with respect to the benefits they promise to the United States or other countries as a result of increased cooperation. In an attempt to establish a meaningful priority ranking of technologies suitable for cooperation, the task force evaluated 18 energy technology sectors on the basis of five criteria: 1) the existence of unexploited opportunities; 2) the existence of useful technology abroad; 3) the potential for reduction of energy deficit; 4) the transfer time to commercial use; and 5) the lack of legal or proprietary barriers involved. Employing these criteria, the task force concluded that the areas of coal technology, energy conservation, environmental protection, geothermal energy, resource assessment, and transportation systems offered the most attractive prospects (from the U.S. standpoint) for increased international cooperation.[29] Second order priorities—based on the length of time to technical and commercial feasibility, the extent of present industrial involvement, or the extent of cooperation already achieved— included the areas of fusion, energy conservation, fuel transport systems, hydrogen economy, nuclear reactor safety, and solar energy. The lowest priority sectors included nuclear reactor technology and oil and gas technology, since these sectors had already reached the stage of full commercialization.[30] Furthermore, the study concluded that the most technologically advanced nations, such as Canada, Japan, and Western European nations were the most desirable partners for cooperation in most of the energy technology sectors.[31]

On December 12, 1973, Secretary of State Kissinger officially launched the major U.S. initiative to establish a multilateral framework for dealing with the energy crisis. In his Pilgrim speech Secretary Kissinger proposed that the nations of Europe, North

America and Japan "establish an Energy Action Group of senior and prestigious individuals with a mandate to develop within three months an initial action program for collaboration in all areas of the energy problem."[32] This group would have as its goal, the coordination of an international program of research to develop new technologies that use energy more efficiently and provide alternatives to petroleum.[33] Kissinger emphasized that the "U.S. [was] prepared to make a very major financial and intellectual contribution to the objective of solving the energy problem on a common basis."[34]

On January 9, 1974, President Nixon issued invitations to heads of government of the major oil consuming countries to attend a conference on energy to be held in Washington on February 11, 1974.[35] At this conference, as the President pointed out, the consuming countries would seek to formulate a consumer action program and part of the program "...would be concerned with new cooperative measures...to accelerate the coordinated development of new energy sources."[36]

On February 11, 1974, the Washington Energy Conference held its first session. In his opening remarks, Secretary Kissinger repeated the U.S. offer to share its energy technology in a collaborative alliance response to the energy crisis:

> [The United States is]...willing to share American advances in energy technology to develop jointly new sources of supply and establish a system of emergency sharing; [and] we are prepared to make a major contribution of our most advanced energy research and development to a broad program of international cooperation in energy.[37]

Two policy concerns came together at the Washington Energy Conference to give R and D its prominent place in U.S. energy policy. The first, as we noted in the previous section, was the dismal state of affairs in U.S.-European alliance relations. After the Europeans broke ranks in the fall of 1973 and refused to allow the United States to use NATO bases in Europe to resupply Israel, Secretary Kissinger made no secret of his desire to rejuvenate alliance unity and resolve.[38] The Washington Energy Conference, therefore, was motivated, "...at least in part by a U.S. desire to use the energy problem as a practical occasion to reaffirm and reconstitute allied relations."[39]

Secondly, U.S. officials and, in particular, Secretary Kissinger, have shown an increasing interest in the role of American science and technology in modern diplomacy and its possible contribution to the solution of world problems. Kissinger has emphasized on a number of occasions that the United States was prepared to offer its science and technology to both developed and developing nations, noting that technology may be America's greatest asset and also precisely what other nations wish to obtain from the United States.[40] Interviews with U.S. agency participants of the Washington Energy Conference confirmed that the U.S. proposals for energy R and D cooperation in the winter of 1973-74 were indeed intended as a trading item to attract Western European and Japanese allies to the Washington Energy Conference.[41]

In other words, the United States extended the offer of energy R and D cooperation as a tradeoff to achieve short term policy goals.[42] Those goals included the creation of a "framework" for cooperation to reaffirm alliance solidarity in the face of the energy crisis, (that is, the International Energy Agency) and agreements on oil sharing in emergencies, conservation programs, and financial arrangements to meet balance-of-payments deficits caused by higher oil prices. In essence this initiative by Secretary Kissinger appears to be a classic example of technology being used as an instrument of foreign policy. That political rather than technical motivations were controlling may be evident in the fact that no substantive agreements in energy R and D have yet been implemented as a result of the discussions arising out of the Washington Energy Conference.

In order to examine why no agreements have been forthcoming, we shift to an analysis of the working groups within which discussions over international cooperation in energy R and D took place.

THE INTRAGOVERNMENTAL LEVEL: BUREAUCRATIC POLICYMAKING IN THE UNITED STATES

Activities at the intragovernmental level revolved around two types of issues: 1) domestic economic and commercial issues, and 2) administrative interagency issues.[43]

Domestic Economic and Commercial Issues

Domestic economic issues that arose during the energy R and D exercise may be usefully categorized into two areas: 1) issues concerned with the allocation of domestic energy funding and the finance of international cooperative efforts, and 2) issues dealing with the commercial involvement and protection of U.S. industry in the areas chosen for possible cooperation.

TABLE 5.4

Federal Energy Research and Development Funding, Fiscal Years 1969-75
(in millions of dollars)

Item	1969	1970	1971	1972	1973	1974[a]	1975[b]
Coal resource development	23.3	30.4	49.0	76.8	85.1	164.4	426.7
Petroleum and natural gas	13.5	14.8	17.5	23.8	18.7	19.1	41.8
Nuclear fission							
LMFBR	132.5	144.3	167.9	237.4	253.7	357.3	473.4
Other civilian nuclear power	144.6	109.1	97.7	90.7	152.8	173.2	251.7
Nuclear fusion							
Magnetic confinement	29.7	34.3	32.3	33.2	39.7	57.0	102.3
Laser-pellet	2.1	3.2	9.3	14.0	35.1	44.1	66.3
Energy conversion with less							
Environmental impact	12.3	22.9	22.8	33.4	38.4	65.5	178.5
General energy R and D	3.0	4.2	8.7	15.4	8.1	28.8	59.8
Conservation including transportation	n.a.	n.a.	n.a.	n.a.	32.2	65.0	115.7
Solar	n.a.	n.a.	n.a.	n.a.	4.0	13.8	50.0
Geothermal	n.a.	n.a.	n.a.	n.a.	4.4	10.9	44.7
	$361.0	$363.2	$405.2	$524.7	$672.2	$999.1	$1810.5

[a]Estimated
[b]Proposed
Notes: n.a. = not available. Data for fiscal years 1969-72 are not exactly comparable to fiscal years 1973-75, as additional programs have been included.
Source: Executive Office of the President. Also published in Ford Foundation Energy Policy Project, Exploring Energy Choices (New York: Ford Foundation, 1974), p. 75.

TABLE 5.5

Energy Research and Development Administration: R and D
(Obligations in millions of dollars)

Program and Type of Activity	1974 Actual	1975 Estimate	1976 Estimate
Conduct of R and D:			
Fossil energy development:			
Coal utilization	70	188	289
Petroleum and natural gas	8	17	23
Oil shale	3	3	8
Solar, geothermal, and advanced energy systems development:			
Solar energy	4	9	57
Geothermal energy	6	14	28
Advanced energy systems	4	12	23
Physical research	253	281	313
Conservation:			
Electric power transmission	2	6	12
Fuel economy	3	10	17
End-use conservation	—	—	3
Nuclear energy development:			
Fusion power	53	85	120
Fission power	272	370	409
Naval reactor development	154	167	186
Space nuclear systems	26	27	31
Nuclear materials	45	51	65
Advanced isotope separation techniques	3	12	24
National security:			
Weapons activities	412	443	495
Laser fusion	37	41	54
Nuclear materials security	4	6	11
Environmental and safety research:			
Biomedical and environmental research	104	130	153
Waste management and transportation	12	20	25
Total conduct of R and D	1,475	1,893	2,346
Total conduct of research, included above	470	594	799
Total conduct of development, included above	1,005	1,299	1,547
Research and development facilities	485	468	503
Total	1,960	2,360	2,849

Source: Office of Management and Budget, Executive Office of the President, Special Analyses, Budget of the U.S. Government, Fiscal Year 1976 (Washington, D.C.: U.S. Government Printing Office, 1975), p. 260.

Table 5.4 exhibits the allocation of domestic energy R and D for 1969-75. In 1974, President Nixon and Congress substantially increased the energy R and D budget and created the Energy Research and Development Administration (ERDA). Table 5.5 presents the ERDA budget obligations for energy R and D for 1974-76. Although the resource allocation for coal R and D has increased significantly during this period, coal is not the priority area for domestic R and D; the development of nuclear energy is. This remains true despite a substantial increase in coal research and development funds administered through the Office of Coal Research (see Table 5.6). In the recent energy R and D discussions, the United States has shown a marked reluctance to cooperate in priority areas, such as nuclear energy. Of the ten areas chosen for possible cooperation, only three deal with nuclear technology, (fusion, radioactive waste management, and nuclear safety), and all of these are remote from commercialization. On the other hand, the United States has displayed considerable willingness to cooperate in secondary R and D funding areas such as coal technologies, even when these areas are close to commercialization.*

Issues also arise over how to finance the costs of cooperative projects and whether the public or private sectors (or a combination of both) should provide the funds.[44] If the funding is public, the projects must be defended before Congress and must be compatible with and benefit our domestic programs in energy R and D. However, there is an understandable reluctance in Congress to commit sizeable portions of domestic budgets to international research projects which are geographically located in other countries and under the control of foreign nationals (or at best—or worst—under the supervision of an international committee which the contributing government does not control). This tension between domestic and international programs suggests the need for close coordination and consultation between Congress and U.S. agencies charged with leadership in each area of possible cooperation. Interviews with U.S. experts in each of the proposed areas, however, disclosed that little or no consultation took place. According to one source, the lack of agency-congressional consultation was no oversight. Rather, the U.S. executive agencies did not seek congressional approval for possible research projects because their negotiating positions would have been disapproved by a majority of the Congress.[45]

---

*This pattern is not peculiar to the United States alone; it seems to be a behavioral characteristic of all countries that consider international cooperation in technical areas in which they place high domestic priority. (See Henry R. Nau, National Politics and International Technology, [Baltimore, Md.: Johns Hopkins Press, 1974], esp. chapter 9.)

TABLE 5.6

Office of Coal Research, Energy Research and Development, Fiscal Years 1975-79
(Obligations in millions of dollars)

Research and Development	1975	1976	1977	1978	1979	Total (1975-79)
1. Coal Liquefaction						
a. Direct Hydrogenation Projects	16.0	20.0	48.0	15.0	5.0	104.0
b. Solvent Extraction Based Projects	10.6	19.5	27.0	25.0	3.0	85.1
c. Carbonization Projects	10.5	31.1	25.0	6.0	6.0	78.6
d. Fischer-Tropsch Variations	7.8	20.0	20.0	6.0	6.0	59.3
e. Design of Prototype Plants	—	50.0	100.0	50.0	—	200.0
Supporting Projects*	34.7	22.1	21.0	21.0	21.0	119.3
Total Coal Liquefaction	79.6	162.7	241.0	123.0	41.0	647.3
2. High-B.t.u. Gas						
a. Pilot Plant Program (with A.G.A.)						
(1) Hydrogasification	3.0	2.3	—	—	—	5.3
(2) Lignite Gasification	2.0	3.3	—	—	—	5.3
(3) BI-GAS	13.2	11.4	2.0	—	—	26.6
(4) Supporting Research:						
(a) Steam-Iron Process	6.0	6.0	—	—	—	12.0
(b) Liquid-Phase Methanation	4.0	—	—	—	—	4.0
(c) Self-Agglomerating Process	1.0	1.8	—	—	—	2.9
(d) Other High-B.t.u. Gasification Projects	.7	—	—	—	—	.7
(e) Demonstration Plant for Pipeline Gas	.7	9.3	100.0	120.0	30.0	260.0
(f) Process Selection, Evaluation, Design and Engineering Assessments	1.2	1.9	3.0	—	—	6.1
Subtotal	31.8	36.0	105.0	120.0	30.0	322.8
b. Support Development						
(1) Equipment Development	2.0	2.0	5.0	5.0	2.0	16.0
(2) Materials Development	2.0	2.0	2.0	2.0	4.0	12.0
(3) Process Development	2.0	1.0	3.0	3.0	4.0	13.0
Subtotal	6.0	5.0	10.0	10.0	10.0	41.0
Total High-B.t.u. Gas	37.8	41.0	115.0	130.0	40.0	363.8

3. Low-B.t.u. Gas					
a. Gasifiers:					
1. Atmospheric	15.0	33.0	39.4	22.8	13.0	123.2
2. Pressurized	31.0	110.0	66.5	65.0	39.5	312.0
b. Cleanup	2.0	9.2	10.2	12.1	8.5	42.0
c. Engineering Evaluations	1.0	1.5	1.5	1.5	1.5	7.0
Total Low-B.t.u. Gas	49.0	153.7	117.6	101.4	62.5	484.2
4. Advanced Power Systems						
a. MHD and Related Projects	12.7	12.0	.5	.5	.5	26.2
b. Comparative Pilot Plants and Demo	—	33.0	36.5	39.5	65.5	174.5
Total Advanced Power Systems	12.7	45.0	37.0	40.0	66.0	200.7
5. Direct Boiler Combustion						
a. Atmospheric Boilers	15.5	25.8	34.5	28.0	12.1	115.9
b. Pressurized Boilers	17.2	42.3	57.4	75.7	30.8	223.5
c. Lab and Process Development	1.2	.6	.5	.4	.3	3.0
Total Direct Boiler Combustion	34.0	68.7	92.4	104.1	43.2	342.4
6. Advanced Research and Supporting Technology	19.14	24.0	29.0	29.0	29.0	130.14
7. System Studies	2.5	7.0	7.0	7.0	7.0	30.5
8. "Pioneer Plant" Projects	42.1	100.0	125.0	100.0	50.0	417.1
Total Projects	276.84	602.1	764.0	634.5	338.7	2,616.14
9. Administration and Supervision	6.56	12.0	15.3	12.8	6.8	53.46
Total Office of Coal Research	283.40	614.1	779.3	647.3	345.5	2,669.60

*Includes: f. Equipment and Materials Development and g. Engineering Support Projects, discussed separately in the text.

Source: U.S. Department of the Interior, Office of Research and Development, Energy Research Program of the U.S. Department of Interior (Washington, D.C.: U.S. Government Printing Office, 1974), pp. 145–46.

Furthermore, international cooperation in several areas—coal conversion, radioactive waste management, and nuclear safety—involve potentially large costs. Public and private funds will no doubt be required. However, just as there were few direct consultations with Congress over funding of potential R and D cooperation, there were few direct consultations with industry representatives in order to ascertain private interest in funding joint cooperative efforts.[46] This development suggests that either the U.S. government was not serious about R and D cooperative efforts, that it was premature to consult with Congress and industry, or that there was unwarranted optimism about the interest of U.S. industry in funding cooperative projects.

With regard to the involvement and protection of U.S. industry, international R and D cooperation is more readily achieved when the activity involved remains relatively remote from the stage of commercial exploitation. At later stages, governmental and commercial constraints arise such as patent protection, licensing agreements, royalties, repatriation of profits, proprietary secrets, regulation of capital imports, and so on. With these considerations in mind, U.S. officials made an effort to eliminate certain R and D areas for possible international cooperation where there was substantial commercial interest or private industry involvement, for example, oil and gas technologies or nuclear (especially breeder) technologies. Fusion and hydrogen, on the other hand, were chosen since these areas were remote from the stage of commercial exploitation. The two additional nuclear areas chosen for possible cooperation—radioactive waste management and nuclear safety—held little commercial interest but were chosen for primarily domestic reasons. The issue here concerned domestic environmental issues associated with the utilization of nuclear energy as a power source. Multilateral cooperation in these two areas, it was thought, might provide greater credibility to safety studies, and thereby facilitate increased sales of U.S. nuclear reactors both at home and abroad.[47]

The other alternate energy technologies selected for possible cooperation (solar, waste heat utilization, conservation, municipal and industrial waste utilization) exhibited varying degrees of commercial involvement. At the time, however, industrial interest was low enough to permit their consideration as international projects.[48]

It is important to note at this point in our discussion that past U.S. cooperative contracts or agreements in energy R and D did not involve government participation in capital costs of commercial ventures (see Chapters 2 and 8 of this study). Now, however, in IEA, the U.S. government is discussing getting involved in joint projects having immediate commercial use (for example, coal fluidized bed combustion project). The problem centers around the possible formation of a government-industry consortium which would operate a prototype plant and then continue in existence after the prototype phase to license and collect revenues on proprietary know-how developed by the project. This possibility raises a number of policy questions:

1. Does the U.S. government want to become involved in a government-industry consortium?
2. Does the U.S. government have the authority to do so where the project goes beyond the R and D phase?
3. Will U.S. industry want to participate in such an extended arrangement?[49]

Administrative Issues

Interagency conflict was not a critical aspect of U.S. energy policy. This was due to a number of reasons. First of all, the entire process—from the initiation of the Washington Energy Conference in February 1974 to the formation of the International Energy Agency in November 1974—took only eight months. This was an unprecedented pace, compared to past efforts, for establishing an institution to promote international collaboration in science and technology. Consequently, there was very little time for jurisdictional, budgetary, or personality disputes to develop among U.S. agency participants. Secondly, very few U.S. agencies were directly involved in the process, and few individuals from these agencies were involved. Additionally, the experts in each area of possible cooperation met on few occasions. For example, only three of the expert groups met as many as four times during the period from May 1974 to May 1975 (the expert groups on coal, nuclear safety, and radioactive waste management). The experts on conservation and waste heat met on three occasions, and four expert groups met only twice (solar, fusion, waste utilization, and hydrogen production). Finally, only general areas were discussed for possible cooperation, the proposals for these areas were left vague, and no agreements were reached on specific projects. As a result, conflict, for the most part, remained "below the surface."[50]

Additionally, a conscious effort was made to maintain a "parallelism" between the R and D working group and the seven policy working groups (confer Table 5.1). During the ECG/ERD phase, when the R and D working group was moving ahead of the policy working groups, the R and D working group was directed to slow down and maintain a pace consistent with the slower progress of the policy groups. This strategy reflected the U.S. desire to use R and D cooperation as an incentive to implement immediate foreign policy objectives.[51] Political and diplomatic objectives were to be achieved before technical agreements for energy R and D cooperation were to be concluded. The desire to slow down progress in the R and D discussions helped minimize interagency disputes.

Although interagency disputes were relatively insignificant, several jurisdictional, budgetary, and substantive differences did emerge and deserve some discussion. While minor, these differences illustrate more generic problems of interagency coordination in technology transfer discussions.

The first instance of interagency conflict developed during the selection of the ten areas for possible energy R and D cooperation. In choosing these areas, (see Table 5.7), the federal Energy Administration (FEA) and State/AEC differed over the inclusion of fusion and hydrogen production as potential areas of R and D cooperation.

TABLE 5.7

U.S. Lead Agencies and the Ten Priority Areas for Cooperation

Agency	Priority Area
1. Department of Interior	1. Coal
2. National Science Foundation (NSF)	2. Solar
3. Atomic Energy Commission (AEC)	3. Radioactive Waste Management
4. AEC	
5. AEC	4. Fusion
6. AEC	5. Hydrogen
7. Housing and Urban Development (HUD)	6. Nuclear Safety
	7. Waste Heat
8. Federal Energy Administration	8. Conservation
9. HUD	9. Municipal Waste Utilization
10. NSF	10. System Analysis

Source: U.S. Atomic Energy Commission, Memorandum for the Record, "EGC Ad Hoc Group on Energy R & D" (Brussels, April 8, 1974).

The issue here was FEA's orientation toward near and medium term technical solutions to the energy situation and State's political desire to offer the prospect of cooperation in fusion R and D as an incentive to the oil consumers. FEA stressed that cooperation in fusion and hydrogen production were long-term solutions and diverted valuable domestic resources from near and medium term solutions, such as coal, conservation, solar, and so on.[52] State and AEC, on the other hand pushed fusion because it offered an exciting, showcase area for possible international collaboration and because its inclusion was a matter of "procedural simplicity." That is, work was going forward in fusion in both the United States and abroad and the original charter for the Washington Energy Conference had stressed that both near and long-term international cooperation were to be established among the Western oil-consuming countries.[53] Furthermore, by including fusion as a potential area for international cooperation, the United States could perhaps gain by an infusion of new ideas from European programs in fusion and eventually improve U.S. program planning and development in fusion. Hydrogen production was chosen because it presented a possible long-term energy solution, because the United States could expect economic and research gains here, and because the area enjoyed broad, general acceptance among the countries represented at the Conference.[54]

Thus, the case of fusion illustrates a domestic, U.S. agency conflict between State's political-diplomatic orientation and FEA's near-term technical-resource orientation that appeared a number of times throughout the energy exercise. While State viewed fusion as a means toward political and diplomatic objectives, FEA either misunderstood this intention or disagreed with it in favor of allocating resources to more promising, short-term technical solutions.

In a second example of conflict, State's political-diplomatic orientation was challenged by the AEC/ERDA. This dispute arose over the State Department's proposals that two R and D consortiums be formed in the IEA—one to develop synthetic fuels technology and another to pool R and D resources on longer-term energy solutions.[55] This proposal was apparently made without prior technical study or coordination with AEC. In the case of the R and D consortium, for example, State was unclear as to what specific projects this consortium would undertake.[56] AEC emphasized to the State Department that the consortium concept could be used up to a point as a political instrument but that State should have specific technical follow-up plans or the present and future credibility of political as well as technical objectives might be severely compromised.[57] AEC prevailed since the idea of a broad R and D consortium eventually took a back seat to the concept of a more specific consortium to develop synthetic fuels technology, that is, the coal fluidized bed combustion project.

The third administrative issue arose over cooperation in coal R and D. Three possible projects were proposed at the March 13, 1975 meeting of the coal expert group: 1) establishment of a coal resource international clearing house (in the United Kingdom) and a data bank (in the United States), 2) establishment of a mining technology clearing house, and 3) construction of a $15 million fluidized combustion test bed in the United Kingdom. Jurisdictional conflicts existed between the Department of Interior and ERDA (replacing AEC in the fall of 1974) over the control of projects in these R and D areas. For example, responsibility for the coal conversion area (fluidized bed combustion) moved from Interior to ERDA under the Energy Reorganization Act of 1974; however, the coal mining and exploration areas remained "grey areas" in which jurisdiction over R and D was undecided.[58]

The coal combustion project precipitated another jurisdictional and budgetary conflict between the Environmental Protection Agency (EPA) and ERDA. EPA was interested in expanding its R and D activities to pollution control technology associated with coal combustion. It sought to become involved in the United Kingdom's coal combustion project in order to test its pollutant control devices on a large facility abroad.[59] The issue remains open. If, for one reason or another EPA cannot become involved in the international project, then EPA will attempt either to test their pollutant control devices on ERDA's $15 million domestic fluidized bed facility to be built in the United States, or attempt to acquire funds to build its own $30 million fluidized bed facility in the United States.[60] The EPA desire to add its own pollutant control devices to the coal combustion project in the United Kingdom is not expected to delay or directly influence the project but it does suggest a struggle among competing U.S. agencies for domestic funds for coal combustion facilities. Ultimately Congress and the Office of Management and Budget (OMB) may have to settle this dispute.

A further jurisdictional dispute centered around nuclear safety and radioactive waste management, and involved both the Nuclear Regulatory Commission (NRC) and ERDA. Both agencies claimed jurisdiction over certain areas of R and D cooperation. Resolution of these internal issues may affect the degree to which the United States cooperates with others in IEA, since ERDA owns the facilities and funds for operation of possible projects while NRC has jurisdiction and a strong substantive interest in these areas.[61]

Although international R and D cooperation in four additional areas—solar, conservation, waste heat, and municipal and industrial

ENERGY R AND D

waste utilization—is less likely at this point in the discussions, there are a number of jurisdictional disputes in these areas over agency leadership for joint projects. For example, leadership in the area of municipal and industrial waste utilization is undecided at this point. HUD was designated the lead agency during the ECG phase, while EPA has assumed leadership during the IEA phase. ERDA may also compete for influence in this area. It has enormous advantages over EPA in terms of staff and budget. One EPA official expressed the opinion that EPA had greater expertise than HUD in the area of waste utilization since EPA had established linkages with state and local governments in waste utilization programs. However, EPA has no money for international programs and their domestic program budget for the fiscal year 1974 in waste utilization was only $400,000. Moreover, the EPA staff is relatively small, (20 to 25 persons) and thus would be no match for ERDA if the latter should seek to become the lead agency.[62]

Another administrative difficulty arose in connection with waste heat utilization programs. There are a number of U.S. agencies who have had domestic programs in waste heat such as HUD, FEA, DOD (Department of Defense), and EPA.[63] Although HUD was named the lead agency during the ECG phase, no agency had sole prior expertise in waste heat and, in effect, there was no clear expert in waste heat.[64] A decision as to which U.S. agency will lead in the specific area of cooperation may have to be reached before cooperative international projects can materialize.[65] HUD's position is complicated by the fact that HUD is already involved in international programs in waste heat and municipal waste utilization though its MIUS programs (Modular Integrated Utility System), which in the spring of 1974, became part of the conservation package agreement implemented through CCMS (Committee on the Challenges to Modern Society). MIUS was primarily a domestic program which was expanded internationally when it became part of the CCMS conservation agreement piloted by FEA.[66] If HUD retains leadership in both areas, there is the problem of rival international programs (CCMS and IEA) competing for scarce funds within the same domestic agency. Unless funds were transferred to HUD, it would be forced to borrow from domestic programs to fund international programs.[67] FEA faces a similar problem through its involvement in international conservation programs implemented through CCMS. Furthermore, FEA is not the sole expert in energy conservation. Other U.S. agencies involved in the conservation R and D area include HUD, DOD, NBS (National Bureau of Standards), DOI (Department of the Interior), BOM (Bureau of Mines), DOT (Department of Transportation), and ERDA.[68]

Thus, in these three areas—municipal and industrial waste utilization, waste heat, and conservation—there are a number of agency experts who compete with each other for U.S. agency leadership in IEA cooperative projects. Also these agencies are attempting to retain leadership vis-a-vis ERDA, and eventually either ERDA or other lead agencies must face the issue of rival international programs in waste heat, waste utilization, and conservation implemented through NATO-CCMS. A fourth area—solar energy—raises the same issue since multilateral cooperation exists through CCMS in solar heating and cooling of buildings.* There have been some discussions within the U.S. government that, at some point, CCMS activities in solar projects (and possibly others) would routinely shift over to IEA for implementation and continuation.[69] However, the possible transfer of CCMS activities to IEA raises serious <u>external</u> issues, including foreign policy and international administrative issues. These external issues will be discussed in the next two sections of this chapter on the transgovernmental and international organization levels of analysis.

THE TRANSGOVERNMENTAL LEVEL: THE ENERGY COORDINATING GROUP

Before the specific issues that arose during the transgovernmental phase are discussed, it is appropriate to review the evolution of activities at this level.

As indicated earlier, the first meeting of the ECG (Energy Coordinating Group) was held February 25, 1974 to organize the work program and modalities for implementing the decisions of the Washington Energy Conference. At this first organizational meeting of the ECG, the United States delegation tabled a document proposing some "Terms of Reference for International Cooperation on Energy Research and Development."[70] This document called for the establishment of an ad hoc group of senior R and D officials to examine and make recommendations on the expansion of international cooperation in energy R and D. Specifically, the mandate for this working group proposed that the ad hoc group shall:

---

*Participants in the CCMS solar project agreement include France, Denmark, Greece, Federal Republic of Germany, and the United States. Bilateral cooperation exists in this area between the U.S., Japan, USSR, Italy, France, and Australia.

Develop criteria for mutually advantageous cooperative efforts in energy R & D that could accelerate the availability of alternate energy sources.

Identify those economic, legal, and other institutional factors which currently constrain more extensive international cooperative efforts in energy R & D.

Review the energy R & D programs of the participating nations, now being catalogued by the OECD, to identify projects of mutual interest for cooperation by two or more of the participating nations and render more effective existing international programs and to submit a report of its funding and recommendations to the Coordinating Group.[71]

The U.S. proposal was adopted by the ECG participants,* establishing the ad hoc working group on international cooperation on energy R and D. The first meeting of this group (known as the Energy R and D Working Group or ECG/ERD) was held March 14, 1974, in Brussels, with Dr. Schmidt-Kuester, of the Federal Republic of Germany, as its chairman. The working group began to implement its terms of reference, notably the preparation of a paper by the United States on the criteria for mutually advantageous efforts in energy R and D, and a paper by the U.K. delegation on factors currently constraining more extensive international cooperative efforts in energy R and D.[72] These two papers were to be presented to the R and D working group at its second meeting to be held on March 25, 1974.

The ECG/ERD proceeded to identify specific projects of mutual interest for international cooperation. To accomplish this task, each country was asked to submit a description of national energy R and D programs using a questionnaire prepared by the OECD. In addition, each country was to list research areas or projects of particular interest for international cooperation (either new or expanded), and an inventory of areas in which international cooperation was already under way.[73] This approach was taken after it was agreed that a more efficient manner of gaining information on specific R and D programs and of identifying specific potential cooperative programs was to convene a small group of experts to prepare the initial paper. For this purpose, Dr. Schmidt-Kuester suggested that a group of voluntary

---

* France did not participate in this meeting.

representatives from the United States, United Kingdom, Federal
Republic of Germany, Japan, and Denmark (representing the smaller
countries) meet in Juelich, West Germany on April 4 and 5 to prepare
a matrix of potential areas of cooperation for submission to the energy
R and D group at its next meeting on April 8, 1974.[74] This group,
known as the "Juelich Working Group" reviewed the national energy
R and D programs of participating countries and identified those
areas where effective international cooperation should be established
or improved.[75] Areas were left out where, according to the opinion
of the Juelich group, there was either 1) sufficient international
cooperation; 2) no promising basis for cooperation; or 3) severe
political or commercial problems. Areas were included in which
there was 1) significant governmental involvement in the technology;
2) the possibility of broad international cooperation; and 3) the likelihood of the technology contributing to the solution of the overall energy
problem.[76]

The Juelich working party submitted its report to the third
meeting of the energy R and D working group held in Brussels on
April 18, 1974. After two reviews of the working party's report and
some regrouping of the categorizations used by the Juelich group,
the ECG/ERD selected ten areas for priority consideration in international cooperation.[77] These ten areas were selected not only on
the basis of substantive criteria developed by the United States and
the United Kingdom in the papers referred to above but also on the
basis of individual country interest and involvement in the development of these techniques.[78] The lead countries with special interest
in each of these areas were the United States (fusion, nuclear reactor
safety, and energy conservation in residential, industrial, agricultural,
and transportation sectors), Japan (solar technology), United Kingdom (coal technology), Germany (hydrogen production and waste
heat utilization), the Netherlands (use of municipal, industrial waste
for energy production, that is, bioconversion), and the OECD (radioactive waste management and energy systems analysis and general
studies).[79] At this point in the ECG/ERD discussions only coal
technology gained clear general endorsement for near-term application. Some interest was also expressed in fusion as an important long-term source of cooperation. (The United Kingdom expressed
an interest in cooperation with the United States in coal technology
and the Italians were interested in fusion technology.)

Nevertheless, it was decided that the lead countries would
prepare specific proposals for cooperative programs in each of these
ten areas for the next meeting of the ECG/ERD on April 25, 1974.
All of the other countries were to identify their existing and planned
levels of national effort in these areas. In preparing proposals where
the United States was the lead country, individual agencies were

instructed to present showcase proposals which would highlight the role of R and D and make maximum use of energy R and D as a diplomatic carrot in overall U.S. energy strategy.

Accordingly, at the April 25 meeting of the ECG/ERD, specific proposals were introduced in the ten areas. The British delegation suggested cooperation in coal mining technology (including equipment development cooperation and field trials involving manufacturers and operating companies), and coal conversion (including advanced combustion, that is, fluidized bed). In both cases, active involvement of industry, including architects, engineers, and industry-wide organizations was proposed. Also bilateral and multilateral use of process facilities and pilot plants was suggested.

The United States delegation presented proposals in the areas of fusion, reactor safety, and conservation; the Federal Republic of Germany proposed cooperation on hydrogen production from water, possibly using the European Community Joint Research Center at Ispra, Italy for European activities, and on possible uses of waste heat and power plants. The Netherlands presented a proposal on municipal and industrial waste utilization suggesting cooperation in pyrolysis process. The Japanese delegation presented a detailed outline of their overall solar program, Project Sunshine. The Nuclear Energy Agency (OECD) presented a review of the most significant areas of R and D interest in nuclear waste management including management practices and control of wastes from plutonium fabrication and reprocessing. The final proposal, presented by OECD, focused on coordinated energy studies applying systems analysis methods, surveys on ecological effects, input/output analysis of total energy flows, and so on.[80]

After the group discussed each proposal, it was agreed to have expert groups convene before the next meeting and examine the draft proposals in greater detail. The experts were instructed to present amendments to the proposals for consideration at the next meeting of the ECG/ERD.

In comments on the proposals U.S. officials noted that most of them "tended to be general rather than specific" suggestions for cooperation. Little discussion centered on administrative arrangements or the extent of individual country participation in each area. Except for an attempt by the Belgians to include cooperation in High Temperature Gas Reactors (HTGR), there was no further effort to modify the original list of priority areas.[81]

The purpose of the experts' meetings held during May 10-14, 1974, was to define as specifically as possible projects or programs which might be recommended to the ECG as desirable of implementation using the lead country proposals as a starting point.[82] The best attended meetings of these expert groups were those on radioactive waste management and nuclear safety, followed by coal, fusion, and conservation R and D. Japan and Germany were particularly enthusiastic about fusion, and coal was the subject of bilateral discussions between the United States, United Kingdom, Germany, and Japan, as well as of multilateral talks within the EGC. There was much less interest exhibited in cooperation in the production of hydrogen from water, solar energy R and D, waste heat, or municipal and industrial waste utilization.[83]

The fifth meeting of the ECG/ERD was held on May 15 in Geesthacht, Germany to coincide with the completion of the expert meetings. A major portion of this meeting was concerned with the recommendations the ad hoc group would make to the ECG on the possible follow-up mechanisms to be employed in the event of R and D cooperation. Four possible options were suggested:[84]

1. the lead countries would assume the responsibility for implementing new cooperative ventures
2. existing institutions such as the Nuclear Energy Agency (NEA) of the OECD would assist in organizing cooperation
3. an existing institution such as OECD, would assist in organizing joint ventures but be restructured to deal more effectively with the energy problems, including R and D
4. a steering group of high level R and D officials would be established to monitor the progress of cooperative ECG R and D initiatives.

The third option was favored by most other countries, while the United States preferred option four. The United States believed that the existing OECD framework would not easily facilitate R and D cooperation. Specifically, the OECD had 25 member nations, twice the number of nations participating in the Washington Energy Conference, thus greatly expanding the size and complexity of the proposed cooperative activity. Moreover, it was believed that the bureaucratic obstacles common to broadly based international organizations would impede the promotion of international R and D projects. In favoring option four, the United States was searching for a mechanism that would substitute for OECD since the existing OECD arrangement was viewed as unable to react quickly to implement policy decisions.[85]

The U.S. position favoring option four had some support from both Denmark and the Netherlands. However, the majority of countries represented on the ECG/ERD favored using the existing

ENERGY R AND D 149

OECD framework. Additionally, the United Kingdom, Japan, and France were particularly concerned about Arab reactions to the establishment of a new institution which could be dominated by the United States. (Japan was especially concerned about avoiding an association with NATO-CCMS.)[86] To mollify these concerns, Secretary Kissinger had previously implied that no new agencies would be created.[87] Actually, the United States preferred a new ad hoc group (option four) but if the pressures toward incorporation of the ad hoc group into OECD became too great, the U.S. contingency position was to create a new informal group within OECD explicitly designed for R and D cooperation. What the United States wanted to avoid most was to give existing OECD organs such as NEA primary responsibility for ECG/ERC actions.[88]

During the course of the fifth ECG/ERD meeting in May, 1974, Chairman Schmidt-Kuester "tried to steer the working group toward option three," while the U.S. delegation "urged the view that the ECG itself, and not the ad hoc group, should decide on the appropriate follow-on mechanisms."[89]

The question of possible follow-on mechanisms was taken up again at the final meeting of the ECG/ERD in Bonn on June 6, 1974. The group agreed not to indicate any preference on the follow-on mechanisms. With the adoption of its report to ECG, the work of the ECG/ERD was completed.[90]

Foreign Policy Issues

During the course of the ECG/ERD discussions, a number of foreign policy issues arose. The first of these occurred during the second meeting of ECG/ERD when the OECD was unwilling to furnish to ECG/ERD copies of country submissions on energy R and D programs being examined by OECD. The issue here was that not all the OECD countries were represented in ECG/ERD, so OECD was reluctant to cooperate.

This suggests that ECG/ERD was operating to some extent in competition with OECD, a factor also brought out by the debate over the most appropriate follow-on mechanism for international cooperation in energy R and D. In one instance, the expert group on radioactive waste management had difficulty in reaching agreement on new projects because of the desire of the Europeans to protect ongoing multilateral cooperative efforts in NEA-OECD.[91] In another instance, the Belgians felt that the OECD Committee on Scientific and Technical Policy was the appropriate follow-on mechanism and the OECD respesentative made outspoken representations that the follow-on effort would most suitably be placed within OECD. At another point in the discussion the Norwegian delegation sought exclusion altogether of the option involving a high level steering group follow-on to ECG.

ECG/ERD may also have been operating in competition with NATO. For example, the Japanese delegation strongly expressed its disapproval of ECG/ERD's formal association with NATO-CCMS in the ten areas for possible cooperation.[92]

These European and Japanese preferences were eventually resolved through a compromise but they indicate the general climate of opinion surrounding the issue of follow-on mechanism.[93] The United States, in contrast to its European allies, wanted to establish a new institution for energy relations since it was felt that OECD and NATO were encrusted organizations that had resisted repeated attempts at reform.

Military-Strategic Issues

Two notable instances of military-strategic issues arose within the transgovernmental context. The first occasion was the separation of the uranium enrichment working group from the energy R and D working group. Although both of these working groups were oriented toward the development of prospects for long-term cooperation, it was necessary to separate the uranium enrichment working group from the R and D working group per se, since uranium enrichment was a highly specific area with political and classification problems. Furthermore, during the course of the meetings of the uranium enrichment working group, there was no talk of cooperative R and D as such, but rather the thrust of the meetings was concerned with the possible transfer of _existing_ technology. The primary concerns of this working group were arrangements for future fuel supplies, the location of enrichment plants, and so on, but there was no mention of cooperative R and D in uranium enrichment technology.[94]

On another occasion, in the area of fusion R and D, the United States proposed an International Fusion Research Laboratory as a possible cooperative project. This project was subsequently dropped since it was believed that Congress would never approve a $5 to 10 million project to be built overseas. In addition, military-strategic considerations militated against such a project.[95]

Foreign Economic Issues

Similarly, a number of foreign economic issues arose which shed additional light on how possibilities for international cooperation emerge (or do not emerge). As we noted before, during the April 25 meeting of ECG/ERD, the Belgian delegation suggested that the list of ten areas for possible cooperation be expanded to include cooperation on HTGR construction. They reiterated this request at the May 15 meeting. However, their suggestion did not receive approval due largely to the fact that this area involved strong commercial interest.[96] The Belgian request illustrates how a country which is lagging in a particular R and D sector will attempt to obtain involve- of its domestic industry through government agreements, and how another country, which already has an extensive private involvement in the area, will seek to block such an attempt.

On another occasion, Japan was reluctant to join in multilateral agreements on solar R and D with the European community (through ECG) because proprietary interests were involved in at least four of its domestic solar R and D programs. Japan's preference in this case was for bilateral arrangements. In addition, several of the ECG/ERD delegations from countries lacking substantial energy R and D resources expressed doubts over U.S. seriousness toward multilateral cooperation in R and D areas of their interest. For example, Table 5.8 illustrates the relative R and D contribution of the U.S. and the 11 other ECG countries to each of the ten energy R and D areas chosen for passive collaboration. One might infer from the table that the United States would most likely cooperate with those countries who could contribute R and D or funds. The United States had less interest in cooperating with those countries lacking R and D or funds. Given this assumption, foreign participants expressed privately their beliefs that the U.S. would cooperate solely with Germany, Japan, and the United Kingdom in areas such as coal, energy conservation, solar energy, fusion, radioactive waste management, and nuclear safety.*

---

* It should be noted that the United States and Japan signed a bilateral energy "agreement to agree" (including solar energy R and D) in July, 1974. (Interview with U.S. State Department Official, Washington, D.C., July 18, 1974.)

TABLE 5.8

Energy Research and Development Expenditures in ECG Countries, Fiscal Year 1974
(In Millions of U.S. Dollars)

Technology	United States	Belgium	Canada	Denmark	Germany	Ireland	Italy	Japan	Luxembourg	Netherlands	Norway	United Kingdom
Coal	164.4	1.2	2.7	—	118.6	.4	—	1.6	—	a	—	17.9
Conservation[b]	42.2	.9	.2	.7	23.4	—	—	3.0	—	2.6	—	15.7
Waste heat	.1	—	—	.3	1.3	—	—	—	—	—	—	.72
Waste utilization	1.1	—	—	—	1.7	—	—	1.5	—	—	—	.24
Solar	13.8	—	5.2	.03	1.0	—	—	3.2	—	—	—	.70
Fusion	101.1	.37	—	.60	23.4	—	—	3.7	—	—	—	7.2
H_2	.2	—	—	—	.09	—	—	.9	—	—	—	.05
RWM	6.2	—	.5	.07	5.2	—	—	.20	—	—	.28	3.8
Nuclear safety	48.6	.33	.5	3.0	24.8	—	—	14.5	—	—	.41	7.2
Systems analysis	17.3	.15	—	—	1.7	—	—	—	—	.4	—	2.4

[a] Funding comes exclusively from industry.
[b] Utilization and conservation of energy.

Source: Organization for Economic Cooperation and Development, Energy R & D (Paris: OECD, 1975), pp. 103-10.

THE INTERNATIONAL ORGANIZATION LEVEL:
THE INTERNATIONAL ENERGY AGENCY

Negotiations over the summer and into the fall of 1974 were directed toward institutionalizing the work of the Energy Coordinating Group and its nine working groups. The first result of those negotiations was the International Energy Program (IEP) unveiled in September.[97] The International Energy Program was primarily concerned with an oil-sharing arrangement but also included long-term cooperation on energy which embodied the original eleven areas for possible R and D cooperation (the original ten areas plus uranium enrichment) selected by the ECG/ERD. Cooperative programs were to be implemented through an International Energy Agency. Thus, the follow-on mechanism that ultimately emerged from the options suggested in the ECG/ERD final report[98] was the International Energy Agency (IEA), an autonomous agency within the OECD. The IEA represented a compromise between the British, German, and Japanese preference for utilizing an existing OECD agency, and the U.S. preference for the autonomous agency.[99]

Although the IEA was symbolically created within the framework of OECD, it is in reality independent of OECD with its own council and weighted voting arrangement. It is composed of the following organs:[100]

- a governing board
- a management committee
- standing groups on
  1. emergency questions
  2. the oil market
  3. long-term cooperation
  4. relations with producer and other consumer countries

The Standing Group on Long-Term Cooperation is authorized by its charter to examine and report to the Management Committee on cooperative R and D action including concrete projects and jointly financed projects in the eleven areas of energy R and D originally selected by ECG/ERD.[101] (See Table 5.2.) The old ECG energy R and D working group was reconstituted in IEA under the Standing Group (hereafter referred to as SLT/ERD). The SLT/ERD met on January 6, February 20, March 20, and May 7, 1975 in Paris, in an effort to further define areas of interest for possible R and D cooperation. The expert groups in the ten areas met at irregular intervals during these five months, some being more active than others. For example, three of the expert groups met on four occasions (coal, nuclear safety, and radioactive waste management), while expert groups on conservation and waste heat met only twice.

The second meeting of the SLT/ERD on February 20, 1975, received the progress reports from the expert groups on the formation of program proposals. After a review and discussion of each of the ten areas, the committee concluded that the areas of coal, nuclear safety, and radioactive waste management were the top priority areas for possible cooperation. The committee also agreed that, to speed up its work, proposals would be further defined in these areas and commitments made before July 1, 1975.[102] At this meeting, the United States also presented its proposal to establish an international R and D consortium first espoused by Secretary Kissinger in his Washington speech of February 4, 1975.[103]

The March 20, 1975 meeting of the SLT/ERD was concerned with further discussions of the expert group proposals, especially in the areas of coal technology, nuclear safety, and radioactive waste management. Information exchanges in the areas of waste heat utilization, municipal and industrial waste utilization, and hydrogen production from water were to be implemented immediately, while proposals in the areas of fusion, solar energy, and conservation R and D were still to be formulated.[104]

The SLT/ERD also received the report of the March 13, 1975 meeting of the coal experts which, as we noted earlier in our discussion of intragovernmental activities, proposed 1) the establishment of a coal resource international clearing house in the United Kingdom, and a data bank in the United States; 2) the establishment of a mining technology clearing house; 3) construction of a $15 million fluidized bed coal combustion facility to be built in the United Kingdom; and 4) later establishment of a coal science and technology information service and technical economic studies on extraction costs, conservation technology and the value of products in the end use.[105] Since the coal fluidized bed combustion proposal raised a number of difficult technical, legal, and economic issues, the United States, United Kingdom, and the Federal Republic of Germany (FRG) attempted to develop general guiding principles regarding intellectual property matters to present to the SLT/ERD committee. The SLT/ERD committee reviewed these principles, but delayed further discussions on them due to insufficient time for analysis.[106]

One additional proposal was made during this meeting by the Italians. They suggested (and the United States supported their suggestion) that the IEA sponsor geothermal expert meetings to discuss the progress and results of national R and D activities in this area.

This suggestion was to be discussed at the next SLT/ERD meeting in May, 1975.[107]

The May 1975 meeting of the SLT/ERD involved general discussions of differences between the United States and the Europeans on national approaches to near commercial ventures, such as the proposed coal combustion facilities. These differences concerned: 1) protection of information, technical data and know-how developed in cooperative activities and consortia having commercial significance, 2) the collection of royalties and license fees and their subsequent distribution to consortium partners, and 3) the strategy for marketing technology developed under consortium arrangements, including the avoidance of inequitable market domination by a single country.[108]

In summary, major discussion within the SLT/ERD centers at the time of this writing around international cooperation in the coal combustion project, nuclear safety, and radioactive waste management. Cooperation in these areas awaits resolution of a number of difficult issues for both the United States and others who may participate in these projects. Cooperation in other areas (solar, fusion, hydrogen production, conservation, waste heat, and waste utilization) involves several difficult issues and appears to be even less likely in the future. We discuss some of these issues below in terms of foreign policy, economic and social-environmental implications.

Foreign Policy Issues

One of the more visible foreign policy issues in the IEA arose over Japan's desire to see solar cooperation under the CCMS program shifted to a non-NATO context, such as IEA, while France threatened withdrawal from all CCMS programs if CCMS energy programs were transferred to the IEA. The United States was also considering the possibility of transferring the follow-on of CCMS energy pilot studies to the IEA in order to minimize duplication of efforts in these areas and alleviate domestic concerns over program duplication. Other countries such as Canada, Ireland, and the United Kingdom likewise expressed concern over duplication in conservation, waste heat, and waste utilization with CCMS projects. One foreign representative agreed that cooperation in these three areas already existed through CCMS, and there was no need for additional programs in the IEA.[109]

Other foreign policy issues arose during the discussions. On one occasion, strong sentiment was expressed for expanding the NEA of OECD into an Energy Development Cooperation Agency; on another instance, it was debated whether leadership for radioactive waste management should be assumed by NEA-OECD or by one of the member countries of IEA (especially the Federal Republic of Germany). These issues reiterated the concern over the most appropriate follow-on mechanism that first arose during the ECG/ERD discussions.[110] They also expressed concern over how to cooperate with non-IEA OECD countries and non-OECD countries. The restricted membership of the IEA created a problem in this regard.

A final foreign policy issue, implied during the discussions of both the ECG/ERD and IEA phases, was the questionable seriousness of the U.S. commitment to undertake cooperative energy R and D. Although this doubt was never openly expressed during the energy discussions, evidence suggests that it was, nevertheless, a concern of several participants.[111]

Foreign Economic Issues

The major economic issue that emerged during this phase of the discussions concerned the possibility of international cooperation in the coal fluidized bed plant proposed by the United Kingdom. This venture was neither strictly commercial nor solely governmental, and therefore, a model of international collaboration had to be found which could accommodate public and private interests. The central issue was over what type and extent of government participation would be compatible with the different economic and industrial structures of the participating countries. For example, in the proposed coal fluidized bed project, the United Kingdom suggested that a consortium be formed which would hold, own, and license resulting intellectual property throughout the world, with royalties being divided up equitably among the consortium members. If the U.S. government insisted on U.S. industry being licensed for free within the United States in accordance with normal practice, presumably this loss of revenue would be made up to the other two countries by a larger share of the royalties given to the United Kingdom and Germany. Ownership of intellectual property would require the consortium to extend beyond the term of the R and D project and would involve the U.S. government in a commercial venture beyond the demonstration of the technology.

This approach appears to be quite acceptable to the United Kingdom and Germany but is quite foreign to U.S. government policies. Traditionally, the United States has stayed out of commercial ventures and not attempted to justify public appropriations through expected revenues from government-owned technology. These considerations underscore the difference between the United States and Europeans in their government-industry relationships. The United Kingdom and Germany have a much greater tendency to retain government-developed know-how and technical data as proprietary information to be licensed at reasonable royalties. The United States, on the other hand, is much freer with its information and at present U.S. statutes severely restrict the U.S. government's ability to treat such information as proprietary.[112]

There was also discussion over the issue of European domestic industry protection vis-a-vis U.S. industry. For example, both the United Kingdom and Germany sought a degree of R and D investment protection such that the governments would agree not to duplicate each other's work. If the consortium agreed to pursue several coal gasification concepts and it was agreed that the United Kingdom would pilot plant one concept, the U.S. government would not be able to fund separate pilot plants or process development work on the same concept. The United Kingdom and Germany were also interested in some protection against U.S. domination of world markets in technology derived from a consortium activity. They proposed, for example, a sharing of royalties from licenses issued in third countries, in proportion to the R and D investment made by the consortium partners. They also sought protection from U.S. firms marketing consortium-developed technology in the FRG and United Kingdom. This protection would be provided either by leaving the U.K. and German markets solely to their own national firms or by having the United States charge a royalty to U.S. firms marketing in the United Kingdom and Germany to place them in the same competititve position with U.K. and German firms. The latter governments charge royalties to their own industry for using government-financed technology.[113]

Furthermore, there is the associated issue of the rights to intellectual property by IEA members not participating in a particular cooperative project. Belgium, for example, expressed the concern that smaller nations must share equitably in commercial exploitation of the results of cooperative R and D projects.[114]

Other areas, such as solar energy, conservation, nuclear safety, and radioactive waste management may also lead to a consortium arrangement. These areas have various levels of industrial involvement and hence similar issues may arise. For example, in the area of nuclear safety, issues arose over how to finance international cooperation in this area. Since the sellers of nuclear reactors are the ultimate beneficiaries of cooperation in this area (that is, international cooperation in this area was proposed in order to alleviate concern over the safety of nuclear energy and thereby increase sales of nuclear reactors worldwide), Switzerland proposed that the sellers of the reactors should include the cost of nuclear safety R and D in the price of the reactors.[115]

Social-Environmental Issues

During the February 20, 1975 meeting of SLT/ERD, the issue of sea bed disposal of radioactive waste was discussed. Especially critical problems of world-wide acceptance and the reaction of the LDCs including the legal problems associated with sea bed disposal, emerged.[116] At the present time, ERDA has been assigned responsibility for U.S. agency input into this problem area and discussions are continuing.

CONCLUSIONS: IMPLICATIONS FOR FUTURE COLLABORATION

In this chapter, we have argued that political rather than technical motivations were behind the initiation of the U.S. offer to share R and D resources in multilateral energy R and D cooperation. In addition, we have identified political and economic issues (internal and external to the United States) which suggest the range of factors that serve either to facilitate or to limit the possibilities for technology transfers in the energy sector. While political (as opposed to technical) factors contributed toward the original motivation for the attempted multilateral cooperation, both political (that is, administrative and foreign policy) and economic factors inhibited subsequent implementation of the proposed cooperation. All of these factors together determine the type and characteristics of technology that are ultimately transferred in relations between the United States and advanced Western countries. The findings of our case study can be summarized in terms of several trends and generalizations which may serve as a useful guide in future technology transfer efforts in the energy sector.

The technology that will ultimately emerge for international transfers tends to be either of three types. Technology, as used in this instance, refers to the exchange of commercial processes and/or management techniques, and excludes scientific information exchanges. First, technologies are transferred which are relatively remote from commercialization. Examples drawn from our discussions include fusion and hydrogen production technologies. Ironically, however, possibilities for international technology transfer in fusion are minimal given individual country R and D capabilities, military-strategic considerations, and rival existing cooperation. And international collaboration in hydrogen production from water held very little interest for ECG and IEA participants.

The more likely technologies to be transferred are secondary priority technologies. These transfers tend to involve technologies which receive only a moderate share of national R and D expenditures relative to higher priority technologies. An example within the current framework of discussions is the coal combustion project. Clearly, this technology is an important one in terms of our energy supply requirements. However, technologies associated with coal utilization received only 16 percent of federal energy R and D funding for the year 1974, compared to 63 percent for nuclear energy technology (see Tables 5.4, 5.5, and 5.6). The point here is that coal technologies are not the priority technologies in the U.S. energy budget, and consequently international cooperation in these areas does not pose an immediate threat to domestic objectives. In addition, these secondary technology transfers, for example, coal combustion technologies, tend to move in directions where there is perceived mutual benefit. For example, such transfers are likely to be restricted to countries that can contribute R and D or funds, such as the United Kingdom, the Federal Republic of Germany, or Canada. Furthermore, cooperation involving these countries is likely to be bilateral, due to their disproportionate R and D capabilities and/or their proprietary interests. Eventual cooperation, of course, further depends on successful resolution of issues relating to different industrial sectors and different systems of government-industry relationships.

A final characteristic of technology transfer among advanced countries is the increasing interest in software activities concerned with the regulation of commercial processes. Examples from our case study are the nuclear safety and radioactive waste management technologies. An interesting development has occurred in which this type of technology transfer is perceived as a new means for alleviating domestic and international environmental concerns associated with nuclear proliferation. It is believed that international nuclear safety studies are more credible than domestic ones and pave the way for increased reactor sales both at home and abroad. In addition, this type of technology transfer holds out the novel possibility that private industry may pick up some of the costs, since industry is assumed to be the ultimate beneficiary of the cooperation.

Regardless of the type of technology ultimately transferred, there are a number of issue areas which affect either the initiation or the implementation of technology transfer and which require attention. One category of issues relates to the agency-Congressional linkage and involves the question of funding for international energy R and D projects. The essential question is how to provide an orderly method of funding in order to accommodate Congressional oversight, as well as to allow for maximum flexibility within the Executive agencies charged with the implementation of the program.

Presently, international program support must come from domestic program funds since no funds have been explicitly set aside for international programs. This does not apply, of course, to the Department of State or the National Science Foundation. Therefore, international program funding must compete with domestic programs for scarce resources. Given this situation, the important question becomes whether an individual Executive agency should have a line item appropriation for international R and D exchange programs.

From the point of view of the Executive agency charged with implementation of the development project, there are advantages, as well as disadvantages, to line item appropriations. First, line item budgeting provides an independent source of funding to the agency and does not force competition with the domestic program budget (which might be subjected to reduced amounts during periods of federal spending cuts). However, a major disadvantage of line item appropriations is the fact that this approach would expose the international project to Congressional scrutiny. At present, Executive agencies may conclude international R and D agreements without Congressional approval. A line item appropriation, however, provides Congress with an inviting target for reduction of funds for international R and D projects. Several members of Congress are reluctant to commit resources to international research projects not located in the United States or under U.S. control. Furthermore, members of Congress have expressed concern over future competition from an unequal exchange of technology.[117]

Another argument against line item appropriations maintains that, under present conditions, domestic R and D funds diverted to international projects must be compatible with and supplement domestic technological goals and objectives. Line item appropriations, on the other hand, tend to direct attention toward the advancement of bureaucratic goals and objectives, such as program expansion, regardless of the technology involved.[118]

From a Congressional perspective, line item appropriations would allow for Congressional oversight into program efficiency and practicality, and essentially provide Congress with effective control over future technology transfers. Secondly, increasing the number of formal and informal consultations with Congress over international R and D programs would ensure that appropriate Congressional actors

ENERGY R AND D

clearly understand both the rationale and the objectives of the technology transfer component of U.S. foreign policy. Clearly, these consultations were absent during the ECG and IEA discussions.

A second set of issues relates to interagency linkages. These issues are concerned with the desirability of a revision of agency charters to allow for participation in international programs where these difficulties exist, and with the improvement of coordination among the Executive agencies involved in international cooperation.

The Department of Interior has no clear mandate in its charter to engage in international R and D programs. Congressional concern over Interior's international activities led in 1975 to the elimination of appropriations for Interior's Office of International Programs. International R and D activities continue to be conducted by other offices, but the situation suggests the precariousness of foreign involvements by some domestic agencies. The Federal Energy Administration likewise has no explicit mandate for its foreign activities, although its enabling legislation allows for interpretation with regard to international R and D programs. The Energy Research and Development Administration, on the other hand, is expressly chartered to engage in such activities.

In the present energy discussions, charter restrictions do not pose a significant problem since ERDA has been designated the lead agency for eventual implementation of international projects in eight of the ten areas for R and D cooperation. Jurisdiction for projects in coal mining and exploration has remained within the Bureau of Mines of the Department of Interior, while EPA and the Nuclear Regulatory Commission are the lead agencies for waste utilization and nuclear safety respectively. ERDA may eventually acquire leadership in these latter two areas as well.

To the extent that future international R and D projects are constrained by agency charter restrictions, revision of agency charters to allow for international program participation may be necessary. However, the more critical question implied by this discussion is whether or not future international cooperation in energy R and D should be centralized within one Executive agency. A more pluralistic approach would perhaps allow for greater innovation in policy planning, as well as provide essential criticism, for possible candidate projects in future discussions.

Secondly, there is the issue of interagency coordination since in some instances in this exercise, U.S. agency actors misunderstood (or disagreed with) the foreign policy objectives of the negotiations. While interagency leadership was effective in mobilizing the bureaucracy to implement the primary objectives of the energy exercise, there was inadequate attention paid to several interagency concerns.[119]

Our final category of issues concerns government-industry relationships. A most difficult issue here includes trying to develop new structural forms that go beyond traditional government contracting. This necessity is illustrated by discussions over international cooperation in fluidized bed coal combustion in which an international consortium would be formed which would hold, own, and license intellectual property throughout the world. As we discussed earlier, this is a dramatic departure from past U.S. policies of staying out of commercial ventures beyond the R and D phase.

A less difficult option for improving government-industry linkages includes involving industry in consultations over proposed international activities, early in the process, in order to ascertain their degree of interest in participating in such projects. Active participation by industry is a prerequisite for the success of international programs in energy R and D. However, government-industry consultations were not a notable characteristic of the ECG and IEA discussions. While it is not too late to engage industry representatives in discussions over proposed projects, a solicitation of their interest in participation would be advisable at an earlier stage in future negotiations.

Industry options include at least three possibilities. First, industry could cooperate with other countries entirely outside of a governmental framework, although this raises the difficult problem of reconciling market forces and objectives with political and diplomatic objectives. Often these objectives conflict, which again suggests the need for close coordination between government and industry. Secondly, industry could fund international cooperation in regulatory technologies, e.g. radioactive waste management technologies, by including the cost of cooperation in the price of their reactors. This option is based on the fact that industry is the ultimate beneficiary of the cooperation and therefore should share in its cost. Finally, industry could participate in joint industry-government funding of cooperative projects. This option may, as we noted previously, require unprecedented action on the part of government and industry where their cooperation is required beyond the R and D phase.

In conclusion, we have suggested that political considerations were the driving force behind the original initiation of the energy R and D exercise, while economic and political considerations arose during the negotiation phase and inhibit implementation. No attempt has been made to rank these issues (and their possible options) in order of significance. Rather, an attempt has been made to identify likely candidates for international technology transfers, and to suggest critical areas which require further attention before present and future international cooperation in energy R and D may be successfully implemented.

NOTES

1. This working group's activities and implications are explored in a separate paper. See Edward F. Wonder, "Competition in Collaboration: Uranium Enrichment in American-European Relations." Ph.D. dissertation, University of Virginia, 1975, chapter 4. Mr. Wonder prepared this chapter to deal with matters of interest to the project on "Technology Transfer and U.S. Foreign Policy."

2. See Energy Coordinating Group, "International Cooperation on Energy R&D," Final Report, June 6, 1974.

3. See Agreement on an International Energy Program, in U.S. Congress, Senate, Committee on Interior and Insular Affairs, International Energy Program, Hearings, 93d Cong., 2d sess., November 26, 1974, pp. 72-96.

4. For a more complete discussion of past and current U.S. activities in energy R and D cooperation, see Herman Pollack and Michael B. Congdon, "International Cooperation in Energy Research and Development," Law and Policy in International Business, July/August, 1974, pp. 677-724.

5. See Warren H. Donnelly, Commercial Nuclear Power in Europe: The Interaction of American Diplomacy with a New Technology, prepared for the U.S. Congress, House, Subcommittee on National Security Policy and Scientific Developments of the Committee on Foreign Affairs (Washington, D.C.: U.S. Government Printing Office, 1972).

6. For a review of agreements currently in force, see U.S. Department of State, International Cooperation in Energy Research and Development, A Report to Governor John A. Love, Director, Energy Policy Office, from William J. Casey, 1973.

7. For detailed history of CCMS and its various projects, see James R. Huntley, Man's Environment and the Atlantic Alliance (Brussels: NATO Information Service, 1972). See also Harry Blaney, "NATO's New Challenges to the Problems of Modern Society," Atlantic Community Quarterly, vol. 11, 1973. Also see Patrick Kyba, "CCMS: The Environmental Connection," International Journal 29 (Spring 1974).

8. Pollack and Congdon, op. cit., p. 687.

9. Organization for Economic Cooperation and Development, Energy Research and Development (Paris: OECD, 1975).

10. See Ford Foundation's Energy Policy Project, A Time to Choose: America's Energy Future (Cambridge, Mass.: Ballinger Pub. Co., 1974), pp. 156-57.

11. See Joseph A. Yager andEleanor B. Steinberg, Energy and U.S. Foreign Policy, (Cambridge, Mass.: Ballinger Pub. Co., 1974), esp pp. 385-915.

12. See Richard B. Mancke, "Petroleum Conspiracy: A Costly Myth," Public Policy (Summer 1974): 8.

13. Ibid.

14. New York Times, December 9, 1973.

15. See "No Rush to Build Refineries," Business Week, (December 15, 1973), p. 36, Prior to President Nixon's decision of May 1, 1973 to abolish oil-import quotas, no new refineries had been built for several years. Following his decision, at least six new refineries were announced as scheduled for completion.

16. See Pollack and Congdon, op. cit., p. 678, for an explication of these specific, short-term policy shifts.

17. See U.S. President, Message to Congress Concerning Energy Resources, (H.R. Doc. No. 85, 93d Cong., 1st sess., April 18, 1973), Richard M. Nixon, 1973.

18. This conceptualization is derived from a fusion of subnational models involving transnational actors and bureaucratic decision models. Essentially, U.S. foreign policy towards multilateral cooperation in energy R and D is characterized as the outcome of a stream of decisions and actions taken by officials in a range of agencies and at several bureaucratic levels. See especially Robert O. Keohane and Joseph S. Nye, Jr. (eds.) Transnational Relations and World Politics, (Cambridge: Harvard University Press, 1972), pp. ix-xxix. See also Graham Allison and Morton Halperin, "Bureaucratic Politics: A Paradigm and Some Policy Implications," World Politics 24 (Spring 1972).

19. For a full development of this argument, see Henry R. Nau, "U.S. Foreign Policy in the Energy Crisis," The Atlantic Community Quarterly 12 (Winter 1974-1975): 426-39.

20. Ibid., pp. 428-29, and Washington Post, June 29, 1975.

21. Washington Post, August 28, 1975.

22. See Address before the Seventh Special Session of the United Nations General Assembly, New York, September 1, 1975, Bureau of Public Affairs, U.S. Department of State.

23. U.S., President, Message to Congress Concerning Energy Resources, (H.R. Doc. No. 85, 93d Cong., 1st sess., April 18, 1973), Richard M. Nixon, 1973.

24. U.S., President, Statement of June 29, 1973, in U.S. Congress, Senate Committee on Interior and Insular Affairs, Presidential Energy Statements, 93d Cong., 1st sess., 1973, (Washington, D.C.: Government Printing Office, 1973).

25. Memorandum from Governor John A. Love, Assistant to the President, to William J. Casey, Under Secretary for Economic Affairs, U.S. Department of State, July 30, 1973. (On file at the U.S. Department of State).

26. Executive Agencies were the Departments of Commerce, Defense, Housing and Urban Development, Interior, State, Transportation, AEC, CIA, CEQ, EPA, NASA, and NSF.

27. See United States Department of State, International Cooperation in Energy Research and Development, A Report to Governor John Love, Director, Federal Energy Office (1973), p.5.

28. Ibid., pp. 10-11.

29. Ibid., p. 4.

30. Ibid., p. 4.

31. Ibid., p. 5.

32. See Department of State Bulletin 69, (December 31, 1973): 781.

33. Ibid., p. 781.

34. Ibid., p. 782.

35. See Department of State Bulletin 70 (February 4, 1974): 123.

36. See President Nixon's invitation to the conference on energy, ibid.

37. Statement by Secretary Kissinger on February 11, 1974, at Washington Energy Conference, See ibid., p. 202.

38. See Department of State Bulletin 70 (January 21, 1974): pp. 48, 223; also see DSB 70 (March 4, 1974): 223, DSB 70 (March 25, 1974): 291.

39. Henry R. Nau, "U.S. Foreign Policy in the Energy Crisis," p. 427.

40. See Nicholas Wade, "Kissinger on Science: Making the Linkage with Diplomacy," Science 184 (May 17, 1974): 180-81.

41. Interview with official at U.S. Atomic Energy Commission, Germantown, Maryland, October 22, 1974.

42. Interview with U.S. State Department official, Washington, D.C., October 8, 1974.

43. This discussion draws on both published and unpublished documentation of U.S. agencies and multiple interviews with agency participants in the R and D discussions. To preserve the confidentiality of the policy process, no references are made to unpublished documentation or to individual respondents. The Appendix displays the number and location of individuals interviewed during the period from October 1974 to May 1975.

44. These issues were discussed during the second meeting of the IEA R and D working group on February 20, 1975.

45. Washington Post, June 29 and July 7, 1975.

46. Those U.S. officials interviewed were almost unanimous in suggesting that there was no need for consultations with industry since each agency knew whether industry was interested or not through their prior domestic program contacts.

47. Interview with U.S. Energy Research and Development Administration (ERDA) official, Germantown, Maryland, May 12, 1975.

48. Ibid., May 12, 1975.

49. These questions were raised during a recent session of the Technical Advisory Board of the Department of Commerce that dealt with "Industrial Participation in International Energy R & D," held May 21, 1975.

50. Interview with official at U.S. Department of the Interior, Washington, D.C., May 13, 1975.

51. Interviews with officials at U.S. AEC, Germantown, Maryland, October 22, 1974, and U.S. Department of the Interior, Washington, D.C., May 13, 1975.

52. Interview with FEA official, Washington, D.C., May 20, 1975.

53. See Energy R and D: Opportunities for International Cooperation. A Background Paper prepared for the Washington Energy Conference, February 11-12, 1974, and Department of State Bulletin, March 4, 1974. Also, interviews with officials at U.S. Department of State, Washington, D.C., May 20, 1975, and USAEC, Germantown, Maryland, October 22, 1974.

54. The Federal Republic of Germany was especially interested in this area.

55. See Address by Secretary of State Henry A. Kissinger before the National Press Club, February 3, 1975, in Washington, D.C.

56. Interview with official at U.S. Energy Research and Development Administration, Germantown, Maryland, May 12, 1975.

57. Ibid., May 12, 1975.

58. Interview with official at U.S. Department of Interior, Washington, D.C., May 13, 1975. See also U.S. Congress, House Science and Technology Committee Subcommittee on Energy Research, Development and Demonstration (Fossil Fuels), 1976 ERDA Authorization and Transition Period—Fossil Fuels, Hearings held February 18, 19, 20, 27, and 28, 1975, pp. 882-83.

59. Interview with EPA representative, Washington, D.C., May 21, 1975, and interview with official from U.S. Department of State, Washington, D.C., May 20, 1975.

60. Interview with U.S. ERDA official, Washington, D.C., May 23, 1975. According to members of House Science and Technology Committee, the likelihood of EPA acquiring funds to build a

rival domestic fluidized bed facility is very slim. ERDA officials, on the other hand, felt that EPA might be able to build its own domestic facility, since "EPA has some very powerful friends." EPA has been engaged in fluidized bed combustion technology since 1967. See EPA, Office of Energy Researh "Fluidized-Bed Combustion Program", mimeographed, paper prepared by the Mitre Corporation, March 1975.

    61. Interview with official at U.S. Department of State, Washington, D.C., May 20, 1975, and interview with ERDA official, Washington, D.C., October 10, 1975.

    62. Interview with EPA representative, Washington, D.C., May 19, 1975. The HUD representative was unavailable for comment on this area of possible cooperation.

    63. See O.E.C.D., Energy R & D, (Paris: OECD, 1975), p. 225.

    64. Interview with FEA representative, Washington, D.C., May 9, 1975.

    65. Interview with ERDA official, Washington, D.C., May 12, 1975.

    66. Interview with FEA representative, Washington, D.C., May 9, 1975.

    67. Interview with HUD official, Washington, D.C., May 16, 1975.

    68. See O.E.C.D., Energy R&D, (Paris: OECD, 1975), pp. 227-30.

    69. The source for the assertion is a note by the U.S. government to the IEA/SLT/ERD on February 20, 1975.

    70. Energy Coordinating Group, "Terms of Reference," (ECG/5), (Brussels, February 24, 1974). Terms of reference for the other eight working groups were also presented.

    71. Ibid.

    72. See Energy Coordinating Group, Ad Hoc Group on Energy R & D, "Minutes of First Meeting," (Brussels, March 14, 1974), ECG/ERD/3).

    73. U.S. Atomic Energy Commission, Memorandum for the Record, "Ad Hoc Group on Energy R & D Meeting in Brussels," (Washington, D.C., March 25, 1974).

    74. Department of State Telegram, March 25, 1974, to Secretary of State Henry A. Kissinger (Summary of ECG/ERD Group Meeting).

    75. See "Report of the Juelich Working Group," (ECG/ERD/11), (Brussels, April 4, 5, 1974). Canada and Italy did not submit a report at this time. Luxembourg's report to the OECD questionnaire indicated that it was not conducting R & D in the energy field.

    76. Ibid.

    77. U.S. Atomic Energy Commission, Memorandum for the Record, "ECG Ad Hoc Group on Energy R & D," (Brussels, April 8, 10, 1974).

78. Ibid. For example, the United States pushed the adoption of fusion as a priority area; the Germans were interested in hydrogen production and waste heat utilization; OECD was interested in and involved in research in overall energy systems analysis, and so on. Also, this was confirmed in an interview at U.S. Atomic Energy Commission, Germantown, Maryland, October 22, 1974.

79. See Energy Coordinating Group, "Summary Minutes of the Third Meeting of Ad Hoc Group on Energy R & D," (ECG/ERC/15), (Brussels, April 8, 1974). In addition to these areas for possible cooperation, a "B" list was also developed for which individual nations were encouraged to further discuss possible cooperation. See Energy Coordinating Group, "International Cooperation on Energy R & D," Final Report, June 6, 1974.

80. See U.S. AEC, Memorandum for the Record, "Meeting of Agency Representatives on International Energy R & D," Washington, D.C., April 10, 1974). The U.S. proposals on fusion and nuclear safety were prepared by the AEC, and the conservation proposals by FEA.

81. See U.S. AEC, Memorandum for the Record, "Meeting of ECG Ad Hoc Group on R & D,: (Washington, D.C., April 25, 1974).

82. See U.S. AEC, Memorandum for the Record, "U.S. Experts Attending ECG Ad Hoc R and D Group Meeting," (Washington, D.C., May 10, 1974).

83. See Energy Coordinating Group, "Report of the Expert Group," (ECG/ERD/43-52), (Brussels, May 10-14, 1974).

84. Energy Coordinating Group, "Summary Minutes of the Ad Hoc Group," (ECG/ERD/53), (Brussels, May 15, 1974).

85. Interview with official at U.S. Department of State, Washington, D.C., October 8, 1974.

86. See U.S. AEC, Memorandum for the Record, "Ad Hoc Group on Energy R & D Meeting in Brussels," (Washington, D.C., March 25, 1974).

87. See address of Secretary Kissinger before the Washington Energy Conference, Department of State of State Bulletin 70 (March 4, 1974).

88. The source document for this assertion is not available for attribution.

89. See U.S. Atomic Energy Commission, Memorandum for the Record, "ECG Ad Hoc Energy R & D, Group Activities," Washington, D.C., May 15, 1974).

90. See Energy Coordinating Group, "International Cooperation on Energy R & D," Final Report, June 6, 1974.

91. U.S. AEC, Memorandum for the Record, "ECG Ad Hoc Energy R & D Activities," (Washington, D.C., May 15, 1974).

92. U.S. AEC, Memorandum for the Record, "Meeting of ECG/ERD," (Washington, D.C., March 25, 1974).

93. U.S. AEC, Memorandum for the Record, "Conclusion of Work of ECG/ERD," (Washington, D.C., June 11, 1974).

94. Interview with U.S. AEC official, Germantown, Maryland, October 22, 1974.

95. Interview with U.S. ERDA official, Washington, D.C., May 12, 1975 and October 10, 1975.

96. See U.S. AEC Ad Hoc Group on R & D," Washington, D.C., April 25, 1974).

97. Washington Post, September 21, 1974, and New York Times, September 30, 1974.

98. See Energy Coordinating Group, "International Cooperation on Energy R and D," Final Report, June 6, 1974.

99. Interview at U.S. Department of State, October 8, 1974. The IEA was established as a permanent, autonomous body under the auspices of the OECD to implement the IEP. A system of weighted voting for decision-making purposes was established under which the United States holds 34 percent of the combined weighted votes. Most decisions will be made by a majority requiring 60 percent of the total combined voting weights as well as the votes of at least eight countries. More stringent voting majorities have been established to prevent the activation of the emergency program and oil sharing commitments in the face of a general embargo. Decisions involving new obligations on participating countries require unanimous approval.

100. See Agreement on an International Energy Program, chap-IX, Article 49, p. 28.

101. Ibid., chapter VII, Article 42, p. 25.

102. See U.S. ERDA, "Summary Minutes of IEA/SLT/ERD," (Washington, D.C., February 21, 1975).

103. See Henry A. Kissinger, "Energy: The Necessity of Decision," An Address by Secretary of State Henry A. Kissinger before the National Press Club, Washington, D.C., February 3, 1975.

104. See U.S. ERDA, "Summary Minutes of Third Meeting of IEA/SLT/ERD," (Washington, D.C., March 20, 1975).

105. Ibid.

106. Ibid.

107. Ibid.

108. See U.S. Department of State, Telegram from IEA R&D Subgroup, May 7, 1975. (On file at U.S. Department of State).

109. See U.S. ERDA, "Summary Minutes of SLT/ERD," (Washington, D.C., February 20, 1975). The CCMS project in conservation includes cooperation in waste heat and waste heat utilization. This project was implemented in 1974.

110. Ibid.

111. This conern was expressed in a government memorandum not available for attribution.

112. See U.S. ERDA, "Summary Minutes of Third Meeting of IEA/SLT/ERD," (Washington, D.C., March 20, 1975).

113. Ibid.

114. Ibid.

115. U.S. ERDA "Summary Minutes of SLT/ERD," (Washington, D.C., February 20, 1975).

116. Ibid.

117. See U.S. Congress, House Science and Technology Committee, Subcommittee on Domestic and International Scientific Planning and Analysis, U.S.-U.S.S.R. Cooperative Agreements, Hearings held November 20, 1975, pp. 224-27.

118. This characteristic behavior of government bureaucracies is fully discussed in Aaron Wildavsky, The Politics of the Budgetary Process (Boston: Little, Brown and Company, 1964).

119. See the administrative issues discussed at the intragovernmental level of analysis.

CHAPTER

6

BAUXITE-ALUMINUM INDUSTRY: U.S. TECHNOLOGY TRANSFER TO RESOURCE-RICH DEVELOPING COUNTRIES

Mary M. Allen

The case study in aluminum-bauxite affords a look at the politics of raw materials supply and the role of technology transfer, primarily through the private industrial sector, as a potential mechanism to guarantee future access to stable raw materials supplies. It examines current trends toward nationalization, cartelization, and other economic actions on the part of resource-rich developing countries and the resultant capacity of these countries to purchase advanced technology with higher foreign exchange revenues.

The aluminum-bauxite case study, like the overall technology transfer discussion in this book, follows a framework of issues and actors, looking first at the different perspectives which bear on the particular issue-area and then at the implications of these perspectives for individual actors and mechanisms (direct investment, and so on) involved in technology transfer. The actors in this case are the U.S. government, the U.S. aluminum industry, and foreign bauxite suppliers. Specifically, the case study examines the role of technology transfer in the development of an international industry and in the potential reconfiguration of that industry through cartelization and/or other economic structures of bauxite production by developing countries. The context in which the change may occur involves 1) the increasing hostility of foreign bauxite-supplying countries toward U.S. direct investment manifested in the wholly-owned subsidiary; 2) increased competition for bauxite resources; and 3) increasing demands of supplying countries for technology as payment for secure access to bauxite supplies. The issues include the economics of substitution, supply and demand, foreign investment, and trade policy. National security and foreign policy issues are also examined.

Trends are identified which suggest possible shifts in industry-government relationships within the United States and in industry-foreign supplier relationships. An example of the latter is the increased willingness of aluminum companies to accept partnerships with minority equity ownership in which they provide the needed technology to supplier countries in return for continued management and market access to raw material supplies. An example of the former is the possibility of government-industry programs to develop domestic nonbauxitic supplies as an alternative to bauxite imports from unreliable foreign suppliers.

BAUXITE SUPPLIES AND U.S. INTERESTS

Over the past two years, developing mineral-exporting countries have been speaking increasingly with one voice in international forums calling for a "new international economic order." On May 4, 1975, the United Nations General Assembly adopted the "Declaration on the Establishment of a New International Economic Order" proclaiming a new international economic order "based on equity, sovereign equality, interdependence, common interest and cooperation among all States."[1] The document further declared the following principles with regard to raw materials.

> Full permanent sovereignty of every state over its natural resources and all economic activities. In order to safeguard these resources, each state is entitled to exercise effective control over them and their exploitation with means suitable to its own situation, including the right to nationalization or transfer of ownership to its nationals . . .
> Just and equitable relationship between the prices of raw materials, primary commodities, manufactured and semi-manufactured goods exported by developing countries and the prices of raw materials, primary commodities, manufactures, capital goods and equipment imported by them . . .
> Facilitation of the role which producers' associations may play within the framework of international cooperation . . .[2]

On December 12, 1974, the "Charter of Economic Rights and Duties of States" (CERD) was adopted by the General Assembly.[3] This document listed specific rights and duties of states in promoting and establishing the new international economic order. Among these rights is the right of states to nationalize foreign property. If controversy over such nationalization should develop, the Charter recognizes the right of the nationalizing state to settle the dispute under the latter's domestic laws, implying no recourse to international law.

These documents suggest the changing relationship between political (world peace and reduction of world tensions) and economic issues (that is, price, demand, and supply of commodities) in the present international system. Today, economic, as opposed to security, issues are providing the reasons for political tensions between states or rather, between groups of states.

In the past, the economic system reflected the political predominance of the United States. The United States, however, is no longer the dominant member of the economic system. Western Europe and Japan have recovered from the ravages of World War II and are competing with the United States for world markets and resources; the Eastern bloc is increasing economic relations with Western countries; and, as illustrated above, developing countries are demanding a more equitable position in the economic system.

Given these circumstances, it has been suggested that the United States may no longer be able to obtain unhindered access to necessary raw material supplies from developing countries, especially through the multinational company. The recent oil shortage is seen as an example of this phenomenon. The options for the United States then must include resource independence, if that is practical, or cooperation in some form: either with other developed consumer countries or with developing producer countries.

Thus far, the response of the U. S. government to this new situation has been hesitant. Traditionally, the United States has been reluctant to support commodity agreements. As long as prices of imported commodities were low, the United States as an importing country had little incentive to favor price agreements. Mineral-exporting developing countries were the principal advocates of price stabilization schemes. Now that commodity prices have gone up and may go higher, importing countries are also considering stabilization schemes such as price floors, and so on. At the United Nations Seventh Special Session in September 1975, Secretary of State Kissinger announced that the United States was ready "to discuss new arrangements in individual commodities on a case-by-case basis."[4]

This chapter attempts to examine the changing relationship between the United States and developing, mineral-exporting countries and the implications of this change for technology transfer. In particular, it examines the bauxite-aluminum industry which, because of its importance to an industrial society and the special issues regarding security of bauxite supply, illustrates the problems of access to raw materials in a changing world economic order. The prospect arises that advanced consumer countries such as the United States may purchase access to future raw material markets through the transfer of industrial technology to supplier countries.

Before focusing on bauxite, however, it is necessary to compare bauxite with other raw material commodities and to suggest the unique and general significance of a case study of bauxite for commodity issues as a whole.

In considering the importance of the problem of raw material supplies to the United States one fact should be kept in mind: over two-thirds of the U.S. industrial raw material imports come from Canada, Australia, South Africa, and other developed countries.[5] Therefore, an improved relationship with the developing world is not essential in order to secure adequate raw materials for U.S. industry and may explain the reluctance of the U.S. government to intervene in markets for raw materials. However, the United States is dependent on developing country imports for selected critical commodities including bauxite, manganese, tin, natural rubber, and cobalt. The first three of these are included among the 13 basic raw materials deemed critical to a highly industrialized society.[6]

In order to appreciate the context in which problems of bauxite supply may be applicable to other commodities, it is necessary to divide imported raw materials into three categories according to source of origin: imports from developed countries; imports from developing countries; and imports from oil-rich countries, which is a separate case of the previous category (for reasons given below). This study is not concerned with the first category of imports and should not be judged applicable to natural products within that category. It is also less relevant to oil imports than to other imports from developing countries. To understand this latter point, let us look at some of the similarities and dissimilarities between bauxite and oil, and bauxite and other commodities imported from developing countries.

The United States imports both oil and bauxite from developing countries (for origin of U.S. imports of bauxite, see Appendix, Table A.5). In addition, the price of bauxite, like oil, was artificially raised to a level beyond that which might have been expected under free market conditions.[7] Beyond these two facts, however, there is little similarity between the two commodities. Bauxite does not approach petroleum in terms of its significance to the U.S. economy. According to a report by the Council on International Economy Policy issued in December 1974 "our petroleum imports amounted to $7.5 billion in 1973, or 11 percent of our total imports, compared to $0.7 billion (about 1 percent) for iron ore, our second ranking net import." By contrast, bauxite imports totalled $0.143 billion or one quarter of one percent of our total imports.[8] Furthermore, bauxite price increases do not increase the prices of the end products as much as crude oil prices. For example, bauxite, as a raw material input, contributed only 7 percent to the total selling price (excluding retail sales taxes) of aluminum in 1974, while crude oil contributed 85 percent to the total selling price of heavy fuel, 55 percent to the price of home heating oil, and 40 percent to the total selling price of gasoline.[9]

A final difference between oil and bauxite involves the ability of producers to disrupt supply by embargoes or cartel-like action. Two reasons seem to rule out an embargo by bauxite producers in contrast to oil producers: lack of unifying political objective and lack of sufficient foreign exchange reserves to carry out an embargo without great internal hardship.[10] Opinions differ on the possibilities of cartel action on the part of the International Bauxite Association (IBA).[11] However, the view of Australian Deputy Prime Minister Jim Cairns that controlling worldwide prices of bauxite is neither desirable nor feasible[12] assures the United States of at least one powerful ally in IBA.

Comparisons can be drawn between bauxite and other imported commodities from developing countries with respect to current market structure and trends (in terms of demand and supply), the possibilities for commodity agreements, and the possibilities for cartel-like action. The following comparisons for bauxite, manganese and tin, the three critical industrial materials for which the United States is dependent on developing countries, serve to emphasize differences between commodities within the category of imports from developing countries.[13]

U.S. aluminum demand is expected to increase in excess of 6 percent annually through 1980. Since bauxite demand is directly related to aluminum demand, bauxite should be in the short run relatively insensitive to price changes. However, in many applications, depending on relative prices, magnesium, copper, steel, zinc, wood, and plastics could be used as substitutes for aluminum. Thus, over the long run, substitution for aluminum products could reduce demand for aluminum and bauxite, making these commodities more sensitive to price. By contrast, there are no satisfactory substitutes for metallurgical grade manganese in its use as a desulfurizing agent in steel production. Over the next five to ten years manganese consumption is expected to increase 2.5 to 3.5 percent annually. There are many substitutes for tin in its final uses, but some of these substitutes (such as steel, glass, aluminum) are themselves in short supply. Demand is likely to remain strong with some slackening of demand for tin solder (for which there is no satisfactory substitute).

TABLE 6.1

U.S. Net Imports of Bauxite, Manganese, and Tin

Commodity	Net Imports as Percent 1973 Consumption*	Major Suppliers (percent)	
Bauxite	90	Jamaica (54)	Surinam (23)
Manganese	82	Gabon (35)	Brazil (33)
Tin	65	Malaysia (64)	Thailand (27)

*In quantity terms. Calculated by dividing net imports by total consumption. In some cases consumption includes withdrawals from government and/or private stocks.

Source: Special Report: Critical Imported Materials, Council on International Economic Policy (December 1974), p. 24.

In terms of supply, world reserves of bauxite, manganese, and tin are very large, but few reserves are available in the United States. Table 6.1 summarizes U.S. imports of these commodities.

Despite heavy dependence on developing countries for imports of these materials, the individual situations differ. Substitutes exist in the United States for bauxite which could become competitive if bauxite prices were increased substantially (see below). This situation does not obtain for manganese and tin. Another difference is the ratio of reserves to current production worldwide. For bauxite, current major producers do not hold the largest reserves (see Appendix, Table A.4). This means that the option of switching to alternative suppliers is open. The USSR possesses about one-third of total manganese reserves. Production could be increased rapidly in the USSR and other suppliers if necessary. In the longer run, ocean seabeds could be an important source of manganese—a fact which has complicated efforts to create an international regime for the exploitation of the deep seabeds. With the exception of Brazil (which is believed to have significant undeveloped reserves), world tin reserves are distributed among producers roughly in proportion to their current production capacity.

The only commodity price agreement in existence today is the International Tin Agreement which has just been negotiated and includes all major producers and consumers. The United States has signed the new agreement but it must still be approved by Congress.[14] The strength of the Tin Agreement lies in the fact that both producers and consumers have been sufficiently interested in price stability to finance a buffer stock which buys when world price falls and sells when it rises. Producers are required to impose export controls if such action is deemed necessary by the International Tin Council. The United States retains some leverage in its ability to sell tin from its strategic stockpile if U.S. industry is forced to pay exorbitant prices.

Recently, the Economic Policy Board concluded that it is not possible to construct a commodity agreement for bauxite. What are the differences between tin and bauxite that account for this conclusion? One reason is that the tin industry is not vertically integrated like the aluminum industry. Hence there are open exchanges and numerous buyers for tin which renders the marketing job easier for tin producers.[15] This situation can be contrasted with the aluminum industry in which outlets for bauxite are controlled by a few major firms (for data on integration of aluminum industry, see Appendix). In addition, the price of bauxite varies considerably due to differing quality and transportation costs thus making it technically difficult to establish ceiling and floor prices.

Cartel-like action is not expected for either tin or manganese. In the case of tin, substitutes and conservation potential rule out an effective cartel. The diversity of manganese producers and possibility of seabed recovery of manganese dictate against cartel-like action for that mineral.

Factors affecting the possibility of success for cartel-like action on the part of bauxite producers can be categorized as internal to the International Bauxite Association and internal to the United States. In the long term, substitutes for both aluminum and bauxite are available for U.S. industry thereby negating the effect of cartel-like action. Within IBA, divergent strategies have divided bauxite producers and reduced the possibility of a cartel. These differences can be seen by comparing Australia and Jamaica. Australia's share of world reserves of bauxite exceeds its share of current world production while exactly the opposite holds for Jamaica (see Appendix, Table A.4). Therefore Australia, as a reserve country, seeks to keep the price of bauxite down in order to expand production and avoid forcing consumers to use substitutes. On the other hand Jamaica, as a current producing country, seeks to keep the price up and exploit its diminishing reserves while it can. The reasons for this are suggested by Zuhayr Mikdashi:

> . . . a price-raising or output restricting commodity agreement may still be a good idea (for commodities with substitutes), even if it encourages a search for substitutes, since it would yield larger foreign exchange receipts in the short-run which the producing countries could put to good use by

diversifying their economies, and increasing flexibility and productive capacity . . . Some developing countries have reason to fear that their natural resources could face market obsolescence resulting from technological changes, which may explain their desire to exploit the market rapidly.[16]

This does indeed seem to be the strategy of Prime Minister Manley of Jamaica. However, it is doubtful a bauxite cartel could succeed without the cooperation of the reserve countries such as Australia, Guinea, and Brazil.

The ensuing discussion takes a closer look at these prospects for cartelization, as well as other issues and options raised for U.S. government and industry policy in the bauxite-aluminum sector.

INTERNATIONAL BAUXITE ASSOCIATION

Although the phenomenon of cartel formation is ostensibly economic, it is a function of governmental policy-making as well. The ramifications can effect an entire economy (witness the results of the oil cartel) and therefore tend to be discussed, if not resolved, in the political sphere. With regard to bauxite, an economic action has given rise to various political and economic issues which have had an impact upon both governmental and industrial policy-making.

The International Bauxite Association (IBA) was established in March 1974, in Conakry, Guinea as a "producers' association." The original seven members—Australia, Jamaica, Surinam, Guyana, Sierra Leone, Guinea, and Yugoslavia—have been joined by the Dominican Republic, Haiti, and Ghana. Together, they control approximately 75 percent of the world's production of bauxite. According to the final act of the conference in Guinea, the objectives of the IBA are spelled out in Article III:

(a) to promote the orderly and rational development of the bauxite industry;
(b) to secure for member countries fair and reasonable returns from the exploitation, processing and marketing of bauxite and its products for the economic and social development of their peoples bearing in mind the recognized interests of consumers;
(c) generally to safeguard the interests of member countries in relation to the bauxite industry.[17]

Nowhere in the final act is there provision for a common price for bauxite. Indeed, the association seemed to stimulate a unilateral, rather than an association-wide set of actions to improve the position of the bauxite producers relative to the foreign aluminum companies. In March 1974, Jamaica began renegotiations on contracts with the six aluminum companies operating there. The companies included Alcan, Alcoa, Revere, Alpart (a consortium of Reynolds, Kaiser, and Anaconda), Kaiser, and Reynolds. In June 1974, in the middle of these negotiations, the Jamaican government imposed an increase in the tax on bauxite from $2.50 a ton to $11.72 a ton and the royalty from 28 cents a ton to 56 cents a ton retroactive to January 1, 1974. The "Jamaican formula" calculated the levy on bauxite as a fixed percentage of the fluctuating price of its end product, aluminum ingot, so that Jamaica's take was indexed against inflation (and would drop if the price of ingot dropped).[18] Since then, the governments of Guyana, Surinam, the Dominican Republic, Haiti, and Guinea have also imposed stiffer levies. The fact that Australia has not is important since it is one of the principal countries with large reserves in excess of current production (see Appendix, Table A.4) and could therefore become an alternate source of supply.

At the November 1974 IBA meeting in Georgetown, Guyana, no firm decisions were made in the areas of pricing and taxation. Instead the question was referred to a group of specialists who began considering possible formulas. On March 10, 1975, the executive board of IBA began a week of closed sessions aimed at "organizing" the price member countries receive for their bauxite. The board's apparent objective is to see if it is possible to develop a common formula to set the price of any given bauxite ore. According to the Wall Street Journal:

> Apparently the association has already decided it can't impose a single floor price for all bauxite. Instead, sources say, each country's deposits would be valued by a complex formula that would account for variables such as the quality of the bauxite, the distance of the deposit from its market and the mining costs.[19]

The development of such a formula involves the examination and comparison of "reams of technical information" gathered from each country. A formal decision based on the results of this study is not expected until November of 1975, when the top ministers of the ten member countries hold their annual meeting.

IBA, as well as OPEC, testifies to the increasing confrontation between rich consumers and poor producers in various international forums. At the Paris meeting in April 1975, oil consumers and producers fell out with one another over the issue of linking energy with other raw material commodities and indexing raw material prices to prices of manufactured goods. At the conference of 33 British Commonwealth nations in Jamaica on April 29, 1975, Guyana's Prime Minister, Forbes Burnham, speaking for the Caribbean nations, stressed the need to link commodity prices to those of industrialized products and to remove trade barriers on goods from developing nations.[20]

The situation described above and demands for what is becoming known as a "new international economic order" give added significance to the issues associated with aluminum-bauxite supply. Below we discuss these issues in greater detail, first in terms of their substantive character and then in terms of the interests and policies of the three principal actors in the aluminum-bauxite drama - the United States government, the foreign suppliers, and the U.S. aluminum industry.

DOMESTIC ECONOMIC ISSUES
FOR THE UNITED STATES

Supply

On the supply side, the topic generally stressed is the research and development of domestic, nonbauxitic sources of aluminum. This subject is well documented by Congressional and Bureau of Mines sources.[21] There is little doubt in anyone's mind that alternative sources should be developed. However, there are varying opinions as to whether the U.S. government should intervene in the support of such R and D efforts through subsidies or other price mechanisms. Another factor is whether the threat to develop alternative sources should be used primarily as a bargaining tool to put a ceiling on bauxite producers' price increases or whether this development should be pursued as a viable commercial undertaking.

Recently, economic stockpiles have received attention as a possible means of insuring security of supply for some key materials. This is another indication of the shift in emphasis from national security to economic issues in U.S. resource policy. Stockpiles in the past have been justified only on strategic grounds. A bill was introduced in the 93rd Congress to amend the Strategic and Critical Stock Piling Act for the purpose of applying the provisions of that act to materials needed to prevent disruption of the national economy, specifically, "when significant shortages of these materials threaten to disrupt, or are disrupting output and employment in domestic manufacturing or agriculture, or both."[22] The bill was not acted upon in the 93rd Congress, mainly due to a fundamental disagreement over the advisability of interfering in the free market system. This domestic pattern of opposition to managed markets contrasts to the movement away from a free market in the international sphere (for example, the formation of resource cartels). Nevertheless, if an economic stockpile could be agreed upon, it would serve many purposes:[23]

1) providing (future) governmental income through sales;
2) stimulating the supply of scarce materials by guaranteeing the market price during times of decreasing demand;
3) providing buffer stocks of scarce materials, that is, government purchase of excess supply to stabilize prices;
4) stimulating domestic production from new sources by maintaining a price level through 2) and 3) above;
5) deterring threats from foreign cartels and consortia by maintaining buffer stocks as a bargaining tool; and
6) providing incentives for new large-scale recycling ventures and technologies.

The third major issue on the supply side is that of recycling. Only 4 to 5 percent of old scrap (after the aluminum has been discarded by the consumer) is now recycled. The President of the Aluminum Association, David P. Reynolds, called on the industry to lift the annual metal supply through recycling by one billion pounds a year instead of the present rate of 660 million pounds. He added "It would save mining and importing 2 million tons of bauxite and, based on today's most efficient smelting requirements it would save about 6.5 billion kilowatt hours of electrical energy. And, at today's cost, it would save a capital investment of at least $1 billion."[24]

As indicated above in the remark of David Reynolds, electrical energy consumption is a prime consideration in the production of aluminum (especially in the smelter from the alumina to the aluminum states - see Appendix). This fact can and does determine to a large extent the location of aluminum smelters. Government estimates indicate that energy costs account for 23 percent of the price of finished aluminum products.[25] Industry is researching the possibility of utilizing new energy-saving smelting processes, but implementation seems to be some time away. An example of these new processes is the Toth-Pechiney process in which aluminum chloride from bauxite or clay reacts with hot manganese to produce aluminum.[26]

Two related issues on the supply side are cost and substitution for bauxite. According to the Senate Government Operations Committee print on aluminum, industry and government officials believe the price of producing a ton of alumina from imported bauxite is "approaching, if not equal to, the cost of recovering a ton of alumina from one of the more promising domestic alternatives."[27]

Demand

The primary emphasis within U.S. industry and government has historically been on the supply side of the question. Even in contrast to oil, there has been little concern for conservation in the bauxite sector. However, if a situation of short supply should develop, conservation may take on more importance. Trends in this direction might include the diversion of raw material from such consumer uses as aluminum wrapping paper - a strategy already followed by one major aluminum company.

Another fact of conservation is improving the efficiency of aluminum usage. One way to achieve this is to reduce the amount of new scrap which results in the fabricating plant when new metal is shaped and extruded to form finished or semfinished products.

Finally, since the demand for aluminum is moderately elastic (that is, sensitive to changes in price), widespread substitution would eventually occur if the relative price of aluminum were to rise significantly. As we noted, depending on relative prices, magnesium, copper, steel, zinc, wood, and plastics could be substituted for aluminum.[28]

FOREIGN ECONOMIC ISSUES FOR THE UNITED STATES

Foreign economic issues center around the U.S. balance of payments with regard to U.S. imports of bauxite and the export of U.S. investment to Caribbean nations. Historically, since the mining operations of U.S. companies in the Caribbean have been wholly-owned subsidiaries, technology has been transferred to these nations within the multinational company. Mining facilities operated as a branch of a foreign parent usually contribute little technology to other sectors of the developing country.[29] With the new arrangements negotiated by Jamaica, a new trend may appear, with a trade account deficit as a result of higher bauxite prices, a retrenchment of U.S. investment as aluminum companies assess the higher risks involved in investing in bauxite-supplying countries, and an outflow of process technology to facilities controlled and owned by the Caribbean countries. The issues of trade policy, investment, and technology transfer are summarized below.

Trade Policy

The Trade Act signed by President Ford on January 3, 1975 grants authority to the president to engage in multilateral trade negotiations aimed at reducing trade barriers and overhauling world trade rules. The trade bill also contains a retaliatory provision which can be used against those countries engaging in cartel-like action by denying them trade preferences. This provision could be used against the members of IBA if their actions discriminate against U.S. import purchases.

In another development, the Ford Administration is reassessing commodity agreements in preparation for the reopening of the General Agreement on Tariffs and Trade (GATT) negotiations. As we noted, the Economic Policy Board judged bauxite to be unsuited for a traditional commodity agreement with a buffer stock. Consequently, bauxite has not been singled out as one of the highest priority items for negotiations. According to government sources, no crisis presently exists with regard to supply.

Investment

The area of investments also encompasses the issues of technology transfer and government guarantees of investment abroad. Government guarantees in the past have included a depletion allowance (22 percent domestic and 14 percent foreign), the Western Hemisphere Trade Corporation and the Overseas Private Investment Corporation. The main variable is the changing investment and technology transfer patterns which are evolving between the foreign bauxite producers and the aluminum companies. In Jamaica, for example, bauxite operations have traditionally been wholly-owned by parent companies. At present Jamaica is negotiating contracts with the aluminum companies in which the Jamaican government will own at least 51 percent of the equity of separate mining operations being established. Agreements have been reached with Revere, Kaiser, and Reynolds. As a result of this type of arrangement and the availability of minority shares in joint government operations (such as the Mexican-Jamaican venture discussed below) the question arises as to whether American companies will be as willing to transfer technology if denied equity control. Will there be a progression from the wholly-owned subsidiary tactic to joint ventures or some licensing arrangement? Will divestment occur as aluminum companies concentrate on producing aluminum from domestic sources?

Technology Transfer

As noted above, technology has been transferred to Caribbean countries largely through the mechanism of wholly-owned subsidiaries. As a result of recent actions by Jamaica and Guyana, U.S. companies no longer own majority equity shares in the mining operations located in those countries. Guyana has nationalized all operations, while the agreements between the aluminum companies and Jamaica leave the latter 51 percent equity ownership. If U.S. companies take an interest in ventures in which they do not have equity control, there is a possibility that technology may be transferred in the future without direct investment. In other words, the U.S. aluminum industry may concentrate on selling technology and services to bauxite suppliers and on purchasing from them finished aluminum products rather than bauxite (see section on "U.S. Aluminum Industry Options"). This strategy entails the risk of loss of proprietary technology with accompanying loss of foreign markets, a decline in U.S. exports, loss of American jobs, and general economic malaise. Much would depend on the price at which technology and services are sold to foreign suppliers. This is an issue we discuss at considerable length in chapters 3 and 8 of this study.

NATIONAL SECURITY ISSUES FOR THE UNITED STATES

The strategic stockpile is the focus of attention in this area. The stockpile as it exists today is a combination of two principal inventories of strategic and critical materials:

1. The National Stockpile established under the Strategic and Critical Materials Stock Piling Act of June, 1939 (amended in July, 1946) to "avoid dangerous and costly dependence on foreign sources of materials for meeting essential needs in limited war . . . and general war. . ."[30]

2. The Defense Production Act (DPA) Inventory established by the Defense Production Act of 1950 which provides broad authority for meeting national security needs, including (a) the expansion of

productive industrial capacity; (b) the making of purchases and commitments to purchase metals, minerals, or other materials; and (c) the encouragement of exploration, development, and mining of strategic and critical minerals and metals.[31]

The Director of the Office of Preparedness, General Services Administration (GSA), has had the responsibility of administering the stockpile since July 1, 1973. Previously, this was the function of the Office of Emergency Planning. Goals and procedures for administering the stockpile are based on guidance from the National Security Council and on advice from other executive agencies having competence in estimating requirements and supply. The National Stockpile requires authorizations from Congress for disposal while the DPA Inventory is under the sole authority of GSA.

The primary issue revolves around whether the present one-year stockpile requirement (instituted by President Nixon on April 16, 1973) is adequate for defense purposes. On March 5, 1975, the Subcommittee on Seapower and Strategic and Critical Materials of the House Committee on Armed Services approved the use of a three-year objective (as existed before April 1973) for stockpiles.

To date, the objectives for aluminum, Surinam-grade bauxite, and refratory-grade bauxite are zero, while the objective for refractory-grade bauxite is 4,638,000 long dry tons (see Appendix, Table A.9). The General Accounting Office has recommended that Congress authorize no further disposals until a review of stockpile objectives has taken place.

FOREIGN DIPLOMATIC ISSUES FOR THE UNITED STATES

The foreign policy of the United States in relation to developing nations must adapt to the realities of Third World alliances. After the success of OPEC, numerous conferences provided occasions for alliance-building. In addition to examples cited above, the New York Times reported on February 6, 1975, that "Ministers from 110 third-world nations meeting at Dakar in a conference on raw materials established a special commission to set out guidelines on products ranging from aluminum and bananas to peanuts and zinc." A sample of newspaper headlines accentuates the situation:

"Major Commodity Exporters Ask OPEC Aid in Stabilizing Prices" (New York Times, March 4, 1974);
"Latin American Bargaining Unit Urged—Mexico and Caracas Plan Price Defense of Raw Materials" (New York Times, April 21, 1975);

"Gulf Widens in Viewpoints of Rich and Poor Nations" (Washington Post, April 20, 1975).

This changing economic order has already elicited a response from the U.S. government in the form of the Trade Bill passed in the 93rd Congress. This bill gives the President the power to deny tariff concessions to countries engaging in OPEC-like cartel activities. This retaliation measure has already strained relations with Latin America as a result of the exclusion of Venezuela and Ecuador from concessions because of their membership in OPEC.

Another issue involves development assistance policies. In 1942 the U.S. government created an institution known as a "Western Hemisphere Trade Corporation" (WHTC) within the Internal Revenue Code to encourage U.S. industry to invest in Latin America. This was meant to assist Latin American economic development. In order to qualify, the company must be a U.S. based company which conducts all its business in the western hemisphere, receives 95 percent of its gross income from outside the United States, and receives 90 percent of its gross income from active conduct of trade or business.[32] The following quote explains the mechanics of this and other tax incentives as they affect aluminum industries in Jamaica:

> While there is no way to determine exactly how the companies operate, statistics suggest that they operate as branches (or file consolidated returns) and very possibly as Western Hemisphere Trade Corporations. A Western Hemisphere Trade Corporation is a domestic (not a foreign) corporation, meaning that there is no deferral of income or payment of dividends. Western Hemisphere Trade Corporations are allowed a special deduction which reduces their tax rate from 48% to 34%.
>
> Western Hemisphere Trade Corporations are also allowed to take percentage depletion (14% for foreign mined bauxite) which a foreign subsidiary cannot take. Also, they are eligible for the foreign tax credit.[33]
>
> The latest published statistics for foreign income are for 1964 and show four returns filed in the primary metals industry which had income from Jamaica. These four returns had $44,534 thousand in taxable income from Jamaica and paid $8,791 thousand in taxes. No dividends were received. These four companies may be assumed to be the aluminum companies operating in

Jamaica, particularly since total taxable income received by all corporations from Jamaica was only $44,702 thousand. The Western Hemisphere Trade Corporation deduction for all companies which had operations in Jamaica was $15,551 thousand. If all four companies had taken the WHTC deduction then an implied deduction would have been a little over $17,000.

The data above then suggests that the aluminum companies operate in Jamaica as Western Hemisphere Trading Corporations, that they do not defer income in subsidiaries and that at least at that time Jamaican taxes did not exceed the U.S. rate of 48%, but were instead around 20%.[34]

If the U.S. government alters such tax incentives, or if aluminum companies decide to divest regardless of tax incentives, Jamaica would be deprived of substantial revenue. The point is then made that the government should continue tax incentives and discourage divestment (that is, by not subsidizing the aluminum industry's R and D to develop alternative domestic resources). This would mean that Jamaica would not be deprived of income and thus Jamaica (or other Caribbean nations) would not petition the United States for foreign assistance. This point was emphasized by a statement from one congressional researcher: "How rational is it for the U.S. Government to make the U.S. aluminum industry self-sufficient and then turn around and give the foreign suppliers foreign aid because we have deprived them of their revenue?"

The above issues are obviously interrelated and involve the perceptions and actions of the three aggregated actors (the U.S. government, the U.S. aluminum industry, and the foreign bauxite suppliers). The following section attempts to examine the situation from the different viewpoint of each actor to sort out the ambiguities which exist.

U.S. GOVERNMENT OPTIONS

Perceptions of the U.S. government are divided into congressional and executive branch viewpoints. While there are a few differences in details, the overall impression is the same: the impact of the price increase has been minimal, the crisis is over, no immediate policies are being planned. Congressional opinion concentrated on the domestic economic issues while those in the executive gave equal time to foreign economic and foreign policy issues.

However, in the summer of 1975, a difference of opinion developed within the executive branch. The Economic Policy Board in the White House had been studying the possibility of negotiating commodity agreements on six nonfuel minerals: copper, lead, tin, zinc, iron ore, and aluminum/bauxite. In a preliminary conclusion, aluminum/bauxite and iron ore were not found amenable to commodity agreements. In a parallel development, Secretary of State Henry Kissinger announced that the United States would now consider consulting both industrial and developing nations in efforts to manage raw material markets. He made the point in a series of three speeches: the first on May 13 to the Kansas City International Relations Council; the second to the International Energy Agency in Paris on May 27; the third to the Organization for Economic Cooperation and Development ministerial council also in Paris on May 28.

As a result of these speeches, controversy arose between Secretary Kissinger and the Economic Policy Board. According to James Reston, "the members of the board didn't mind his proposal for consultation with other countries, but thought it a bit odd that he didn't consult with them, and Secretary of the Treasury Simon was particularly incensed by his [Kissinger's] talk of a new world economic order, a popular phrase with the poor and the Communist nations, which suggested that the old economic order was no good."[35] Treasury Secretary Simon prefers a policy which emphasizes the "values of the free enterprise system and the dangers of negotiating commodity agreements rather than leaving prices to the market place."[36] As of this writing, the Kissinger approach seems to have come out on top rhetorically if not substantively, as the Administration seeks to compromise with raw material exporters.

Opinion on Capitol Hill is influenced by those analysts who see no problem with regard to the price and supply of bauxite. In the appendix of a Senate Government Operations Committee print on aluminum, Jane Gravelle analyzed the impact of the increased Jamaican tax on the price of U.S. aluminum products. She indicates that the increase in aluminum prices was a function not only of the Jamaican tax, but also of rising energy costs. Despite this increase in the price of primary aluminum metal, Gravelle concludes that "the increase in aluminum product prices due to the tax is likely to be slight to the final consumer."[37] This is in contrast to the situation with regard to oil, as was pointed out in the introduction. Furthermore:

> The fabricated aluminum industry tends to be substantially more competitive than the primary aluminum industry and

the expectation is that the primary aluminum price increase would be passed on to the end product. The possibility of substitution of other materials in the final consumer product is significant, and may limit the impact on the end product.[38]

Gravelle adds that the impact of the Jamaican tax as a cost is also related to the ability to substitute other sources of bauxite—both foreign and domestic. In conclusion, "the high elasticity of demand and the existence of substitutes would probably present no substantial barriers to passing on the Jamaican tax increase."[39]

There is no concerted effort anywhere on Capitol Hill to resolve the bauxite situation. Aluminum is only another commodity and as such, is included in legislation and hearings on recycling, and strategic and economic stockpiles, which are the issues most discussed. There is no comprehensive materials policy either in the White House or on the Hill—a fact deplored by some analysts in both places. However, the Office of Technology Assessment is presently conducting studies on recycling, stockpiles, and materials information systems. It is hoped that especially the latter effort will serve as the basis for a comprehensive policy.

The possibility of R and D subsidies to industry was described as unlikely. Dealing specifically with aluminum, the fact that it is highly energy-intensive and that there are substitutes for the final products militate against any subsidies on behalf of the aluminum companies.

The attitude of Congress is epitomized by a statement from an analyst of the Congressional Research Service who feels there has been an "unwarranted cry of doom" over increased bauxite prices.

If anything the perception of the executive branch (at least in the Treasury Department) is even more laissez-faire than that of the Congress. Several studies have been done concerning raw materials (especially the Council on International Economic Policy Report) but the conclusions with regard to bauxite have been optimistic because of the availability of substitutes and the nonexistence of a crisis. As to R and D funding (amounting to cash subsidies to the aluminum industry) beyond the present Bureau of Mines miniplant project (see Appendix), the following views were expressed by staff members of:

Council on International Economic Policy—no one in the government espouses subsidies to the aluminum industry

Department of Treasury—it would be hard to single out the aluminum industry as a hardship case

Bureau of Mines—subsidies to the aluminum industry are not justifiable

The Bureau of Mines insists that the relationship of cost and nonbauxitic substitutes is now on the competitive edge with imported bauxite. The switch from bauxite to nonbauxitic sources is a function of technology and cost. Since no new technological breakthroughs are expected, the new sources could be utilized if the prices of bauxite rose drastically. However, if the new facilities were brought onstream and then the bauxite exporters lowered their prices, the industry would be left hanging. Therefore, in the view of two officials at the Bureau of Mines, the new technology for extracting alumina from nonbauxitic materials will not be used commercially but will be used as a bargaining tool to establish a ceiling on the price of imported bauxite.

With respect to external issues, some movement seems to be taking place. There is the Economic Policy Board review of commodity agreements with the goal of stabilizing the cyclic swing of prices mentioned above. Favorable opinions are also expressed with regard to technology transfer and new investment arrangements which would locate processing and manufacturing facilities in developing countries. There is an awareness of problems such a national security and U.S. jobs, yet a protectionist stance is seen as dangerous by risking a backlash.

The past and present policy as viewed by an official of the Treasury Department is one of noninvolvement in the affairs of industry. The extent to which this posture will be modified by the Department of State remains to be seen.

This policy of noninvolvement, however, has been challenged by the U.S. labor movement. In a study released on September 9, 1975, the industrial union department of the AFL-CIO urged the United States to take steps to insure long-term raw materials stability. The study by the consulting firm of Ruttenberg, Friedman, Kilgallon, Gutchess and Associates considered "the possible consequences to American industry if vital raw materials become subject to the same kind of price and quantity manipulations practiced by the oil-producing nations."[40] On the basis of the study, several conclusions were reached: if national materials policy is to be effective there must be a continuation of the strategic stockpile; the U.S. government must take positive actions to assure access to adequate raw materials supplies; defensive actions should also be taken to protect the United States from the harmful effects of cartels and/or the negative impact of multinational corporation activity. A ten-point program was advanced to cope with threats to raw material supply from foreign sources and to develop domestic resources. The recommendations were:

1. The United States should enter into specific agreements with supplier nations to insure that this country has a continuous flow of raw materials in return for the capital and technical assistance needed by those nations.
   2. The federal government should establish an agency to mobilize research and development of new materials technologies, sources and substitutes.
   3. The government should assume responsibility for the development of materials from the ocean floor.
   4. Economic stockpiles of critical materials should be established to safeguard against economic disruptions resulting from attempts to inflate prices or restrict supplies.
   5. Standby facilities for the production and processing of materials should be built and maintained.
   6. The United States should take steps to strengthen its industrial base by removing tax incentives for establishing manufacturing facilities abroad and recognizing this nation's interests in the location within United States boundaries of plants for the fabrication and manufacturing of essential commodities.
   7. Antitrust laws to prevent domination of the materials industry by a few corporations should be enforced.
   8. Conservation measures such as recycling, should be expanded.
   9. A strong American maritime industry should be developed to remove dependence on foreign-owned ships for imports of essential raw materials.
   10. A Federal Commission on National Resources should be established with representation from labor, industry and consumers.[41]

FOREIGN BAUXITE SUPPLIER OPTIONS

> The third world has been driven by its poverty and the inexorable workings of the free trade system to the discovery of the producer association. The Organization of Petroleum Countries [sic] has changed fundamental equations of economic power as decisively as did the Industrial Revolution.[42]

The above statement was made by Jamaica's Prime Minister, Michael Manley, at the conference of British Commonwealth nations on April 29, 1975. In June 1974, as we noted, the government of Jamaica legislated a new formula of production levies

on aluminum companies operating in Jamaica. The new levy is
a graduated percentage (7.5 percent in 1974, 8.0 percent in 1975,
8.5 percent in 1976) based on the prices of aluminum ingot. The
new formula also establishes minimum levels of production for
each company operating in Jamaica in order to secure some stability
in government revenues.

Since then, the government of Jamaica has concluded new agreements with Kaiser (in November 1974), Revere (in December 1974), and Reynolds (in April 1975). In each case Jamaica acquired all lands and 51 percent of the mining operations owned by the companies. Under each agreement a new company is set up administered by an executive committee with equal membership by the government of Jamaica and the foreign aluminum company. A seven-year management contract is included in which the foreign aluminum company manages the operations without a fee.

Another option which bauxite producing countries possess is nationalization. The government of Guyana nationalized mining operations owned by Alcan in 1971 and those owned by Reynolds on January 1, 1975. At present, there are no foreign aluminum companies operating subsidiaries in Guyana.

To understand Jamaica's perspective and to some extent, other bauxite suppliers as well, statements made by Prime Minister Manley before the Jamaican Parliament on May 15, 1975 are informative.

In general, the realization that Jamaica's natural resource (bauxite) is finite has led the government of Jamaica to the conclusion that 1) unlike oil, substitutes for bauxite exist which are now on the competitive edge commercially and therefore, rates of extraction should be increased; and 2) in order to reap the most benefit from this depletable natural resource (that is, by rapid depletion at a high price for reasons noted earlier) Jamaica must control bauxite reserves and bauxite mining operations.

In discussing the government's proposals for a tax increase, Prime Minister Manley cited the following background factors:

1. Companies operating in Jamaica are wholly owned subsidiaries of American and Canadian multinational companies and are classical examples of fully integrated companies. In the case of bauxite, approximately 80 percent of the raw material is carried through mining to alumina processing, to primary metal, and then to fabrication by the same company. This leaves the company free by adjusting transfer prices to determine where the profits should be shown, that is, either at the mining, the alumina processing, the primary metal, or the fabricating stage.

2. Revenue (income tax plus royalty) to government from each ton of bauxite mined and exported as bauxite from Jamaica by Reynolds, Kaiser, and Alcoa has been approximately $2.60 per ton of ore, little more than 2 percent of the value of the primary metal extracted from a ton of ore when the price was 25 cents per pound. The total payments made by Alcan in respect to income taxes and royalties have been roughly equivalent to those made by the companies exporting raw bauxite. In the case of the three alumina companies (Alcoa, Revere, Alpart) the government revenue has been 26 cents per ton of bauxite used for this purpose. In 1972, 3.5 million tons of bauxite converted into alumina by the latter companies produced only $900,000.

3. The companies together hold under lease or ownership some 1.5 billion tons of bauxite reserves or over 80 percent of the estimated reserves of the whole country. The companies have furnished the government with no plans to accelerate extraction of the bauxite in Jamaica, so that accordingly Jamaica would be denied the potential benefit of the exploitation of the remainder of the reserves. At current rates of extraction, the present stock of reserves will be entirely depleted in about 100 years. The government has taken the view that the needs for economic development in Jamaica are too urgent for the country to wait for such a long period of time in order to secure addition to income and employment from these reserves. However, if present reports are correct the time may not be too distant when technological progress will begin to yield substitutes for bauxite. In view of these two considerations the government has formally decided that all possible steps be taken to achieve a substantial increase in rates of extraction.

4. After 25 years of exploitation of bauxite reserves in Jamaica, all the bauxite mining and alumina processing companies in Jamaica remain wholly foreign owned and controlled. There is no local share in the ownership or control of any of the enterprises.

Important points stressed by the foreign suppliers are ownership of their natural resources and the importance of value-added which would extend to the processing of alumina and aluminum (see Appendix). With regard to the latter, new institutional investment arrangements are taking shape. The governments of Jamaica and Mexico announced in November 1974 an agreement for a bauxite-aluminum venture. Ownership will be as follows:

Bauxite facilities (located in Jamaica)	Jamaica	51 percent
	Mexico	29 percent
	Others	20 percent
Alumina plant (located in Jamaica)	Jamaica	51 percent
	Mexico	29 percent
	Kaiser	20 percent
Aluminum smelter (located in Mexico)	Mexico	51 percent
	Jamaica	29 percent
	Kaiser	20 percent

These arrangements are in the planning stages. Kaiser will supply the needed technology as a partner without equity control. Venezuela is also invited in this venture and has agreed to buy 400,000 tons of bauxite for three years starting in 1979, 200,000 tons of alumina for ten years starting in 1979, and 500,000 tons of aluminum for the next seven years. Venezuela has its own aluminum smelters. The agreement is flexible and given Venezuela the option of buying 10 percent of the Mexican-Jamaican facilities. In return, Venezuela has agreed to supply oil to Jamaica for the next ten years.

Another joint venture involves Jamaica, Trinidad, and Guyana in which aluminum smelters will be built in the latter two countries. The Trinidad smelter will use natural gas and a feasibility study on implementation has been completed. However, Guyana's smelter is contingent upon the development of hydroelectric power and such a plant is only in the formative stages and in need of financing. The technology for these facilities could be obtained from other Eastern European countries (such as Yugoslavia) with which the Caribbean nations are associated.

Efforts to increase value-added processing facilities also continue with the foreign aluminum companies in Jamaica. No company is being considered for reduced production levies under the new agreements unless they are committed to assume the cost of building a minimum of 200,000 tons capacity for the new Jamaican-Mexican alumina plant in South Manchester, Jamaica. For example, Reynolds, who agreed to participate, will not be a shareholder, but will finance the cost of expansion of 200,000 tons to the plant, whose capacity will be increased to 900,000 tons.

With the revenue generated from such arrangements the government of Jamaica presumably will be able to solve some of the problems cited in the defense of the production levy:[43]

BAUXITE-ALUMINUM INDUSTRY

More and more money is urgently needed to carry out programs of development on behalf of the country and its people:

- Houses to be built
- Jobs to be provided
- Illiteracy to be wiped out
- Agriculture to be revitalized
- Foreign goods to be paid for
- Numerous other services to be provided

U.S. ALUMINUM INDUSTRY OPTIONS

The attitude of the aluminum industry on the issue of bauxite supplies is by no means unified. Although most companies agree, at least in public, that the exploitation of commercially feasible non-bauxite sources is imminent, the emphasis placed on this source varies. According to a recent study by the U.S. Department of the Interior, there are at least three reasons why the aluminum industry may not have a strong incentive to develop alternative domestic sources of aluminum:

1. The U.S. aluminum companies have invested some $600 million in bauxite production and alumina production facilities in Jamaica and about $1,500 million in other countries. Even though Jamaica, for example, may levy a royalty on bauxite so high that the cost of building and operating a new plant for producing alumina from domestic resources would be cheaper than building a new plant in Jamaica and consequently paying royalties, there may be no incentive to switch existing production from Jamaica to the United States. The explanation for this is that the investment in facilities in Jamaica represent sunk costs and can only be used for production in Jamaica. As long as the operating costs plus royalties in Jamaica are less than the sum of capital costs and operating costs in the United States, aluminum companies will continue to produce in Jamaica.

2. To some extent, the aluminum companies are shielded from the effects of large price increases in bauxite caused by a commodity action because of their ability to pass on the cost increases in the form of high prices. In the short run when the demand for aluminum is quite inelastic, the quantity of aluminum sold by the companies will not be reduced greatly at higher prices, and thus their profits will be

largely unaffected. However, in the long run the aluminum companies must face the possibility of substitution away from aluminum to competing materials such as steel, plastics, plywood, glass, etc.

3. The aluminum industry is dominated by three large companies. One concern for major aluminum companies may be that opening up production from domestic resources may lead to an increase in the competitiveness of the industry by allowing new firms to begin the production of aluminum.[44]

The situation is still evolving, however, and several factors can be introduced which may have a bearing on the outcome.

Because of the publicity involved in the Jamaican situation, this section again focuses on that country. Given the attempts to present a unified front, however, generalizing to other Caribbean supplies is not unrealistic. In this section aluminum company views on four topics are explored: reaction to Jamaica's policies, adjustments in contract relationships with bauxite suppliers, adjustments in internal company programs to develop nonbauxite sources, and perceptions of the role the U.S. government should play.

According to the Wall Street Journal,[45] the three major U.S. aluminum companies import the following percentages of their total bauxite supply from Jamaica: Kaiser, 70 percent; Reynolds, 60 percent; and Alcoa, 16 percent. This fact is important, and although not stated explictly, may be a reason for the positions taken by individual companies.

The U.S. aluminum industry recognized Jamaica's need for higher revenues. In a statement dated June 17, 1974, Cornell Maier, President of Kaiser Aluminum and Chemical Corporation said:

> Throughout our discussions with Jamaica officials, we have not disagreed, nor do we now disagree, with the propositions that Jamaica should now receive a higher return from its bauxite resource. In light of current world economic conditions, we believe Jamaica is now entitled to substantially higher revenues from bauxite. The only point at issue in this regard is how much higher is fair to both parties—particularly in terms of the level of costs that can be charged for bauxite to improve returns to Jamaica and yet maintain profitable growth of the aluminum industry, which is of importance to both Jamaica and the companies. We feel that the level set by Jamaica is too high.

The reaction to the unilateral abrogation by Jamaica of the contracts, however, was not favorable. The companies involved filed complaints to the International Center for the Settlement of Investment Disputes, a World Bank affiliate, in an effort to force fulfillment of their original agreements. These complaints were withdrawn as the companies agreed to new contracts with Jamaica. However, some distrust remains—especially on the part of U.S. banks making investment loans to the aluminum companies.

Concerning adjustments in contract relations with bauxite suppliers, reference has already been made to the new agreements between Jamaica and Kaiser, Revere, and Reynolds. It is accurate to say that future agreements with Jamaica, and with other Caribbean countries, will be on a joint venture rather than a wholly-owned subsidiary basis. However, new developments are occurring on two fronts: the search for new supplier countries which are more dependable, and the new trend toward supplying technology and skills to bauxite suppliers, creating technology transfer without equity control.

Because of transportation costs, sources of bauxite supply relatively close to aluminum smelters (that is, Caribbean as opposed to European countries) are very attractive. However, given the uncertainty of the Caribbean supply, the aluminum companies have increased exploration in other countries. Brazil is a case in point. Brazil is believed to be rich in bauxite deposits and at least one company, Alcoa, has expended much time, effort, and money examining the possibility of setting up operations there. A consortium of five Japanese firms has already planned a bauxite-to-aluminum project on the Amazon River.

The second development involves arrangements in which U.S. aluminum producers supply technology to bauxite suppliers to enable the latter to set up their own downstream facilities for alumina and even aluminum productions. This service role of U.S. industry is repudiated in public by some aluminum companies as "disastrous," however, the situation is being forced upon the companies in Jamica and given the value-added push which is gaining popularity, it may become even more widespread. This trend may not be unique to the aluminum sector. According to C. Fred Bergsten:

> In the modern world, pursuit of an optional international division of labor determined solely by market forces might well produce a steady transfer of manufacturing jobs to LDCs from the industrialized world which would in turn devote an increasing share of its output to services.[46]

What has been the internal response of the industry to the higher prices of bauxite and the demand for downstream technology? There are conflicting views on the subject. Some analysts contend that industry is not spending much money on developing nonbauxitic sources. This suggests that industry may have figures showing the cost of nonbauxitic sources to be prohibitive, barring very drastic price hikes by bauxite suppliers. Publicly, however, the stance is quite different. According to Kaiser Aluminum and Chemical Corporation:

> Kaiser Aluminum, like most companies in the aluminum business, has been actively testing processes for obtaining alumina from lower grade bauxites and other ores for many years. Because of the work provided by nature, bauxite economics have far surpassed those of any alternate ore. This has become even more true in recent times due to the energy shortages and costs. The Jamaican tax, has, however, reduced the differential to a point where secure, domestic alumina-containing ores must be seriously developed as possible alternates.[47]

Toward that end, Kaiser Aluminum is participating in the joint government-industry process development program on domestic ores operated by the U.S. Bureau of Mines (see Appendix). Kaiser is also studying processes on clay, coal shale, anorthosite, alunite, and oil shale with particular regard to relative energy consumptions. In addition, Kaiser is continuing a detailed survey of domestic ore locations in concert with process economic studies and has an active task force of explorations, process engineering, and R and D personnel working on the definition of Kaiser's alternatives.

Kaiser anticipates that extraction from non bauxite ores will prove to be technically feasible within a period of three to five years. Economic competitiveness between these processes and bauxite will depend upon the rising costs of energy and other essential commodities as well as trends in bauxite costs from the Caribbean and elsewhere. Thus, whether nonbauxitic sources become a reality commercially or remain largely a threat useful for bargaining purposes hinges on other exogenous factors besides the price of bauxite such as the price of energy to process nonbauxite sources and the availability of bauxite from other supplying countries such as Australia, Guinea, or Brazil.

Recycled aluminum is another source of supply—one about which the aluminum companies are not enthusiastic. Again, according to Kaiser:

> There is increasing emphasis on recycling of aluminum, not as a result of pressures, but because it makes economic good sense. As you know, there is a substantial energy saving in the recycling of aluminum. For this reason it is very attractive to the aluminum industry. However, the cost per pound of metal produced is still cheaper from the original bauxite source than through the collection and recycling despite the energy saving. There are constant refinements being made in this process, however, and recycling could become competitive at some future time. The push toward that end will be from pressures of energy conservation rather than any other reason.[48]

It has been suggested to this author by an official of another aluminum company, however, that recycled aluminum will not become competitive with primary metal precisely because recycling does not conserve substantial amounts of energy. According to this view, if all aluminum companies were to recycle all old scrap (after consumer use) not now recycled, the energy saved would be one-half of 1 percent (0.5 percent) of all energy utilized by the aluminum industry in a year. The emphasis on recycling, it is contended, is merely a public relations device to divert attention from the huge amounts of energy consumed by the industry.

Perceptions of the role to be played by the U.S. government depend upon the individual positions of the aluminum companies. Kaiser has made direct accommodating overtures to Jamaica and seems to have worked out a satisfactory relationship. Thus, Kaiser feels that the U.S. government should not take a more active role at this time—either through economic support of the aluminum industry or external pressure on bauxite suppliers. Other companies, however, do not share this view. Some senators and congressmen have been lobbied on measures ranging from direct subsidies to industry to support R and D, to economic stockpiling, to pressure on Jamaica by denying trade preferences.

CONCLUSIONS

The changing of relationships between rich and poor countries has been labelled the "threat from the Third World" by C. Fred Bergsten of the Brookings Institution. The implications of the "threat" vary depending upon the perspective of the different actors involved. This case study has attempted to view the relationships among a consuming nation (the United States), a group of producing nations (the foreign bauxite producers) and a U.S. industry (the aluminum industry) from the perspective of each actor. The issues which result from this situation determine a variety of policy options. This concluding section presents five trends in the bauxite aluminum sector and the policy options available to each actor as a result of these trends. Some of these trends and options may apply more widely to other raw material sectors (see Introduction).

The New International Economic Order

The international economic environment is changing. A new relationship is emerging between the industrialized and developing countries. According to C. Fred Bergsten:

> The United States, in fact, faces the wholly unanticipated specter of the Third World which is often far more unified on key issues than the erstwhile First World of rich, industrial countries. . . . And developing countries which host multinational firms are increasingly sharing their experiences to enhance their national bargaining positions, while the United States, the largest home country, sits idly by.[49]

In developing a policy to enhance the U.S. "bargaining position" and anticipate rather than merely react to commodity crises, the U.S. government has both accommodating and competitive policy options. Policies of competition with supplying countries include:

1. A unilateral response by the United States to insure security of supply through (a) an economic stockpile and/or (b) subsidies or price supports for U.S. industry to encourage the development of domestic resources including recycling.

2. A coordinated response on the part of consumer nations to finance joint stockpiles and/or coordinate attempts to produce aluminum from nonbauxitic sources.

On the other hand, there exist policies of accommodation vis-a-vis the supplying countries. These policies include:

1. The negotiation of commodity agreements with buffer stocks to decrease price fluctuations thus insuring supply for consumers and a stable price for suppliers;

2. Encourage industry to negotiate contracts with developing countries with greater local participation and transfer of downstream technology through incentives such as the Western Hemisphere Trade Corporations and the Overseas Private Investment Corporation (this policy was recommended by the House of Representatives report on OPIC in 1973[50]); or

3. Maintain the policy of noninvolvement and allow demand and supply to be controlled by the market.

These issues and policies involve raw materials in general. The following three trends deal specifically with bauxite.

Foreign Bauxite Suppliers: The Value-Added Approach

The second trend results partly from the new economic order described above and partly from the example set by the oil producers. There is a realization that producing countries can extract a higher price for their natural resources. Therefore, in part to assuage the balance of payments problem resulting from higher oil bills, bauxite suppliers have espoused the value-added approach. That is, they have decided to increase revenues by expanding to the alumina and aluminum phases of production. This expansion requires technology now available from the major aluminum companies and such Eastern European countries as Yugoslavia. This trend has been manifested in two ways:

1. The first method involves the intergovernmental joint ventures by the suppliers in which U.S. companies are invited to join. An example of this is the Mexican-Jamaican venture in which Kaiser will have an equity share of only 20 percent (see "Foreign Bauxite Supplier Options.")

2. The second method has been implemented by Jamaica and involves the renegotiation of present contracts. An example of this method is Jamaica's agreement with Reynolds in which the latter will assume the cost of expanding Jamaica's new alumina facilities by 200,000 tons although Reynolds will not be a partner in the facility. In return Reynolds pays a preferential level of tax for its bauxite.

In this demand for downstream industry the foreign suppliers of bauxite have economics on their side. Alumina, the intermediate product of aluminum, has a higher content of the final product but yet costs no more to transport than bauxite (see Appendix for more detailed discussion). Economically, then, it would make more sense to import alumina rather than bauxite. The situation was distorted when the U.S. government sold alumina facilities to aluminum companies on very easy terms (especially Reynolds and Kaiser) after World War II—thus it was more profitable for industry to import the crude ore than to establish alumina plants in the Caribbean (see Appendix).

The United States Aluminum Industry: Investment Without Equity Control

The third trend deals with the same demands of bauxite suppliers as above—that is, value-added—but from the perspective of the U.S. aluminum industry. One of the interesting trends of this study is that the aluminum industry may be moving toward a service role with regard to the bauxite suppliers. That is, the time may come when aluminum companies are no longer only in the business of producing aluminum for export from imported bauxite but also in the business of selling technology and the skills to service that technology in the bauxite supplying countries. An example of this trend is the participation of Kaiser in the Mexican-Jamaican joint venture. Along the same lines, an Alcoa subsidiary is reportedly being set up which will deal exclusively in the selling of technology. If this trend materializes it would mean a change in the U.S. balance of trade—a change in the composition of U.S. exports and the outflow of capital. The net effects of these shifts will depend upon the price at which technology and services are sold and the forms of payments permitted by the bauxite supplying countries.

This trend toward investment without equity control is subject to the policies of the bauxite suppliers. Two such policies have emerged—first, nationalization as in Guyana, and second, contracts such as in Jamaica. An example will serve to illustrate both the trend in Jamaica and the cautious nature of the conclusion because the situation is still evolving.

Kaiser concluded an agreement with Jamaica in which Kaiser has 49 percent equity ownership while Jamaica owns 51 percent equity of the new mining operations which replaces Kaiser's wholly-owned subsidiary. However, the board of directors of the operation

BAUXITE-ALUMINUM INDUSTRY

will be divided equally—four for Jamica and four for Kaiser. Also, Kaiser has a seven-year contract to manage the operations without a fee with local participation in management. This situation can be viewed in two ways—or rather, as two options for Jamaica. Each of these options implies a different relationship with Kaiser.

    1. In the first option (known as the Mideast option in the oil area) Jamaica may view the arrangement of 51 percent equity control as satisfactory from a domestic and political point of view. Prime Minister Manley can say that Jamaicans own their bauxite while leaving the control of management entirely to Kaiser.

    The implications of this for Kaiser are favorable. Kaiser has a secure supply and need not worry too much about the added cost incurred by shifting to the use of nonbauxitic U.S. sources of aluminum.

    2. However, the second option for Jamaica (in the oil area, the Mexican option) is to plan the eventual takeover of the entire operation—equity and management. If this is the case numerous options are available to both the U.S. industry and the U.S. government.

Industry options include:

    1. Divestment in the Caribbean and the search for new suppliers such as Australia or Guinea;
    2. Bringing onstream full scale commercial plants utilizing nonbauxitic domestic materials such as anorthosite, alunite, oil shale, dawsonite, and so on.
    3. Further movement toward the service role discussed above supplying technology and skills without equity or management control.

The U.S. government may also be pressured to act if such a scenario should develop. The options for the U.S. government would then be:

    1. Do nothing.
    2. Protect U.S. industry through retaliation utilizing trade preferences and authority from the 1974 trade bill.
    3. Secure supply through anticipatory measures such as economic stockpiles and incentives for industry to develop domestic resources—both of which can be used as bargaining tools with Jamaica.

The United States Government: Security of Supply

The fourth trend again flows from the scenario above in which industry is forced or decides to divest its operations in the Caribbean and turn to domestic nonbauxitic sources. The issue is whether the U.S. government should become involved in industry's search for a secure supply through domestic resources. The government options can be anticipatory or reactionary and are as follows:

1. To do nothing and let industry bear the cost of developing domestic sources;
2. To subsidize the aluminum industry directly for R and D of domestic supplies;
3. To use a price support scheme to provide incentives and protect a domestic-based industry;
4. To increase support for the Bureau of Mines miniplant program and construct at least one pilot plant to make the bargaining tool of domestic supplies credible. (This policy has been recommended by the Office of Minerals Policy Development of the U.S. Department of the Interior.)[51]

Up to this point the four trends listed have followed from one another: first, the reality of a changing economic order which has influenced producer country demands—the second trend of value-added. As a response to these demands, industry is being forced to rethink traditional investment patterns and is also putting pressure on the U.S. government to act.

One conclusion of these four trends is that the efforts by both private industry and the U.S. government to develop alternative nonbauxitic sources of aluminum up to the point the domestic price will support will act as a constraint on foreign bauxite suppliers. This constraint will affect the leverage of these suppliers both with regard to the price of bauxite and the demands for value-added and downstream industry.

Materials Policy

The fifth and final trend deals with the fragmented approach to materials policy in the U.S. government today. Not only is there little communication between Capitol Hill and the Administration but there is also an interagency struggle between the Departments of

State and Treasury. The ideological debate between free versus controlled market advocates in commodity areas reflects bureaucratic conflicts as well as more fundamental philosophical differences.

Although the issue of raw materials is often discussed in the government, the lack of a crisis militates against any comprehensive policy. If any policies do emerge they will do so as a result of anticipatory thinking by policymakers who are aware of the possible damages inherent in not acting at all.

NOTES

1. United Nations, General Assembly, Sixth Special Session, April 9-May 2, 1974, Resolutions Adopted by the General Assembly during its Sixth Special Session, A/9559, Supplement no. 1, p. 3.
2. Ibid., p. 4.
3. United Nations, General Assembly, Dec. 12, 1974, Charter of Economic Rights and Duties of States, Resolution 3821 (XXIX), Reprinted from the UN Monthly Chronicle (New York: United Nations Office of Public Information, 1975).
4. See address before the Seventh Session of the U.N. General Assembly, New York, September 1, 1975. Obtained from Bureau of Public Affairs, U.S. Department of State.
5. Council on International Economic Policy, Special Report: Critical Imported Materials (Washington, D.C.: U.S. Government Printing Office, December, 1974), p. 4.
6. U.S. Congress, House, Committee on Foreign Affairs, Global Commodity Scarcities in an Interdependent World, Foreign Affairs Committee Print, 93d Cong., 2d sess., 1974 (Washington, D.C.: U.S. Government Printing Office, 1974), p. 11.
7. Council on International Economic Policy, Critical Imported Materials, pp. 9, 17.
8. Ibid., pp. 23, A-2.
9. Ibid., p. 25.
10. Ibid., p. 16.
11. See Part 2, "International Bauxite Association," and three articles appearing in Foreign Policy which discuss the possibilities: Zuhayr Mikdashi, "Collusion Could Work," Stephen Krasner, "Oil Is the Exception," and C. Fred Bergsten, "The Threat is Real," Foreign Policy 12 (Fall 1973).
12. "Australia Sees Little Prospect for Price-Fixing Bauxite Cartel," New York Times, November 5, 1974.

13. See the relevant sections in the Appendix of the Council on International Economic Policy's Critical Imported Materials.
14. Henry Kissinger, in his speech to the United Nations on September 1, 1975, said: "President Ford has authorized me to announce that the United States intends to sign the tin agreement, subject to Congressional consultations and ratification." (Washington, D.C.: Department of State, 1975.)
15. Mikdashi, op. cit., p. 66.
16. Ibid., p. 61.
17. Final Act of the International Conference of Bauxite Producing Countries, International Bauxite Association, Conakry, Guinea, March 8, 1974.
18. Wall Street Journal, April 23, 1975.
19. Wall Street Journal, March 10, 1975.
20. New York Times, April 30, 1975.
21. See especially, U.S. Department of Interior, Bureau of Mines, Alumina from Domestic Resources: A Miniplant Project to Evaluate Alumina Recovery Processes mimeographed, January 1974; and U.S. Congress, Senate, Committee on Government Operations, Materials Shortages: Aluminum, Appendix I, "Alternatives to Imported Bauxite: Domestic Potential Sources of Aluminum," by Stephen M. Phillips, Government Operations Committee Print, 93d Cong., 2d sess., 1974 (Washington, D.C.: U.S. Government Printing Office, 1974).
22. Congressional Research Service, National Materials Stockpiles by William C. Boesman, Issue Brief No. IBF4111 (March 21, 1975), p. 3.
23. Ibid., p. 4.
24. New York Times, November 1, 1974.
25. Wall Street Journal, March 31, 1975.
26. New Scientist (August 9, 1973), p. 326.
27. Senate Committee on Government Operations, Materials Shortages: Aluminum, p. 19.
28. Council on International Economic Policy, Critical Imported Materials, p. A-3.
29. Jack N. Behrman, Decision Criteria for Foreign Direct Investment in Latin America (New York: Council of Americas, 1974).
30. General Services Administration, Strategic and Critical Materials: Descriptive Data (Washington, D.C.: U.S. Government Printing Office, December, 1973), p. ii.
31. Ibid.
32. Mira Wilkins The Maturing of the Multinational Enterprise: American Business Abroad from 1914-1970, (Cambridge, Mass.: Harvard University Press, 1974), p. 262N.

33. According to Theodore H. Moran: "The deferral feature of the Foreign Tax Credit in effect provides subsidiaries of U.S. businesses with an interest-free loan amounting to the U.S. tax liability of unremitted profits. In less developed countries, the absence of a 'grossing-up' requirement on the Foreign Tax Credit means that taxes paid to a host government relieve a company of much more of its tax liability than taxes paid to the U.S. government." "New Deal or Raw Deal in Raw Materials", Foreign Policy 5 (Winter 1971-72): 127.

34. Senate Committee on Government Operations, Materials Shortages: Aluminum, Apendix II, "An Analysis of the Impact of the Increase in the Jamaican Bauxite Tax on the Price of Aluminum Products in the United States," by Jane Gravelle, p. 45-46.

35. New York Times, May 30, 1975.

36. Ibid.

37. Senate Committee on Government Operations, Materials Shortages: Aluminum, Appendix II, p. 41.

38. Ibid., p. 43.

39. Ibid., p. 44.

40. "Stability Urged in Raw Materials", New York Times, September 10, 1975.

41. Ibid.

42. New York Times, April 30, 1975.

43. Press kit for the Government of Jamaica prepared by A.F. Sabo Associates, 1974.

44. U.S. Department of Interior, Office of Minerals Policy Development, Critical Materials: Commodity Action Analyses; Aluminum, Chromium, Platinum and Palladium (Washington, D.C.: U.S. Government Printing Office, March 1975), pp. 41-42.

45. Wall Street Journal, November 21, 1974.

46. The Future of the International Economic Order: An Agenda for Research (Lexington, Mass.: Lexington Books and D.C. Health and Company, 1973), p. 20.

47. Personal correspondence from Richard L. Spees, Corporate Director, Public Affairs, Kaiser Aluminum and Chemical Corporation. May 14, 1975.

48. Ibid.

49. "The Response to the Third World," Foreign Policy 17 (Winter 1974-75): 12.

50. U.S. Congress, House, Committee on Foreign Affairs, The Overseas Private Investment Corporation, H. Rept. 93-672, 93d Cong., 1st sess., 1973, p. 8.

51. U.S. Department of Interior, Critical Materials: Commodity Action Analyses, p. 43.

CHAPTER

7

IRRI SMALL AGRICULTURAL MACHINERY PROJECT: U.S. TECHNOLOGY TRANSFER TO RESOURCE-POOR DEVELOPING COUNTRIES

Ann L. Becker
Carol A. Ulinski

In June 1965, the Agency for International Development (AID) signed a three-year contract with the International Rice Research Institute (IRRI) to "adapt, test and develop [in the Philippines] more suitable rice-producing equipment in those cases in which currently available equipment obviously does not perform efficiently."[1] Under this contract, the Agricultural Engineering Department (AED) of IRRI concentrated primarily on testing existing agricultural equipment developed and manufactured in industrialized countries. Beginning in 1967, however, the project gradually shifted its focus to include the design and development of rice production and processing technology which would be locally produced in the country's small metalworking shops. In 1969 AID signed a second contract with IRRI to finance product development activities of the AED. By 1971, IRRI had a sufficient

---

There are many people who have given much time and invaluable assistance to the work that follows. Those to whom we are especially indebted include Dr. Amir U. Khan and Dr. J. Bart Duff of the Agricultural Engineering Department of the IRRI. They contributed to the productivity and success of two months of field research conducted in the Philippines during the summer of 1975 under a contract from the U.S. Agency for International Development (AID/TA-C-1242, Evaluation of Factors Affecting the Rate of Adoption of IRRI Small Farm Equipment). Their continuing interest, advice, and encouragement helped immeasurably. We also wish to acknowledge the help and suggestions of many officials of the Technical Assistance Bureau of the Agency for International Development, and the countless Filipinos without whom this study would not have been possible.

number of completed designs to justify industry involvement and shifted some of its energies from R and D to commercialization of the designs. December 1974 marked the termination of the AID contract, at which time the R and D activities of the AED were incorporated into the core budget of IRRI. In 1975 a third AID contract was signed with IRRI to promote the international extension of IRRI designs to Thailand and Pakistan. IRRI/AID contracts are summarized in Table 7.1

Known as the Small-Scale Agricultural Machinery Project, the AID/IRRI experiment over the past ten years represents an interesting example of what is today being called appropriate or intermediate technology transfer. Although the AID/IRRI effort was not originally conceived in these terms, it has many of the characteristics of the new concepts. An evaluation of this effort, therefore, could provide us with an early assessment of the feasibility and potential of appropriate technology transfer to developing countries. This assessment seems particularly valuable in light of the new emphasis of U.S. foreign aid legislation. In the Foreign Assistance Act (FAA) of 1973, Congress laid down new guidelines for U.S. aid programs which stress many of the objectives—transfer of technical assistance, increase in employment, and so on—which appropriate technology concepts are also designed to achieve. This case study, consequently, enables us to gain some insight into future issues and problems that may be associated with U.S. foreign policy and technology transfer to poor developing countries.

By definition, appropriate technology is one "which is as responsive as possible to the capital, manpower, natural resource, institutional and social realities of a particular country environment."[2] Simply put, it is the technology which utilizes local factors of production most efficiently. Experience has shown that the majority of currently available agricultural machinery produced and marketed primarily by the Western industrialized countries and Japan is inappropriate to conditions in developing tropical areas. Large four-wheel tractors, for example, have been designed to function in areas whose environmental conditions and factor endowments are radically different from those of tropical, less developed countries (LDCs). In the case of Japanese equipment, the power tiller is functionally appropriate to the conditions in the Philippines but is too expensive and sophisticated for the typical farmer.[3]

Appropriate technology is a broad concept referring to technology at any level of sophistication appropriate to local circumstances. Intermediate technology refers to technology at a middle level of sophistication, falling "somewhere half-way between the age old 'traditional' technologies and the large-scale capital-intensive 'modern' technology."[4] Some important characteristics of intermediate technology are that it can be produced by the nonmodern, rural sector with labor

TABLE 7.1

IRRI/AID Contracts

Date	Contract Number	Project Title	Activities
June 1965	csd-835	"Research on Farm and Equipment Power Requirement for Production & Processing of Rice and Associated Food Crops in the Far East & South East Asia"	Research on economics and engineering aspects of existing agricultural equipment, concentrating on four-wheel tractors.
June 1969	csd-2541	"Agricultural Equipment Development Research for Tropical Rice Cultivation"	Design and development of rice production and processing technologies which can be locally produced and satisfy the needs of small farmers.
June 1975	AID/ta-C-1208	"Industrial Extension of Small-Scale Agricultural Equipment Developed at IRRI"	International transfer of the IRRI designs to Thailand and Pakistan.

Source: Office of Contract Management, Bureau for Programs and Management Services, Agency for International Development, Washington, D.C.

intensive production methods and local resources. It is relatively inexpensive in terms of production cost and selling price, and is simple to fabricate, operate, maintain, and repair.[5]

The equipment technologies produced by the AID/IRRI project meet all these criteria. The IRRI axial flow thresher, for example, offers an alternative to the backbreaking job of threshing by hand, and is cheaper and less disruptive than a combine-harvester. It can be manufactured in the small metalworking shops scattered throughout the Philippines with the existing level of skills and production equipment. It is simple to operate and can be repaired by local machine shops. In essence, it offers Filipino farmers an alternative both to traditional technologies, which may limit local productivity and output, and to expensive capital-intensive technologies which are produced and utilized under circumstances unique to the industrialized world.

The IRRI project is particularly relevant when viewed in light of the revised FAA of 1973 (see text and note 25, Chapter 2). Its characteristics correspond to the three major directives of this new legislation. These directives include:

1. Content of aid: the United States should place greater emphasis on technical assistance as opposed to capital transfers.
2. Target of aid: U.S. foreign assistance should benefit the poor majority who have largely been bypassed in past aid efforts.
3. Means of aid: Aid is to be channeled through private and multilateral institutions whenever possible.

The IRRI Small Agricultural Machinery Project, which was initiated almost five years prior to the 1973 changes in the legislation, is remarkably in accord with these revised policy directives. First, the project does not entail large-scale transfer of capital resources from rich to poor countries. The emphasis is on harnessing available technological know-how and expertise for the purpose of design and development of farm machinery in the local environment itself. Second, the target is the poor majority. IRRI engineers tailor the designs to meet two criteria: 1) the product can be produced in small metal-working shops with local resources and skills, and 2) the product satisfies the needs of small rice farmers and is a viable technology for small farm holdings ranging from two to ten hectares (one hectare = 2.47 acres). And third, the aid has been channeled through the International Rice Research Institute, which is a multilateral, nonprofit organization supported by a number of countries and private foundations.

STAGES OF THE IRRI PROJECT

There are three identifiable stages in the evolution of the IRRI project over the past ten years. The first stage, which represents the function and responsibility of the project, was to conduct research and development activities in the area of farm mechanization. The second stage, which commenced in 1971, entailed the transfer of the designs from IRRI to the local industrial community. The third stage involved the actual sale and use of the finished products by the farmer. The feedback mechanism completed the circle, linking the farmer and R and D stages. Obviously, these stages overlapped chronologically. Farmer surveys were conducted at the outset to ascertain local requirements for new equipment designs. R and D activities have continued throughout the second and third stages. Nevertheless, the emphasis of the project shifted with each stage. The problems encountered in the R and D stage, which represents the transfer and application of know-how from abroad (IRRI project directors and key staff were largely western trained), are quite different from the problems encountered in transfer of that know-how within the local country itself. Figure 7.1 sets out this primary level of relationships in the IRRI project.

At another level, the particular activities associated with the AID/IRRI project may have spinoffs into R and D, manufacturing, and marketing activities of other sectors of the local economy. IRRI efforts in the different stages may prompt local groups to assume similar, independent activities. In the R and D stage, firms and local research institutes may begin product design activities of their own; in the manufacturing stage, additional investments may be encouraged; and, in the marketing stage, word may spread that the product is a worthwhile investment. IRRI involvement at this second level has been indirect but significant. IRRI engineers continue to provide needy firms with the technical assistance required to overcome engineering problems. The role of government, however, becomes extremely important at this level and may be directly responsible for the success or failure of the project at this level. Figure 7.2 illustrates these second order relationships.

At a third and most important level, the indigenization process is completed. Local institutions and actors perform all activities initially undertaken by IRRI, thereby obviating the need for a foreign or international input. This level is characterized by the existence of (1) developed, well operating R and D capabilities, and (2) mechanisms for transferring research designs into the commerical sector and ultimately into the hands of consumers. As with the second level, government policies impact heavily on the possibility and pace at which

FIGURE 7.1

First Sequence of Relationships, IRRI Project

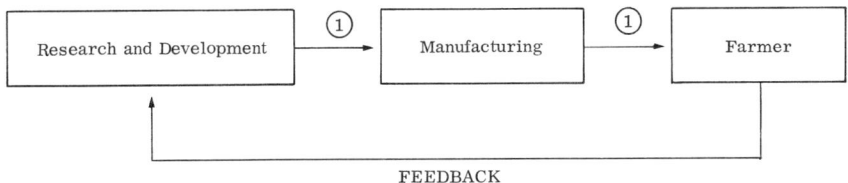

FEEDBACK

Source: Compiled by the authors.

a country reaches this highest level. Figure 7.3 portrays this final self-sufficient set of relationships.

The following discussion describes and evaluates the IRRI project through the three primary stages of R and D, manufacturing and farmer activities. Spinoffs from the IRRI project and progress toward local self-reliance are discussed in the context of each of these stages. Finally, an additional section examines the important role of government policies in the IRRI project and in the transfer of appropriate technology as a whole. Our interest lies with determining how IRRI made the transition from one stage to another, and from one level to another. In evaluating the success of the project, we look primarily at the linkages at the primary level. It is still too early to evaluate the strength of the secondary and tertiary linkages. Ultimately, of course, the success of the project will be determined by the level of indigenization attained.

THE RESEARCH AND DEVELOPMENT STAGE

The activities of the Agricultural Engineering Department (AED) have evolved over time to include the design and development of farm machines which meet specified criteria. To date, the majority of this work has been performed by the AED but involvement of Filipino private and public actors is on the upswing.

FIGURE 7.2

Second Sequence of Relationships, IRRI Project

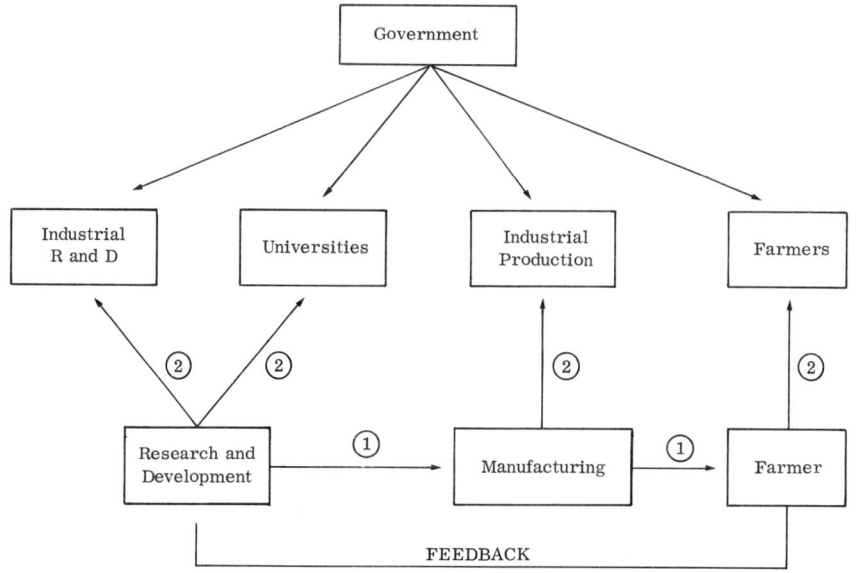

Source: Compiled by the authors.

FIGURE 7.3

Third Sequence of Relationships, IRRI Project

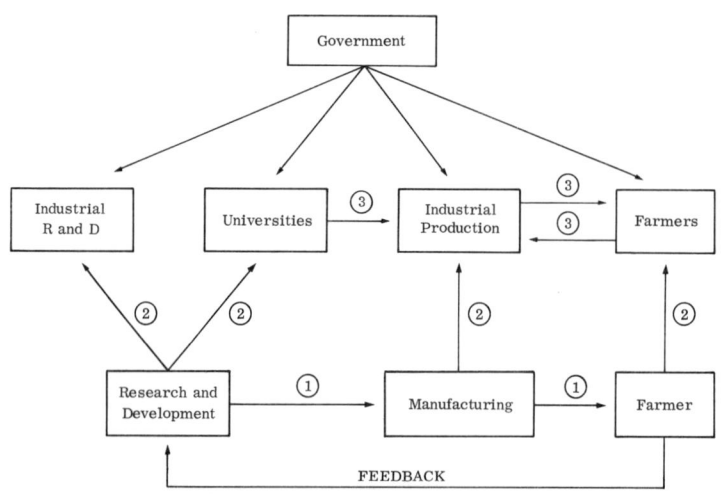

Source: Compiled by the authors.

Project Objectives

The first director of the IRRI Mechanization Research Project was Loyd Johnson, an agricultural engineer and staff member at IRRI since its inception in 1960. Under his stewardship, the project concentrated on a number of studies and surveys, principally in Central Luzon which is the rice bowl of the Philippines. Data of an agronomic, engineering, and economic nature were compiled, the region's cropping patterns, water use, soil conditions, and annual yields were scrutinized, and potential bottlenecks to increasing productivity were identified.[6]

The objective of the project, as noted previously, was to test the performance of currently available machinery (mostly designed abroad) in rice growing regions of the Philippines and to make the necessary modifications. Working in close cooperation with the National Tillage Machinery Laboratory of the U.S. Department of Agriculture (USDA), the project tested the performance of different wheels, rotor blades, and spade lugs under flooded soil conditions. Because of severe limitations on money and manpower, the Agricultural Engineering Department (hereafter AED) of IRRI was unable to conduct tests on many machines already on the market; instead the Department's activities entailed observation of machine performances in rice paddies, with suggestions for modification directed to the appropriate industry engineers. Where observation was not possible, the AED borrowed equipment from manufacturers and conducted the tests at IRRI.[7]

The project maintained close contacts with industry. These contacts were necessarily with companies in the developed countries— especially those in the United States and Japan. An agricultural machinery industry was virtually nonexistent in the developing countries. Loyd Johnson visited numerous manufacturers and machinery centers in Japan, Taiwan, Australia, Canada, and the United States, including International Harvester, Massey Ferguson, and the Food Machinery Corporation. During the years 1966 and 1967 representatives from several companies, including John Deere and Case, also visited the Agricultural Engineering Department at IRRI. They hoped to "obtain some idea of how their respective companies could fill the needs of rice producers."[8] As these contacts with industry suggest, the project was not intended to act as a substitute for R and D performed by industry. Any company, especially U.S. firms, showing an interest in producing equipment which satisfied the needs of the rice farmer was to be encouraged. According to the terms of the AID contract, "where U.S. manufacturers show distinct interest in the development of suitable equipment, the Contractor (AED) will submit a proposal to 'AID/W' that development funds be made available."[9]

The focus and strategy of the AID/IRRI project began to shift in 1967. In that year, Dr. Amir Khan became the director of the project. Dr. Khan had considerable industrial work experience behind him; he managed his own industry in India, worked for a large diversified industrial company in India, and later served with the Ford Tractor Division in the United States. While at Ford, he worked on the development of a high speed planter, and participated in the planning of the "Developing Nation Tractor," an agricultural machine designed specifically for small farmers in LDCs. This attempt by Ford to design and develop a product specifically for the LDC market met with failure; the "Developing Nation Tractor" proved to be too expensive and did not have all the features desired by Latin American farmers.[10]

Dr. Khan, with his earlier experience in the mechanization of tropical agriculture, believed that adaptation of machinery developed outside the Philippines for temperate zones was only a partial solution to the needs of tropical zone rice farmers. The requirements of mechanization for small-scale farms and the local production of agricultural machines, he felt, were two facets of the same problem. Further, he was convinced that the actual design of the machine and its production process were intimately related. In other words, the mechanization problem in the field could not be solved until the bottlenecks to indigenous machinery production had been overcome.

Khan identified a significant gap in existing technology and, more specifically, a lack of designs for simple agricultural machines which could be produced with indigenous resources. With the support of Dr. Robert F. Chandler, Jr., who was at that time director of the IRRI, Khan changed the focus of the project to the invention and innovation of new, simple designs for agricultural equipment.[11] In the first semiannual report published after Khan's arrival, the shift in approach was justified in the following manner:

> The agricultural machinery research underwent a change in emphasis during the latter part of the year. A review of machinery research in the developing countries indicated that in order to have a significant impact on mechanization, it was essential that the results of the research must be incorporated in commerically produced machines. To achieve such a goal, it was necessary to orient the research activities towards the manufacturers of agricultural equipment located within as well as outside the tropical rice producing countries.[12]

Khan was operating under two major assumptions. First, he argued that agricultural equipment must be suited to the social, economic, and industrial environment. He attributed the failure of LDCs to absorb foreign technology to the incompatibility of the technology to local environmental conditions. Second, as noted above, he stressed the relationship between the design and manufacture of a product. The product design largely determines the production process; the failure of the development of a labor-intensive farm equipment industry in LDCs was largely due, he believed, to the unavailability of appropriate designs.[13]

Under the leadership of Khan, the objectives of the project are twofold: 1) to develop agricultural machines which are economically suitable to small farms, ranging from 2 to 10 hectares in size;* and 2) to design equipment which could be produced with locally available resources.[14]

Initial program strategy included 1) a survey of small farms to determine the equipment/machinery needs of the farmer;[15] 2) a survey at the firm level to appraise local production capabilities;[16] and 3) a survey of part shops to determine which components were readily available. With these findings in hand, IRRI engineers set out to design machinery appropriate to the needs of the farmer and the availability of local skills and resources.[17]

Product Design and Development of IRRI Threshers

Threshers

One of the first pieces of equipment to be developed by the AED was a thresher. In the developed countries, the advent of the combine harvester eliminated the need for a thresher. Many companies in the developed world therefore no longer manufactured this particular piece of machinery. For a number of environmental, economic, and social reasons, the combine harvester had not gained wide acceptance in the developing countries. Hence, the thresher was still very much in demand but "due to a lack of suitable threshers," as one report put it, "the farmers in many tropical countries [were using] machines which were originally developed over 50 years ago."[18] In response to this need the AED commenced work on two models: a drum type power thresher and a table type power thresher.

The first designs of the drum type power thresher were released to industry as early as 1968. This particular model proved to be a

---

*According to Dr. Khan, the farmer with a holding smaller than two hectares does not have the requisite resources for investment in agricultural machinery.

failure because it was not commercially profitable. In the case of the table type thresher, a number of years were required to resolve the major engineering problems inherent in the design. Despite its lower production costs and simpler design, however, this second model was also unsuccessful commercially. Farmers appeared to be uninterested in the hold-on type nature of both threshers. They also desired a machine with greater capacity.[19] Consequently, IRRI engineers developed a third model—the axial flow thresher—which is the throw-in type and has four times the capacity of its predecessors. This last model is currently being produced by local firms and has been relatively popular.

Power Tillers

The most successful design measured in terms of commercial acceptability is the four- to six-horsepower tiller, which was released to manufacturers in 1972. Until the AED designed a tiller for local production, all hand tractors were imported, the majority coming from Japan in completely knocked down form and assembled in the Philippines.[20] The Japanese models were expensive and the devaluation of the peso in 1970 substantially increased the price of imports. Consequently the sales of tractors declined slightly.[21]

Dr. Khan recognized at the time that "the high cost of imported power tillers [was] a serious bottleneck in the mechanization of rice cultivation in the developing countries." Local manufacture of the Japanese tiller within the Philippines was not a viable alternative because ". . . these machines [were] basically designed for capital-intensive, mass-production techniques."[22] Seventy-eight percent of Philippine companies are small and the complex Japanese designs could not be produced with local capabilities and simple methods of production. The AED, familiar with the success of Thai engineers in developing designs of agricultural equipment which could be produced in domestic small machine shops, set out to develop a small lightweight tiller.[23]

In designing the tiller, engineers had to pay particular attention to the 1) weight of the final product, 2) simplicity of design, and 3) production costs. The tiller must be light enough for two to three men to lift it if it should bog down in mud. It must be simple so that farmers can understand how it works and local job shops can produce it. It must be designed in such a way that it can be produced with local resources.[24] And it must be cheap enough so that the small farmer can afford it.

The final product—a 4-6 hp. tiller—meets these criteria and is without a doubt one of the most successful machines developed at IRRI. This particular model can be produced with local components with the

SMALL AGRICULTURAL MACHINERY PROJECT 219

exception of the engine, roller chains, sprockets, bearings, and seals which must be imported. It is relatively light (112 kg.), of sturdy construction, and can perform a number of operations, including plowing, puddling, cultivation, and hauling. Operation and maintenance costs are low. Repairs can be done quickly and cheaply with locally available components and labor skills. And it is inexpensive: in 1973 the Philippine model could be purchased for 4,000 pesos whereas the Japanese tiller, with the same performance specifications, sold for 7,000 pesos.[25]

A survey conducted in early 1972 has indicated that imported tillers in the 8-14 hp. range are very popular among Philippine farmers.[26] The demand for the more powerful product, coupled with the overwhelming acceptance of the 4-6 hp. tiller, induced IRRI engineers to develop a slightly larger model. The design has been released to five Philippine companies and prototypes are currently being built. These should be available for testing by IRRI engineers sometime in 1975. It also appears that a number of distributors are equipping the IRRI tiller with a more powerful engine (8-10 hp. range) at the request of the customer.

Production and Postharvest Equipment

Besides the axial flow thresher and the power tiller, the AED has designed, developed, and disseminated to manufacturers blueprints for a seeder, rotary power weeder, and rice hull furnace. Current projects include the development of a small riding tractor (15-20 hp.) which is tailored specifically for use on medium-sized farms and by small custom operators.

More recently, increasing attention has been directed to development of equipment for postharvest operations such as drying and processing. Adoption of the new seed-fertilizer-water technology by a greater number of farmers has resulted in increased yields which cannot adequately be handled by the traditional postharvest system.[27] In response to this need, IRRI engineers have designed a batch dryer which is currently being manufactured by several Filipino firms. (The Japanese manufactured a batch-dryer, but it's a mass-produced item and is therefore, not suitable to the production facilities available in the Philippines, and its selling price is too high for the typical Asian farmer. Consequently, the AED developed a simple batch-type dryer similar to the Japenese design.)

Indigenous Research and Development

So far the discussion has focused entirely on the research and development work carried on by IRRI. Similar or complementary activities were also being conducted by several local actors. Under a program jointly funded by the government of the Philippines and the United Nations Development Program, the University of the Philippines at Los Banos (UPLB) designed a flatbed dryer which is easy to operate and can be manufactured locally. This particular model has not been widely accepted by the local industrial sector for reasons which will be discussed in the next section. The two important points to be made here are that 1) there has been little or no interaction between IRRI and UPLB in spite of the fact that they are located within a half mile of each other; and 2) the two institutes have each developed a dryer which is remarkably similar in design. This seeming lack of communication, cooperation, and coordination in R and D activities has produced a duplication of efforts and a waste of scarce resources.

Research and development capabilities of industrial firms in the Philippines are extremely limited, and separate R and D facilities are usually found only in the larger companies such as Marsteel. Although there are a number of examples where a creative owner-operator has designed and developed a farm technology which satisfies local needs, the local inventor is often unable to undertake the expensive process of testing and evaluating the performance of the product (which is part and parcel of the product design and development process). In addition, these models frequently have structural defects which the innovator has trouble correcting.

Adoption of IRRI designs by local firms has indirectly strengthened the R and D capabilities of Filipino firms. In almost all instances of firms adopting the IRRI technology, some degree of product adaption has been required. Each manufacturer must fit the design to his particular production facilities and this may entail some, often minor, changes on the design. There are also instances in which the owner-operator of a given firm has made some product improvements on the IRRI machine,[28] which is a step above and beyond product adaption.

THE MANUFACTURING STAGE

Since 1971 the Agricultural Engineering Department (AED) has focused its energies on promoting acceptance and adoption of IRRI-designed farm equipment by the commercial sector. The task has not been an easy one, and a number of problems still remain to be resolved. The following discussion is partially based on interviews conducted in the summer of 1975 with AED staff and Filipino manufacturers.

Involvement of Foreign Business

During the first few years when AED's activities required close cooperation between IRRI and industry in the developed countries, there were only a few developed country firms that expressed an interest in manufacturing the kind of simple, labor-intensive equipment IRRI engineers were designing. An American company based in Michigan gave serious consideration to the possibility of producing the IRRI grain cleaner for the U.S. market. And an Australian company expressed an interest in manufacturing the IRRI thresher for export to Asian countries. The latter decided the enterprise was too risky, however, after its request for exclusive production rights was turned down by IRRI.[29]

A Japanese company was the first to successfully produce and market an IRRI design. On a visit to the Philippines, Mr. Ohtake of Ohtake Agricultural Machinery Company Limited became interested in the power paddy weeder. He returned to Japan with copies of the design, which he obtained at no cost, and developed a mini-cultivator. The machine has enjoyed a high degree of success in Japan, and recently two competing firms—Mametora Company and Konma Company—commenced production of the weeder.[30]

Except for these few cases, however, industry involvement has been minimal. The incentives for R and D, manufacture and marketing of simple equipment do not appear to exist. The only possible justification for industries in the industrialized countries to produce this type of equipment would be to secure a place in the market in anticipation of future sales.[31] To date, no industries within the developed countries—the Japanese companies being the exception—are producing the IRRI designs and there does not appear to be any sign of interest on the part of the companies in catering to the small, tropical rice producer.

Local Production

There appears to be a direct correlation between the introduction of the IRRI designs and the growth of the local agricultural equipment industry. Prior to 1972, this industry was underdeveloped, and the Philippines was almost wholly dependent upon foreign sources for supplies of agricultural equipment. U.S. multinationals dominated the market for tractors (Ford Motor Company's share of the market has exceeded 40 percent since 1967)[32] and Japan was the major supplier of power tillers. A few Filipino innovators had designed some simple farm machines and were successful in selling a limited number of units, but for the most part the industry's potential remained latent. In 1971 IRRI released its design of the power tiller and actively undertook a campaign to attract the interest of local firms. During the next few years the local agricultural equipment industry experienced rapid growth. The ensuing development of local industry was reflected by two phenomena. The first of these was the relative reduction in imports of power tillers. In 1972, for example, imports accounted for 85 percent of total power tiller sales in the Philippines. In the following year the percentage of imports to total sales of power tillers dropped to 35 percent.[33]

The second important indication of local industry growth was reflected by the increased demand for small gasoline engines. Although IRRI engineers designed the tiller for local production with indigenous resources, the Philippines did not have the capabilities to manufacture a number of essential components. The major import was a gasoline engine in the 5-8 hp. range. Consequently, the demand for Briggs and Stratton engines—the most popular foreign brand in the Philippines— doubled in each of three successive years. (See Table 7.2) Noel Reyes, President of Muller and Phipps (the sole distributor of Briggs and Stratton engines in the Philippines) attributed this dramatic jump in engine sales to the introduction of the IRRI designs.[34]

TABLE 7.2

Sales of Briggs and Stratton 7-8 hp Engines, 1970-73

Year	Total Sales 7-8 Hp.
1970	1,100
1971	2,000
1972	5,300
1973	9,500

Source: Noel Reyes, Muller and Phipps, Philippines.

Philippine Metalworking Industry

Before embarking on a discussion of local industry involvement in the IRRI project, a brief description of the metalworking industry in the Philippines is in order. The industry as a whole is composed of 1,907 firms which employ a total of 49,520 people. The majority of firms—about 76 percent—are small-scale, both in terms of total employees and the level of capitalization. In terms of geographic distribution, 59 percent are situated in the Greater Manila Area, with an additional 20 percent in Central Luzon and Southern Tagalog.[35] This concentration of metal-working firms is largely determined by the location of final markets as it is "the tendency of firms to choose locations that are near the market centers."[36] Marketing strategy is usually a function of size: the small-scale operators utilize the direct selling technique, relying heavily on personal contact and advertisement via word of mouth. Similarly, the R and D capabilities of small firms are extremely limited, and in some cases nonexistent.

Development of the metalworking industry, of which the farm equipment sector is a major component, could significantly contribute to the overall development process in the Philippines. Small, labor-intensive metalworking shops are scattered throughout the country and are a potential source of employment in rural areas. Stimulation of the industry could result in productive work opportunities and sources of income for some of the underemployed at the rural level, with the effect of slowing down rural-urban migration and ameliorating income distribution. In addition, local production would permit considerable foreign exchange savings by lessening the country's dependence on expensive imports.*

Stimulating Industrial Involvement

One responsibility of the AED, as stipulated by the second AID contract, is to design and develop farm equipment which can be fabricated in the local metal working shop, utilizing indigenous resources and the available level of technical skills to the greatest extent possible. By 1972 IRRI had a sufficient number of designs to warrant involvement of local firms in production of the new technologies. At this point IRRI shifted some of its energies from product design to transfer of the fruits of its research to the industrial sector.

Initial difficulty was experienced in attracting the interest of local manufacturers. IRRI launched an extensive advertising campaign, but few firms showed any interest in manufacturing the machines despite the fact that the designs were being offered at no cost. Small firms were reluctant or unable to shoulder the financial risks involved in producing and marketing a new product. In a last ditch attempt to capture industry's interest, IRRI assumed some of the risk by contracting with a number of firms to build prototypes.

Procedures for releasing the IRRI designs to manufacturers are not formalized, but nevertheless follow a readily identifiable pattern. When R and D on a design has been completed, drawings and a bill of

---

*The availability of local models has resulted in saving of foreign exchange, itself a scarce resource in developing countries. Engineers at IRRI have designed farm machinery which will maximize utilization of local resources. In the case of the power tiller, for example, the import content averages about 35 percent. The major imported component is the engine which costs approximately 1450 pesos for the standard 8 hp. model. If we assume that the foreign content of a local tiller is 35 percent of the selling price, the foreign exchange cost is about 2,100 pesos. In comparison, the foreign exchange cost of a Kubota tiller is approximately 15,000 pesos.

materials are released to manufacturers who have expressed an interest in the machine in question. Each participant, after careful examination of the information, submits a cost estimate for the production of a prototype. IRRI selects a few manufacturers to perform the job, basing its choice on the cost estimates and on the firm's production facilities. More than one firm is chosen in order to encourage competition and hence cost consciousness on the part of the manufacturer.[37]

Upon its completion, the prototype is shipped to IRRI where its performance is tested and evaluated. The prototype is then returned to the manufacturer with suggestions for improvements. At this point the manufacturer must decide for himself if he wants to commercially exploit the technology. If so, he must sign a "Memorandum of Agreement" by which he consents 1) not to obtain any patents on IRRI equipment, 2) to produce a quality product, and 3) to submit any changes he may make in the product design to IRRI for testing.

Marsteel Corporation, A Catalyst

IRRI efforts to stimulate local industry involvement did not meet with a great amount of success until 1972, at which time the Marsteel Corporation—an importer of Kubota power tillers and tractors—commenced production of the 4-6 hp. tiller. At this time, Luis Bernas, Marsteel's marketing manager, became concerned about the impact the revaluation of the yen might have on Marsteel's sales in the Philippines. Consequently in February 1972 Bernas went to IRRI to examine the drawings of the tiller. By June of the same year the company had constructed six prototypes and soon thereafter commenced full-scale production of the tiller. The company had no difficulty selling all the units it produced, an indication of fairly strong demand for the IRRI power tiller.[38]

Marsteel's contribution to stimulating the agricultural machinery industry in the Philippines was twofold:

1. It demonstrated the marketability and profitability of the IRRI designed equipment. The old cliche—"nothing succeeds like success"—is particularly relevant when introducing a new product. The fact that a large company was successfully manufacturing and marketing the tiller offered visible inducement for small firms to follow suit.

2. Marsteel's widespread marketing structure facilitated the distribution of IRRI tillers throughout the Philippines. Farmers and small metalworking shops in outlying areas were exposed to the IRRI designs for the first time. This was, in effect, the beginning of the process of developing consumer and producer awareness, an essential step in introducing a new product into a market.[39]

Production and Marketing Problems of Small Firms

After a firm makes the decision to manufacture an IRRI developed design, a number of problems must be successfully tackled before the product reaches the ultimate consumer. These include keeping a lid on production costs, pricing an unprotected technology, and marketing the finished product.

A firm in a developing country experiences great difficulty in keeping production costs low. Imports and interest rates are principal causes of inflated production costs. Because the metals industry in the Philippines is relatively undeveloped, local firms must rely on expensive imports to fulfill their needs for raw materials.[40] Purchases of raw materials and components are financed by short-term credit, frequently obtained at exorbitant rates of interest. These costs are partially offset by the availability of cheap labor and by the simplicity of the IRRI design. However, production costs remain sufficiently high so as to have an adverse impact on both the firm's profit margin and the availability of funds for R and D.[41]

The problems faced by the firm in pricing an IRRI-designed product are twofold. First, the lack of protection presents a problem. IRRI designs, as we noted, are universally available at no cost. The selling price must cover production costs and profit while remaining competitive with similar equipment manufactured by other firms.

The second difficulty in pricing IRRI-designed equipment is related to the nature of the market. The agricultural machinery in question has been tailored specifically for small farmers whose resources are limited and to whom the purchase of an IRRI machine represents a major investment. Manufacturers must be sensitive to the pocketbooks of the potential consumer so as not to price him out of the market.[42]

The existence of a marketing system may be critical to the commercial success—measured in terms of sales—of a new product. In the case of larger firms, the factory's physical location may be far removed from the actual market. The distributor, either in the form of a company branch or a dealership, bridges the gap between the factory and the consumer and serves as the vital "link between the company and the end-user."[43] In this respect, the larger companies have a distinct advantage over the smaller firms and local job shops, as the latter often lack a sales organization. In the case of the IRRI-designed equipment,

> Experience has shown that it is desirable to introduce new machines through manufacturers who are well established and have their own sales organization. Custom fabrication shops may be effective in building made-to-order machines but generally do not have the necessary organization to effectively develop the potential for a new machine.[44]

The importance of a marketing system is well illustrated by the case of Marsteel. As we pointed out before, the IRRI machines gained popularity in the Philippines only after this large firm commenced production of the 4-6 hp. tiller. Marsteel has approximately 40 established outlets throughout the Philippines, a situation which has greatly facilitated the marketing of the new machines.

Some of the smaller firms operate through a limited number of dealers. Others, however, have no marketing structure and depend wholly upon direct sales. These same owner-operators expressed reluctance to work through dealers who obtain a 30 percent markup. Rather, they prefer to exclude the middleman, capture some of the marketing profit for themselves, and pass a portion on to the farmer in the form of a lower selling price, thereby enhancing their competitiveness.

Since 1972 a healthy number of small and medium firms have commenced production of IRRI type equipment. The majority of these firms are located in the Greater Manila Area—IRRI's sphere of influence. One should also remember, however, that 59 percent of all Filipino metalworking shops are located in the Greater Manila Area. Explanations for the concentration of firms producing IRRI-designed equipment are several:

1. Proximity to IRRI, thereby permitting maximum contact between IRRI and the firms.
2. Proximity of Manila to the market: Central Luzon is the Philippines' rice bowl.
3. The Land Reform Program has been most fully implemented in Nueva Ecija (Central Luzon). The tiller becomes an attractive and viable technology in an area where rice farms are small, averaging less than five hectares.
4. The progressive nature of Central Luzon. In the past, new ideas have been tested in this region. Farmers have therefore been exposed to new technologies and may be more receptive to new ideas and less resistant to change.

Extension to Remote Areas

To date, extension of the designs to remote areas of the Philippines and other Asian countries has met with little success. Few firms in the outlying regions of the Philippines have commenced production of the IRRI equipment. In the same vein, efforts to transfer the agricultural technology to other Asian countries through the subcontract program have been thwarted. One conclusion we can draw from these past experiences relates to the location and role of IRRI. Involvement of local institutions may be a requisite to successful transfer and

SMALL AGRICULTURAL MACHINERY PROJECT 227

diffusion of new designs. For example, as of this writing no firms in Davao and General Santos (Mindanao) are fabricating IRRI designs. One firm built a prototype of an IRRI power tiller in 1973, which was tested and approved by IRRI engineers. The firm, however, decided not to commence production. Other companies have designed their own equipment or are producing the local variety of the thresher, and are not interested in the IRRI designs.[45] Expressed reasons for this disinterest are as follows:

1. Some manufacturers feel that the IRRI equipment is inappropriate to the particular needs of farmers in Mindanao. The average farm size is relatively large and the tractor can prepare the land much more quickly than the power tiller. Continuous cropping is practiced in the area and timeliness is therefore an important element. As for the thresher, the local variety reportedly has a greater threshing capacity than the IRRI model (35 to 40 sacks per hour as opposed to 20 sacks per hour).[46]

2. One local inventor and enterpreneur, who has designed and is currently manufacturing his own tiller, believes that it is too difficult to imitate someone else's work. He prefers to design his own equipment, for only in this way will he be familiar with all the working parts of the machine.

3. Farmers are not satisfied with the IRRI product. The tiller is too heavy and the belts break easily. The most frequently expressed complaints regarding the thresher are that grain recovery is low and the seeds are cracked and cannot be used for transplanting.

4. Demand for power tillers is weak. One reason for this is the unavailability of credit to the farmer. Requirements for obtaining a loan from the Philippine National Bank (PNB) or Development Bank of the Philippines (DBP) are extremely difficult (and in some cases impossible) for the small farmer to meet. The farmer must put up collateral and in the event that he cannot meet his payments the bank will foreclose if it does not permit refinancing.[47] The farmer's lack of training on how to operate a machine was a second explanation for weak demand. According to several manufacturers, a farmer is reluctant to invest in a technology which he does not understand.

One manufacturer in General Santos, Cotabato did express an intent to commence production of three IRRI designs in the near future. He has recently been granted a loan by the DBP and is in the process of expanding his production capabilities. After his shop is completed, he will manufacture the IRRI tiller, thresher, and seeder. In striking contrast to other manufacturers we talked to, he feels there is a potential market for IRRI equipment for the following reasons: 1) The average farm holding is 8 to 12 hectares, which is sufficient collateral for obtaining a loan. He therefore feels that credit is not a constraint.

2) The opportunities for doing custom work are many, thereby increasing the profitability of investment in agricultural equipment. 3) Farmers in Cotabato are already employing modern farm technologies and are receptive to the idea of using machines. 4) There is a marked scarcity of farm labor in the area, due to the presence of banana and pineapple plantations (Stanphilco and Dole).

The experience of the IRRI project seems to indicate that the successful transfer of technology may be in part a function of location. Evidence points to the conclusion that technology may be rapidly absorbed in the areas contiguous to the research institute, but that difficulties will arise when the technology is to be transferred to regions beyond the institute's influence, as in the case of Mindanao.

The spectrum of services provided by IRRI—research, development, publicizing the availability of designs, providing designs at no cost, contracting with manufacturers to build a prototype, testing and evaluating industry prototypes, provision of technical assistance—may be invaluable to the process of dissemination and diffusion of a new technology. The importance of these functions is supported by the experience of the University of the Philippines, Los Banos (UPLB), which designed a flatbed dryer but has not actively promoted diffusion of the technology because it lacked the necessary financial resources.[48] The number of firms actually producing the UPLB dryer are limited, in contrast to the IRRI model of the dryer, which has gained greater acceptance among local firms. The failure of the UPLB design to catch on may in part be attributed to the inability of the University to provide the follow-up services which IRRI can and does furnish. The initial difficulties faced by IRRI in obtaining industry involvement and the minimal diffusion of the UPLB design suggest that more is involved in successful technology transfer than simply producing appropriate designs which can be obtained at no cost. This is supported by the example of a manufacturer in General Santos who has obtained copies of all IRRI reports and blueprints but perceives no market for these designs. As a result, the latter are now stacked neatly in a corner of his shop covered with two inches of dust. (His stated reason for not producing IRRI-designed equipment is its apparent unsuitability to the needs of the local farmer. In essence he does not perceive a market for the equipment. His competitor, however, is planning to commence production of IRRI tillers, threshers, and weeders.)

It cannot be realistically expected that IRRI can provide these services to all areas within the Philippines and Asia as a whole. It would appear that local and national institutes, such as universities and government-sponsored research facilities, may be the appropriate vehicle for facilitating the transfer of technology from the institute to the commercial sector. By assuming responsibility for some of the

SMALL AGRICULTURAL MACHINERY PROJECT

services, national institutes would relieve IRRI's burden and simultaneously facilitate the technology transfer process. This approach has the additional benefit of developing the capabilities of national institutes to take over the activities currently performed by IRRI—that is, indigenization of the R and D and domestic technology transfer process. This could serve to enhance the country's problem solving capabilities and reduce its reliance on foreign aid.

Potential Problem Areas

In the course of the study, a number of potential problem areas were identified. The first of these centers on IRRI's patent policy, which was formulated with the objective of encouraging small firm participation but which may stifle local innovativeness and work to the advantage of the large corporate firm and/or limit the growth of the export industry. The second important issue is the compatability or incompatability of the small and large firm in the agricultural equipment sector.

Patents

Recognizing that few firms can afford to pay for the designs, IRRI has opted to disseminate its blueprints to interested manufacturers at no cost, subject to a few provisions. Two conditions are particularly relevant to a discussion on patent issues. The first states that no firm can "obtain patents or other encumbrances on any component or part originating from IRRI designs." The second condition stipulates that any improvements engineered by the manufacturer are to be submitted to IRRI, who retains the right "to distribute such information to manufacturers located outside the country in which the improvement originated."

Universal availability of the IRRI designs to interested manufacturers may be the optimum strategy if one's objective is to stimulate an underdeveloped industry. This policy has undoubtedly been a factor in encouraging the smaller firms to commence production of the designs. These firms operate with extremely tight budgets and are unable to buy blueprints or rights to production. However, the impossibility of obtaining exclusive rights to production may discourage some firms from producing the technology.

Two larger firms, GAMI and Durasteel, expressed dissatisfaction with the policy: they noted that market development is a costly and unprofitable venture for unprotected products. GAMI, for example, has high overhead costs and is interested only in products with exclusive features which cannot be easily copied by small shops.[49] Marsteel, on the contrary, is unconcerned about the free availability of the design. Luis Bernas, Marketing Manager of Marsteel, informed us that his company is actually encouraging small firms to enter the market. According to Bernas, proliferation of small firms manufacturing agricultural equipment is a low cost, effective method for developing the market for said products. Once the market has been developed, the battle will be to capture the largest possible share of total sales. Bernas hinted that when the time is ripe, Marsteel can temporarily lower product prices, driving smaller competitors who are unable to respond in like fashion out of the market.[50]

With respect to patent rights, it is unclear if local entrepreneurs are prohibited from obtaining patents on design changes they may make on IRRI equipment. The first company to market an IRRI technology—Ohtake in Japan—did not sign a written agreement with IRRI; it has since obtained a number of patents on changes it has made on the weeder. However, Filipino firms have also made a number of changes on the original design and to our knowledge none has obtained patents on these changes. For example, Arsenio Dungo of Kaunlaran, in response to the complaints and feedback from customers, outfitted the axial flow thresher with an oscillating tray, an innovation which has resulted in cleaner grain. To his chagrin, Durasteel—a larger competitor—has copied his innovation. Dungo told us that he has spent many sleepless nights, knowing that his design improvement is unprotected and can be copied by others. He is reluctant to make further innovations.[51]

Bonifacio Isidro of C and B Crafts has also made a number of improvements on the thresher, one of which has reduced threshing losses. He is proud of his accomplishment and is pleased that IRRI has taken note of, and in some cases has used, his design changes.[52] Isidro's generous attitude may be attributable to his relative isolation from other manufacturers of the axial flow thresher. He may become more protective of his innovations if a competitor moves into his sphere of operation.

As of this writing, the number of firms producing IRRI-designed agricultural equipment is limited. As the market grows and more firms initiate production of the designs in response to growing demand, marketing spheres will begin to overlap. This is already beginning to occur in Cabanatuan City, where there may be as many as 52 local dealers of agricultural equipment. To attract customers and corner a larger portion of the market, firms will wish to differentiate their product from those of competitors. One current method of achieving product differentiation is by color of the paint job, but this will be insufficient when competition becomes keener.

The current patent policy may discriminate against the small firm. A company such as Marsteel—with ready access to credit, considerable R and D resources and a national network of dealerships—can exploit a small firm's innovations and simultaneously make modifications which cannot be copied with the limited production facilities of small, labor-intensive firms. According to Luis Bernas, Marsteel will respond to the growing sophistication of farmers by offering a number of options and accessories to its machines. He noted that these changes would be difficult, if not impossible, for the smaller firms to imitate and would enlarge Marsteel's share of the market.[53] Smaller companies would be at a distinct disadvantage and could ultimately be forced out of business.

IRRI's policy regarding dissemination of information on design changes to manufacturers outside the country of origin has some potential implications for export opportunities. At the time of this writing the export market for IRRI equipment is small and therefore this policy does not currently affect Filipino firms. It is conceivable that as the export market grows, this policy could inhibit firms from improving their product as they would not be assured of recouping R and D expenses—the raison d'etre of patents. While this issue is not of immediate concern in regards to local industry, it may merit consideration in the future as an export industry develops.

Compatibility of Large and Small Industry

An important issue which should receive more attention is the compatibility of large firms like Marsteel and small metalworking shops. Marsteel, as noted above, has played an important role in encouraging small firms to commence production of IRRI equipment. However, it should be recognized that Marsteel could also conceivably snuff out local competition when it is to its advantage to do so. Luis Bernas has already mentioned that he perceives the battle as being one of obtaining the largest possible share of the market. One way to achieve this is by temporarily cutting prices, forcing competitors unable to retaliate out of the market.[54]

Marsteel's advantages over the smaller firms are many. It is a large, well established company which could absorb temporary losses to gain a monopoly. It has ties with the Marcos family, and therefore has political influence. It has benefited from the IRRI designs, but, unlike the majority of firms in the Philippines, has the necessary resources to support an R and D function. It can purchase raw materials and imported components (such as the Briggs and Stratton engine) in bulk, thereby cutting its production costs and ultimate selling price. It can modify its product in a manner which cannot be easily copied by the small firm, thereby achieving a degree of product differentiation.

It was not the intent of the IRRI project to benefit large powerful companies. In a program which makes its designs freely available to interested parties, how can one prevent the large companies from gaining the benefits to be derived from production of the designs? This question is important because 1) the project is partially missing the target, which is the small firm, and 2) if large firms get control of the market, does this put the small company in jeopardy?

Furthermore, large local and foreign agricultural equipment companies have formed an Agricultural Machinery Dealers Association (AMDA) whose function is to represent the industry and its interests. This entails interaction with government officials on policy issues relevant to the health and well-being of the industry. In addition, lending institutions such as the Central Bank or the Development Bank of the Philippines are more favorably inclined to grant loans to AMDA members for the reason that AMDA polices its members. This is a particularly valuable benefit in view of the difficulties involved in obtaining financing.[55]

To become a member, a firm must submit an application to the membership committee, which assesses the company's capability to maintain specified standards. Membership dues amount to 600 pesos a year, a fee most small firms cannot afford to pay. Importers of four-wheel tractors and Japanese power tillers, as well as the larger local manufacturers of agricultural equipment, are members of the AMDA.

As of this writing, small firms do not have an organization of this nature to protect or represent their interests. Mr. Dungo of Kaunlaran has requested the assistance of the University of the Philippines Institute of Small-Scale Industries (UP-ISSI) in organizing small firms producing IRRI equipment into an association.[56] The functions of this organization would be twofold: to protect its members from big industry, and to represent the interests of small firms before the government. The ISSI has written to a number of firms about this proposal, but has to date received only a few responses from companies indicating an interest. If small firms can organize themselves into such an association, they may be less susceptible to exploitation or manipulation by their larger counterparts. It must be recognized, however, that there are great difficulties involved in attempting to organize firms which are producing the same product and therefore are essentially competitors themselves.

One method of promoting and maintaining the competitiveness of the small firm is through the formation of industrial cooperatives. Membership in a cooperative would entitle the firms to a number of services which could cut production costs and permit a wider distribution of the finished product. For example, purchase of raw materials and imported components in bulk by the cooperative would substantially

SMALL AGRICULTURAL MACHINERY PROJECT

lower the cost of these materials to the small firm. Second, technicians maintained by the cooperative could provide firms wishing to expand production and sales with assistance to overcome the technical, managerial, and financial implications of such a change. And third, the cooperative could operate a clearinghouse of information on potential government contracts, export opportunities and availability of new technologies.

The preceding discussion has focused primarily on the benefits to be derived from the mobilization of small firms producing agricultural equipment. It has assumed that each firm produces the entire unit on its own, and suggests cooperation among small firms in areas other than production. The idea of joint production of farm machinery has been promoted by Dr. Bart Duff of AED and has been initiated in Mindanao. At Dr. Duff's suggestion, the Davao Metal Industrial Association has been organized to manufacture and market agricultural equipment. The Association consists of 33 firms, each of which will contribute a component or service in which it has a comparative advantage. More specifically, some firms will build parts, one firm will assemble the machine and another will be responsible for sales and marketing. This approach, when it becomes operational, will promote horizontal integration and will result in the production of better quality, lower priced machines. As of this writing, the Association has not gotten off its feet, and one member expressed the opinion that the Association could not function without some government assistance. The nature or scope of the required aid was not specified.[57]

The Marsteel Corporation provides us with an example of both the cooperative and joint production approach. It relies on nearby metalworking shops to provide it with components which cannot be economically produced at the Marsteel factory. The company has subcontracted with anywhere from 12 to 62 firms at any given time to perform specific jobs.[58] Marsteel has also begun to purchase completed threshers from Durasteel and Kalayaan. Luis Bernas explained to us that the current market for threshers is small and does not justify mass production with capital-intensive production methods. The thresher, as designed by IRRI, requires labor-intensive production processes which are too costly for Marsteel's mode of operation. Bernas pointed out to us that smaller firms can economically fabricate the thresher but do not have adequate marketing and distribution systems. The current arrangements benefit both parties involved: the small firms sell the completed product to Marsteel, which in turn performs the marketing function after attaching the Marsteel label to all units.

THE FARMER STAGE

During the course of field work on this study, interviews with 45 farmers were conducted in one province in Central Luzon (Nueva Ecija) and two provinces in Mindanao (Davao and South Cotabato). The interviews were designed to garner impressions as to the relative rates and reasons for adoption and nonadoption of the IRRI-designed equipment.

Regional Prefences

While it appears that locally designed power tillers are being purchased at a rapidly accelerating pace in Central Luzon, the tiller has not yet received widespread acceptance and usage in Mindanao. This is probably due to the larger size of land holdings in Mindanao encouraging the use of four-wheel tractors rather than tillers, a difference in soil conditions which does not make the IRRI-type tiller feasible for usage in the south, and the proximity of IRRI to the Central Luzon region.

While power tiller sales have been steadily increasing since production commenced in 1972, imported tillers are also being sold in increasing numbers. This is true in spite of the price differential of more than four to one favoring local tillers. Farmers interviewed said they often preferred the imported type because of its greater power, durability, and other features such as the steering clutch.

The other IRRI-designed machine which has received a considerable amount of attention and is presently being produced in Central Luzon is the axial-flow thresher. While this machine has seen relatively little use to this date in comparison to the power tiller, the thresher has only been in the market for two years. Given the current pattern of demand, it may well be that future sales of the thresher will rise gradually.[59] However, the cost of the thresher is almost double that of the power tiller, and many farmers in Nueva Ecija do not feel it is a feasible investment to use on their small farms.

In Mindanao the Cotabato-type double drum thresher has been widely used since the mid-1950s. It was originally designed by Gabaldon, a native of Cotabato. At this date, the IRRI thresher has seen no usage in this region.

SMALL AGRICULTURAL MACHINERY PROJECT

Incentive to Invest

Available literature suggests several reasons as to why a farmer chooses to invest in farm machinery instead of continuing to rely on the traditional form of energy, the water buffalo, known in the Philippines as the carabao. These include more timely land preparation, particularly for double cropping; more complete tillage to aid in weed control; and less time out of the field taking care of the carabao.

The machine is not a simple substitute for the carabao, however. The overwhelming majority of farmers surveyed in both Nueva Ecija and Mindanao did not sell their carabao after purchasing a machine; instead they continued to use the carabao for plowing the edges of the field where machinery is not as effective. They found caring for the carabao to be of little nuisance and did not feel land devoted to the carabao for food consumption was in competition with the land area of crop production.

No clear-cut relationships between machine adoption and increased yields or income could be discerned. While the productivity and income of farmers using IRRI machines increased, this increase could not be attributed directly to use of the machines. It undoubtedly depended on a range of factors, such as the existence of irrigation to allow for double or triple cropping, and so on. The main advantage that tiller use provides is more free time to do other chores in the fields and around the home. Additional time and effort devoted to the soil, of course, may have an impact on productivity and eventually increase income.

The key factor influencing the farmer's decision to risk a new investment in a machine was that of fellow farmer influence. Many farmers had no knowledge that a machine had been designed by IRRI, indicating that the IRRI name did not play a substantial role in encouraging machine adoption. While manufacturers and dealers attribute sales to field demonstrations which they conduct, farmers adopting the machines overwhelmingly cited a neighbor's or relatives' influence as the primary factor affecting purchase and choice of equipment.

An example of the strength of the communications link among farmers and the importance of additional free time was provided through interviews in the village of Baluarte, Nueva Ecija where many of the farmers had purchased locally manufactured brands of power tillers since 1972. Three farmers jointly interviewed who had all previously farmed with a carabao, cited fellow farmer influence as the major incentive in their decisions to buy a local brand. For them added expenses incurred from operating the machine such as the cost of gas and oil were viewed as worthwhile in light of all the advantages the machine provided. While the time saved by the tractor in land preparation was felt to be important, all three farmers agreed that the major advantage was the additional free time they had since they had made their purchases. They spent their new time around the home and cleaning and mending dikes in the field.

Financing

As other studies also suggest, it appears that lack of access to credit is a major bottleneck inhibiting machine adoption. Many farmers who had purchased machines said that they had paid in cash, suggesting that they may have had more available resources than the small farmers who indicated a desire to purchase a machine but cited capital as the major constraint. Rural bankers who still view the farmer as a risky venture and available statistics from the third CB:IBRD loan program (see next section on government policies) indicate that a marked bias remains against small farmer lending for the purchase of agricultural machinery.

Servicing and Spare Parts

While fellow farmer influence is significantly greater than the role of the manufacturer or dealer in a farmer's decision to purchase a machine, there is substantial feedback from the operator to supplier. In contrast to imported hand tractors and large four-wheelers, farmers owning locally manufactured tillers found no problems getting their tillers repaired or in securing spare parts for the machine. Repairs could usually be made in local machine shops. When local expertise could not resolve a mechanical difficulty, the machine would be sent back to the factory, often located in the Greater Manila Area. While this may be a time constraint for the farmer, it is certainly less severe than having to send an imported brand back to its home factory.

The Impact of Mechanization on Employment

Although definitely not the major concern of our investigations from the outset, a few questions concerning the impact of agricultural equipment on employment were asked during the course of our surveying. While recognizing that labor displacement is a highly controversial subject and that, due to the general nature of our field research,

SMALL AGRICULTURAL MACHINERY PROJECT 237

our results are by no means definitive, we did gather the following impressions.

1. In Baluarte, Nueva Ecija, where approximately 80 percent of the farmers are owner-operators of power tillers, little hired labor was used prior to purchase of the machine. The labor saved in most cases was that of the owner-operator, indicating that the machine does not replace hired labor whose sole source of income may be derived from working during the planting-harrowing stage.

2. In Mindanao, where the Cotabato thresher is popular, the amount of hired labor displaced by the thresher again appears to be minimal. According to barrio captains (village spokesmen) in the General Santos area of South Cotabato, threshing was accomplished under a system of labor exchange among the farmers prior to adoption of the machine. Several interviews with farmers in this area seemed to indicate that family labor was, in some cases, the primary source of labor for the threshing process, thereby resulting in family labor savings when machines were used.

3. In those areas in the Philippines where harvesting-threshing operations are traditionally performed by hired labor, the introduction of IRRI-type threshers may have adverse effects on rural employment. However, the introduction of IRRI-type threshers could generate employment opportunities in areas where the large McCormick-type thresher has traditionally been used.

4. The above mentioned factors are concerned with employment and opportunities on the farm level. In addition, the development and growth of the local agricultural equipment industry is contributing to job opportunities at the manufacturing level and to the development of an industrial semiskilled and skilled labor force. In almost all cases, manufacturers stated a preference for unskilled labor, which they subsequently trained. In this way industry is performing a valuable service and is contributing to the economic development of the country.

THE ROLE OF GOVERNMENT POLICIES

In determining the strength of the secondary and tertiary linkages generated by appropriate technology programs (see discussion in first section of this chapter), sensitivity to the political context in which a project such as IRRI's is operating is <u>essential</u>, for the political environment and policies permeate activities at all levels and often have a stronger impact than anything else on the potential for success or failure of such a program. Governmental actions which may have stimulated a demand for farm equipment, the encouragement of small and medium-scale industries,* and credit policies have held much significance for the program to date.

Since the commencement of martial law in September 1972, the Philippine government has instituted several socio-economic reforms in an effort to create an appropriate setting and to mobilize resources for development. Two reforms in particular, which may have been instrumental in creating a climate favorable for the diffusion of the IRRI designs after the initial R and D sequence, are the restoration of peace and order and the acceleration towards agrarian reform; both may have contributed to a growth in interest in small farm equipment in the Philippines around this time. For many, the reinstatement of law and order diminished the fear of having valuable possessions stolen and simultaneously increased the opportunity for the poor to have more recourse to justice. In many respects, the risks in making a new investment were lessened. Secondly, when President Marcos announced Presidential Decree No. 2, proclaiming the entire nation as a land reform area, new emphasis was placed on small land holdings and benefits for the small farmer. Coupled with these reforms, other factors which may have played a role include the devaluation of the peso in 1971, causing a substantial increase in the price of imported equipment and the establishment of a governmental support price for rice, providing the farmer with incentive to increase his production.

Small and Medium-Scale Industries

One reform announced by the Philippine government, the creation of additional employment opportunities, has been incorporated into the first development objective of the Philippine Four Year Development Plan FY 1974-77. This reform calls for "maximum utilization of the labor force, or more specifically, promotion of employment and minimization of underemployment."[60] In contrast to virtual neglect of this objective in the past,[61] government policies now aim to stimulate labor-intensive production processes and the growth of small and

---

*Although commonly referred to as small and medium-scale industries, it should be noted that this also includes cottage industries, those which are usually family-operated and carried on in or near the home. Distinction among cottage, small, and medium vary according to each particular institution's definition; however, the industries are frequently categorized according to the total amount of assets: less than 100,000 pesos for cottage; 100,000 to 1 million for small; 1 million to 4 million for medium.

medium-scale industries such as many of those producing IRRI-designed machines. Small and medium-scale industries not only can help in lessening employment difficulties but also can aid regional development and the decentralization of industrial activity by helping to stem the exodus from rural to urban areas. They are usually labor-intensive and more suitable to the relative factor endowments of the developing countries.

Whereas the University of the Philippines Institute of Small-Scale Industries (UP-ISSI) was until recently the major institutional promoter of small and medium-scale industries, the government is now supporting these industries through a variety of institutional channels and through various policies geared toward economic reform. One such channel is the Department of Industry's Commission on Small and Medium Industries (CSMI), a 12-member agency created in June 1974 to aid the development of small and medium-scale industries through providing technical and managerial assistance.[62] One project of CSMI is the Medium and Small-Scale Industries Coordinated Action Program (MASICAP) under the jurisdiction of the Department of Industry.

> In the context of a development program for small and medium-scale industries, MASICAP . . . assists the rural entrepreneur [in obtaining] bank credit by preparing with him the project feasibility study and assisting him [to] comply with all the loan papers required by financial institutions.[63]

While MASICAP compiles an extensive loan application and the only costs incurred by the small entrepreneur are for materials and secretarial services, the final decision on whether or not the loan is to be granted rests with the particular lending institution. During the fiscal year 1974-75, MASICAP's 11 regional assistance teams prepared a total of 756 small and medium-sized projects.[64] At the time of the writing of the MASICAP Annual Report FY 74-75, the loan proposals of 217 projects had already been decided upon by the particular lending source; of the 217, 215 projects had been approved for loans. MASICAP undertook 32 agri-implement projects between November 1973 and August 1975. While eight of those projects have already been approved, lending institutions have not yet made decisions on the remaining 24.

In addition to MASICAP, CSMI established four Small Business Advisory Centers in 1974 in Zamboanga, Tacloban, San Fernando La Union, and Legaspi City. These centers provide management consultancy and analysis of small business problems. It has been projected that an additional seven centers will be built around the country within the next three years.

For several years the Philippine government has encouraged investment in industry through a variety of incentives including such measures as tax exemptions and deductions from taxable income.[65] The Board of Investments (BOI) administers such incentives and also prepares a list of preferential areas for investment known as the Investment Priorities Plan (IPP). The plan is a list of industries in which investment should be encouraged because there is a gap between potential demand and present capacity. Industries that have excess capacity are not included in the IPP and are therefore not eligible for the government incentives listed above. Industries now on the BOI's priority list include animal feed and animal husbandry, poultry farming, and agricultural implements and machinery.

Early Investment Priorities Plans were criticized for overly general objectives and no clear-cut rationale for many of the industries listed as "priority".[66] Many of the IPP's objectives now reach beyond simple encouragement of investments to develop local industrial production capacity for certain products. Newer and more specific policy considerations include promotion of small and medium-scale industries and encouragement of regional development. Despite this shift, however, the International Labor Organization in its report entitled Sharing in Development—A Programme of Employment, Equity, and Growth for the Philippines, contends that little change has actually occurred.

> Actual BOI registrations in 1972 show a continuation of large-scale and capital-intensive concentration of the past, in spite of efforts to the contrary. What is of particular concern is the fact that, even with the best intentions, it is administratively difficult for the BOI to reach the smaller and more regionally dispersed firms. And yet these represent a very important untapped potential for output generation and employment growth. It is virtually necessary for a firm to have a Manila office to obtain a BOI registration.[67]

Available data regarding the power tiller industry appears to support this statement. As of April, 1974 the BOI had two companies, Marsteel and Seacom, registered for the production of power tillers. Even though both companies manufacture IRRI-designed machines, Marsteel and Seacom are two of the largest Filipino firms devoted to agricultural machinery production, and both are located within the confines of Manila.

In early 1973 the government revised the Tariff and Customs Code in order to encourage the manufacture of locally made products with a maximum amount of indigenous resources, thereby discouraging an excess reliance on imports. However, while the tariff rate on power tillers is 30 percent, threshers are only subject to a 10 percent duty.

SMALL AGRICULTURAL MACHINERY PROJECT 241

With the Cotabato-type thresher having been available since the 1950s and the recent commercialization of the IRRI axial-flow thresher, the tariff rate for threshers should probably be comparable to that for power tillers if imports are actually to be discouraged.

The 10 percent duty on four-wheel tractors is a more debatable issue. On the one hand, there is no local industry which presently manufactures four-wheel tractors and could be stifled by the imported ones. Four-wheelers may in fact be the most suitable types of tractors for larger land holdings, especially in areas where sugarcane is grown. On the other hand, locally produced power tillers are now replacing the use of four-wheelers in several areas, indicating that the former may actually be more appropriate for those areas than the latter. This is an instance where locally produced equipment is in competition with imports, and if the government is encouraging local production through its revised tariff structure, perhaps a second look should be given to duty rates on four-wheel tractors.

While the government has supported the growth of local industry with many new policy changes, Presidential Decree No. 287, signed by President Marcos on September 6, 1973, appears to be in direct contradiction to this trend. According to the decree, local industry was unable to meet the immediate machinery needs of Filipino farmers; therefore, 140 million pesos were allocated to the Department of Agrarian Reform (DAR) to finance the acquisition of 5,000 hand tractors. In 1973, the DAR purchased 5,000 Kubota tillers from Japan which were provided on suppliers' credit. Repayment was to be made in U.S. dollars over a period of seven years at 9 percent rate of interest. Marsteel imported the tillers and sold them to the DAR.

The approximate cost per unit was 28,000 pesos; the cost to the farmer was substantially less, 17,894 pesos for a 10 hp. tiller,[68] the difference being absorbed by the government. According to officials at the DAR, power tillers obtained under this particular program have been distributed.

The government consummated the contract with Kubota during a period when the local agricultural equipment industry was gaining momentum. Available production figures suggest that local industry, if given the opportunity, could have provided the government with a portion of the total. BOI statistics show that nine firms manufactured 4,014 units and sold 2,935 in FY 1974. There was, therefore, a minimum of 1,079 units available locally which could have been purchased by the government. This could have supported local industry, represented a foreign exchange savings, and a savings to the farmer (the local variety sells at about one-third the price of the subsidized model).

As we noted in the previous section, studies indicate that the allocation of credit has historically discriminated against the development of small and medium-scale industries; lending institutions have leaned heavily towards short-term loans and required collateral instead of recognizing projected revenue and growth potential of small and medium-scale industries as the crucial elements in considering loan repayment possibilities.[69]

One example of a government effort to provide credit for small and medium-scale industries that has been largely unsuccessful in fulfilling its objectives is that of the Industrial Guarantee and Loan Fund (IGLF). The IGLF was established in 1965 with AID and the International Bank for Reconstruction and Development (IBRD) assistance. Operating under the Central Bank, the IGLF guarantees loans which banks have made from their own resources and also makes loans to banks to be reloaned for IGLF-approved projects. In spite of the fact that the IGLF was created with the promotion of small and medium-scale industry as its major objective, large firms have received most of the benefits. Loans have averaged about 670,000 pesos, and two or more loans have been channeled to over one-third of the borrowers.[70]

> The IGLF has gone badly astray in the past, favouring large instead of small firms. Even after recent recommendations for change, which indicate some improvement, the final decision on loans is still highly centralized.[71]

The Philippine Four Year Development Plan recognizes the importance of adequate credit facilities as an influential tool to stimulate the development of small and medium-scale industries; an increase in the supply of institutional credit is one of eight activities enumerated in the plan for encouraging small and medium-scale growth. Several financial institutions now have special small-scale financing programs.* It is apparent that there has been no lack of recent recognition on the part of the government or lending institutions of small and medium-scale industry's need for financial assistance. Whether these firms have actually benefitted from that recognition is not at all clear. In the course of our interviews, it appeared that announcements of available financing have not necessarily been coupled with adequate liberalization of loan terms to allow the small manufacturer to benefit. Stringent collateral requirements and the amount of time necessary for loan processing were the two factors most frequently cited by small

---

*These include First National City Bank—Finance, Inc., General Bank and Trust Company, Private Development Corporation of the Philippines, Rizal Commerical Banking Corporation, and the Development Bank of the Philippines.

manufacturers we interviewed as the major bottlenecks in efforts to obtain institutional credit.

Meeting the Needs of the Small Farmer

Along with promotion of employment-enhancing activities, another important objective of the Four Year Development Plan is more equitable distribution of wealth and income. The use of credit as a policy instrument to stimulate production, increase the adoption rate of new technologies, and subsequently increase farmers' incomes has received growing attention from the Philippine government over the past few years.[72]

Credit policies of the past greatly neglected the needs of the small farmer and were largely channeled to export activities and to the wealthier farmer. Statistics available prior to the land transfer decree of 1972 indicate the inequities in the distribution of credit were especially blatant. It was estimated that small farmers (defined here as those with less than ten hectares of land) were only receiving 20 percent of the total amount of agricultural credit in spite of the fact that they comprised 95 percent of total farmer population and operated 70 percent of total cultivated land area. However, the inequities become even greater when one considers those farmers with less than three hectares of land and no collateral. Although they constituted 73 percent of all farmers and were responsible for 39 percent of the cultivated lands, it was estimated that they received only 1.6 percent of all available production credit.[73]

In order to help meet the goal of self-sufficiency in rice production, the Masagana 99 program was launched in May 1973 with one element being a revised credit scheme to allow program participants to obtain short-term production loans.

While it appears that Masagana 99 loans are reaching the small farmer (the majority of farmers we surveyed had such loans), loans for the purchase of agricultural machinery do not seem to be as easily accessible. Difficulties in obtaining adequate funds appear to be a significant constraint to the adoption of farm equipment. In a survey undertaken by Dale Porter for the Board of Investments in February 1974, lack of funds was overwhelmingly cited (61 percent) the major reason why farmers have not bought or hired the machinery they want.[74]

> Larger and higher income farmers, mostly in the better-off regions, have been the major beneficiaries of the expansion of the institutional credit system, obtaining low-priced credit in a country where its scarcity price is very high.[75]

Interviews conducted with bankers both in Manila and the provinces indicate that one of the main reasons for not providing the farmer with a loan is fear of repayment difficulties; as we noted before, many bankers continue to perceive loans to the small farmer as risky ventures.

Several specific policies and practices of formal lending institutions appear to be major bottlenecks which have prevented the small farmer from gaining access to available credit. First, institutional lenders have traditionally placed heavy reliance on collateral rather than potential capital to be generated by a loan project.[76] Our research findings support this statement. For instance, according to Mr. Rimorin, Chief of Loans and Discounts at the Davao branch of the Philippine National Bank, two loans have been made to farmers for the purchase of four-wheel tractors in Davao during the first half of 1975; by contrast, 12 farmers had applied for loans for the purchase of power tillers and all these loans were denied because the farmers' collateral and paying capacity were too low.[77] Another example of stringent loan requirements exists at the General Santos branch of the Development Bank of the Philippines; in order to receive a loan to buy a rice thresher, a farmer must own at least eight hectares of land. Romualdo Limsiaco, presently the proprietor of Steelpride Industries, Inc. and formerly a loan officer of the DBP-General Santos branch explained that the bank does not feel it is feasible for a farmer with fewer than eight hectares to purchase a thresher. The fact that a farmer often does custom work which supplements his income and could help with his loan repayment is not given consideration by the bank.[78]

One other likely factor influencing the accessibility of agricultural credit to the small farmer which should be noted is the length of time necessary in order to obtain a loan. Time involved in processing a loan can be as much as six to eight months; each provincial bank with which we had contact noted that it was subject to a loan ceiling which could not be exceeded without approval of the main branch in Manila, usually requiring an estimated additional two months of loan processing work.

The interesting point which deserves mention here is that although farmers cited lack of credit as the major constraint to purchasing a machine, very few had actually applied for a loan and been denied. Most expressed reluctance to even submit a loan application because they felt they could not meet all the necessary loan requirements.

Initial overly severe loan requirements were widely publicized as a major bottleneck in the implementation of a government sponsored emergency program which evolved in response to the foot-and-mouth epidemic affecting many of the carabao in Central Luzon in the summer of 1975. Central Luzon, the predominant rice growing region of the Philippines, is composed largely of small farm holdings. Under the emergency program, liberalized loan requirements for hand tractors were made available by the Land Bank of the Philippines for farmers whose animals had been stricken by the disease. Prerequisites for obtaining a loan included farm size of at least three hectares and membership in a Samahang Nayon, a village cooperative. Shortly after the program commenced, it became clear that the loan requirements could not be met by many of the small farmers whose carabao were diseased. According to an article in the Manila Bulletin dated August 28, 1975, "Most of those farmers whose carabaos were afflicted with the foot-and-mouth disease are poor and cannot afford to rent power tillers and/or are disqualified from the Land Bank for the purchase of hand tractors."[79]

After this, Land Bank requirements were liberalized even more. A farmer could now apply for the hand tractor if his farm size was a minimum of two and one-half hectares; however, if his holding was smaller, he could apply for a joint loan with other farmers if their total land area met the necessary hectarage requirement. Samahang Nayon membership was no longer a prerequisite, and delinquencies in amortization payments for Phase III of Masagana 99 would not disqualify a loan application. As of September 4, 1975, 702 hand tractor loans had been approved. Lack of existing information precluded the determination of the beneficiaries of the emergency program's loans at that time.

The impact of another special credit program on the promotion of farm mechanization also deserves special mention here; this is the Central Bank-International Bank for Reconstruction and Development (CB:IBRD) Farm Mechanization Loan Programs (see Table 7.3). The first of three loan programs was begun in 1966 and was designed specifically to promote small-farm mechanization.[80] Although tiller sales increased greatly during the first and second programs, the value of the loans made for four-wheel tractors far exceeded the amount allocated for power tiller purchases.[81]

> While the CB:IBRD loan program may have been a strong single factor in the promotion of small farm mechanization, loans have been granted selectively, resulting in limited participation by small farmers. Since all loans have been made on the basis of collateral available rather than on productivity of investment, more than half of all loan applications have been denied each year. The extension of medium and long-term credit has benefited mostly farm owners.[82]

The third loan program was begun in May 1974. Although farm size requirements have been adjusted to allow eligibility to any farmer not owning more than 50 hectares of land, the following figures indicate

TABLE 7.3

CB:IBRD Credit Financing, May 15, 1974—June 30, 1975

Loan Team	Power Tiller		4-Wheel Tractor	
	Number	Amount[a]	Number	Amount[a]
Southern Mindanao	283	7,638,475	26	3,116,513
Nueva Ecija	57	927,292	163	18,361,644
Panay	16	393,959	53	6,680,586.88
Panagasinan	9	303,959.50	163	19,739,068
Manila	282[b]	2,736,991	242[b]	26,970,248
Bicol	8	148,441	14	1,808,976
Cebu	39	996,303	56	7,358,016
Cagayan Valley	108	2,868,440.70	174	21,264,022.70
Bacolod	19	419,743.50	147	17,592,289.86
Totals	770	16,433,604.70	1,029	122,891,364.44

[a]Pesos
[b]more recent figures (July 3, 1975)
Source: Central Bank Department of Rural Banks and Savings and Loan Association.

that the majority of available funds has still gone overwhelmingly towards the purchase of four-wheel tractors.

AN EVALUATION OF THE IRRI PROJECT

First Sequence: Primary Linkages

The involvement of a multilateral, nonprofit research institute in the design, development and diffusion of products for commercial exploitation is extremely unusual. In a developed economy private industry normally bears the costs associated with product design and development. In the developing countries, however, a number of factors have discouraged private industry from fulfilling this function. First, the majority of firms in the LDCs are small scale and financial constraints—primarily a lack of risk capital and a tight cash balance—preclude them from establishing R and D staffs.[83] Although there are a number of examples in the Philippines where creative owner-managers have made innovations on existing technology or designed their own version of technologies which satisfy local needs, this by no means represents a steady flow of innovations. Moreover, the innovations are, almost without exception, restricted to the locale in which they originated. A second factor is the lack of a national policy in many LDCs for industrial development. Inventors do not have guarantees of patent protection and many developing countries have not instituted effective incentive-oriented tax policies. Finally, a shortage of design engineers with a commercial orientation places limits on R and D possibilities.[84]

The Agricultural Engineering Department has designed and developed agricultural equipment for rice which meets two criteria: 1) the machinery can be produced by small local metalworking shops with available resources, and 2) the machines satisfy the needs of small rice farmers and are economically viable on farms ranging in size from two to ten hectares.[85] To date the AED has initiated a total of 35 projects; six machines are currently being commercially produced in Asia and Latin America.[86]

Transferring designs from the research to the industrial sector has never been an easy process, and the case of IRRI is no exception. In 1971 the Institute launched a fairly extensive advertising campaign in an effort to attract the interest of local firms. Few firms expressed an interest in initiating production despite the fact that the designs were being offered at no cost. IRRI then contracted with a number of firms to build prototypes of the machines, which it subsequently tested. The link between the R and D and manufacturing stages was tenuous until Marsteel Corporation began producing and marketing the 5-7 hp. tiller on a large scale, an occurrence which greatly strengthened this link. Marsteel's successful experience proved that the designs could be profitably manufactured and that demand for the end-product existed. A number of small firms in the Greater Manila Area quickly joined the ballgame.

Marsteel's role in the commercialization process suggests that small firms may be reluctant to shoulder the risks inherent in the manufacture and introduction of a new product, unless they are relatively sure of success. Once the profitability and marketability of a product have been proved, there is no limit to the number of firms entering the market hoping to capitalize on demand. In Mindanao, for example, no firms have as yet commenced production of the IRRI machines and the demand potential for the technology remains to be established. Among the entrepreneurs cognizant of the existence of IRRI equipment, there are great differences of opinion regarding the suitability and marketability of the machines in Mindanao. One owner-manager plans to commence manufacture of IRRI designs in the near future and his success or failure may influence other local competing firms, as did Marsteel in the Greater Manila Area.

IRRI's role in transferring the completed designs from the industrial to the agricultural sector has been limited to testing the prototypes. Performance of the machines is evaluated in the field, and farmers are exposed to them in this way. It is at this stage that engineering and technical problems with the machines can be identified and dispatched to IRRI engineers; this is the feedback which completes the circle. Figure 7.4 indicates the activities undertaken by IRRI at this first sequence.

In summary, the results of the project are localized. The overwhelming majority of firms and farmers who have accepted the IRRI technology are located in the Greater Manila Area where the Institute's influence is at its peak.

Second Sequence: Secondary Linkages

In the second sequence, some of the activities heretofore performed by IRRI are taken over by local actors. This phase implies some degree of financial commitment and risk-taking by local participants in R and D manufacturing and marketing of IRRI designs.

Research and Development

In the case of the Philippines, each firm undertaking production of the IRRI designs must at a minimum make some changes necessary to accomodate the designs to its respective production facilities. In most cases these changes are minor, as the designs have been tailored specifically with the production facilities of small firms in mind. In other cases the changes have been extensive; Marsteel has radically changed the design of the 5-7 hp. tiller so that it can be manufactured with capital-intensive production processes.

Several firms have gone a step further and made changes which enhance machine performance. Two of the firms are small-scale and do not have official R and D personnel. In both cases the owner-manager has made the innovations in response to the complaints and/or

FIGURE 7.4

First Sequence: Primary Linkages

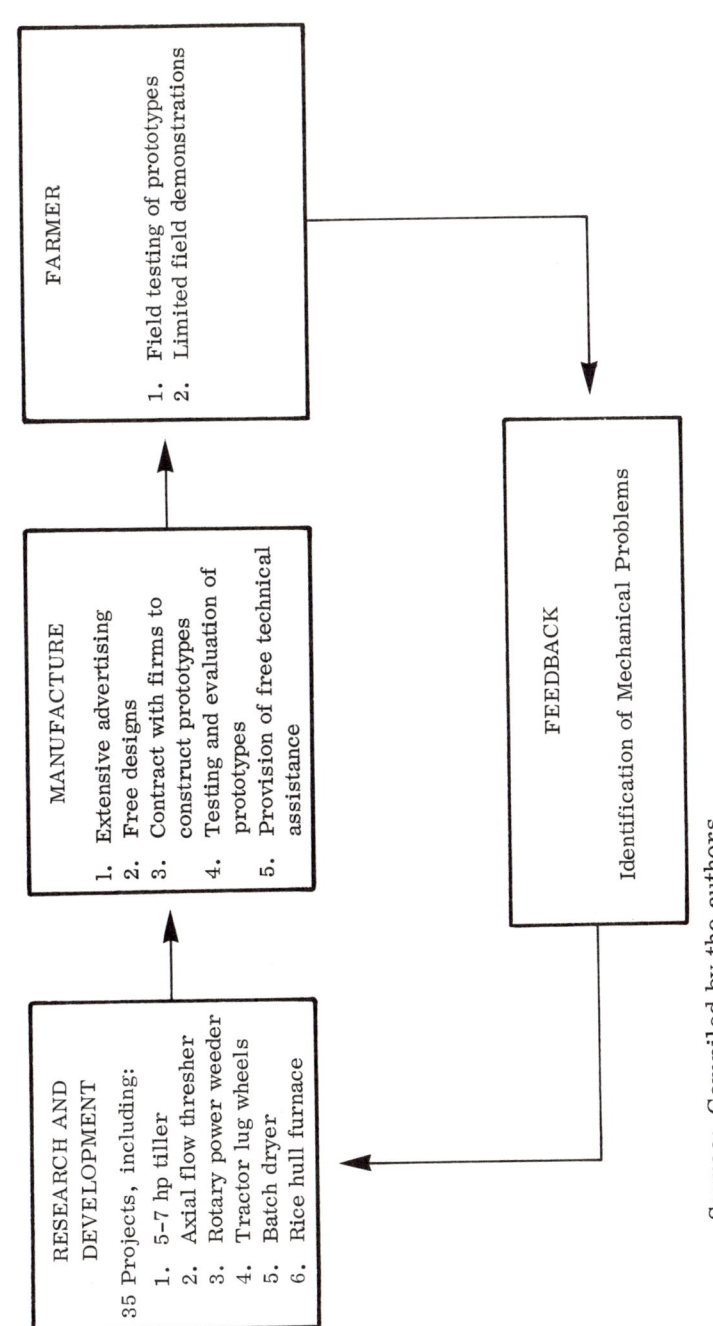

Source: Compiled by the authors.

suggestions of his customers.* Larger firms, such as Marsteel, have R and D capabilities which were established prior to production of IRRI designs.

At this time there appears to be little involvement by local research institutes and universities in product design and development. The only case we are aware of is the design of the flatbed dryer at the University of the Philippines at Los Banos (UPLB). Because of a lack of financial resources, the University has not played an active role in transferring the design to the industrial sector and does not anticipate further involvement in product design and development.

Three important points must be made with reference to the UPLB experience. First, only a few firms are allegedly fabricating the dryer, which suggests that an active role must be played by the design institute, in this case UPLB, to insure widespread transfer to industry. As we have seen, IRRI has provided a package of services which has greatly facilitated the transfer of designs from the research to industrial sector. Second, IRRI has not actively solicited participation of local research institutes. A striking illustration of this fact is the relative absence of cooperation and interaction between IRRI and UPLB, which are a mere half-mile from each other. And third, the lack of cooperation and coordination of activities has resulted in a wasteful duplication of efforts. The dryer designed by UPLB bears remarkable resemblance to IRRI's.

Manufacture

At this point, local firms make the decision to commence production of IRRI designs and take on some of the risks associated with this step. Although the experience of a large company—Marsteel—may have demonstrated the profitability of entering the market, no firm can be absolutely assured beforehand that a new venture will be successful. Problems will inevitably arise in both the production and marketing of the technology and the success of the venture will be dependent on the firms' ability to resolve these problems.

The IRRI project has been extremely successful when evaluated in terms of the number of firms producing the technology in Luzon. Small metalworking shops and large companies in the Greater Manila Area, Nueva Ecija, Laguna, and Bulacan have commenced production of IRRI-designed farm machinery. Although the majority of these firms have had some degree of contact with IRRI, there are some firms which have had no contact and have simply copied an IRRI-type tiller. (Yazon

---

*The two innovators are Arsenio Dungo of Kaunlaran and Bonifacio Isidro of C and B Crafts.

SMALL AGRICULTURAL MACHINERY PROJECT 251

Trading Company in Cabanatuan City, Nueva Ecija is a case in point. The company bought an IRRI-type tiller, took it apart and copied it. The company has made one prototype and has sold three additional units. To date, there has been no contact between Yazon and IRRI. In Naga City there are a number of firms which have had no contact with IRRI, but are producing IRRI-type designs.)

The links between IRRI and areas outside its sphere of influence are weak. As was noted previously, no firms in Mindanao are currently fabricating the designs although one firm has expressed an intent to do so in the near future.

Farmer

IRRI's involvement in market development has been negligible and has largely been left to the various manufacturers of farm machinery. This stage is characterized by consumers' decisions to invest in IRRI-designed equipment. The factors which appear to influence the farmer's decision to invest in a power tiller are as follows:

1. The farmer has been influenced by a fellow farmer who owns a machine.*
2. The farmer has been present at a field demonstration sponsored by the manufacturer or dealer;
3. The farmer is willing to invest in a technology which will speed up the land preparation cycle, thereby allowing him more spare time.

From our limited number of interviews performed in Nueva Ecija, we found that many owners of the power tiller are unaware of the fact that the equipment was originally designed by IRRI.

As in the case of manufacturers, the majority of farmers who have adopted IRRI farm machines are concentrated in Luzon. This is probably attributable to the location of the firms producing the equipment, many of which lack extensive marketing/distribution systems and depend on direct sales.

Feedback

Small firms which are close to the market, and have special relationships with customers are in an ideal position to identify and

---

*This phenomenon has occurred in Baluarte, an irrigated barrio in Nueva Ecija. Fellow-farmer influence was cited frequently as a major reason for investment in the power tiller. Almost 8 percent of the farmers in Baluarte own a power tiller.

resolve mechanical difficulties as they arise. They are also able to identify local needs which may require development of new technologies. This may not be the case for a large company which has a widespread marketing/distribution system but whose R and D staff is located in Manila. Any problems which arise at the local level would have to be referred to Manila, in itself a time-consuming process.

Third Sequence: Tertiary Linkages

The success of the IRRI project can be judged ultimately by what has occurred within the third sequence. Ideally speaking, all activities originally undertaken by the multilateral institute, in this case IRRI, should be indigenized, thereby obviating the need for such an institute. Figure 7.6 portrays the accomplishments at this level to date.

In the R and D phase, the development of problem-solving capabilities by local research institutes to include product design, development, and introduction of the designs into the commercial sector is still very young. While there has been some contact between the AED of UPLB and local firms, that contact has been minimal. Attempts to spark the interests of local firms have been limited almost solely to periodic advertisements and articles in local newspapers, a far cry from promotional efforts undertaken by IRRI. UPLB's very minimal degree of success in encouraging local entrepreneurs to produce the flatbed dryer may well indicate that what is needed is a wide range of services similar to those performed by IRRI in order for the machine designs to be successfully diffused. If national research institutes had the necessary financial resources, perhaps they would be better equipped to take over many of the responsibilities presently undertaken by IRRI and simultaneously could indigenize R and D capabilities and diffusion of designs into the commercial sector.

At the manufacturing level isolated instances exist where local innovators have designed equipment which has subsequently been manufactured by local firms. However, it is difficult to assess the overall impact, if any, which IRRI has had in any of these situations. Obviously, one can conclude that Gabaldon, a native of Cotabato who has been designing and manufacturing his own thresher since the 1950s, developed his capabilities autonomously of IRRI. A number of manufacturers are now producing his design.

Both Duhaylungsod of Davao and Isidro of Bulacan are self-proclaimed inventors. While both have had varying degrees of contact with IRRI, only Isidro is producing IRRI-designed machines. Duhaylungsod, who has designed and is presently manufacturing his own tiller, prefers to design his own equipment rather than copy blueprints

FIGURE 7.5

Second Sequence: Secondary Linkages

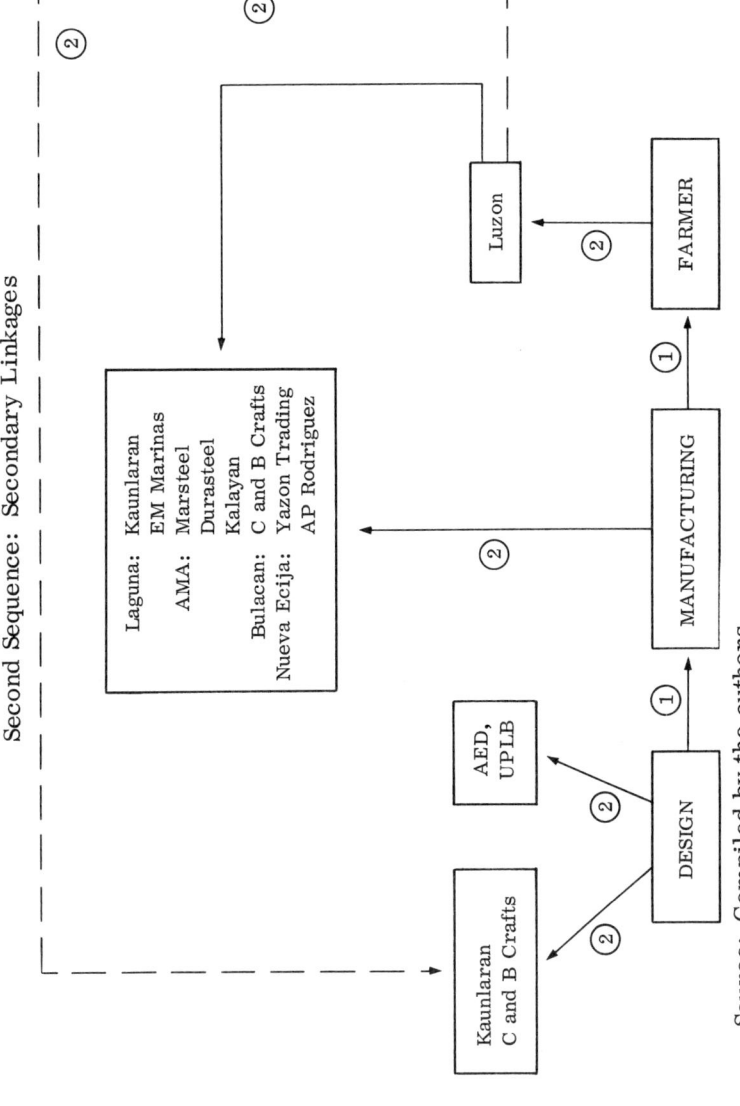

Source: Compiled by the authors.

designed elsewhere. While Isidro is presently selling the IRRI thresher, he is also selling a self-designed thresher, a dough roller, and pumps for home use.

To this date, the only firm which has its own officially established R and D department is Marsteel. It has recently designed, fabricated, and subsequently patented a rice mill. Once again, the actual impact which IRRI has had on the development or progress of this firm's R and D capabilities may be tenuous as Marsteel had its own R and D staff in operation before it began to manufacture IRRI-designed equipment in 1973.

At this time it is the link between the local firm and farmer which is the strongest and where the role of IRRI is negligible. Firms which manufacture IRRI-designed machines either sell directly or through distributors. While many of the smaller firms expressed reluctance to work through distributors because of fear that they would absorb excess profit and thereby increase the price of the product to the end-user, several of the larger firms have established extensive distributor networks throughout the Philippines.

Manufacturers and dealers advertise the machines with in-store and on-farm demonstrations. It is evident that these and fellow farmer influence are much more significant factors than the IRRI name in the farmer's decision to take the risk and purchase a machine for many farmers interviewed did not even know what IRRI meant. The feedback mechanism is also strong at this level as the farmer deals directly with the dealer or manufacturer himself when he encounters machinery maintenance or spare parts problems. Figure 7.6 summarizes this sequence.

The Role of Government

While activities undertaken during the first sequence do not appear to be significantly influenced by government policies, the existence or absence of government policies becomes much more significant at the secondary and tertiary levels. Several areas in which the Philippine government may play a crucial role include industry promotion, credit, and communication. These are enumerated in Figure 7.7.

The promotion of small and medium-scale industries by the Philippine government is fairly recent, and it is difficult to assess the net effect of government policies as they impact on the development of rural entrepreneurial capabilities at this time. A program such as MASICAP has a good track record to this date; however, very few manufacturers indicated awareness of its existence. The Tariffs and Customs Code which was revised in late 1972 has raised the tariff rate

FIGURE 7.6

Third Sequence: Tertiary Linkages

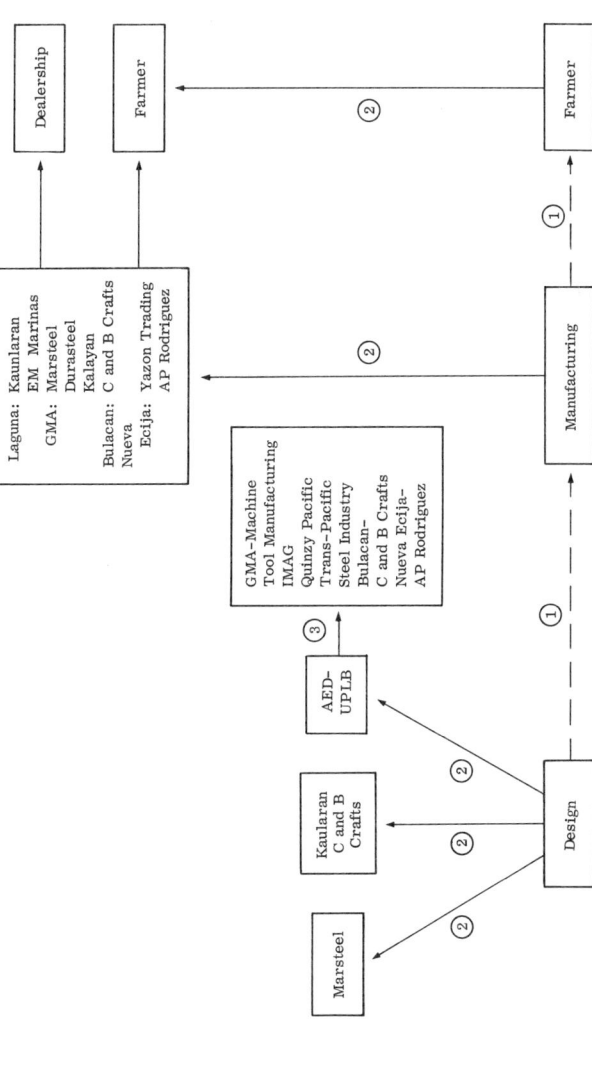

*While UPLB ads say that C and B Crafts is producing the dryer, the manufacturer made no mention of it when interviewed.

Source: Compiled by the authors.

on power tillers to 30 percent while threshers continue to be subject to a 10 percent duty.

Some official shifts in government policy may mean little in contrast to what has happened in reality. Such appears to be the case with the BOI's Investment Priorities Plan, where, in spite of more specific objectives, BOI registrations continue to be concentrated in large capital-intensive efforts. A more blatant inconsistency in government policy was the importation of the 5,000 Japanese Kubota power tillers authorized under Presidential Decree 287 at a time when local sales could have met some of the demands of the land reform farmers; had the government thoroughly surveyed the capabilities of local industry to meet this demand before the issuance of the decree, this could have provided another avenue for use of the domestic labor force and simultaneously fostered more growth of indigenous industrial capabilities.

While it is apparent that the Philippine government is no longer neglecting the demands of small and medium-scale industries, fairly new programs and frequently changing policies do not allow for a clear picture of what the government's overall role has been in furthering indigenization at this time. However, the potential for government yielding a significant influence in the indigenization process at the manufacturing level is great.

Often small and medium-scale industries may be more appropriate for dealing in local rural markets; this includes the ability to operate well with a less sophisticated infrastructure and maintain close personal contact with customers. The importance of the latter cannot be stressed enough, for close links between manufacturer and consumer are crucial in determining what types of technologies a rural town or village needs. An understanding of farmers' needs stems from an understanding of local culture and traditional value systems; obviously, the local entrepreneur who may come from the same village as the farmers or a nearby town will have a more accurate perception of local needs than a large firm based in Manila.

Governmental assistance to stimulate industrial activity in rural areas may also tap technological innovation in areas where it was previously dormant due to any number of reasons, including lack of credit, technical assistance, and so on. Encouragement of technological innovation through the avenues of small and medium-scale businesses also widens the range of technological choices available to the consumer, the entrepreneur, and the government planner. To be able to choose from among a wide variety of technologies enables one to discover those technologies which are most suitable for local conditions; in the Philippines it is evident that the four-wheel tractor is still appropriate for certain regions while local power tiller sales indicate a preference for a new technology which many people, now given a choice among different types of technologies, feel is more appropriate for local conditions.

Along with small and medium-scale industry promotion, credit received an increasing amount of governmental attention. Credit options designed to encourage small and medium-scale industrial development are frequently changing and expanding, but whether or not such changes have actually benefited the small entrepreneur is not clear. Overly strict collateral requirements and the amount of time necessary for a loan to be processed were the two factors most often cited by small manufacturers we interviewed as impeding their efforts to obtain financial assistance.

Credit appears to be the major bottleneck which has inhibited the small farmer from purchasing agricultural machinery. The majority of farmers interviewed expressed reluctance to even submit a loan application because they felt they could not meet all the necessary loan requirements.

It is difficult to get a clear perspective of what governmental involvement has meant to small farmer credit programs. Although the Philippine government relaxed initial overly stringent loan requirements in response to the foot-and-mouth disease epidemic during the summer of 1975, lack of information precluded the determination of the loan beneficiaries at that time; it is not known whether loan requirements were liberalized to such a degree so as to allow the small farmer to benefit.

Available statistics from the CB:IBRD Farm Mechanization Loan Program indicate that this is one governmental program which, in spite of having been designed to help promote small farm mechanization, has channeled the majority of its available funds to the purchasers of four-wheel tractors rather than the purchasers of power tillers.

Gaps in communication emerged continuously during our investigations as bottlenecks which may often inhibit the small producer and small farmer from availing of all the ingredients necessary to establish a small business or to purchase a locally manufactured piece of agricultural equipment. As indicated earlier, very few entrepreneurs know of MASICAP's existence. Also, with the promotion of credit as a major policy instrument to help increase production, new and expanded sources of credit arise frequently, making it difficult to be constantly tuned in to new credit opportunities. Lack of knowledge about the wide range of machine brands, operational and repair know-how may also be factors which discourage machine adoption.

One must look at such constraints to communication within the larger context of overall development efforts in the Philippines and the impact they may have on slowing down the achievement of such objectives as creating more employment opportunities, lessening the income gap between rich and poor, and promoting regional development. From this, we may infer that the technological hardware, in this case the locally manufactured agricultural machinery, is perhaps

FIGURE 7.7

Governmental Role in Indigenization of Technology

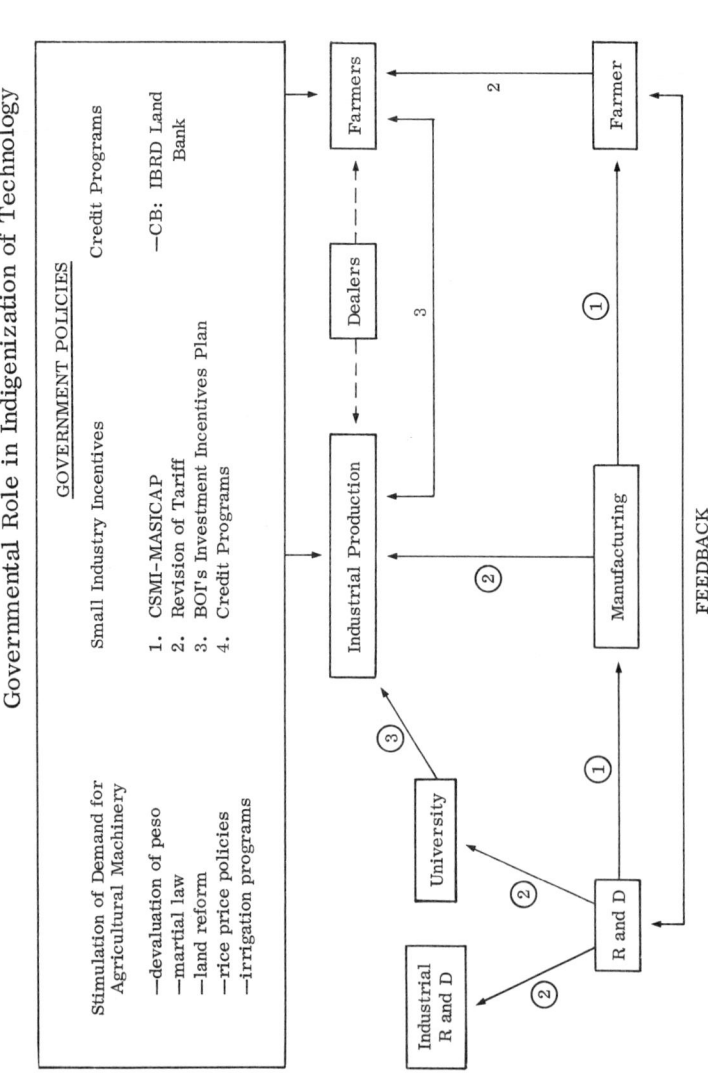

Source: Compiled by the authors.

far less important than problems dealing with the software, that is, technical and managerial assistance, financial assistance, information, and education, if such technologies are to play an influential role in the development process.

Figure 7.7 depicts the crucial role of government programs and policies in the eventual indigenization of technological skills initially transferred from abroad.

NOTES

1. Agricultural Engineering Department, International Rice Research Institute, Semi-Annual Substantive Report No. 1 for the period ending December 31, 1965 (Los Banos, Philippines), p. 2.

2. Office of Science and Technology, Agency for International Development, Appropriate Technologies for International Development: Preliminary Survey of Research Activities (Washington, D.C.: AID, September 1972), p. 30.

3. Agricultural Engineering Department, International Rice Research Institute, Semi-Annual Substantive Report No. 3 for the period July 1, 1966 to February 8, 1967 (Los Banos, Philippines), p. 5.

4. Organization for Economic Cooperation and Development Center, Low Cost Technology—An Inquiry into Outstanding Policy Issues, January 1975, p. 10.

5. Organization for Economic Cooperation and Development, Choice and Adaptation of Technology in Developing Countries: An Overview of Major Policy Issues (Paris: OECD, 1972), p. 161.

6. Semi-Annual Report No. 3, p. 1.

7. Ibid., p. 9.

8. Ibid., p. 5.

9. Loyd Johnson and Stanley Johnson, Annual Report for the period July 1, 1966 to June 30, 1967 (Los Banos, Philippines), p. 2.

10. Amir Khan, private interview held in Washington, D.C., April 10, 1975.

11. Amir Khan, private interview in Los Banos, Philippines, August 1975.

12. Agricultural Engineering department, International Rice Research Institute, Semi-Annual Substantive Report No. 5 for the period of July 1, 1967 to December 31, 1967 (Los Banos, Philippines), summary.

13. Amir Khan and Bart Duff, "Agricultural Mechanization Technology Development at the International Rice Research Institute" (a paper presented at the seminar on Priorities for Research on Innovating and Adapting Technologies for Asian Development, Woodrow Wilson

School, Princeton University, New Jersey, September 20-23, 1972), p. 6.

14. Khan and Duff, op. cit., p. 12.

15. Results of the farmer surveys conducted in Central Luzon during 1966-67 can be found in the Semi-Annual Substantive Report No. 5. Profiles on farmers who have invested in hard tractors or other equipment are contained in the following reports: Semi-Annual Report No. 10 for the period January 1 to June 30, 1970 and Semi-Annual Report No. 13 for the period July 1 to December 31, 1971 (Los Banos, Philippines); and Stanley Johnson's "Terminal Report on the General Engineering and Economic Research Portion of Contract AID/csd 834" (Los Banos, Philippines: International Rice Research Institute, 1969).

16. The definition and description of a small Filipino firm can be found in Semi-Annual Progress Report No. 13, pp. 16-17. For the results of a study undertaken by the Agricultural Engineering Department in conjunction with the Harvard Advisory Group to identify production and marketing problems faced by small firms, see Semi-Annual Progress Report No. 12 for the period January 1 to June 30, 1971 (Los Banos, Philippines), p. 23.

17. Bart Duff, private interview held in Washington, D.C., March 13, 1975.

18. Agricultural Engineering Department, International Rice Research Institute, January 1 to June 30, 1969 (Los Banos, Philippines), p. 16.

19. Amir Khan, private interview in Los Banos, Philippines, August 1975.

20. Agricultural Engineering Department, International Rice Research Institute, June 30, 1972 (Los Banos, Philippines), p. 22.

21. Ibid.

22. Semi-Annual Report No. 13, p. 8.

23. Ibid.

24. Ibid.

25. Steven Breth and Thomas Hargrove, "IRRI Tiller Fills Asian Machinery Gap," The IRRI Reporter II (1973).

26. Agricultural Engineering Department, International Rice Research Institute, Semi-Annual Progress Report No. 15 for the period July 1 to December 31, 1972 (Los Banos, Philippines), p. 5.

27. The New York Times (November 16, 1975) reported that the Philippines has harvested a record rice crop this year. The record yields are attributed to the "Green Revolution" technology and favorable weather conditions. A shortage of warehouse facilities for storing the rice has been cited as a major problem.

28. Two firms we visited in the course of our research have made product improvements on the axial flow thresher. The two firms are C and B Crafts in Bulacan and Kaunlaran in Laguna.

29. Semi-Annual Report No. 10, p. 7.
30. Bart Duff, private interview.
31. Bart Duff, letter to James Urano, October 17, 1974.
32. Edilberto Uichanco, private interview in Quezon City, Philippines, August 1975.
33. D. N. Porter, The Market For Farm Machinery, Working Paper for Agricultural Machinery Sector Survey, Manila, Philippines, March 1974 (Manila, Philippines: Board of Investment, 1974), p. 19.
34. Noel Reyes, private interview in Manila, Philippines, August 4, 1975.
35. Philippines, National Science Development Board, Metal Industry Research and Development Council, Metalworking Industry of the Philippines, II (Philippines, 1974), pp. 1-2.
36. Ibid., p. 5.
37. Bart Duff and Amir Khan, "Development of Agricultural Mechanization Technologies at IRRI," paper presented at a seminar on Agricultural Equipment Development Research for Tropical Rice Production, Reston, Virginia, September 23, 1973, p. 12.
38. Luis Bernas, private interview at the Marsteel Corporation in Manila, Philippines, August 11, 1975.
39. Bart Duff, private interview.
40. Luis Bernas, "Profiles of the Agricultural Machinery Manufacturing Industry—Production and Marketing Strategies: Large Firms," paper presented at the Workshop on Agricultural Mechanization and Indigenous Production of Agricultural Machines in the LDC, Los Banos, Philippines, May 6-9, 1975, p. 5.
41. Ibid., p. 9.
42. Ibid., pp. 6-7.
43. Ibid., p. 9.
44. Semi-Annual Report No. 8, p. 5.
45. These research findings were compiled during the summer of 1975. Davao and General Santos are located in Mindanao, one of the southernmost islands of the Philippine archipelago. This particular area was examined because of its relative distance geographically from Los Banos, thereby providing the researchers with the opportunity to view the technology transfer process to an area falling outside of IRRI's sphere of influence.
46. Gabaldon, a native of Cotabato, designed a thresher in the 1950s. A number of local manufacturers have copied his design, and it has gained popularity among farmers in parts of Mindanao.
47. We talked with officials of PNB, DBP, and a Commerical Bank in Davao, and were informed that they were reluctant to grant loans to small farmers because of the risk involved. None of the banks has approved a loan to a small farmer for purchase of agricultural equipment, although the PNB and DBP have received applications for such loans.

48. Carlos Del Rosario, private interview at the Agricultural Engineering Department of the University of the Philippines at Los Banos, September 1, 1975.

49. Edilberto Uichanco, private interview.

50. Luis Bernas, private interview.

51. Arsenio Dungo, private interview in Laguna, Philippines, July 29, 1975.

52. Bonifacio Isidro, private interview in Bulacan, Philippines, August 5, 1975.

53. Luis Bernas, private interview.

54. Ibid.

55. Edilberto Uichanco, telephone conversation in Manila, Philippines, August 30, 1975.

56. Dr. Herminia Fajardo, private interview in Quezon City, Philippines, August 1975.

57. Mr. Martinez, private interview at the Mindanao Machine Shop, Inc. in Davao, Philippines, August 1975.

58. R. A. Jaurique, Engineering Manager, Marsteel Corporation, private interview in Quezon City, Philippines, August 1975.

59. D. N. Porter, Survey of Farmers, Working Paper for Agriculture Machinery Sector Survey, UNDP/IBRD Technical Assistance Project, February 1974, p. 11.

60. National Economic and Development Authority, Four Year Development Plan FY 1974-77, Manila, 1973, p. 18.

61. International Labor Organization, Sharing in Development: A Programme of Employment, Equity, and Growth for the Philippines (Geneva, Switzerland, 1974), p. 541.

62. Members of the Commission include: Department of Industry; University of the Philippines Institute for Small-Scale Industries (UP-ISSI); Development Academy of the Philippines; Bureau of Domestic Trade; National Manpower and Youth Council; Food Terminal, Inc.; Development Bank of the Philippines (DBP); Philippine International Trading Company; Design Center Philippines; National Economic and Development Authority-Central Bank; Industrial Guarantee and Loan Fund (IGLF); National Cottage Industries Development Authority (NACIDA); Department of Local Government and Community Development (DLGCD)

63. Department of Industry, MASICAP Annual Report FY 74-75, Manila, p. 1.

64. Each MASICAP team is assigned to a particular region of the country in order that local needs may be more effectively met within each area. Regions are as follows:

I—Ilocos Region
II—Cagayan Valley
III—Central Luzon
IV—Southern Tagalog
V—Bicol

VI—Western Visayas
VII—Central Visayas
VIII—Eastern Visayas
IX—Western Mindanao
X—Northern Mindanao
XI—Southern Mindanao

65. For further details, see International Bank for Reconstruction and Development, "Industrial Development Problems and Prospects in the Philippines," Vol. I—general issues (Industrial Projects Department Report No. 280 PH: November 13, 1973).

66. Ibid., p. 17.

67. Sharing in Development: A Programme of Employment, Equity and Growth, op cit., p. 167.

68. D. N. Porter, Policy Issues, Working Paper for Agricultural Machinery Sector Survey, UNDP/IBRD Technical Assistance Project, April 1974, p. 15.

69. Sharing the Development: A Program of Employment, Equity and Growth for the Philippines, op. cit., p. 235.

70. "Industrial Development Problems and Prospects," op. cit., p. 48.

71. Sharing in Development: A Programme of Employment, Equity and Growth, op. cit., p. 162.

72. National Economic and Development Authority, Strategy for Action: Food and Agriculture Sector, Manila, p. 40.

73. Orlando J. Sacay, "Small Farmer Credit in the Philippines," paper for A.I.D. Spring Review of Small Farmer Credit, vol. XIII, February 1973, p. 8.

74. Porter, op. cit., p. 28.

75. Sharing in Development: A Program of Employment, Equity, and Growth for the Philippines, op. cit., p. 96.

76. Ibid., p. 235.

77. Mr. Rimorin, private interview held at Philippine National Bank, Davao, Philippines, August 19, 1975.

78. Mr. Romualdo Limsiaco, private interview held at Steelpride Industries, General Santas City, Philippines, August 21, 1975.

79. Pedre M. Garcia, "Ecija Farmers now use muscle power," Manila Bulletin, August 8, 1975.

80. Small farms were then defined for purposes of the program as not less than five or greater than 50 hectares in spite of the fact that only 18.7 percent of all Philippine farms fell within that category and over 81.8 percent were less than 5 hectares. See Ida Estioko, "Farm Mechanization in the Philippines and the International Bank for Reconstruction and Development Loan Program" (Paper prepared for the seminar on Farm Mechanization in Southeast Asia, Penang and Alor Star, Malaysia, November 27-December 2, 1972), p. 3.

81. For more detailed information on the first and second loan programs, see Ibid.

82. Ibid., p. 7.

83. Report of the Advisory Group Meeting at the IRRI (Los Banos, Philippines: March 29-30, 1974), p. 25.

84. Ibid., p. 23.

85. Khan and Duff, op. cit., p. 6.

86. The six machines which are currently being manufactured by industry are the 5-7 hp. tiller, the axial flow thresher, the rotary power weeder, the tractor lug wheels, the batch dryer, and the rice hull furnace. For more detailed information on these machines, consult the Semi-Annual Reports and the Terminal Report for AID/IRRI Projects No. csd-834 and csd-2541 (May 21, 1975) published by the Agricultural Engineering Department, International Rice Research Institute, Philippines.

CHAPTER

8

NATIONAL AND CASE STUDY PERSPECTIVES ON TECHNOLOGY TRANSFER: AN INTEGRATED VIEW

The case studies of the previous chapters provide some illuminating examples of the broader trends we discussed in Chapter 3. These examples, of course, are only suggestive and do not constitute confirmation of broader trends. There is a significant gap, at the moment, between the aggregate data presented in Chapter 3 and the case study data of Chapters 4 through 7.

In Chapter 9 of this study, we suggest a series of further studies which will be needed to begin to fill in this gap. A primary purpose of our effort has been to suggest the extreme inattention which has been paid to these matters in the past and to urge immediate follow-up studies to compensate for our lack of knowledge and even awareness of policy issues concerning one of America's most important foreign policy resources, that is, its commercial technology abroad.

The case study findings may be presented within our basic framework of trends in issues and actors associated with the international transfer of U.S. technology:

Issues

1. the increasing importance of economic-social as well as military-strategic criteria for evaluating technology transfers and the corresponding focus on the pricing of technology exports
2. the shift from product and capital exports to service or disembodied technology exports occasioned by increasing hostility to foreign direct investment abroad and by relative growth of the service sector at home

Actors

1. the declining relative role of government funding of R and D in the industrial sector
2. adjustments in government-industry relationships and mechanisms to cope with a changing external and internal economic environment
3. adjustments in interagency relationships and mechanisms to meet changing political and economic conditions affecting the use of U.S. technology in the international system

ECONOMIC-SOCIAL CRITERIA FOR EVALUATING TECHNOLOGY EXPORTS

The case studies were selected to highlight the importance of new economic issues in the international transfer of U.S. technology. As noted previously, these issues concern the distribution of returns from the transfer of technology, both between source and recipient countries and between groups within these countries individually.

The Kama River truck plant study, for example, is most interesting for what it tells us about industrial negotiations and technology transfer processes between free enterprise and planned economy countries.* The principal issues affecting the distribution of returns from technology transfer in these relationships may be summarized as follows:

1. How do U.S. companies cost out their technology for sale to the Soviet Union, if they do so at all? Swindell-Dressler, an engineering design firm, sold the designs for the Kama foundry plant through an

---

*Military issues were involved in the initial contacts by U.S. firms concerning the Kama project, as suggested by the dispute between Henry Ford of the Ford Motor Company and Melvin Laird, then Secretary of Defense. These issues, however, were more of a foreign policy than strategic nature. While it was true, as Laird asserted, that Kama trucks could be used to fight against American soldiers in South Vietnam, it was probably also true that Laird was more concerned about the timing of this move symbolizing detente with the Soviet Union than he was about the actual military contribution Kama trucks would make to Soviet military capabilities or Soviet military assistance to North Vietnamese allies. The Vietnam War, at least U.S. participation in it, was very likely to be over before Kama trucks would begin to roll off the assembly line.

initial lump sum cash contract. Swindell officials maintained that this first contract returned a profit by itself, independent of a second contract involving subsequent equipment sales to Kama. At one point in the negotiations, however, Swindell officials also complained about being whipsawed by Soviet partners to lower price in relation to alleged offers by competing firms. If, nevertheless, the first contract was profitable, the question remains how that profit was calculated, that is, on what cost basis. Indeed, was cost accounting involved at all or did Swindell sell its designs solely on the basis of the price the market would bear? As we discussed in Chapter 3, externalities may be involved in either case, raising the issue of the role of public policy in the pricing of technology exports.

2. The issue of pricing technology transfers to the Soviet Union (or, for that matter, other communist countries) is closely linked to the length of time or duration of industrial agreements with Soviet partners. The Soviet Union, up to the present time (and most Eastern European countries until recently), has preferred one shot transactions with Western partners (involving, at the most, turnkey arrangements such as the contract with FIAT for a passenger car plant at Tol'yatti) rather than long-term arrangements involving the continuous exchange of technology over a period of time going beyond the start-up phase of new plants in the Soviet Union.[1] By contrast, many Western firms prefer long-term associations as the only way to guarantee a continuous and adequate stream of income from sale of manufacturing equipment and know-how. (For example, even Swindell officials expressed their hope, that the initial contracts with the Kama project would lead to longer-term arrangements with the Soviets in which Swindell know-how could be exchanged under normal licensing conditions.) If Western firms were permitted to share in future sales and profits through royalty or minority equity arrangements, the matter of one time pricing of technology sales to the Soviet Union would become less problematic. Firms would no longer be required to recoup costs and extract profits from a single contract. Of course, the transfer of technology under longer-term arrangements denying majority control of equity might still be less profitable than foreign direct investment (as we noted in Chapter 3), but it would seem likely to be more profitable than one shot transactions. A serious problem with the latter, as the Swindell case illustrates, is the high and often unexpected costs encountered in delivering and installing equipment in the Soviet Union under management and working conditions controlled by the Soviets. Longer-term arrangements would absorb these costs as front-end installments on an anticipated, profitable, long-term relationship.

The Kama study only partially illustrates another factor determining relative economic gains from technology transfers between source and recipient countries. This factor is more important among industrialized Western countries and concerns the effect of the technology transfer on the international economic competitiveness of the recipient country and the ability of that country to increase its share of exports to third markets and perhaps eventually to home markets of the source country as well. Through foreign direct investment multinational firms exercise some control over this eventuality by dividing up subsidiary export markets. When direct investment is denied, however, as in the case of the communist countries and, more importantly for U.S. exports, in the case of Japan (until recently when Japan relaxed somewhat its controls against direct investment), the risk of export losses increases. In a strict economic sense, therefore, the immediate and long-run returns from technology transfer, especially under conditions short of majority equity control, must be discounted against the ability of the recipient country to increase its competitiveness in future export markets.

The Kama study showed, for example, some concern that the Soviet Union might not be able to absorb the sudden increase in truck production afforded by Kama and might have to resort to export sales. The concern was based on the experience of the FIAT-constructed passenger car plant at Tol'yatti. Although original plans for Tol'yatti called for all cars to be sold internally within the Soviet Union, the plant, within three years of operation, was exporting about one-third of its total production to the West. Since it is widely believed that Soviet traders are free to set prices for export purposes at whatever level they choose, Western apprehension grows at the prospect of East-West industrial cooperation contributing to widespread dumping of Soviet products on Western markets. (At a recent meeting of the Technical Assistance Board of the Commerce Department a top official of an American automobile company complained about the "dumping" prices at which Tol'yatti cars were being sold in West Germany.)

International competition involves more than price, however. Quality, reliability and servicing of products are also important. Because the Soviets lack many of these capabilities in international markets, the threat of export competition from Soviet products is much less than from products produced by technology transfers among industrialized countries (United States, Canada, Western Europe and Japan). Unfortunately, our case studies do not address this problem among industrialized countries, since we found it impractical in the university context to do a case study of technology transfer within the private sector (except as in the case of Kama, where there is a public record of sorts). The bauxite-aluminum study, however, suggests that the problem of future competition from technology transfers, while remaining most serious vis-a-vis developed country competitors, may become increasingly important vis-a-vis an intermediate group of countries, that is, the more advanced communist countries (for example, Eastern European countries) and the raw-material rich developing countries (such as Iran). For example, what would be the likely competitive effects for U.S. aluminum exports of the large scale transfer of U.S. aluminum process technology to bauxite-supplying countries? Or what would the transfer of fertilizer production capabilities to oil-producing states mean over the long run for U.S. fertilizer exports? Some U.S. officials, including Secretary of State Henry Kissinger, believe that American technology is an important asset to be traded for secure raw material supplies. These officials correctly sense that raw material producing countries need and demand U.S. products and know-how for industrialization programs. Nevertheless, the consequences for U.S. exports of geographic shifts of production occassioned by such transfers cannot be overlooked. Much depends on whether this production technology can be absorbed in recipient countries. Paradoxically, the more successful technology transfer is, the more international competition U.S. exports may undoubtedly confront.

An assessment of the consequences of geographic production shifts is also important for understanding the impact of technology exports on the internal distribution of resources in source and recipient countries. Labor's argument in the United States that foreign direct investment costs domestic jobs and hence domestic income seems to be contradicted by many existing studies of this problem.[2] But it should not be discarded because it can be shown that, <u>overall</u>, foreign direct investment has been beneficial to the U.S. economy. There is still the possibility that foreign investment has been more beneficial to management than to labor. Moreover, it may have occasioned a shift in the composition of jobs in the United States, away from blue collar workers to highly skilled and service-oriented workers, sectors where labor unions are still relatively weak. Thus the distributional and hence political significance of the issue would remain, even in the face of macroeconomic data demonstrating the positive effects of foreign investment on total domestic employment.

Our case studies shed little light on this distributional issue. One conclusion of the Tariff Commission study bears noting, however. This study found that, under certain assumptions, high technology firms have a lower ratio of foreign sales by affiliates to new MNC-related exports from the U.S. than medium and low technology firms.[3] This suggests that high technology affiliates abroad erode U.S. export markets more slowly than medium or low technology affiliates. Now, if medium and low technology affiliates, among which are included the bauxite-aluminum and other natural resource industries, are the ones initially and increasingly nationalized by foreign governments, and if these newly nationalized industries are less efficient than former U.S.

affiliates in supplying foreign markets, U.S. exports may increase as a consequence of recipient country actions. Comparatively, this should improve the situation of blue collar workers (assuming that workers in low and medium technology sectors benefit more from direct exports than from returns on high technology direct investments abroad). The improvement, of course, may be only temporary. As we noted above, if nationalized or private foreign competitors are able effectively to absorb U.S. technology (for example, the process technology being supplied by U.S. aluminum companies to bauxite-supplying countries), they may be able to pick up full supply of third markets and perhaps of some of the home markets of former parent companies as well. As or if, under these circumstances, exports from low and medium technology industries decline, adjustment assistance to retrain blue collar workers for employment in more skilled, high technology industries may be justified on grounds of technology export, no less than on traditional grounds of import competition. Again, the issues here concern the slicing of the economic pie, which even if growing, may not be shared equitably or, at least, to the mutual satisfaction of all the domestic groups involved.

These economic issues in source countries are mirrored in recipient countries. While source countries are concerned about the underpricing of technology, recipient countries are concerned about the overpricing of technology. As Jamaican behavior in the bauxite-aluminum study suggests, these countries seek to peel away the separate layers of the direct investment package and to obtain technology at a price freed from links with repatriated earnings from majority-owned subsidiaries, tied-product purchases from parent companies, or restrictive clauses limiting export development. As our AID/IRRI study suggests, they also demand more appropriate technologies suited to their own local resource conditions rather than to the problems and factor endowments of advanced countries.

These shifts in recipient country demands raise new issues for U.S. policy. Such issues concern primarily the consequences of the struggle over returns from technology transfer for institutional relationships in the United States, principally government-industry relations. We discuss these consequences more fully in another section below.

This discussion of economic issues associated with technology transfer is not meant to diminish the continued importance of foreign policy and military-strategic considerations in the management of U.S. technology exports. Indeed, our energy R and D case study reveals a classic example of the use of American technology to achieve largely foreign policy, diplomatic objectives, even, if necessary, at the cost of some technological and commercial assets. The energy study, on the other hand, also suggests the new obstacles to the traditional foreign policy use of technology transfer. U.S. industries were not particularly enthusiastic about government initiatives to share technology in the energy sector, particularly by the offer to share enriched uranium technology internationally before this technology was fully commercialized domestically. (By contrast, U.S. industries were eager to follow government initiatives in the late 1950s to share nuclear reactor technology with Western Europe.)[4] Likewise, domestic-oriented government agencies and the U.S. Congress are more skeptical today about any programs that can be interpreted as giving away American technology.

We have emphasized economic issues because they are new, not because they are by any means predominant or should weigh more heavily in technology export evaluations than traditional strategic and foreign policy concerns. U.S. policy makers have had some experience with the military-strategic evaluation of technology exports, however controversial that experience may have been. These officials have had no such experience with economic issues. We are only debating today whether economic evaluation of technology exports is justified and, if so, on the basis of what guidelines. Present legislation permits the control of exports of agricultural and raw material products under carefully limited and, until recently, seldom used short supply conditions. Current debate concerns the extension of these controls to exports of industrial technology and know-how and the development of more general economic-commercial criteria going beyond limited short supply conditions. Similarly, as we noted in our bauxite-aluminum study, an economic rationale for stockpiling raw materials is being debated for the first time. At the moment, security arrangements are the sole basis of existing stockpile legislation. Economic stockpiles would serve to support raw material prices, encourage the domestic development of alternative sources, and increase independence of foreign material supplies. This would avoid the need to pay for stable foreign supplies through large resource, including technology, transfers.

GROWTH OF DISEMBODIED TECHNOLOGY EXPORTS

The issue of pricing technology to maximize economic returns may become more important and also more difficult the more disembodied the form of technology transfer becomes. It may become more important because the "purer" forms of technology transfer (see Figure 1.1) have potentially wider implications for development than product forms. An electronics engineer is likely to make a broader contribution to development over time than a single computer incorporating static technology. The pricing of such technology may become more difficult, because more intangibles are involved. If we know little about the costing practices of high technology product firms, we know less about the costing practices of high technology design and service firms (such as management consultant firms, and so on). For the latter, pricing is presumably a function of the market place alone. Optimum returns depend heavily on knowledge of the market place. Is U.S. management and service know-how unique and are there monopoly rents to be obtained? These are difficult questions to answer, but developments in foreign and domestic markets require that we, at least, begin to ask them.

These developments, as we noted in Chapter 3, include increasing hostility to U.S. direct investment (and foreign direct investment in general) and relative growth of the service as compared to manufacturing sector at home. The case studies offer some examples of both phenomena.

In the bauxite-aluminum study, for example, we observe the pattern of nationalization of U.S. mining operations in bauxite-supplying countries and of demand in these countries for U.S. aluminum process technology apart from direct investment control. The joint alumina plant and aluminum smelter being built by Jamacia and Mexico involve only minority equity participation by Kaiser and financial contributions by Reynolds and other U.S. companies operating in Jamaica without any equity participation whatever. Yet Kaiser is supplying most of the technology for these processing or value-added installations. Jamaica is engaged in another joint venture with Trinidad and Guyana to construct two further aluminum smelter plants, one each in the latter two countries. The technology for these plants may be obtained from Eastern European suppliers, such as Yugoslavia. This latter possibility suggests the competitive factors operating in the present international economic system to facilitate the unbundling of U.S. technology from the traditional direct investment package. If U.S. firms do not accede to customer demands to sell technology separately, other suppliers will do so in their place.

If direct investment becomes an increasingly less acceptable mode of technology transfer in developing and even advanced Western, as well as communist, countries, U.S. firms may be compelled to do more licensing of manufacturing know-how and outright selling of management and marketing skills. Since licensing of know-how is most significant when accompanied by technical assistance agreements, the transfer of personnel (as opposed to capital) is likely to be a primary ingredient of U.S. technology exports in the future. In the bauxite-aluminum sector, for example, Kaiser will continue to manage its mining operations in Jamaica, despite 51 percent Jamaican ownership. Guyana, on the other hand, will manage as well as own its newly nationalized mining industries. It may, from time to time, purchase selected services from former parent companies.

American industries may already be making adjustments to meet these foreign developments. One aluminum company is setting up a new subsidiary to do nothing but develop and sell aluminum processing technology. Gulf Oil Company has recently created a new subsidiary, known as Geoman, to sell Gulf's engineering and technical services abroad on a straight contract basis.[5] In the past, Gulf has used these services only internally in connection with its direct investment activities in foreign areas.

No conclusions can be drawn from these isolated examples. But the Kama study suggests that we should start asking some questions not only about the price of U.S. technology exports but also the content or ingredients of these exports. For example, did Swindell sell only designs, equipment and operational know-how to the Soviet Union, or did it also include, consciously or inadvertently, significant amounts of manufacturing, management and marketing know-how? Swindell maintains that no know-how was involved in its Kama contract. Yet more than one hundred Soviet engineers and specialists have been present over a three-year period at Swindell offices in Pittsburgh. Similarly, Swindell engineers are now present in the Soviet Union advising on the installation and start up of Swindell equipment. What is the range of know-how being exchanged? Do we even have adequate classification categories of strategically or economically important software know-how comparable to our classification lists of hardware technology?

In posing these questions, we are aware of the undesirability of restricting interpersonal relationships with foreigners any more or less so than restricting such relationships among U.S. citizens. Moreover, some people argue that U.S. know-how in software areas, such as organizational management, is irrelevant to many foreign societies, particularly centrally planned and directed economies. Yet repeatedly we hear that what U.S. firms have to offer to communist as well as other foreign partners is not so much their products, which many foreign competitors can now also supply, but their knowledge and experience, especially with the integration and management of large-scale systems.[6] If this know-how is demanded in the future increasingly apart from products (finished and intermediate products, and capital equipment), we will have to begin to address the question of what these forms of software, services, or disembodied technologies are worth. At first glance, there would seem to be many more public externalities involved in the development of these technologies (for example, the education of a professional engineer) than in the development of more specific, product technologies. As an initial hypothesis, therefore, we might expect private and public value to diverge considerably, raising the issue of public intervention to insure adequate returns on public investments. We are not saying public intervention is necessary or a good thing. But simply that, without further study (which we strongly advocate in Chapter 9), there is a stronger prima facie case for public intervention in the case of "people" technologies than in the case of "product" technologies.

DECLINING GOVERNMENT FUNDING OF INDUSTRIAL R AND D

The case studies amplify only marginally the decline of government funding of industrial R and D in the United States. This trend, however, is already firmly evident in the aggregate data presented in Chapter 3 (see Tables 3.1, 3.2, and 3.3).

The bauxite-aluminum study deals with an industrial sector where government R and D funding has been historically small. Compared to defense and space industries, this is true of all raw material or resource industries. Table 3.3 (last column) shows the small absolute amount of R and D done in the nonmanufacturing sector. The government share is high, but this may be overstated since some R and D in nonmanufacturing areas are done by integrated manufacturing industries and entered elsewhere in the SIC code. One consequence may be that government is not in a position, either by historical habit or by actual control of relevant technology, to assume the initiative in raw material sectors (energy may be the exception because of government development of nuclear energy). Our aluminum study shows that there is little propensity in government to take action on bauxite supply problems despite the fact that bauxite prices have increased as much and as rapidly as oil prices. The relaxed attitude is also the result, of course, of important differences between the bauxite and oil sectors. The former is much less susceptible to sustained cartelization than oil (due to existence of substitutes, and so on), and the impact of bauxite prices on aluminum end products, let alone the economy as a whole, is minuscule compared with the impact of oil prices. Nevertheless, the lack of traditional government leverage in the aluminum sector contributes to inaction. A greater propensity to act might be present, even if action were unwise, if government had more knowledge about and influence over technological developments in the aluminum industry. By comparison, government intervention may have been no wiser in the energy R and D sector but occurred anyway because government had information about and control over (in the case of uranium enrichment technology) important energy R and D resources.*

Swindell's initial contacts with the Soviet Union preceded the signing of the 1972 U.S.-USSR Science and Technology Agreement which encouraged industrial contacts under Article 4. Once the latter agreement sanctioned such contacts, however, industrial liaisons between East and West mulitplied. The U.S. government had little knowledge about what these contacts involved. In the absence of information in Commerce, the Department of State initiated an effort through the Industrial Research Institute to determine the number and extent of East-West industrial discussions. The government's lack of information, in this case, cannot be traced directly to its declining R and D support of the particular companies involved. But it is not unwarranted to view this incident as symptomatic of larger patterns in which private industries have greater leeway to do what they want with their own technology developed through their own resources.

The issue is highlighted in the oil sector where government agencies, such as the Federal Energy Administration, are wholly dependent on information and data supplied by the oil companies. The latter control the information, not only about R and D (which we are considering here) but about all facets of company policy. They decide upon the dissemination of this information in both amount and content.† What I am suggesting here is that defense and space industries may be acquiring similar leverage. Whereas in the past, heavy government R and D

---

*Some believe, for example, that while government action was necessary in the face of the energy crisis, government funding of R and D, especially in government laboratories, was a continuation of an uneconomical mode of technological development, begun under Cold War exigencies of strategic-military competition but now increasingly unacceptable in a world of heightened economic and commercial competition. (For the case against government-conducted R and D, see George Eads and Richard Nelson, "Government Support of Advanced Civilian Technology: Power Reactors and the Supervision on Transport" Public Policy 19, no. 3 [Summer 1971]: 405-27.)

†This dependence on oil company data and discretion is sufficiently troublesome for all advanced industrial countries that a program to improve the oil market information system (i.e. principally liaison between governments and private oil companies) was a principal part of the International Energy Program agreed upon by the allies in September 1974. (See International Energy Program, Hearing, Committee on Interior and Insular Affairs, U.S. Senate, 93rd Cong., 2nd Sess., November 26, 1974 [Washington, D.C.: Governmental Printing Office, 1975].)

funding in these industries ensured significant public access to and influence over private industrial activities, including technology outflows, the lower shares of government funding today may have diminished this access and influence.

ADJUSTMENTS IN GOVERNMENT-INDUSTRY RELATIONS

The fact that State, which has few existing ties with domestic industry, rather than Commerce which has traditional responsibilities in this area, had to take the initiative to find out about U.S.-Soviet industrial contacts under the Science and Technology Agreement suggests the adjustments that may be taking place in technology relations between government and industry. As the case studies indicate, there are hesitant steps on the part of both industry and government to search for new arrangements.

Industry, for its part, is aware of the need to work with government under certain circumstances, if only to avoid antitrust violations. For example, when the aluminum companies desired to get together in 1971 to discuss the pricing policies of bauxite-supplying countries, they had to do so in the White House to avoid collusion charges. Similarly, other companies, in dealing with foreign cartels such as OPEC or foreign trading monopolies such as trade ministries of socialist countries, have recognized the need for a government role to permit information exchange among U.S. companies so as to reduce the latters' vulnerability to whipsaw and other monopolistic bargaining tactics. A Rand Corporation report has called for an institution like the British Board of Trade before World War II to develop and analyze Soviet industry and technology and provide some overview of the numerous contacts and experiences between U.S. and Soviet business officials (the British Board did the same with respect to German industry).[7] The establishment of the U.S.-USSR Trade Council, a partly private, partly public institution to assist U.S. and Soviet business representatives during initial contacts, may be viewed, at least in part, as a response to this need.

Traditionally, U.S. industries have found as many reasons to detach themselves from direct or formal identification with the U.S. government abroad as to seek government support in extreme cases of nationalization, and so on. Our bauxite-aluminum study showed, for example, that industrial feelings continue to diverge widely on the need for government interference or support in relations with bauxite-supplying countries. In relations with more industrialized partners, the preference is still very strong to keep government out.

External pressures, however, are working against this preference. Our energy R and D case study illustrates this fact quite well. The U.S. government proposed an industrial consortium within the framework of the International Energy Agency to operate and develop a coal gasification pilot plant. The British refused to consider this project unless the U.S. government would participate in the capital costs of the consortium. British officials were reluctant to expose the British coal industry, a nationalized sector, to commercial arrangements with aggressive private American partners without a U.S. government involvement and stake in the proprietary results of the project. To acquire this stake, the Energy Research and Development Administration (ERDA) proposed a radical departure from past U.S. government practices. If the project is realized, ERDA will contribute to the capital costs of the pilot plant, thereby becoming a full partner in the disposition of proprietary know-how developed by the project. In the past, ERDA's predecessor, the AEC, refrained from contributions to the capital costs of commercial projects even within the United States. It limited its intervention to R and D costs, with patent and licensing rights generally given to private contractors. Now it may contribute to the capital costs of a plant constructed in Great Britain and remain a partner in this project even after the plant is shut down so as to collect the licensing and royalty fees resulting from the project.

In principle, the British demand for U.S. government participation in this project is not that different from demands by Latin American and other developing countries that the U.S. government exercise some leverage, if not supervision, over U.S. private company activities in the transfer of technology to developing countries. Such demands have prompted within some government agencies a search for new alternatives to relate private and public institutions in the United States to deal with technology exports. From a certain point of view, the experimentation with joint industrial commissions to broaden cooperation with some countries in economic and technological areas and the recent establishment of an advisory committee to the State Department on multinational companies reflect this accelerating search. These developments may not be consciously intended to link private resources and public purposes in foreign affairs, but it is not unwarranted to assume that they may be useful toward this end.

The need to structure new relationships at the government-industry interface may arise not only from demands of foreign governments but also from the desire of our own government to retain an American private industrial presence and influence abroad. With the increasing imposition of political constraints abroad, American companies may simply decide to withdraw from foreign markets (divestment) or, at least, reduce their enthusiasm for foreign expansion. U.S. companies, for example, were not at all happy about the prospect of dealing with the British nationalized coal industry in the coal gasification project discussed above. To obtain industrial participation under such circumstances, U.S. policy may have to sugar the pill, as it has done for so many years in encouraging private industry to support U.S. aid programs in developing countries.

It is not only a matter of maintaining private industrial enthusiasm for participation in foreign markets but also motivating private industries to implement domestic programs that support foreign policy initiatives. For example, in energy, Secretary of State Kissinger seeks to coordinate allied policies on the development of alternative conventional, as well as new, energy sources. To do this, certain cooperative demonstration projects are needed, such as the proposed coal gasification pilot plant. But more importantly, coordination of domestic R and D policies is required. How to support private industry in the development of new energy sources is a controversial issue involving directly the interface of public-private relations in the United States, as well as other industrialized countries. Price floor schemes, a government corporation (the so-called Energy Independence Authority), and direct loan guarantees to private industry have all been proposed.[8] Each involves a somewhat different relationship between the public and private sector in the United States. Perhaps no development illustrates better the ferment that is occuring at the private-public interface and the resultant requirement, stressed in this report (see especially Chapter 9), to study these phenomena than these latest events in the energy sector.

Anticipated changes in foreign assistance programs offer another illustration. Aid programs in the past have relied heavily on tying U.S. foreign assistance to the purchase of U.S. products. As Table 8.1 shows, the largest portion of AID assistance since 1962 has been commodity and capital aid (less than 20 percent has been technical assistance—percentage figure in column 2). In the case of commodity aid, 90 percent or more of the products have been purchased in the United States (percentage figure in column 3). Food aid is the other major source of U.S. economic assistance. Of the totals shown in Table 8.2, all but a tiny fraction has been spent for U.S. products. In the future, however, as our AID/IRRI study shows, U.S. foreign aid may involve an increasing amount of technical, as opposed to commodity or capital, assistance. What is more, this technical assistance may not be aimed, as in the past, at training foreign recipients to use and therefore purchase American products and technology but at the development of new or adapted technologies appropriate specifically and perhaps exclusively to the conditions of developing societies. U.S. industry (not to mention Congress) may not be too enthusiastic about spending aid money on technologies with no or limited application in Western markets. Yet the new foreign assistance legislation also stresses continued

TABLE 8.1

AID Expenditures, Fiscal Years 1962-73
(thousands of dollars)

Fiscal Year	Grand Total	Technical Assistance	Commodity Purchases
1962	1,832,274	280,432 (15)	883,900
1963	2,033,329	328,716 (16)	1,170,000 (79.4)
1964	1,980,814	308,968 (16)	1,165,200 (86.6)
1965	2,036,665	299,461 (15)	1,287,800 (92.1)
1966	2,142,983	311,899 (15)	1,231,600 (90.2)
1967	2,319,693	306,613 (13)	1,402,300 (96.2)
1968	2,033,888	317,502 (16)	1,161,200 (98.4)
1969	2,011,861	276,856 (14)	1,024,600 (98.9)
1970	1,819,382	261,745 (14)	995,100 (98.0)
1971	1,899,022	277,169 (15)	975,000 (99.8)
1972	2,022,805	257,505 (13)	829,900 (95.5)
1973	1,939,271	258,079 (13)	684,900 (94.5)

Note: numbers in parentheses in the "Technical Assistance" column refer to percentage of the grand total; those in parentheses in the "Commodity Purchases" column refer to the percentage procured in the United States.

Source: U.S. Agency for International Development, Operations Report, FY 1973 (Washington, D.C.: Statistics and Reports Division, Office of Financial Management, June 1973), pp. 47, 56.

TABLE 8.2

Food for Peace Total Expenditures
(thousands of dollars)

Fiscal Year	Total Title I[a]	Total Title II[b]
1962	1,616,975	477,650
1963	1,800,364	476,427
1964	1,683,036	573,499
1965	1,715,409	358,186
1966	1,562,428	413,196
1967	1,289,428	380,966
1968	1,134,841	343,279
1969	868,409	363,013
1970	895,328	348,945
1971	851,104	393,499
1972	769,604	521,386
1973	744,471	393,855
1974	578,111	383,161

[a]Title I includes payments only to U.S. agricultural, processing and flagship industries.

[b]Title II includes payments only to U.S. agricultural and processing industries; the vast majority of flagship freight payments goes to U.S. flag ships.

Notes: Table includes all CCC costs: commodity purchases, processing, and flagship freight payments.

Source: U.S., Department of Agriculture, Agricultural Stabilization and Conservation Service, The Fiscal Division.

and even increased reliance on nongovernmental agents, particularly private industry, to implement future aid programs. What incentives will be needed to encourage private industry to participate in the development of products whose markets, at least for the moment, are confined to small developing countries and, even within these countries, to low-income, rural consumers? Without new incentive structures, U.S. aid programs may lose one of their principal domestic rationales, that is, the financing of sales of American-made products around the world.

In sum, both industry and government in the U.S. may have to recognize the need for a new partnership in foreign industrial and economic relations. This is not to say that greater government influence, let alone control, is the answer. Even if desirable (which it probably is not), government influence today is more difficult, given the enhanced control by industry of relevant commercial technologies. While industry was limited to an advisory role in the strategic-military evaluation of technology transfers (the TACs, see Chapter 2), it is almost sure to have some policy role in the economic-commercial evaluation of these transfers. Thus, the new arrangements that emerge at the government-industry interface will reflect industrial, no less than governmental, requirements. Industrial trade associations may become more prominent partners of government in foreign economic relations. We noted the State Department's use of the Industrial Research Institute to learn about U.S. industrial contacts with the Soviet Union. The Council of the Americas, a nonprofit business association, may be another example. The Council was involved in 1974 with State and other agencies in technology transfer discussions with Latin American countries.

ADJUSTMENTS IN INTERAGENCY RELATIONS

Just as neat separations of U.S. government policy and private industrial activities in foreign technological relations may be a thing of the past (the end of Cooper's two-track system—see Chapter 3), neat distinctions between domestic-oriented and foreign policy-oriented government agencies in these relations may also be increasingly passe. Interagency adjustments fuzzing over such distinctions may result both from internal realignments between government and industry and from external pressures toward greater multilateralization of U.S. foreign assistance and private industrial activities.

As international industrial relations become more and more politicized, government agencies are likely to become more and more polarized around free market versus managed market advocates. In raw material sectors, for example, State has emerged as the principal advocate of measures to stabilize commodity prices and insure a more favorable investment climate (the effect, for example, of minimum safeguard price schemes in energy, long-term sales agreements with the Soviet Union in grains, and buffer stock schemes in certain raw material sectors). By contrast, more domestically oriented agencies such as Treasury, Commerce, Agriculture, and even Interior, urge a reliance on free market mechanisms. The trade-offs here are complex, and it is not simply a matter of State placing foreign policy over domestic interests or the other agencies doing the reverse. For example, minimum safeguard prices for energy products, which may be desirable to develop alternative sources and to reduce dependence on OPEC, may be bad for American consumers but good for American energy producers. Similarly, managed grain sales to the Soviet Union, which may be desirable to shield detente from domestic backlash, helps American consumers (by ensuring greater price stability in grain markets) but may hurt American farmers (by preventing extreme price fluctuations upwards as well as downwards). Whatever the balance between these interests, State and other agencies are likely to differ because they are responding to different environments. Domestic U.S. interests, however, are at stake in both environments.

What may be changing in contemporary foreign economic policy-making is not the relative weight of foreign versus domestic interests but the mechanisms for coupling the two. As we noted, U.S. technology-related foreign policy initiatives in the past could be implemented largely by technical and private U.S. institutions without explicit coordination by high-level policy officials. Such coordination may now be more necessary. The most interesting and perhaps novel developments, therefore, may occur at the interagency level. These developments may emphasize mechanisms of coordination rather than shifts of influence from domestic to foreign policy agencies, or vice versa. As in the case of adjustments in government-industry relations, we need to look less for shifts of influence or control from one institution to another (implying a zero-sum contest) than for new arrangements to interrelate a larger number of institutions and policy issues.

A good example of what these new arrangements may look like is found in our energy R and D case study. Traditionally, as a recent study notes, the State Department has been weak in technological and economic issue areas, such as energy.[9] The real muscle in foreign technological affairs was exercised by domestic, technical agencies (all of which added international branches during the postwar period, much as business corporations did in the early stages of their multi-nationalization). On energy, however, the State Department has played a leading role from the outset. This role, as the R and D case study shows, was not established without some interagency friction and indeed conflict. Surprisingly, however, this conflict was not obtrusive, perhaps reflecting a new deference on the part of technical agencies to foreign policy organs. Today, the Bureau of Economic and Business

Affairs (EB) in State coordinates all aspects of U.S. foreign policy in energy, including energy R and D. On R and D issues related to the IEA, ERDA goes through EB, while on all other international R and D agreements, ERDA has a relatively free hand, nominally relating to OES (the newly created Bureau of Oceans and International Environmental and Scientific Affairs). Reportedly, EB is also looking at other commodity areas besides energy to determine coordination possibilities and requirements. Assistant Secretary for Economic and Business Affairs, Thomas Enders, led the American delegation to the United Nations special session in September 1975, where a series of commitments covering a wide range of commodities was agreed upon.

A recent development in food policy, which does not concern technology directly, provides a further example of enhanced foreign policy direction of economic and technical issues. In preparation for the World Food Conference in November 1974, the U.S. government was badly fragmented on food issues.[10] As a result, U.S. policy at this conference was much less decisive or effective than it was, for example, at the Washington Energy Conference where State played a leading coordinating role.[11] Today, U.S. food policy continues to be fragmented but State may be assuming a greater role. In September 1975, a high-level State Department official, Under Secretary for Economic Affairs Charles Robinson, led a delegation to the Soviet Union to negotiate a long-term grain sales agreement. As commentators noted, this was the first time State rather than Department of Agriculture officials headed a negotiation of food policy.[12]

None of this implies that foreign policy agencies necessarily have more influence or, as we already noted, that foreign policy interests are dominating domestic ones. Moreover, these developments may only reflect the power and personal energies of the present Secretary of State. We are inclined to believe, however, that they also represent adjustments to a changing foreign economic environment which no longer permits technically oriented government or private U.S. actors to operate on their own in foreign technology-related issue areas. These actors may not only have to coordinate more explicitly with U.S. foreign policy officials, but also to multilateralize their foreign activities to include government and private counterparts abroad. In the case of private industrial actors, the coal gasification consortium we have discussed may be one example. In the case of government technical agencies, the revised role of Comsat in the Intelsat organization is an example.

Our AID/IRRI study suggests a further implication of a possible pattern toward multilateralization of U.S. technology-related activities abroad. This project was carried out in a public, international research center which finds it difficult to discriminate among private institutions in the licensing of proprietary information. If, as the 1973 foreign assistance legislation urges, more U.S. foreign aid and in particular, technical assistance is to be carried out in the future through multilateral institutions, U.S. private industries will have to learn to relate to these institutions, no less than to the U.S. government. If exclusive licensing privileges are denied by these institutions, U.S. companies may have to form consortia with foreign counterparts to ensure adequate markets to cover development costs without proprietary protection. Multilateralization at the level of intergovernmental R and D, in other words, may bring with it multilateralization at the level of industrial R and D. The reverse may also occur, as British insistence on government participation in the industrial consortium for a coal gasification plant suggests.

Two other interesting examples of governmental and industrial multilateralization may be mentioned. In addition to the coal gasification project discussed above, the United States also proposed within IEA the establishment of an R and D consortium, pooling national resources on the development of new energy sources such as solar and fusion. This consortium was to manage joint facilities, including at one point the possibility of an international fusion laboratory. The consortium to date has not been realized. But again the novelty of such a consortium needs to be recognized. In the past, as we noted in Chapter 2, agencies such as the AEC, preferred coordination of parallel national programs and expenditures over establishment of joint facilities as the appropriate instrumentality for R and D cooperation. Now, in the consortium concept, ERDA is discussing the possibility of joint facilities. The problems of handling proprietary information developed in such facilities are comparable to those we noted above in connection with multilateralization of research under foreign aid programs.

Industries may also find increasing incentives to multilateralize, that is, move more toward joint ventures and other arrangements as opposed to direct investment. Interestingly, just as government-initiated multilateral organizations may assume R and D and operational, as well as regulatory (preferred in the past—see Chapter 2), roles in technology-related areas, industries may be motivated into multilateral regulatory, as well as R and D and operational, activities. For example, an interesting possibility noted in our energy R and D case study is that industries may decide on their own at some point to finance safety and environmental studies and procedures to self-regulate the sale of potentially dangerous products in foreign markets. Clearly, industries have an interest in removing safety and environmental obstacles to commercial sales and may be willing to assume some of the costs and responsibilities (under overall intergovernmental control, of course, as in the case of nuclear energy and the IAEA) to ensure that broader social interests and demands are met. Clearly, the credibility of industrial self-policing in international areas may be difficult to establish. But international industrial self-regulation, with the checks of competition among rival national industries, may be more credible to the public than national industrial self-regulation. In connection with parallel intergovernmental arrangements, such as we referred to above, international industrial arrangements of this sort may become quite plausible. Once again, pressures toward multilateralization in one sector bring with them pressures toward multilateralization in another.

These pressures toward multilateralization will exert strain on traditional relations between Congress and the Executive in foreign technology-related activities. Congressional support of U.S. technological initiatives in the past, from the Atoms for Peace Plan to foreign aid programs, has been based in large part on returns to private and domestic-oriented U.S. institutions. If these returns have to be increasingly shared with foreign partners, Congressional support may wane. Perhaps, as our energy R and D case study suggests, Congress will have to authorize separate and larger budgets for international programs of domestic agencies. As long as domestic agencies are required to divert domestic money for international projects, U.S. private industry and its supporters in Congress are likely to oppose meaningful international cooperation. On the other hand, as we noted in Chapter 5, authorizing separate budget line items for international activities may also give Congress the opportunity to hold international programs to a minimum. Domestic agencies may have to continue to be convinced of the technical and/or political necessity of such cooperation by foreign policy agencies, without going to Congress for separate budget allocations.

Where defense-related technologies are involved, the Department of Defense (DOD) is also likely to oppose multilateralization. Indeed, DOD has a right to be unhappy about a number of trends we have projected in this study. The declining role of U.S. government funding of industrial R and D is occurring in precisely the defense and space technology sectors where DOD has been most influential in the past. As less of the technology being developed in the industrial sector is funded by defense contracts and hence subject to the scrutiny of DOD contract monitors, other agencies, such as State and Commerce, have had to step into the gap to find out what private industries are doing in technological contacts abroad. Defense leverage may have correspondingly declined. Perhaps in response to this, as we noted in Chapter 3 of this study, congressional supporters of the Defense Department have sought to strengthen DOD's position in the export review process. An amendment to the 1974 export administration legislation required Defense to be informed of all requests for validated licenses (and not just those requests that surfaced in the interagency operating committee). If government's share of industrial R and D funding continues to decline, however, Defense may be facing a secular shift in its influence on technology transfer issues. Our case studies were not designed to get at the implications of this shift, but it would seem to be one of the prime areas that calls for further research and analysis. The last chapter of this study goes on to make a series of recommendations for further research of this and other issues. Our inquiries have identified but hardly resolved many of these problems.

NOTES

1. The generalization applies only to manufacturing sectors. In extractive sectors, the Soviet Union has accepted certain long-term arrangements involving buyback of resultant products, as in the fertilizer contracts signed with Occidental Petroleum Company. For a full discussion of this distinction between "one shot" and long-term arrangements, see Eric W. Hayden and Henry R. Nau, "Manufacturing Enterprise Relationships in East-West Technology Transfer: Theoretical Models and Practical Experiences," Columbia Journal of World Business, 10, no. 3 (Fall 1975): 70-83.

2. See, in particular, United States Tariff Commission, Implications of Multinational Firms, for World Trade and Investment and for U.S. Trade and Labor. Report to the Committee on Finance of the United States Senate, TC Publication 537, Washington, D.C., January 1973, vol. III, p. 671.

3. Ibid., pp. 577-78.

4. See Chapter 2, Note 27.

5. See "The Experience of Gulf Oil in the Transfer of Technology," paper prepared by the Gulf Oil Company for presentation at the Seminar on the Management of the Transfer of Technology within Industrial Cooperation, U.N. Economic Commission for Europe, Geneva, July 14-17, 1975.

6. See, for example, the results of interviews conducted by the East-West Industrial Cooperation project directed by Professor Paul Marer of Indiana University (mimeographed), and Herman Kahn and William Schneider, Jr., National Security Policy Issues in U.S. Soviet Technology Transfer, prepared by the Hudson Institute for the Defense Advanced Research Projects Agency, HI-2016RR, June 14, 1974.

7. See Charles Wolf, Jr. U.S. Technology Exchange with the Soviet Union: A Summary Report, prepared by the Rand Corporation for the Defense Advanced Research Projects Agency. R-1520/1-ARPA, August 1974, p. 14.

8. See newspaper reports, Washington Post, September 23 and 24, 1975, and October 4 and 11, 1975.

9. See Science and Technology in the Department of State, prepared for the Subcommittee on International Security and Scientific Affairs of the Committee on International Relations, U.S. House of Representatives, by the Science Policy Research Division, Congressional Research Service, Library of Congress (Washington, D.C.: U.S. Government Printing Office, June 1975. This study is part of a series on "Science, Technology and American Diplomacy," directed by Franklin P. Huddle.

10. See Leslie H. Gelb and Anthony Lake, "Less Food, More Politics," Foreign Policy, no. 17 (Winter 1974-75, 176-90.

11. See an essay by this author, "Interpreting U.S. Foreign Policy in Food and Energy," paper presented at the Annual Convention of the American Association for the Advancement of Science, Americana Hotel, New York, New York, January 1975.

12. Washington Post, October 17, 1975.

CHAPTER

9

U.S. FOREIGN POLICY FOR TECHNOLOGY TRANSFER: RESEARCH NEEDS AND POLICY DIRECTIONS

The case studies reviewed in the previous chapter offer practical manifestations of general trends identified in Chapter 3. They are not intended to confirm these trends. Our task has been one of working at two widely separated levels—an abstract, conceptual level seeking to synthesize postwar and contemporary trends in U.S. technology transfer policy, and an empirical case study level examining specific industries or projects of technology transfer. Our purpose was to begin to sketch out the problem areas between these levels, on which very little previous research has focused. There was no alternative to this approach, given the fact that few existing efforts have gone beyond the examination of individual technology transfer cases or considered these problems in more than one of the several policy sectors involving technology transfer (that is, they have looked at these problems in the strategic-military, foreign assistance, or private industrial policy sector but not among these sectors).

A principal objective of our study, therefore, was to establish a framework for identifying the central issues and actors or mechanisms currently associated with international technology transfer by the United States. These issues and mechanisms set the context for current policymaking, which goes on even in the absence of the resolution of these issues or a clear understanding of current mechanisms (for example, what the concept of unbundling implies for U.S. foreign direct investment). It is far from being too late, however, to address these issues and mechanisms and to seek to throw more analytical light on the current and intensifying debate over technology transfer.

In this chapter, therefore, we suggest possible areas for future research and study. These areas can be grouped into three broad categories: 1) international—studies of what is happening to U.S.

commercial assets in foreign markets and how these external developments are affecting the form of U.S. technology exports and the returns from these exports in the balance of payments; 2) national—studies examining the relationship between the U.S. government and private industry as this relationship bears on information and criteria for formulating national policy toward international technology transfer and on mechanisms and structures for implementing this policy; and 3) industrial—microlevel studies of how firms behave with respect to the international transfer of technology. In the first part of this chapter, we discuss briefly eight types of studies falling into these different categories.

We conclude the chapter by drawing together the implications of this study of U.S. technology transfer policy for U.S. foreign economic and diplomatic policy in general. Technology, we argue, remains an important asset of U.S. policy in foreign affairs. But U.S. technological superiority of the kind experienced in the 1950s and early 1960s is clearly a thing of the past and is unlikely to be retrieved, if at all, without unacceptable cost to other domestic and foreign policy goals. Rather than across-the-board technological leadership, therefore, a selective type of technological interdependence, especially with Western Europe and Japan, may offer the best model in the future for relating technology to U.S. economic and diplomatic objectives in foreign affairs.

RESEARCH NEEDS

Aggregate Data on Unbundling

Despite increasing interest in and rhetoric about unbundling the foreign direct investment package, U.S. direct investment outflows remain high and indeed continue to climb (see Table 2.2). More work needs to be done to clarify these concurrent trends. Is unbundling only a threat in less developed countries, or are Western European countries also increasingly following Japan's example and bargaining for U.S. technology separately from capital and marketing assets?

A more serious problem is how one would detect unbundling, even if it were occurring. Published balance-of-payments data do not provide sufficient detail. Long-term capital outflows are reported as direct investment if U.S. ownership of equity in foreign facilities equals or exceeds 10 percent. All other long-term outflows are treated as portfolio investments.

It is assumed, in short, that 10 percent equity ownership constitutes management control. Now, the greatest part of U.S. direct investment in the past, as we have noted, has involved wholly—or majority—owned subsidiaries, that is, 51-100 percent equity ownership. In the future, however, U.S. firms may be required to accept equal or minority participation in overseas ventures. Under these circumstances, the degree of U.S. control of foreign operations may go down. This could happen while total new direct investment outflows, reported in balance-of-payments data as anything more than 10 percent equity participation, stayed the same or even went up. For example, a U.S. firm exporting $100,000 of long-term capital in one year to establish 100 percent equity ownership of a new subsidiary abroad might export the same amount of capital the next year to initiate three minority shareholding operations (at 33 1/3 percent equity ownership each). The same amount would be reported each year as direct investment in the balance-of-payments, but the control position of the firm would have changed considerably.

If control of foreign operations is significant in terms of what firms can expect to obtain in payment for their technology transferred abroad, this decline in degree of U.S. equity ownership and associated control may bring with it a decline in U.S. earnings on technology. The Tariff Commission study gave preliminary evidence that direct investment (defined as control) is a more flexible and, for the donor, profitable instrument for pricing technology in international business relations than joint ventures or indirect investment (licensing unaffiliated partners). Unbundling poses the threat of rolling back U.S. foreign direct investment and thereby reducing the level of returns on U.S. technology transfers. Yet balance of payments data offer no measurement of this phenomenon. Between the critical ranges of 10 to 50 percent equity ownership, it is still assumed that U.S. firms exercise control of the foreign enterprise.

When it could be assumed that most U.S. direct investment involved 51 to 100 percent equity ownership, there may have been no need for finer investment data reporting. A share reported to be above 10 percent could be safely assumed to be actually above 50 percent. If unbundling should acquire meaningful proportions, however, this could no longer be assumed. A 30 percent share might still be reported as direct investment but not necessarily involve the advantages of control and flexible pricing of assets in international exchanges previously associated with direct investment.

Technological Balance of Payments

The last point suggests that there are multiple means of payment for technology in international economic exchanges. Some, but by no means all, of these payments are recorded in the so-called technological balance-of-payments (licensing, royalty, and management fees). As we noted in Chapter 3, however, reporting of these payments is afflicted by all sorts of data problems—structural, definitional, and operational. More work needs to be done to improve our understanding of the means of payment for technology and how these payments get reported in the balance of payments. This seems especially necessary if foreign countries are increasingly going to restrict the means of payment for technology (by preventing direct investment and hence transfer pricing, by restricting repatriation of net earnings, and so on). It may also be necessary to counter foreign claims that the price of U.S. technology is excessive. Andean Common Market countries, for example, have already calculated these costs for themselves. Unless we are to accept their calculations, we will have to come up with some total payments estimates of our own.

Classification of People Services

If the direct investment package is unbundled, disembodied technology or what we might more broadly call people services (since information is usually accompanied by people—see Table 1.2) will become more important in U.S. technology outflows. We need to develop some classification of these people services in order to know what we are exporting and its approximate worth. What do we mean, for example, by the broad desgnation "management services"? How do we distinguish management services from routine administrative services or from other private services (as defined in the balance of payments and found in column E of Table 2.2)? What are the economically most valuable forms of management service? We have developed some rough but nevertheless useful distinctions between high and low technology when referring to hardware, that is, final products and capital equipment. These distinctions contribute to our understanding of the value and usefulness of hardware exports. What are the comparable distinctions between high and low management or software technology?[1] Unless we seek to make these distinctions systematically from an economic perspective, they may emerge ad hoc from individual cases of military export review. (An example might be the General Electric license to manufacture B-1 jet engines in France. The license was approved only after GE agreed to maintain overall management activities within the United States. Presumably, location of management activities in the United States was considered to be necessary to preserve certain economically valuable management assets, no less than military secrets.)

Service Versus Product Firms

Related to the need to develop more sophisticated classifications for exports of people services is the need to understand more broadly how service firms behave in the export of technology. In the case of product firms, we have a rough explanation of export behavior in the product-cycle theory. What is the comparable explanation for export behavior of service firms? The latter have been historically confined to local or contiguous markets (for example, civil construction services). But, in the modern economy, professional services abound (such as, consulting, marketing, construction engineering). These services are no more geographically limited than manufacturing firms, indeed perhaps less so. What impact can we expect on the U.S. technological or overall balance of payments from the increasing number and activity of these firms in domestic and foreign markets?

Industrial Disclosure Policy

Some of the above problems concerning reporting of investment data, transfer pricing, management exports, and so on, relate to a larger problem of public and private requirements in the handling of proprietary and internal company information. This is a delicate area in government-industry relations and is accordingly ignored in many studies. But there is little point in ducking relevant research into this problem, even if it has to be done largely through nongovernment sources. The point is to be aware of and to study the implications of the ongoing struggle over information between Congress, the Executive, and private industry. This struggle is going on in individual industrial sectors, as in the current case of oil companies, or to influence the economy as a whole, as in the case of recent congressional proposals for national economic planning. There are trade-offs in these economic areas between protecting national economic interests and upholding private <u>industrial</u> rights, comparable to more familiar trade-offs in military areas between protecting national security and upholding private <u>individual</u> rights and liberties. Only through careful study and vigilance can these trade-offs be balanced. In the case of technology transfer, we need to define the limits of what government needs to know to protect legitimate public interests and what industry needs to conceal to protect private property.

Implications of Decline of Government Support for Industrial R and D

Related to the information problem is the need to know far more than we do about the implications of the decline of government funding of R and D in the industrial sector. This trend, as we noted in Chapter 3, is already well advanced. At an abstract level, it seems to suggest that government has less information about and therefore less influence over what industry is doing in areas of new technology. As a result, industry may be in a stronger position to do what it wants with its technology, both at home and through export.

From an ideological point of view, this may be applauded or deplored. We are suggesting neither. First, the facts have to be established. Studies are needed of government contract monitoring procedures to establish what, if any, relationship exists between the level of government R and D funding in a particular firm or industry and government knowledge of and influence over the full range of R and D activities of that firm or industry. Is there a threshold percentage of government R and D funding in certain firms and industries below which government influence over what is done with publicly funded innovations or spin-offs from publicly funded innovations is sharply reduced? Moreover, from the standpoint of control of technology in export situations, what are the implications of a move from direct government support of R and D in U.S. industries to indirect government influence over industrial innovation through demand-oriented policies?[2] At first glance, at least, such a move would seem to reduce government leverage over technology transfer issues, since it removes government contractors from an inside relationship with private industry.

Even if it were established that government knowledge and hence influence had declined, this might not be significant for technology export. Studies would have to be done to see if the industries in which government R and D funding is going down are also the ones in which technology exports are going up. Even then, the exports involved may not be that significant from the standpoint of public interest, either in security or economic terms.

Institutional and Procedural Devices to Relate Government and Industry in Technology Export

If these exports were significant, however, some government intervention might be justified. This, as we have noted, might be necessary to protect public interests at home as well as to counter

public interventions in private markets abroad. Given the apparent
evidence that industry has acquired greater leverage over technology
transfer policy within the United States at the same time industry,
chiefly multinational companies, is losing leverage outside the United
States (due to increased competition and unbundling), particular attention needs to be directed to the interface of U.S. government-industry
relations and the adjustments that may be taking place to accommodate
these cross-cutting developments. Industry would seem to have the
initiative but for traditional reasons may be reluctant to exercise it.
(In the energy sector, for example, industry has been extremely reluctant to proceed without government guidelines and agreement in
Congress on a national energy policy. Even with considerable government encouragement, as we noted in the case of a fourth uranium enrichment plant, private industry has preferred to delay. This hesitancy, as we also noted, has complicated U.S. offers of international
transfer of uranium technology, as discussed in Chapter 2). Government may try to seize the initiative in industry's place, but being ill
informed, may make ill suited proposals. We need to study what is
happening and analyze some of the institutions and procedures that may
be emerging intentionally or unintentionally at the government-industry
interface (some of which we noted in our case studies). Only then will
we be able to judge what we want or how we might modify our institutions without abandoning our fundamental economic philosophy of free
enterprise.

Economic Criteria for Technology Export

To make wise policy in the face of new political and economic
conditions affecting technology transfer, we need to do a great deal
more work on economic criteria for evaluating technology exports.
In one of the few papers that addresses this problem seriously, there
is a large gap, which the authors themselves admit, between the conditions they describe facing American exporters of technology and the
criteria they propose to evaluate and regulate such exports.[3] We need
to close this gap, to fill in between our general sense of changing international economic conditions and our specific understanding of how
technology is managed at the firm or microeconomic level. At the
moment, the argument that technological innovation is a microeconomic
phenomenon too often serves as a argument against any macroeconomic
policy altogether. Perhaps, instead, we should recognize that a better
understanding of the microeconomic evolution and management of technology may contribute to sounder macroeconomic policy, not to its
superfluousness. If externalities are carefully studied, they become

less of an excuse for ill prepared government intervention as well as for a lack of intervention altogether.

Microeconomic Studies of Technology Transfer

Our theoretical understanding of the economic issues attending technology export is likely to be advanced inductively as well as deductively. We need many more case studies of how firms manage their technology in international exchanges. We have few such studies now either within the multinational company or between independent enterprises. The former type of study, of course, is difficult to do, as testified by our choice not to pursue such a study in this project. Even projects that have the full support of high levels of government as well as industry encounter difficulties in getting industrialists to speak frankly about firm-level policymaking with regard to technology exports.[4]

The multinational company and hence studies of these companies may be less important in the future, however, than in the past. Licensing between independent enterprises may acquire greater importance. Licensing arrangements also present problems of information acquisition, but they may at least be more fully documented than internal transfers, permitting ex post facto studies to be done after particular licensing agreements have expired or been significantly modified.*

POLICY DIRECTIONS

This list of future research needs is only partial and suggestive. But it reflects the evident requirement to rethink the relationships between technology and U.S. policy in contemporary foreign affairs. For most of the postwar period, international technology transfer was perceived in the United States largely within the limited context of defense and prestige considerations. Today it is recognized as a much broader instrument of U.S. foreign policy, entailing economic, social and environmental, as well as defense and diplomatic, consequences. By becoming less exclusively associated with defense issues, however,

---

*The Labor Department has recently awarded a contract to a Washington consulting group, Developing World Industry and Technology, to undertake a series of case studies of international licensing of technology between private firms.

technology transfer policy has become not less but more important. It continues to retain its significance for defense and foreign policy objectives and is now also critical for the achievement of important economic and social objectives. Indeed, given the concerns about technological dependence abroad, in developed as well as developing countries, technology policy is as likely to be coopted in the future by national security and economic policy considerations, intensifying international technological competition and conflict, as it is to attract new attention to non-security, commercial relationships promising increased international technological cooperation and interdependence.

To the extent that technology policy is integrated with national policy, international technology transfer may decline or assume a radically different form. Each country will seek a minimum degree of technological independence, limiting transfers that involve foreign control. On the other hand, it may encourage transfers that involve the training and education of local personnel to solve their own technological problems with local resources and manpower. The latter is particularly likely in future technology relations with developing countries. If developed countries assist this process, they will increasingly transfer technology through the form of people-embodied exports, such as we have emphasized in this study, rather than through product- or capital-embodied exports. As the member nations of the United Nations Conference on Trade and Development (UNCTAD) and United Nations Environmental Program (UNEP) declared at Cocoyoc, Mexico in October 1974, they want technology transfers in the future to focus "on adaptation and the generation of local technology . . ., reliance on the capacity of people themselves to invent and generate new resources and techniques to increase their capacity to absorb them, to put them to socially beneficial use, to take a measure of command over the economy, and to generate their own way of life."[5]

There is little doubt, in this writer's mind at least, that the focus of developing countries' policies in the technology field in the future will be on national self-reliance and technological independence, rather than transnational cooperation and technological interdependence. This mades sense from their point of view, since, as the Cocoyoc declaration further notes, "it is impossible to develop self-reliance through full participation in a system that perpetuates economic dependence." What is less clear is how developed countries will respond to the cross-cutting tendencies to subordinate technology policy to national self-reliance or to pursue technology strategies of selective development accompanied by international technology transfer and interdependence.

How the United States responds will be especially important. Some analysts have recently argued that the United States is losing its technological edge in world economic competition.[6] These analysts believe that new policies of technological innovation are needed to rejuvenate the U.S. economy and to restore U.S. world leadership. In the absence of positive government actions, they fear the United States will incur long-term economic consequences from living off past U.S. technological achievements, as well as short-term political consequences from reactionary pressures to throw up protective barriers around America's declining industries.

These observers correctly perceive the need to preempt forces pushing U.S. technology policy in the direction of national self-encapsulation but, in the view of this writer, they advocate the wrong remedy. They argue, for example, that the United States, unlike Japan, cannot afford to rely on import of foreign technology, especially given the increasing restrictions that are being applied to the free flow of technology in international markets, forcing even Japan to pay more attention to indigenous innovation. Yet, it is precisely because of the increasing restrictions on international technology transfer (especially, as we have noted in this study, on the direct investment mechanism) that a U.S. strategy of renewed technological leadership or self-reliance is fraught with potentially undesirable consequences. Such a strategy, as we noted, requires positive government intervention to restructure innovative incentives in the private sector. Given the strength of labor unions today, this intervention could easily be turned against its original purposes and acquire protectionist or quasi-protectionist characteristics. Even if it did not, however, a strategy of technological leadership, in the present world of greater competition, smacks too much, in this writer's view, of a strategy of technological independence, reflecting an unwillingness on the part of the United States to accept even a small degree of dependence on the international economic system, while its European and Japanese competitors remain significantly dependent. Instead of regarding the postwar narrowing of the technological gap with these allies as threatening and conflict-producing, the United States should recognize that the current level of international industrial and technological competition is far more normal and indeed healthier than the very unusual situation characterized by U.S. dominance in the 1940s and 1950s. Moreover, international technological leadership may be less important to the United States today than it was before, both in terms of U.S. foreign policy interests and in terms of stimulation of the domestic economy.

In terms of foreign policy interests, U.S. technological superiority and resulting current account surpluses were considered necessary in the past in large part to offset long-term capital account deficits created by government military and foreign assistance programs abroad and private direct investment outflows. Now, if, in the future, government outflows are likely to be less, in line with the retrenchment of U.S. defense commitments under the Nixon doctrine, and if private direct investment outflows are also likely to be smaller given foreign opposition to direct investment, the need to run current account surpluses fueled by technology-intensive exports of the same magnitude as in the past also diminishes. Concrete foreign policy considerations do not justify it, and even the psychological or prestige advantages of technological leadership are vastly reduced today compared to the 1950s.

In terms of stimulation of the U.S. domestic economy, a strategy of technological leadership may take us off in the wrong direction. It has always seemed somewhat forced, in the case of the United States, to argue the need for a domestic economic strategy in terms of international competitive requirements, given the relatively (in comparison to our allies) small role international markets play in overall U.S. economic production. This may have been justified in an era when U.S. foreign policy leadership required relative subordination of domestic interests to foreign policy objectives. But this is less true today than before. Thus, if the United States is suffering from a relative decline of productivity and industrial growth, due perhaps as William Nordhaus has suggested to a secular shift from high productivity growth sectors, such as the technology-intensive industries, to low productivity growth sectors, such as government and services,[7] then, for domestic purposes, the United States may be better off focusing on technological innovation and improvements in the lower productivity growth sectors while relying more on the technological import from abroad in some of the high technology sectors.

The argument is not an either/or proposition, suggesting an excessive dependence on high technology imports. It is instead an attempt to argue that, in contrast to postwar policies of across-the-board technological leadership, U.S. policy in the future should aim more at selective leadership accompanied by selective imitation and adaptation of foreign technologies. The result would be a slight but significant shift from a strategy of technological independence to a strategy of technological interdependence.

Two characteristics of this strategy should be emphasized. We are talking about interdependence primarily in high technology industrial sectors and, related to that, interdependence primarily with our advanced country allies (Western Europe, Japan, and Canada). Technological interdependence with oil-producing or other resource-rich developing countries and with socialist or planned economy countries entails different consequences. Here bargaining inequalities will continue to force a close integration of technology policy with national political and security considerations. In some sense, the problem in relations with these countries is how to build up technological interdependence to serve political objectives of securing raw material supplies and of diffusing military and strategic tensions between the superpowers. In relations with advanced industrial countries, the problem, as we note below, is how to preserve a limited autonomy of technological and industrial relations from national political and security considerations and to prevent the latter from poisoning and rolling back the high levels of technological and industrial interdependence already achieved.

In pursuit of this latter objective, a strategy of selective technological interdependence holds two advantages over a strategy of renewed technological leadership. First, it may not require any more government intervention in high technology sectors than currently exists, and is therefore less vulnerable to domestic protectionist pressures. For example, as we have emphasized throughout this study, even though R and D spending by U.S. industry has levelled off in real terms over the past five years, industry today funds a larger share of industrial R and D than in the past, due to the decline of government funding of industrial R and D. Total R and D may have levelled off, but more commercially relevant R and D controlled by industry is being done. This enhanced importance of commercial as opposed to defense and space criteria in industrial research will lead, in our view, to more careful assessments of technological costs and opportunities. Rather than reinventing the wheel, companies will be more inclined to search out what is being done abroad and to screen foreign technologies for import. Many industries, which have traditionally conducted little of their research abroad, are already taking a greater interest in technological opportunities in foreign markets and beefing up their R and D capabilities overseas to improve monitoring of local technological activities. With little change in current policy, therefore, one might expect high technology industry to move on its own toward greater interdependence and exchange of technology with advanced country competitors.

Secondly, a strategy of technological interdependence would direct our R and D efforts at home to domestic sectors where innovation is most needed, that is, the lower productivity as opposed to the high technology sectors. One is speaking here principally of the government and service sectors—health, education, transportation, housing, professional services, and so on. Unlike a strategy of technological leadership, which would take us off in a direction well traveled over the past 30 years focusing on electronics, aerospace and instrumentation sectors, a strategy of technological interdependence would force us to think anew our domestic needs and to put our international position into proper perspective vis-a-vis these needs. It would also give us the chance to be on the leading edge of the next technological revolution. While the high technology sectors were the leading edge of the second industrial revolution, government and service sectors may comprise the key sectors of the postindustrial revolution. Indeed, if the United States developed solid capabilities in areas of social and organizational innovation, the export situation of the United States might take care of itself. As we have suggested in this study, the export of services or people-embodied technologies is likely to become more important in the future. If the United States pioneered in the development of new service technologies designed to improve urban life and the quality of life in general, these services would very likely be in great demand overseas. The idea that services, no less than products and capital, may be exported is relatively novel, but it should not obscure the fact that most modern, professional services (information, transportation, management, and other specialists) are highly mobile. Such services are also, as we noted in the case of Cocoyoc Declaration, increasingly in demand, especially among developing countries who see people-embodied transfers of technology as the only answer to the development of indigenous capabilities and long-term self-reliance and independence in technological areas.

The inevitable narrowing of U.S. technological dominance after World War II and the increasing interest of foreign countries in developing indigenous technological capabilities suggest that technology may not be as fungible an asset of U.S. foreign policy in the future as it has been in the past. By fungible, we mean it may not be as readily or easily traded for political or economic advantage. In some sense, Secretary Kissinger himself has noted this fact. As we observed at the outset of this study, he believes that "science and technology are becoming our most precious resources." He is undoubtedly right that, as a _resource_, science and technology remain powerful tools of diplomatic policy, particularly in an era of resource shortages. Science and technology hold out the prospect of stretching these shortages, if not eliminating them altogether. On the other hand, he is also correct in noting that this resource is _precious_. It is no longer, as President Truman observed (see Chapter 2), "inexhaustible," at least not without great cost to promote further development. The United States, it would seem, need not and probably should not try to bear this cost alone. A selective policy of technological interdependence among advanced allies would help to spread such cost. It would ensure that, at least in some areas, technology transfer would be subjected to more systematic technical and economic, as opposed to political and prestige, examination.

This type of limited technological specialization among developed countries would maximize the potential of these countries to use their technological assets to achieve political objectives in relations with developing countries, especially the objective of timely redistribution of resources. For, in North-South relations, in contrast to relations among developed countries themselves, technology transfer is likely to retain its symbolic and foreign policy significance. This fact is less to be deplored than accepted and understood. It presents an opportunity, since few incentives other than political ones exist to motivate technology transfers among radically unequal economies, as well as a problem, since technology transfer relations may succumb to overpoliticization with resultant losses to world welfare, as well as world peace.

NOTES

1. A preliminary and useful effort to distinguish between hardware and software technologies in the manufacturing process is contained in Harvey W. Wallender, "Managing and Evaluating Technology Transfer in Manufacturing Industries," paper presented to the seminar on the Management of the Transfer of Technology within Industrial Co-operation, U.N. Economic Commission for Europe, Geneva, July 14 – 17, 1975. Mr. Wallender is Vice President of Operations and Planning of the Council of the Americas.

2. Influencing innovation through government procurement policies and fiscal and monetary policies affecting overall demand is now the strategy increasingly recommended now for government R and D efforts. See Robert Gilpin, Technology, Economic Growth and International Competitiveness, a report prepared for the Subcommittee on Economic Growth of the Joint Economic Committee, U.S. Congress, 94th Cong., 1st Sess. (Washington, D.C.: Government Printing Office, July 9, 1975).

3. See Raymond Vernon and Marshall I. Goldman, "U.S. Policies in the Sale of Technology to the USSR," paper presented to the Technical Assistance Board of the Department of Commerce, September 15, 1974. For a preliminary critique of this paper, see Thomas A. Wolf, "Preliminary Assessment of Vernon and Goldman Paper," October 10, 1974 (obtained from author).

4. This has been the experience of the East-West Industrial Cooperation project at Indiana University. This project is directed by Professor Paul Marer and sponsored by the Bureau of East-West Trade of the Department of Commerce.

5. For a copy of the full declaration, see John Gerard Ruggie and Ernst B. Haas (eds.), "International Responses to Technology," International Organization 29 (Summer 1975): 893-901. Quotes in the text are from p. 898.

6. A very useful and provocative discussion drawing together and assessing the arguments about U.S. technological competitiveness is offered by the Gilpin study cited in Note 2 above. As Gilpin notes, the evidence supporting the assertion of declining U.S. technological competitive is mixed and incomplete. This evidence hinges on the relative importance of cyclical factors affecting U.S. technology-intensive exports, such as the business cycle and dollar devaluations

of recent years, and secular factors purporting to show a long-term decline of overall U.S. industrial productivity vis-a-vis its major international competitors.

7. See Nordhaus, "The Recent Productivity Slowdown," Brookings Papers on Economic Activities, 3 (1972): 493-545.

APPENDIX

TECHNICAL COMPONENTS OF ALUMINUM

Uses

The process utilized in the production of aluminum involves three materials: bauxite (the ore), alumina (the intermediate stage) and aluminum (the final product—ingot or derived product). In terms of tonnage, approximately 4.5 tons of bauxite yield two tons of alumina from which is produced one ton of aluminum metal. In 1972, 93.4 percent of bauxite consumed in the United States was used in the production of alumina while 93 percent of the alumina consumed in the United States in 1970 went into the manufacture of aluminum. Other uses of bauxite in 1972 include:[1]

abrasives	1.6 percent
chemical applications	1.9 percent
refractory applications	2.6 percent
other applications	0.5 percent

After aluminum ingot is obtained from alumina in the smelting process it is fabricated into mill products and sold for the uses in the United States shown in Table A.1.

Aluminum is classified as a strategic and critical material and is thus included in the National Strategic Stockpile. The uses of aluminum important for strategic purposes include aircraft, missiles, cartridge cases, bridging equipment, and electric power transmission cables.[2]

The fact that 93 percent of the bauxite consumed in the United States is used to produce alumina and 93 percent of the alumina is used in manufacturing aluminum suggests that the aluminum industry is integrated. According to the Council on International Economic Policy (CIEP)[3] six firms control the majority of the noncommunist world's production capacity for bauxite, alumina, and aluminum. These

---

The most comprehensive study on the structure of the aluminum industry is <u>An Economic Analysis of the Aluminum Industry</u>, Charles Rivers Associates, Inc., 1972. Much of the data in this section is derived from the Charles Rivers study.

TABLE A.1

Aluminum Shipments Distribution by Market, 1972 and 1973
(in percent)

Industry	Shipments	
	1972	1973
Building and construction	26.5	24.7
Transportation	18.5	19.3
Containers and packaging	15.2	14.2
Electrical	12.7	12.7
Consumer durables	9.2	9.2
Machinery and equipment	6.1	6.5
Others	7.1	6.0
Exports	4.7	6.5
Total	100.0	100.0

Source: The Aluminum Association, Inc., *Aluminum Statistical Review 1973*, p. 3.

companies are Alcan Aluminum Ltd., Aluminum Company of America, Reynolds Metals Company, Kaiser Aluminum and Chemical Corp., Pechiney Ugine Kuhlmann (France), and Aluminium Suisse S.S. (Switzerland). Because the largest producers of primary aluminum are integrated, only very limited quantities of the intermediate products (bauxite and alumina) are bought and sold.

TYPES OF BAUXITE

The principal ore in the production of aluminum is bauxite. This ore is a

> complex mixture of aluminous materials, mainly aluminum hydroxides but with variable amounts of impurities. The alumina (aluminum oxide, Al_2O_3) content of most bauxites (a complex mixture of aluminum oxides) ranges from 35%

APPENDIX

to 50%, and the most common impurities are quartz, kaolinite (a clay mineral), and materials containing iron oxides. Bauxite ores consist of several types, which are classified according to mineral content, mode of occurrence, use, and source.[4]

There are three types of bauxite classified as Jamaican, Surinam, and European with varying amounts of hydrated aluminum oxide minerals. The higher grade ores contain a larger percentage of alumina (aluminum oxide, Al_2O_3). Table A.2 illustrates the type of hydrated aluminum oxide minerals contained in each type of bauxite.

TABLE A.2

Types of Bauxite

Mineral	Percent alumina	water	
1. Gibbsite (aluminum trihydrate)	65.4	34.6	Jamaican/Surinam
2. Boehmite (alpha monohydrate)	85	15	European
3. Diaspore (beta monohydrate)	85	15	Jamaican

Source: Charles River Associates, An Economic Analysis of the Aluminum Industry, pp. 2-3.

The existence of different types of bauxite is important. The CIEP report on Critical Imported Materials explains the implications:

> Bauxites are not entirely interchangeable, as slightly different grades and impurity levels have led many U.S. plants to specialize in the use of a specific type of bauxite. Changes in type require modifications in processing equipment resulting in temporary loss of production and requiring new investment.[5]

This fact could restrict the options available to the aluminum companies in switching to different suppliers (see below). However, the capital investment necessary to switch production facilities from using one type of bauxite to another type would be modest—on the magnitude of one-half to 1 percent of the total investment needed to rebuild the entire facility.[6] As to the time factor involved in loss of production, stockpiles do exist of Jamaican bauxite which could be used if necessary until the new facilities were in operation.

The alumina content of the bauxite of some of the major suppliers is illustrated in Table A.3. From this table, it can be seen that the bauxite from Surinam and Guyana generally contain higher percentages of alumina than Australian bauxite. Brazilian and West African ores, potential sources of future supply (see Table A.4), also have high alumina contents.

TABLE A.3

Compositional Range of Bauxite Ore for Some Major World Producers
(in percent)

Constituent	Guyana	Jamaica	Haiti	United States	Surinam	Brazil	West Africa	Australia
Water	24-31	23-29	24	29-30	30	28-33	23-30	22-28
Silica	2-12	14	3.4	2-5	2-15	1-7	1-5	5-8
Titania	2-4	2-3	2.8	2-3	2	1-2	1-4	4-6
Iron oxide	1-10	20-30	22	11-21	5-15	1-7	5-20	3-8
Alumina	50-62	48-52	47	45-50	50-63	59-65	48-60	40-51

Source: Wilfred David, The Economic Development of Guyana, 1953-1964 (Oxford: Clarendon Press, 1969), p. 198 (Compiled from U.S. Bureau of Mines, Mineral Facts and Problems, 1956-60.

SUPPLY PATTERNS—WORLDWIDE

The U.S. Bureau of Mines' current estimates of proven world reserves of bauxite are on the order of 15.5 billion tons—sufficient to supply all the world's smelters for more than 230 years at the current consumption rate.[7]

The production and reserves of bauxite worldwide are distributed as shown in Table A.4.

From Table A.4 it is evident that those countries with the largest amount of reserves (Australia and Guinea—52.9 percent) produce less than 23 percent of the total world mine production. This suggests there is the possibility of a shift to these countries as more important sources of bauxite supply.

The United States imports approximately 90 percent of the bauxite used domestically. The main suppliers of bauxite to the United States appear in Table A.5.

A comparison of supplier exports to the United States and supplier reserves is revealing and indicates a possibility of change with regard to supply. For example, the current principal exporters to the United States—Jamaica, Surinam, and Guyana—account for 84.2 percent of the total U.S. imports while they possess only 11 percent of total world bauxite reserves. On the other hand, principal reserve countries—Australia and Guinea—currently export a small percent (5.4) to the United States and could take up a much larger share of production and supply in the future. Table A.6 illustrates these relationships.

TABLE A.4

World Mine Production and Reserves 1973

Country	Reserves[a] Percent	Production[a] Percent
Australia	30.3	22.7
Guinea	22.6	0.04
Brazil	12.9	—[b]
Jamaica	6.5	19.7
Greece	4.5	0.04
Surinam	3.2	10.1
Yugoslavia	2.3	3.3
Guyana	1.3	5.3
Soviet sphere	4.0	4.9
USSR	1.9	7.1
Hungary	1.0	—[b]
All others	12.4	26.86
Total	100.0	100.0

[a] Based on data provided by U.S. Bureau of Mines, 1974.
[b] Not available.

Source: U.S. Congress, House, Committee on Interior and Insular Affairs, Mineral Scarcity, Oversite Hearings before the Subcommittee on Mines and Mining of the Committee on Interior and Insular Affairs, House of Representatives, No. 93-48, 93rd Cong., 2d sess., 1974, pp. 347-48.

The differences reflected in Table A.6 should not be exaggerated. Transportation costs account to a large extent for the primacy of the Caribbean producers. But importing alumina rather than bauxite from sources further away would substantially decrease the transportation costs involved.

TABLE A.5

U.S. Imports of Bauxite, by Source, 1973

Country	Percent	Tonnage*
Jamaica	52.2	7,106
Surinam	21.8	2,969
Guyana	10.2	1,388
Dominican Republic	7.5	1,026
All others	8.3	1,129
Australia	4.3	585
Haiti	2.5	344
Guinea	1.1	143
Total	100.0	13,618

*Thousands of short tons.
Source: U.S. Congress, House, Committee on Interior and Insular Affairs, <u>Mineral Scarcity, Oversite Hearings</u> before the Subcommittee on Mines and Mining of the Committee on Interior and Insular Affairs, House of Representatives, No. 93-48, 93d Cong., 2d sess., 1974, p. 350.

TABLE A.6

Major U.S. Suppliers and Reserves

Country	Percent of U.S. Imports	Percent of World Reserves
Jamaica	52.2	6.5
Surinam	21.8	3.2
Guyana	10.2	1.3
Australia	4.3	30.3
Guinea	1.1	22.6

Source: Compiled by the author from Tables A.4 and A.5.

APPENDIX

The juxtaposition of Tables A.7 and A.8 serves to illustrate the (1) sources of imported alumina to the United States (2) sources of alumina production worldwide. It is evident that the Caribbean countries are correct in their assessment that their natural resource is being depleted almost solely for use in other markets. While these countries process and export some alumina to the United States, they account for only a small percentage of worldwide alumina production (compare Tables A.7 and A.8). This latter percentage is considerably less than their share of worldwide bauxite production (for example, for Jamaica, 9.1 percent compared to 19.7 percent). These figures confirm the fact that bauxite suppliers currently export primarily the raw material which is then processed into alumina in industrialized countries.

TABLE A.7

U.S. Imports of Alumina, by Source

Country	1973[a]		1968-72 average	
	Percent	Tonnage[b]	Percent	Tonnage[b]
Australia	57.4	1,939	50.4	1,120
Jamaica	26.8	904	20.8	461
Surinam	11.3	380	20.3	452
All others	4.5	152	8.5	189
Canada	0.6	21	0.7	15
Guinea	0.6	21		
Guyana	1.0	33	1.2	27
Total	100.0	3,375	100.0	2,222

Note: Virgin Islands included as U.S.
[a]Preliminary
[b]Thousands short tons.
Source: U.S. Congress, House, Committee on Interior and Insular Affairs, Mineral Scarcity, Oversite Hearings before the Subcommittee on Mines and Mining of the Committee on Interior and Insular Affairs, House of Representatives, No. 93-48, 93rd Cong., 2d sess., 1974, p. 351.

Aluminum is unique among nonferrous industries in that the mining of the ore in general represents a fairly small percentage of total costs. The composition of bauxite mining costs, however, has had a noticeable effect on the location of alumina plants. Transport costs tend to be approximately 50 percent of the delivered cost of bauxite in the United States, although the amount varies with the source of the bauxite. The costs of shipping bauxite and alumina are nearly equal per ton mile, but as the aluminum content of alumina is approximately

TABLE A.8

Alumina Production, Worldwide

	1973[a]		1968-72 average	
Country	Percent	Tonnage[b]	Percent	Tonnage[b]
USA	25.7	7,100	30.1	6,857
Australia	14.5	4,000	10.6	2,407
USSR	9.4	2,600	9.7	2,220
Jamaica	9.1	2,500	7.5	1,707
Japan	6.9	1,900	6.2	1,416
Surinam	5.1	1,400	5.2	1,195
Western Europe	14.6	4,013	12.9	2,929
France	4.3	1,200	5.4	1,238
West Germany	4.0	1,100	3.7	815
Soviet Sphere Ex. USSR	4.9	1,350	4.8	1,105
Other Free World	9.8	2,707	13.0	2,964
Canada	4.5	1,250	5.2	1,185
Total	100.0	27,600	100.0	22,800

[a]Preliminary.
[b]Thousands of short tons.
Source: U.S. Congress, House, Committee on Interior and Insular Affairs, Mineral Scarcity, Oversite Hearings before the Subcommittee on Mines and Mining of the Committee on Interior and Insular Affairs, House of Representatives, No. 93-48, 93d Cong., 2d sess., 1974, p. 349.

twice that of bauxite, transport costs (although not necessarily total costs) may be substantially reduced by locating alumina plants near bauxite mines.

The question which naturally arises from this economic reality is why the aluminum companies do not locate more alumina plants in the bauxite-supplying countries—an issue which is frequently raised by the supplier countries themselves. One answer may be that because of the risk of nationalization, or other government controls, the companies (as well as their banks) are unwilling to commit such a large quantity of capital. Another reason which explains Reynolds actions with regard to Guyana has to do with U.S. government policy:

> Reynolds had extensive facilities for processing the ore in the U.S. During World War II, the U.S. government had erected plants to carry out various stages of aluminum smelting in order to augment supplies for the war effort. After the war the government was reluctant to sell these plants to Alcoa against which it had brought an anti-trust

APPENDIX

suit in 1937. It was decided to promote competition by helping Reynolds Metals and Kaiser Aluminum Corporation to establish themselves as integrated units by leasing them most of the plants on favourable terms.

The two companies subsequently bought the facilities on very easy terms and with these initial advantages it has been profitable for the Reynolds Company to ship the crude ore to the U.S. rather than to establish alumina plants in Guyana.

.... for a long time the American tariff fell more heavily on alumina than on crude ore and this discouraged the importation of the former.[8]

SUPPLY PATTERNS—DOMESTIC

While most of the U.S. supply of bauxite is imported, there are bauxite reserves in Arkansas and Georgia, although they are minor when compared to those in other nations. In addition, there are U.S. government and individual company stockpiles of quality bauxite in the United States. The status of the bauxite stockpile is given in Table A.9. The controversy regarding the stockpile has been expanded upon in the section on "National Security Issues for the United States" in Chapter 6.

Since 1914, the U.S. Bureau of Mines has been investigating the possibility of obtaining aluminum from other nonbauxitic aluminum-bearing materials such as clay, anorthosite, laterite, and alunite. In recent years, this effort has been receiving more publicity because of the increasing dependence of the United States on foreign sources for bauxite. With the increasing demand for aluminum, a Bureau of Mines study notes that:

.... it is expected that the use of imported alumina and aluminum as well as bauxite will increase, creating an added burden on the U.S. balance of payments. To complicate matters, competition with other industrial nations for aluminum resources is increasing. Eventually the situation may become analogous to the current one involving the world's petroleum output. From this Nation's standpoint, it is becoming increasingly important to advance a technology that will allow the United States to depend largely on its own ample resources for aluminum production. Because

TABLE A.9

National Strategic Stockpile of Bauxite

Commodity	Unit	Objective	Total Inventory	Excess	Balance of Disposal Authorization
Bauxite, metal grade, Jamaica	LDT[a]	4,638,000	8,858,881	4,220,881	1,370,077
Bauxite, metal grade, Surinam	LDT	0	5,300,000	5,300,000	0[b]
Bauxite, Refractory	LCT[c]	0	173,000	173,000	0[b]

[a]Long Dry Ton.
[b]Legislation is pending for authorization of disposal.
[c]Long Calcined Ton.
Source: General Services Administration, Office of Preparedness, Stockpile Report to Congress, July-December, 1974 (Washington, D.C.: U.S. Government Printing Office, 1974), p. 5.

domestic deposits of high-grade bauxite are almost nonexistent, raw materials such as clay, anorthosite, laterite, shale, alunite, and coal mine wastes must be considered.[9]

This governmental concern is echoed by industry spokesmen. During hearings on mineral scarcity before the House Subcommittee on Mines and Mining C. W. Parry of the Aluminum Company of America (Alcoa) was asked a question about the necessity of developing substitutes for imported bauxite. Mr. Parry replied: "We have made the corporate decision to move toward commercial scale processing [of nonbauxitic materials] in the United States."[10]

The recent imposition of a sixfold increase in taxes and royalties paid by U.S. companies to foreign bauxite suppliers has intensified the interest in alternative domestic sources of alumina by both industry and the U.S. government. As the result of a 1971 meeting which included both government and industry representatives, the Bureau of Mines instituted the "Miniplant Project" to evaluate alumina recovery processes. Eight major aluminum companies joined the venture in fiscal year 1975 contributing $50,000 per company. Meanwhile the

APPENDIX

government's share of the costs of the miniplant rose from $500,000 in FY 1974 to $700,000 in FY 1975 to a projected $2 million in FY 1976 for information and design to select one process to build a pilot plant.[11] Among the ongoing activities of the cooperative program are: processing clay with nitric acid, processing clay with hydrochloric acid, processing anorthosite, processing clay with sulfurous acid, processing alunite and processing dawsonite.

Internally, industry has also been testing nonbauxitic materials. According to the Senate Government Operations Committee print on aluminum:

> The Aluminum Company of America (Alcoa), the world's largest producer of aluminum, has led the industry in attempting to develop anorthosite as an alumina source. In 1972 Alcoa purchased 8,000 acres of Wyoming land containing large anorthosite deposits, at a cost exceeding $1 million. The company has engaged in laboratory work and conducted pilot plant operations using anorthosite for

TABLE A.10

Major Potential Domestic Sources of Aluminum
(Data in million short tons)

Source	Quantity	Alumina Content Quantity	Percent
Alunite	800	120	15[a]
Anorthosite	599,490	158,342	27
Clays:			
Ball	813	243	30
Bauxite	297	125	42
Fire	8,276	2,275	27
Kaolin	3,288	1,076	33
Dawsonite	27,000	9,500	35[b]
Laterite	1,313	384	29
Aluminum phosphate rock	800	164	28
Aluminous shale	810	229	25
Saprolite	–	–	25

[a]Deposits contain 40 percent alunite which is 37 percent alumina.
[b]Deposits contain 12 percent dawsonite which is 35 percent extractable alumina.

Source: U.S. Congress, Senate, Committee on Government Operations, Materials Shortages: Aluminum. Committee Print, 93 Cong., 2d sess. 1974, p. 19.

the past six to eight months in East St. Louis, Illinois. In light of the bauxite import situation, Alcoa's anorthosite work is likely to be accelerated and an announcement in the near future that a commercial anorthosite-processing facility will be constructed would not be unlikely.[12]

The report also notes that a joint venture involving Earth Sciences, Inc., the National Steel Corporation and its aluminum affiliate, Southwire Company, has been operating a $1 million alunite reduction pilot plant in Golden, Colorado and anticipates having a commercial plant on stream by 1978. Being the most recent alternative nonbauxitic sources considered, alunite may also be the first for use in commercial production.[13]

In addition, recycled aluminum scrap is being considered as a potentially significant source of primary aluminum.[14]

Table A.10 lists the major nonbauxitic sources of aluminum in the United States.

NOTES

1. U.S. Department of Interior, Bureau of Mines, Bureau of Mines Mineral Yearbook, 1972 ed., Bauxite Preprint (Washington, D.C.: U.S. Government Printing Office), p. 3.

2. General Services Administration, Strategic and Critical Materials: Descriptive Data (Washington, D.C.: U.S. Government Printing Office, December 1973), p. 1.

3. Council on International Economic Policy, Critical Imported Materials (Washington, D.C.: U.S. Government Printing Office, December 1974)

4. U.S. Congress, Senate, Committee on Government Operations, Materials Shortages: Aluminum, Government Operations Committee Print, 93d Cong., 2d sess., 1974 (Washington, D.C.:U.S. Government Printing Office, 1974), p. 1.

5. Council on International Economic Policy, Critical Imported Materials, p. A-4.

6. However, this percentage applies only in switching from bauxite requiring high temperature digestors (e.g., Jamaican and Australian) to those bauxites requiring low temperature digestors (e.g., Surinam). Since high temperature digestors are the most expensive switching from Surinam (using low temperature) to Jamaican bauxite (high temperature) would require a capital investment on the order of 15 to 20 percent.

APPENDIX

7. U.S. Congress, House, Committee on Interior and Insular Affairs, <u>Mineral Scarcity, Oversite Hearings</u> before the Subcommittee on Mines and Mining of the Committee on Interior and Insular Affairs, House of Representatives, No. 93-48, 93d Cong., 2d sess., 1974, p. 344.

8. Ronald D. Medas, <u>The Guyana-Alcan Conflict: The Multinational Enterprise in a Developing Country</u> (unpublished thesis, August 1974) summarizing Wilfred David (<u>The Economic Development of Guyana, 1953-1964</u> [Oxford: Clarendon Press, 1969]), p. 14, N 12.

9. U.S. Department of Interior, Bureau of Mines, <u>Revised and Updated Cost Estimates for Producing Alumina from Domestic Raw Materials</u>, by Frank A. Peters and Paul W. Johnson (Information Circular IC8648, 1974), pp. 1-2.

10. U.S. Congress, House, Committee on Interior and Insular Affairs, <u>Mineral Scarcity, Oversite Hearings</u>, p. 333.

11. Interview with Bureau of Mines official, April 10, 1975.

12. U.S. Congress, Senate, Committee on Government Operations, <u>Materials Shortages: Aluminum</u>, p. 24.

13. Ibid., p. 25.

14. For contrasting views on this subject see section on "U.S. Aluminum Industry Options" in Chapter 6.

INDEX

Advisory Committee on Export Policy, 26
aerospace technology, 3, 35-37, 41, 68, 275-76
AFL-CIO, 190
Agency for International Development (AID), 7, 208-09, 242, 270, 278, 283
Agricultural Machinery Dealers Association (AMDA), 232
Agriculture Department (USDA), 11, 29, 35, 37, 215, 282, 283
AID/IRRI study, 7, 208-59, 270, 278, 283
Alcan Aluminum Ltd., 179, 192
Alfred, A. M., 47
Alpart, 179, 193
alumina, 193, 194, 197, 202
aluminum, 171-72, 173-74, 175, 185, 188-89, 269, 270, 272, 273, 274
Aluminum Association, 181
Aluminum Company of America (Alcoa), 179, 193, 196, 197, 202
Anaconda Company, 179
Andean Common Market, 291
Apollo program, 30, 35
Arab oil embargo, 73, 124, 128, 129-30
Atomic Energy Act, 36
Atomic Energy Commission (AEC), 22, 29, 35, 36-37, 38, 40, 76, 125, 129, 140-42, 277, 284
Atoms for Peace Plan, 10, 30, 35, 37, 38, 285
Australia, 174, 177-79, 198, 203, 215, 221

B-1 jet engine, 291
bauxite, 7, 171-72, 189, 190, 191-94, 198, 272, 274, 276; supplies, 172-78
bauxite-aluminum industry study, 7, 18, 171-205, 268-69, 270, 271, 272, 274, 276
Belgium, 147, 149-51, 157
Bergsten, C. F., 58, 61, 62, 197, 199, 200
Bernas, L., 224, 231, 233
bilateralism, 38
Board of Investments (BOI), 240, 241, 243, 256
Brazil, 176, 178, 197, 198
Briggs and Stratton engine, 222, 231
British Board of Trade, 276
British Commonwealth nations, 180, 191
Brookings Institution, 199
Bureau of East-West Trade, 26, 27
Bureau of Economic and Business Affairs (EB), 282-83
Bureau of International Scientific and Technological Affairs, 37
Bureau of Mines (BOM), 144, 180, 189, 190, 198, 204
Bureau of Oceans and International Environmental and Scientific Affairs (OES), 37, 283
Bureau of Political-Military Affairs, 27
Burnham (Prime Minister F.), 180
Bush, V., 22

C and B Crafts, 230, 253

316

INDEX

Cabanatuan City, 230
Cairns (Deputy Prime Minister J.), 175
Canada, 3, 60, 121, 130, 155, 192, 215, 268
carabao, 235, 244-45
Caribbean, 182, 187, 196, 197, 202, 204
Case, J. I., Company, 215
Cavalier, F., 108
Central Bank (Philippines), 232, 242, 245, 257
Central Intelligence Agency: Office of Economic Research, 28
Chandler, R. F., Jr., 216
Chase Manhattan Bank, 100
Chile, 78
China (see, People's Republic of China)
coal technology, 123-25, 130, 139, 140, 141, 148, 151, 154; fluidized bed combustion project, 138-39, 142, 147, 154, 156, 159, 277, 278, 284
cobalt, 174
Cocoyoc Declaration, 296, 300
Commerce Department, 11, 26, 27, 28, 73, 91, 92, 100-01, 104, 275, 282; International Trade Office, 22
Commission on Small and Medium Industries (CSMI), 239
Commodity Control List (CCL), 26
Communications Satellite Corporation (Comsat), 35-37, 39, 40, 79
computer technology, 25
Congress, 1, 27, 35, 176, 180, 186, 292; energy program, 125, 129, 135, 138, 150; export control, 28, 95; foreign assistance, 34, 36, 39,

82, 209, 278, 285; materials policy, 181-82, 185, 187-89, 105; and technology transfer, 11, 159-60, 201, 271
Congressional Research Service, 189
Consultative Group-Coordinating Committee (COCOM), 23, 24, 27, 29
Cooper, R., 43, 76, 281
cooperatives, 232-33, 245
copper, 175, 182, 188
Cotabato thresher, 227, 234, 237
Council of the Americas, 281
Council on International Economic Policy (CIEP), 174-75, 189

Davao Metal Industrial Association, 233
Deere, John, Co., 215
Defense Department (DOD), 9, 26, 27, 28, 63, 73, 94, 100-01, 143, 285, 286; Directorate of Research and Engineering, 28
Defense Production Act, 184
Defense Production Act (DPA) Inventory, 184-85
Denmark, 146, 148
Developing Nation Tractor, 216
Development Bank of the Philippines (DBP), 227, 232, 244
Development Loan Fund, 35
direct investment, 14, 41-48, 58-60, 65, 80, 81-82, 184, 265, 268-70, 272, 284, 288-91
Dominican Republic, 178, 179
dryers, 219-20, 228, 250
Duff, B., 233
Duhaylungsod, 252
Dungo, A., 230, 232
Dunning, J., 41
Durasteel, 229-30, 233

East-West Foreign Trade Board, 26
Eastern Europe, 1, 91, 113, 173, 194, 267, 269, 272
Economic Cooperation Administration (ECA), 34-35
Economic Policy Board, 177, 183, 188, 190
Ecuador, 186
Egypt, 32
electronic industries, 56-57, 68
Enders, T., 283
Energy Action Group (proposed), 131
energy conservation, 130, 140-41, 146, 151, 153, 154-55, 157-58
Energy Coordinating Group (ECG), 121, 123, 127, 139, 144-51, 161
Energy Development Cooperation Agency (proposed), 156
Energy Independence Authority, 278
Energy Reorganization Act, 142
Energy Research and Development Administration (ERDA), 79, 80, 135, 141-44, 161, 277, 283, 284
energy technology, 120-62
environmental protection, 130
Environmental Protection Agency (EPA), 142-43
European Atomic Energy Community (Euratom), 35, 38, 40, 123
European Community Joint Research Center, 147
European Recovery Program, 30, 38
Export Administration Act, 24, 62, 95, 285
Export Control Act, 22-23, 24
Export-Import Bank, 35, 100, 102

Farm Mechanization Loan Programs, 245, 257
Federal Commission on Natural Resources (proposed), 191
Federal Energy Administration (FEA), 140, 141, 143, 161, 275
Federal Power Commission, 29
Federal Products Company, 89
Federal Republic of Germany (FRG), 89, 105, 124, 145-48, 152-54, 156-57, 159
FIAT, 89, 112, 115, 116, 267, 268
Food for Peace Program, 35
Food Machinery Corporation, 215
Ford (President G. R.), 183
Ford, Henry, II, 90, 91, 94, 95
Ford Motor Company, 88, 89, 90, 91, 92, 94-96, 97, 221; Tractor Division, 216
foreign aid, 56-57, 209, 211, 229, 278-81, 284, 285
Foreign Assistance Act (FAA), 7, 34, 36, 57, 209, 211
foundry technology, 98, 99
fourth world, 7
France, 121, 149, 155, 291
fusion technology, 125, 130, 138, 139-41, 146-48, 150, 151, 155, 158, 284

Gabaldon, 234, 252
GAMI, 229
Geiger, T., 60-61, 78
General Accounting Office, 185
General Agreement on Tariffs and Trade (GATT), 128, 183
General Electric Company, 291
General Services Administration (GSA), 185
Geoman, 273
geothermal energy, 123-24, 125, 130, 154, 155
Ghana, 178

INDEX 319

glass, 175
Gravelle, J., 188-89
Greenberg, D., 21
Guinea, 178-79, 198, 203
Gulf Oil Company, 273
Guyana, 178-80, 184, 192, 194, 202, 272

Haiti, 178, 179
Haynes, E. S., 92-93, 99, 104
Health, Education, and Welfare Department (HEW), 37
high temperature gas reactors (HTGRs), 147, 151
Hiroshima, 30
Hoffman, P., 64
Housing and Urban Development Department (HUD), 143
Hudson Institute study, 25
hydrogen production, 130, 138, 139, 141, 146, 147, 148, 155, 158

Iceland, 29
Independence Project, 125
indirect investment, 59, 60, 81, 290
Industrial Guarantee and Loan Fund (IGLF), 242
Industrial Research Institute, 275, 281
Institute of American Affairs, 35
Interior Department (DOI), 29, 142, 143, 161, 195, 282
Internal Revenue Code, 186
International Atomic Energy Agency (IAEA), 38-39, 129, 284
International Bank for Reconstruction and Development (IBRD), 242, 245, 257
International Bauxite Association (IBA), 175, 177, 178

International Council of Scientific Unions: Committee on Space Research (COSPAR), 39
International Energy Agency (IEA), 6, 80, 127, 132, 138, 139, 142, 143, 144, 153-58, 159, 161, 188, 277, 283, 284; establishment, 122, 128-29; Management Committee, 153; organization, 153; Standing Group on Long-Term Cooperation (SLT/ERD), 122, 153, 154
International Energy Institute (proposed), 129
International Energy Program (IEP), 121, 129, 153
International Foundry Congress, 92
International Fusion Research Laboratory (proposed), 150, 284
International Harvester Co., 215
International Labor Organization, 240
International Monetary Fund (IMF), 128
International Rice Research Institute (IRRI), 7, 270, 278, 283; Agricultural Engineering Department (AED), 208, 209, 213, 217-19, 223, 233, 247; Agricultural Machinery Project, 208-59
International Telecommunications Satellite Consortium (Intelsat), 36, 38, 79
International Tin Agreement, 177-78
International Tin Council, 178
Investment Priorities Plan (IPP), 240, 256
Iran, 32, 269
Ireland, 155
iron ore, 174, 188
Isidro, B., 230, 252

Israel, 131
Italy, 124

Jackson (Senator H. M.), 11
Jamaica, 178-80, 182, 185, 270; aluminum industries in, 186-87, 192-97, 199, 201, 202-03, 272; bauxite reserves, 177-78, 191-94
Japan, 29, 94, 100, 101, 197; energy crisis and, 124, 128, 130-32, 146, 147-50, 151, 153, 155; technology transfer and, 3, 40-41, 56-57, 59, 60, 268, 289, 297, 298
Johnson, L., 215
Juelich Working Group, 146
Justice Department, 29

Kaiser Aluminum and Chemical Corporation, 179, 183, 192, 194, 196-99, 201-03, 272
Kalayaan, 233
Kama River Purchasing Commission, 102
Kama River Truck Plant (KamAZ), 6, 87-116, 266, 268, 273; contract implementation, 105-10; contract negotiations, 99-105; contacts, 90-98; implications for future U.S.-Soviet commercial relations, 110-16; role in Soviet economy, 111-14
Kansas City International Relations Council, 188
Khan, A., 216-17, 218
Kissinger (Secretary of State H. A.), 95, 128, 188; and energy crisis, 129, 130-31, 154, 278; raw materials statements, 188; science and technology statements, 1, 79-80, 269, 300
Kitchin (Congressman P.), 24

Konma Company, 221
Korean War, 22, 30, 35
Kubota tiller, 224, 241, 256

labor groups, 58, 59, 78, 190, 269, 297
Laird (Secretary of Defense M. R.), 94, 95, 100-01
Land Bank of the Philippines, 245
Land Reform Program (Philippines), 226
Latin America, 1, 31, 35, 185, 186, 216, 247, 277, 281
lead, 188
less developed countries (LDCs), 158, 209, 216, 217, 246-47
Limsiaco, R., 244
Love, J., 130
Love Report, 130
Luzon, 215, 222, 226, 234, 244, 251

Mack Trucks, Inc., 88, 89, 90-92, 93, 95, 96-97, 115
magnesium, 175, 182
Maier, C., 196
Mametora Company, 221
management services, 4, 291
manganese, 174-77
Manley (Prime Minister M.), 178, 191-93, 203
Marcos (President F.), 231, 238, 241
Maritime Administration, 29
Marshall Plan, 29-30, 35, 38
Marsteel Corporation, 220, 230, 231, 233, 250, 254; tiller, 224, 226, 240, 241, 247, 248, 250
Masagana 99 program, 243, 245
Massey Ferguson, Incorporated, 215
Maximov, N. P., 99

INDEX

Medium and Small-Scale Industries Coordinated Action Program (MASICAP), 239, 254, 257
Metallurgimport, 92, 93, 98, 99, 103, 107
Mexico, 183, 185, 193-94, 201-03, 272
Middle East, 32, 94, 128
Mikdashi, Z., 177-78
Mindanao, 233, 234, 235, 237, 247, 248, 251
Modulated Integrated Utility System (MIUS), 143
Morfee, D. J., 99
Muller and Phipps, 222
multilateralism, 38, 39, 65, 124-27, 130-31, 138, 151, 158, 176, 283-85
multinational corporations (MNC), 7, 74, 73, 78, 79, 173, 192-93, 221, 268, 294; Tariff Commission study, 60, 81-82, 269, 290; technology transfer and, 2, 6, 7, 40-48, 59-60, 65, 76, 123, 182, 277, 295
Munitions Control Board, 27-28, 62
Mutual Defense Assistance Control Act (Battle Act), 23
Mutual Security Act, 23

Naberezhnyye Chelny, 87
Nagasaki, 30
National Academy of Sciences, 39
National Aeronautics and Space Act, 36
National Aeronautics and Space Administration (NASA), 27, 36, 38, 39, 76, 79
National Bureau of Standards (NBS), 143
National Science Foundation (NSF), 22

national security, 11, 13, 22, 23, 25, 58, 171, 185, 190, 271, 292
National Security Council, 102, 185
National Stockpile, 184-85
National Tillage Machinery Laboratory, 215
natural gas, 124-25
Navy, 22
Nelson, R., 41
Netherlands, 73, 146, 147, 148
Nixon (President R. M.), 95, 101, 102, 128, 135, 185, 297; Washington Energy Conference, 125, 131
Nordhaus, W., 298
North Atlantic Treaty Organization (NATO), 23, 27, 29, 131; Committee on the Challenges to Modern Society (CCMS), 124, 143, 144, 150, 155
North Vietnam, 94
Norway, 121, 150
Nuclear Energy Agency (NEA), 147, 148, 155
nuclear energy technology, 30, 57, 76, 125, 135, 138, 158, 271
nuclear reactor safety, 130, 135, 139, 146, 148, 151-55, 157, 159
Nuclear Regulatory Commission (NRC), 29, 142
Nueva Ecija, 234-36, 250, 251
Nye, J. S., Jr., 46

Occidental Petroleum, 96
ocean materials, 79, 176, 191
Office of Emergency Planning, 185
Office of Export Administration (OEA), 26, 28, 91, 92, 100
Office of International Security Affairs, 28

Office of Manpower and Budget (OMB), 142
Office of Munitions Control, 27
Office of Preparedness, 185
Office of Science and Technology (OST), 37
Office of Scientific Research and Development (OSRD), 21, 22
Office of Technology Assessment, 189
Ohtake Agricultural Machinery Company Limited, 221
oil, 123, 128, 129, 131, 138, 153; embargo, 73, 121, 124, 128, 129-30; imports, 121, 124, 125, 174-75
Organization for Economic Cooperation and Development (OECD), 3, 60, 124, 145, 146-49, 153, 155, 156, 188; Committee on Scientific and Technical Policy, 149-50; Development Assistance Committee, 40; Energy Committee, 124
Organization of Petroleum Exporting Countries (OPEC), 7, 31, 32, 34, 60, 64, 80, 129, 179, 185, 186, 191, 276

Pakistan, 209
patents, 229-31, 247, 277
Patolichev (Foreign Trade Minister N. S.), 102
peaceful nuclear explosions (PNEs), 37
People's Republic of China, 28, 30
Peterson (Secretary of Commerce P.), 102
Philippine National Bank, 227, 244
Philippines, 208, 209, 211, 213; Department of Agrarian Reform (DAR), 241; Department of Industry, 239; Four Year Development Plan, 238, 242, 243; Tariff and Customs Code, 240, 254, 256
plastics, 175, 182
Point IV Program, 30, 35
Poland, 124
pollution control technology, 142
Porter, D., 243
Pullman, Inc., 88, 89, 93, 96

radioactive waste management, 135, 139, 146, 147, 149, 151, 154-56, 157, 158, 161
Rand Corporation study, 25, 276
recycling, 181, 189, 191, 199
Renault, 89, 99, 112, 116
research and development (R and D): by aluminum industry, 180, 187, 189, 199, 204; energy, 6, 120-62, 270, 277, 278, 282, 284-85; government funds for, 55, 56, 59, 63, 65, 68-76, 266, 277, 293, 299; industrial, 55, 63, 65-73, 266, 274-76, 299; IRRI study, 209, 212, 220, 222, 223-24, 229, 238, 247, 248-50, 252, 254; by multinational corporations, 42, 59
Reston, J., 188
Revere Copper and Brass, Inc., 179, 183, 192, 193, 197
Reyes, N., 222
Reynolds, D. P., 181
Reynolds Metals Company, 179, 183, 192, 193, 194, 196, 197, 201-02, 272
Rimorin, 244
Robinson, C., 283
Romania, 124

INDEX 323

rubber, 174
Ruttenberg, Friedman,
　Kilgallon, Gutchess, and
　Associates, 190

Samahang Nayon, 245
Satra Corporation, 91, 92
Saudi Arabia, 32
Schmidt-Kuester, W. F.,
　145-46, 149
Seacom, 240
seeders, 227
semiconductors, 46
service technology, 61, 81, 184,
　197, 265, 272-74, 291, 299-
　300
Sharing in Development — Pro-
　gramme of Employment,
　Equity, and Growth for the
　Philippines, 240
Sierra Leone, 178
Signal Corporation, 91
Simon (Secretary of the
　Treasury W. E.), 188
Small Business Advisory
　Centers, 239
Small-Scale Agricultural
　Machinery Project, 208-59
solar energy, 123, 125, 130,
　138-41, 142, 144, 146, 148,
　151, 157, 284
South Africa, 174
Southeast Asia, 30, 56
Soviet Union (see, Union of Soviet
　Socialist Republics)
Stans (Secretary of Commerce
　M.), 101
State Department: export con-
　trol, 22-23, 26-27; foreign
　economic and technology
　policy, 1, 10-11, 36-37, 76,
　100, 275, 276, 277, 281-82,
　283; materials policy, 204-
　05; Washington Energy

　Conference role, 125, 129,
　140-41, 283
steel, 175, 182
Steelpride Industries, Inc. , 244
Stingel, D. , 93, 97, 99, 103,
　104
stock piling, 180, 184-85, 271
Strategic and Critical Stock Piling
　Act, 180, 184
Sunshine Project, 147
supersonic (SST) aircraft, 57
Surinam, 178, 179, 185
Sushkov, V. N. , 93
Swindell-Dressler, division of
　Pullman, Inc. , 6, 88, 89, 92-
　94, 97-98, 99-100, 266-67,
　273
Switzerland, 157
synthetic fuels technology, 141-42

Tagalog, 222
Tariff Commission study, 60, 82,
　269
Technical Advisory Committees
　(TACs), 27
technological interdependence,
　76-80, 289, 296, 298-301
technology gap, 23, 41, 56, 297
technology transfer: administra-
　tive agency problems, 2, 10-
　11, 26-29, 127, 138-44, 282-
　83; to advanced countries, 120-
　62; appropriate, 208-59; con-
　temporary developments, 55-
　82; definition, 14-19; economic
　aspects, 2, 4-6, 10, 40-48,
　55-57, 62, 65, 111, 127, 132-
　39, 151, 156-58, 266-74, 281,
　288, 294-96; foreign policy,
　2-3, 4-6, 10, 29-40, 56-57,
　58-59, 65, 76-80, 127, 171-72,
　270-71, 282, 283, 288 ff. ; in-
　dustrial disclosure policy,
　293; military-strategic policy,

1-2, 5, 6, 9-10, 21-29, 55-56, 58, 63, 64, 150, 159, 265, 270-71, 281, 288; by multinational corporations, 2, 6, 7-8, 40-48, 59-60, 65, 76, 123, 182, 277, 295; national perspective, 1-19; postwar history, 21-46; to resource-poor developing countries, 208-59; to resource-rich developing countries, 171-205; social-environmental aspects, 10, 57, 64, 127, 158, 295-96; to USSR, 11, 87-116
Thailand, 209, 218
third world, 7, 185, 191, 199
threshers, 211, 217, 219, 227, 230-31, 233-34, 237, 240-41, 252, 254, 256
tillers, 234, 235, 245, 254, 256; IRRI design, 218-19, 221-22, 224, 225-27, 234, 236, 240-41, 247-48, 250; Japanese, 209, 218, 221, 224, 232, 241, 256
tin, 174, 175, 176, 177, 188
Tol'yatti automobile project, 267, 268
Toth-Pechiney process, 181
tractors, 209, 216, 218, 219, 224, 232, 234, 241, 244-45, 256
Trade Act, 183, 186, 203
Trade Reform Bill, 4
Trading with the Enemy Act, 23
transnationalism, 77-78, 296
Transportation Department (DOT), 37, 144
Treasury Department, 11, 29, 189, 190, 204-05, 282
Trinidad, 194, 272
Truman (President H. S.), 30, 300

Union of Soviet Socialist Republics (USSR), 23, 28, 30, 34, 62, 64, 73, 87, 93-95, 100-01, 124, 176, 282; automotive industry, 115; Communist Party, 87, 114; contract procedures, 104-06, 109-10; Five Year Plan, 87, 112; Kama River Truck Plant (KamAZ), 6, 87-116; Ministry of Foreign Trade, 91-93, 98, 102, 103; planning and management, 105-07; Politburo, 88; State Committee for Science and Technology, 90, 92, 96, 98; Supreme Soviet, 115; technology transfer to, 1, 11, 25, 87-116, 266-68
United Kingdom (U.K.), 142, 145-47, 148, 149, 151-57, 159, 277-78, 284
United Nations (UN), 38, 39, 129, 173, 283; Charter of Economic Rights and Duties of States (CERD), 172-73; Declaration on the Establishment of a New Economic Order, 172-73; General Assembly, 1, 172
United Nations Conference on Science and Technology, 32
United Nations Conference on Trade and Development (UNCTAD), 296
United Nations Environmental Program (UNEP), 296
United States (U.S.): agreements, 32, 34, 37, 73, 102, 176-78, 183, 188, 201; balance of trade, 101, 289, 290-91; Congress (see, Congress); energy crisis, 128-29; export control policy, 22-24, 26-29, 95, 100-02, 285-86, 294; foreign aid, 7, 29-40, 56-57, 209, 211,

INDEX 325

229, 278-81, 284, 285; <u>International Economic Report of the President</u>, 1; R and D funding, 55, 56, 59, 63, 65, 68-76, 266, 275, 277, 293, 299; raw materials supplies, 171-74, 180-81, 187-91, 195, 205, 269, 281-82; stock piling program, 184-85, 190, 191, 199, 200-01, 271; technology transfer (<u>see,</u> technology transfer); trade policy, 3-4, 95, 183; science and technology, 1-3, 21-26, 30, 32, 269, 296-300 (<u>see also,</u> specific U.S. government agencies, bureaus, departments, and offices)
U.S.-Soviet Commercial Agreement, 102
U.S.-USSR Trade Council, 276
University of the Philippines: Institute of Small-Scale Industries (UP-ISSI), 232
University of the Philippines at Los Banos (UPLB), 220, 228-29, 250, 252
uranium enrichment, 40, 121, 150, 153, 271, 275
USSR (<u>see,</u> Union of Soviet Socialist Republics)

value-added concept, 194, 201-02, 204
Vasiliev, L. B., 107, 115

Venezuela, 186, 194
Verzahntechnik, 105
Vietnam, 36, 94, 101
Volga Automobile Plant, 115

Washington Energy Conference, 121, 123, 124-27, 129-32, 139, 141, 144, 148, 283; Energy Coordination Group, 6
waste utilization, 138-40, 142-43, 146-48
weeders, 221
West Germany (<u>see,</u> Federal Republic of Germany)
Western Europe, 3, 38, 56, 59, 60, 79, 94, 101, 112, 173, 268, 271, 289, 297, 298; energy R and D and, 121, 123-24, 128, 130, 131, 151, 153
Western Hemisphere Trade Corporation (WHTC), 183, 186, 187, 201
White House (the President), 28, 34, 36, 37, 76, 129, 187-88, 189, 204, 276
wood, 175, 182
World Bank, 128, 197
World Food Conference, 283

Yaroslavl Engine Plant, 112
Year of Europe, 128
Yugoslavia, 178, 194, 201, 272

zinc, 175, 182, 185, 188

ABOUT THE AUTHORS

HENRY R. NAU is Associate Professor of Political Science and International Affairs and Deputy Director of the Graduate Program in Science, Technology and Public Policy at George Washington University. During the academic years 1975-76 and 1976-77, he is on leave from the University serving as a special assistant to the Under Secretary for Economic Affairs in the Department of State.

Professor Nau received his B.S. degree in economics and science at the Massachusetts Institute of Technology and his M.A. and Ph.D. degrees in international relations from the Johns Hopkins School of Advanced International Studies. He is author of the book National Politics and International Technology: Nuclear Reactor Development in Western Europe, published in 1974 by the Johns Hopkins Press, and of a number of articles in professional journals.

Professor Nau is a member of Phi Beta Kappa and has received research and fellowship awards from, among others, the Council on Foreign Relations, National Science Foundation and Foreign Area Fellowship Program. From 1971-73, he was Assistant Professor of Political Science at Williams College.

MARY M. ALLEN is a candidate for the Ph.D. degree in political science and research associate of the Graduate Program in Science, Technology and Public Policy at George Washington University.

ANN L. BECKER has an M.A. degree from the Graduate Program in Science, Technology and Public Policy of George Washington University and is co-author of the article "IRRI Design of Small Scale Farm Equipment for Developing Country Production," Development Digest, January 1976.

HARLAN S. FINER is a candidate for the M.A. degree in science, technology and public policy at George Washington University.

HOWARD GOBSTEIN has an M.A. degree from the Graduate Program in Science, Technology and Public Policy of George Washington University and is a science policy analyst with the General Accounting Office.

GEORGE D. HOLLIDAY is an economic analyst with the Congressional Research Service of the Library of Congress and a candidate for the Ph.D. degree in international relations at George Washington University. He is co-author with John P. Hardt of several publications on East-West trade, including <u>U.S.-Soviet Commercial Relations: The Interplay of Economics, Technology Transfer and Diplomacy</u>, Committee on Foreign Affairs, U.S. House of Representatives, 1973.

JAMES P. LESTER has an M.A. degree in political science from the University of Oklahoma and is a candidate for the Ph.D. degree in political science at George Washington University.

CAROL A. ULINSKI is a candidate for the M.A. degree in science, technology and public policy at George Washington University and co-author of the article "IRRI Design of Small Scale Farm Equipment for Developing Country Production," <u>Development Digest</u>, January 1976.

RELATED TITLES
Published by
Praeger Special Studies

CHINESE TECHNOLOGY TRANSFER TO THE
THIRD WORLD: A Grants Economic Analysis
Janos Horvath

*THE MAKING OF UNITED STATES INTERNATIONAL
ECONOMIC POLICY: Principles, Problems and
Proposals for Reform
Stephen D. Cohen

*SOCIAL SCIENCE AND PUBLIC POLICY IN THE
UNITED STATES
Irving Louis Horowitz and
James Everett Katz

TECHNOLOGY AND COMMUNIST CULTURE: The
Socio-Cultural Impact of Technology Transfer
under Socialism
edited by Frederic J. Fleron, Jr.

TECHNOLOGY TRANSFER TO EAST EUROPE:
U.S. Corporate Experience
Eric W. Hayden

*Also available in paperback.

T
23
T4

MAY 25 1979